SUBSCRIPTION NOTICE

This Wiley product is updated on a periodic basis with annual supplements to reflect important changes in the subject matter. If you purchased this product directly from John Wiley & Sons, we have already recorded your subscription for this update service.

If, however, you purchased this product from a bookstore and wish to receive (1) any current update at no additional charge, and (2) future updates and revised or related volumes billed separately with a 30-day examination review, please send your name, company name (if applicable), address and the title of the product to:

Supplement Department
John Wiley & Sons, Inc.
One Wiley Drive
Somerset, NJ 08875
1-(800)-225-5945

PROTECTING TRADE SECRETS, PATENTS, COPYRIGHTS, AND TRADEMARKS

ROBERT C. DORR, Esquire

Dorr, Carson, Sloan & Peterson

CHRISTOPHER H. MUNCH

Professor of Law
University of Denver College of Law

Wiley Law Publications
JOHN WILEY & SONS
New York • Chichester • Brisbane • Toronto • Singapore

In recognition of the importance of preserving what has been
written, it is a policy of John Wiley & Sons, Inc., to have
books of enduring value published in the United States
printed on acid-free paper, and we exert our best efforts
to that end.

Library of Congress Cataloging-in-Publication Data

Dorr, Robert C.
    Protecting trade secrets, patents, copyrights, and trademarks /
    Robert C. Dorr, Christopher H. Munch.
        p.   cm. — (Business practice library)
    Includes bibliographical references.
    ISBN 0-471-51441-1
    1. Intellectual property—United States. I. Munch, Christopher H.
II. Title. III. Series.
KF2979.D67   1990
346.7304'8—dc20
[347.30648]   90-12686
                                                               CIP

Printed in the United States of America

10 9 8 7 6 5 4 3 2 1

PREFACE

The collection of subjects grouped under the broad rubric of intellectual property embraces the world of ideas, the expression of those ideas, how those expressions may come to be associated with a product, service, or source, and the usefulness of the ideas.

This book not only explains the basic principles of intellectual property, but it also (1) provides valuable business tips to minimize future legal liabilities while maximizing their intellectual property interests, (2) provides access to resources including leading references, books, articles, databases, and associations (complete with addresses and telephone numbers), and (3) provides legal checklists, legal forms, and case examples.

This book covers trade secrets, creatures of common law; patents, creatures of a federal statute; unfair competition, a creature of the common law; trademarks, mixed creatures of common law, state law, and federal law (Lanham Act); and copyrights, creatures of a federal statute. These fields are separate, discrete, and yet generally compatible with one another, and on some points the contacts are intimately connected. We also focus on the ramifications of directors' liability arising from use or misuse of intellectual property and the impact on the field of advertising and software.

The common law of trade secrets provides limited protection of commercially valuable information or processes that may or may not be patentable, but that provide a commercial advantage to the holder of the secret. The common law of trade secrets is not per se preempted by either the patent statute or the copyright statute, but subsists only so long as the information or processes remain a secret. In the event they are registered under the patent laws or published under the copyright laws, the trade secrets are no longer secret and their common law protection is extinguished. In the event the secret is not discovered by way of reverse engineering or otherwise, a trade secret could have a perpetual life.

Patents, on the other hand, are designed to protect useful ideas for a limited period of time. Patents, so long as the patent fully discloses the patentable invention, may be used in conjunction with, or as an adjunct to, a trade secret, and the accompanying manuals or drawings could also be protected by the federal Copyright Law. Furthermore, a patented product in commerce could acquire a distinctive trade dress protection if that trade dress did not involve functional features of the product. The product could also bear a trademark that identifies the particular product and the source of the product.

v

The field of unfair competition is, by and large, the product of common law, that is state law. However, the federal trademark law also contains one section that describes two distinct areas of unfair competition which violate the federal statute and which also may be state law unfair competition activities. The patent law and the law of copyrights preempt state law where those statutes apply, except that the copyright law does not preempt the two counts of unfair competition set out in the federal Trademark Act or any other federal statute.

The federal Trademark Act, commonly known as the Lanham Act, provides for the identification of either services or goods in commerce, and protects the source of such services or goods against the likelihood of confusion by either competing or noncompeting products or services. It is in general a statutory form of a part of the common law of unfair competition. The interrelation of the many fields of intellectual property can be illustrated initially by examining a 12 oz. container of a popular soft drink. The label could constitute a distinctive trademark identifying the product and, if specifically artistic, could also be registered as a federal copyright. The beverage contained in the can or container could also be protected by either a federal patent on its formula or, in the alternative, as a trade secret. Similarly, copyright registration protects only the representation of an idea, but that protection may also extend to technical manuals describing the idea and, as mentioned earlier in this paragraph, may also be embodied in the symbol of a registered trademark.

The impact of these major fields of intellectual property in recent years has exposed corporate directors to individual liability for misuse of another's intellectual property which, in many instances, is termed infringement. Finally, the wise and vigorous use of trade dress, trademarks, copyrights, and patents may be extremely valuable in the creation of commercial goodwill through advertising.

Denver, Colorado   ROBERT C. DORR
August 1990   CHRISTOPHER H. MUNCH

ACKNOWLEDGMENTS

The authors express their sincere admiration and well-deserved gratitude to their tireless and gifted research assistant, Ms. Susan Biemesderfer, Esquire. Her tactful reconciliations of the authors' concept of footnotes and citations, the Harvard *Uniform System of Citation,* and the publisher's prevailing criteria, at least in part, made this printing possible.

We also are very grateful for the transcription, and transcriptions, and more transcriptions, of Ms. Vivienne Burrell and Ms. Deloris Stahl. Thank you all so very much.

R.C.D.
C.H.M.

ABOUT THE AUTHORS

Robert C. Dorr is a partner in the Denver, Colorado law firm of Dorr, Carson, Sloan & Peterson. He is the author and coauthor of 20 articles on such diverse areas as solid state physics, computers, and law, and he is a continuing legal education lecturer on all phases of patents, trademarks, and copyrights for the University of Denver, Bureau of National Affairs, the International Practicum Institute, the American Bar Association, the Federal Bar Association, the National Business Institute, and the Southwestern Legal Foundation. Mr. Dorr holds a masters of science degree from Northwestern University and is a graduate of the University of Denver Law School where he served as senior editor of the Denver Law Journal. He has been selected by Marquis's "Who's Who in American Law," Sigma Xi, and Outstanding Young Man of America. He was formerly a member of the Patent and Technical Staffs of Bell Laboratories of the American Telephone and Telegraph Company, and he is the author of "Federal Ex Parte Relief," in *Intellectual Property and Litigation, Patent Preliminary Injunctive Relief,* in Journal of Patent Office Society with Bradford J. Dugt, *Trademark Preliminary Injunctive Relief,* in Journal of Patent Office Society with Bradford J. Dugt, and *Resolving Claims to Ownership of Software and Computer Related Data,* in Computer Law Journal with William P. Eigles.

Christopher H. Munch is a professor at the University of Denver College of Law, and Of Counsel, Dorr, Carson, Sloan & Peterson. He was formerly chairman of the Law Department of the United States Air Force Academy and associate dean of the University of Denver College of Law. He earned a bachelor's degree at the United States Military Academy and a doctor of law degree with honors at the University of Illinois. Professor Munch is a member of the bars of the states of Illinois and Colorado, United States Court of Military Appeals, United States District Court for the District of Colorado, United States Claims Court, the Court of Appeals for the Federal Circuit, the Order of the Coif, and the Order of Saint Ives. He is a legal specialist in patents, trademarks, copyrights, and government contracts. His published books include *Unfair Competition and Intellectual Property, Cases and Materials on Government Contracts,* and he is the coauthor of *Risk Management in*

Construction Contracting. He has taught in the Scholar's Program of the University of Denver Political Science Department, lectured on copyright law in the Graduate School of Library Science, and on agency and partnership law, corporation law, and remedies for a Colorado Bar refresher course. He has also delivered numerous nationwide lectures on patents, trademarks, copyrights, and government contracts.

INTRODUCTION

This book discusses the individual topics of trade secrets, patents, trademarks, copyrights, and unfair competition. This introduction addresses each of these individual topics together to provide overlapping protection for several given fact situations.

The business executive or general counsel typically is faced with the problem of protecting a new product. The following two examples are designed to cover a vast array of different types of products.

Protecting a T-shirt

The T-shirt example is equally applicable to protecting caps, jackets, mugs, and the like. Many businesses use such items as promotional products or as the very basis of their business.

Artwork title. As discussed in the copyright chapter, an outside artist or advertising firm creates the artwork for the T-shirt. At this point an independent contractor relationship exists, and because the artist holds copyright to the artwork, a copyright assignment must be obtained from the artist/agency. Copyright notice should be visibly (although not noticeably) placed on the artwork in the business name. The artistic expression should be protected with a Visual Arts (VA) copyright application, an example of which appears in the copyright chapter.

Celebrity likeness. In the chapters on unfair competition and advertising it becomes clear that should the T-shirt use the likeness of a celebrity such as Joe Montana, a written permission or license must be obtained from Joe Montana.

Building appearance. In the chapter on advertising, we address issues like the appearance of a famous building, car (such as Rolls Royce), or the like and the need to obtain permission from the image owner.

Artwork as trademark. In the chapter on trademarks, if the artwork is also a trademark such as your corporate logo, then consider filing for a trademark registration claiming use of the trademark on clothing products. The Trademark Office may consider the use, however, ornamental and not allow the registration.

Celebrity name.   To use a celebrity name, obtain written permission or a license from the celebrity.

Your trademark.   Make sure you use the encircled R (if federally registered) or the "TM" notation for a product or the "SM" notation for a service (if not federally registered).

Another's trademark.   In the chapter on advertising, you do have the right to use another's trademark according to the guidelines set forth. Usually, in T-shirt designs, another's trademark such as COORS is used prominently and, therefore, a permission or license from Coors Co. must be obtained.

Registering trademark.   A registration for the trademark for clothing can be made in the United States Patent and Trademark Office.

A Computer Peripheral Such as a Modem

A large number of businesses design, manufacture, and sell computer peripheral products such as printers, modems, storage devices, and the like. Protecting such electronic products involves many overlapping principles discussed in this book.

Hardware patents.   In the chapter on patents, a number of important concerns arise. First, during the development stage of the modem, a thorough patentability and literature search should be made of all prior art approaches. Particular attention should be taken to searching for modem patents from competitors. Your own design and development efforts should be carefully documented according to the recording procedures as in an engineering notebook. These should be properly witnessed and understood. It is imperative that all engineers have in their employment agreement a patent assignment clause assigning all their inventions with respect to the modem over to the company. If outside R&D facilities such as consultants are used, patent assignment clauses must be incorporated in such contractual relationships. Vigorously file for utility patent applications on the circuitry, the overall system presented in the modem, the software contained therein, and any error code correcting algorithmic approaches. The housing and packaging design should be protected by design patents.

Copyrights.   Unlike doing a patentability search, it is essentially impossible to search prior software copyrights. Title to your software, however, must be carefully investigated. If the software is completely authored within the business, then title is fairly well assured. It is optional whether or not a copyright assignment clause appears in the employment agreement, but it does not hurt to put it in. If outside programmers are used, title investigation concerns become paramount. The written agreement with the outside programmer should contain a warranty clause that all programming is original with the programmer as well as an assignment clause assigning it over. If your software, of necessity, requires using software interfaces of another company's software, it is important to investigate the requirements of the other company with respect to the use of their software interfaces. Most companies will grant licenses and actually provide the necessary information for you to effectively use their software interfaces. After title has been properly investigated and placed in the business, the business should file a form Text (TX) copyright application according to the example and procedure set forth in the chapter on copyrights by treating it as a trade secret. The actual source code listing should incorporate the proper copyright notice, the label on the floppy or the tape should bear copyright notice, and when the software (if it does) provides an output on the screen the copyright notice should be appropriately flashed on.

Trade secrets. This is a hotly litigated area. When hiring new employees, audit their prior employment experience. To avoid a charge of trade secret misappropriation, do not assign the new employees to the same technological task that they were engaged in with their former employer. Be sure the employment agreement makes it fully clear that they are not to bring with them any trade secrets (especially documents or programs). Implement the trade secret program set forth in the chapter on trade secrets to have full control over visitors and employees, and keep the new product for public announcement as a true trade secret. Trade secret protection is the cheapest of all of the intellectual property protections, and it is a self-help approach.

Trademarks. It is becoming increasingly difficult to pick a trademark in the electronics areas, and therefore a clearance search must be made on all proposed marks. As soon as the mark clears, an intent to use application should be filed to get the federal registration in the works. All advertising for using the trademark must follow proper trademark grammar.

Advertising. If you decide to comparatively advertise the modem with a competitor's modem, follow all comparative advertising guidelines set forth in the chapter on advertising. If the modem is compatible with trademark software or hardware, you certainly have the legal right to use the trademarks of others in advertising your modem, but be careful to follow the proper advertising guidelines with respect to use of their trademarks. Be sure to place proper copyright notice on all advertising although there is no real reason to go to the expense or time of filing a copyright application.

SUMMARY CONTENTS

DETAILED CONTENTS

CHAPTER 1

PROTECTING TRADE SECRETS

§ 1.1   Importance of Trade Secrets

Executives, engineers, and entrepreneurs encounter hundreds of trade secrets daily, especially those pertaining to important new products. Businesses actually have thousands upon thousands of trade secrets to guard and protect, and their own employees represent the highest risk group for stealing valuable secrets. The fact that this group is also highly mobile (that is, easily accepting employment with competitors) only underscores the risks involved.

Legally trade secrets are perhaps the easiest and least expensive intellectual property rights to protect, but doing so requires a business to take affirmative self-help steps. This chapter provides practical legal advice in the area of trade secrets. This advice must be followed because if not, the courts will not protect the trade secrets. It is as simple as that.

Most businesses first become aware of the importance of trade secret protection only after a key employee, who has been hired away by a competitor or has started her own competing company, takes advantage of trade secrets. To ensure that this does not happen, companies need to be on guard to protect their trade secrets. In § **1.16**, an example of a corporate trade secret program is presented.

RESOURCES:

1. Without doubt the best reference is Milgrim, Roger M., *Milgrim on Trade Secrets* (Matthew Bender: 1275 Broadway, Albany, NY 12201) (1990).
2. Callmann, Rudolph, *The Law of Unfair Competition Trademarks and Monopolies* (Callaghan & Co.: 155 Pfingsten Rd., Deerfield, IL 60015) (1990).
3. *Corporate Counsel's Guide to Protecting Trade Secrets* (Business Laws, Inc.: 8228 Mayfield Rd., Chesterland, OH 44026) (1990).

---

§ 1.2   —Trade Secrets Defined

A classic legal definition of *trade secrets* relied upon by many courts across the country is found in the *Restatement of Torts*: "Any formula, pattern, device or compilation of information which is used in one's business, and which gives him an opportunity to obtain an advantage over competitors who do not know how to use it."[1]

---

[1] Restatement of Torts § 757 comment b (1939).

The Uniform Trade Secrets Act (UTSA) provides a more modern definition:

> "Trade secret" means information, including a formula, pattern, compilation, program, device, method, technique, or process that:
>
> (i) derives independent economic value, actual or potential, from not being generally known, and not being readily ascertainable by proper means by other persons who can obtain economic value from its disclosure or use, and
>
> (ii) is the subject of efforts that are reasonable under the circumstances to maintain its secrecy.[2]

Despite these functional definitions, courts have had difficulty in defining trade secrets. As one court said in defining a trade secret, "It is at best a nebulous concept which . . . is somewhat incapable of definition."[3] Secrecy ultimately is a question of fact to be determined within the sound discretion of the trier of fact.[4]

From a practical viewpoint, trade secrets can comprise any information that gives a business a competitive edge over competitors. To aid businesses in determining whether information is protected as a trade secret, the *Restatement of Torts* suggests six factors of inquiry. It states:

> An exact definition of a trade secret is not possible. Some factors to be considered in determining whether given information is one's trade secret are:
>
> 1. the extent to which the information is known outside of his business;
> 2. the extent to which it is known by employees and others involved in his business;
> 3. the extent of measures taken by him to guard the secrecy of this information;
> 4. the value of the information to him and to his competitors;
> 5. the amount of effort or money expended by him in developing the information;
> 6. the ease or difficulty with which the information could be properly acquired or duplicated by others.[5]

This chapter sets forth the practical procedures and examples of the legal forms necessary to comply with these quite functional factors.

---

[2] Uniform Trade Secrets Act § 1(4) (1985), 14 U.L.A. 286 (Supp. 1987).

[3] Kodekey Elecs., Inc. v. Mechanex Corp., 486 F.2d 449, 453 n.3, 179 U.S.P.Q. (BNA) 770 (10th Cir. 1973).

[4] 486 F.2d at 454 n.4 (10th Cir. 1973).

[5] Restatement of Torts § 757 comment b (1939).

§ 1.3 —Examples of Trade Secrets

It is important to recognize trade secrets. Many businesses honestly but quite mistakenly believe they have few, if any, trade secrets. The following are common examples of business information that may constitute protectable trade secrets:

1. Organic Technology
    a. Body creams and cosmetics such as lipsticks, face creams, and hair conditioners
    b. Household products such as soaps, scents, and furniture polishes
    c. Recipes for food products such as soft drinks, salsas, sauces, coatings, and flavorings.
2. Complex Technology
    a. Circuits on integrated chips
    b. Manufacturing techniques
    c. Software programs
    d. Photographic processes.
3. Business Methods
    a. Cost and pricing data
    b. Unpublished promotional material
    c. Marketing techniques and demographic data (for example, location of businesses such as for fast food restaurants)
    d. Food manufacturing and preparation processes
    e. Methods of instruction for ballroom dancing.
4. Customer Lists
    a. Salesman route information
    b. Mail order lists
    c. Characteristics and demographic breakdown of customer traits.
5. Business Knowledge[6]
    a. Lead times in component supply
    b. Existence of alternate suppliers of parts
    c. The names of a customer's key decision makers.
6. Pending Patent Applications

Creativity in defining what is trade secret and, thus, what is protectable, is smart business acumen. Unfortunately, it is a great temptation, especially for technical engineers and software programmers, to believe that nothing

---

[6] *See* SI Handling Sys., Inc. v. Heisley, 581 F. Supp. 1553, 222 U.S.P.Q. (BNA) 52 (E.D. Pa. 1984).

they are involved in is trade secret. This is a dangerous attitude, and corporations, as a matter of procedure, should consider valuable and secret as much information kept internally to the organization as possible.

§ 1.4   —Examples of Trade Secret Theft

As we have stated, a trade secret is legally anything that gives a competitor an advantage or head start. The following are examples based on actual cases of trade secret theft.

Corporate opportunity.   Various opportunities that present themselves to a business constitute trade secret material. Even though the corporate opportunity is not used, an employee does not have the right to leave the company and then use the rejected corporate opportunity. For example, Sally, a geologist, was employed by an oil company. While there, she devised a unique plan for developing an oil and gas area. The company rejected the plan. Sally left and commenced to develop the area according to her plan—and at a profit. The oil company sued for loss of a trade secret corporate opportunity and won.[7]

Head start.   Trade secrets are generally developed through substantial time and cost; the use of trade secrets by another generally eliminates an initial investment in time and materials. For example, Jim worked for a computer company in the development of a memory system. It took 8 months and $150,000 to develop the system. Jim left, and in 2 months and with $25,000, produced a competing memory system. The company sued and won $150,000, the value appropriated.[8]

Enticement.   Trade secrets can be appropriated by means of enticing an employee away. In one case, the successful enticement of 80 percent of a company's executive and skilled employees resulted in the award of $1.2 million in damages and $250,000 in attorneys' fees.[9] When employment contracts are terminable at will, absent wrongful means, there may be no liability for inducing an employee to resign unless a fellow employee is doing the enticing. A number of factors need to be carefully analyzed in these cases.[10]

---

[7] Tlapak v. Chevron Oil Co., 407 F.2d 1129, 1135 (8th Cir. 1969).

[8] Digital Dev. Corp. v. International Memory Sys., 185 U.S.P.Q. (BNA) 136 (S.D. Cal. 1973).

[9] C. Albert Sauter Co. v. Richard S. Sauter Co., 368 F. Supp. 501, 505–08 (E.D. Pa. 1973).

[10] Mulei v. Jet Courier Serv., Inc., 739 P.2d 889 (Colo. Ct. App. 1987), *remanded,* 771 P.2d 486 (Colo. 1989).

Key personnel.   Directors, officers, and key employees have a fiduciary duty to act in the best interests of their employer, whether or not a written contract exists. For example, a group of scientists, engineers, technicians, and others left their former company and formed a new, highly successful company. The court held them to be key personnel because they (a) had worked together for many years; (b) possessed the "knowledge and competence" required to produce the competing product; and (c) had the "understanding" needed to serve the industry. The court awarded more than $1.5 million in profits to the former employer.[11]

§ 1.5   —What Are Not Trade Secrets

If information is in the public domain, then it is probably not a trade secret. Consequently, all advertising literature, technical specifications, operation manuals, and the like, which are freely disseminated to the public, contain information that no longer constitutes trade secrets.

The following three areas deserve special comment:

Patents.   Issued patents are good examples of technical information that no longer constitutes trade secrets. The information contained in a patent application is kept by the Patent and Trademark Office as a trade secret as long as the application is pending. The day the patent is printed by the Government Printing Office, all trade secrets contained therein become public knowledge.

Copyrights.   Be careful with copyrights. If you do not take proper steps to file your copyrights as trade secrets, they are a matter of public record. If software source code or other valuable and trade secret business information is filed with the copyright office, a procedure exists to protect the trade secrets by filing only the identifying portions. Copyrighted material freely distributed or sold to the public loses any trade secret status it had. If the public can ascertain all technical information, trade secret protection is gone. Trade secrets are often protected under contract law by confidentiality clauses added to license agreements. For example, when a business sells or distributes the copyrighted material (such as software) under a license agreement protecting the confidentiality, then the trade secrets are still protectable.

No internal trade secret program.   Perhaps the single most important factor that weighs against the existence of a trade secret is the absence of a

---

[11] Julius Hyman & Co. v. Velsicol Corp., 123 Colo. 563, 233 P.2d 972, *cert. denied,* 342 U.S. 870, *rehearing denied,* 342 U.S. 895 (1951).

planned business trade secret program. Failure to exercise control over trade secrets will result in loss of trade secret protection.[12] The importance of thoroughly reading this chapter, understanding it, and implementing the simple rules and procedures contained herein cannot be overemphasized.

§ 1.6   Bodies of Law Protecting Trade Secrets

No overall federal legislation like that for patents and copyrights exists for protecting trade secrets. The present action for employee appropriation of trade secrets has been traced to Roman law's *Actio Servi Corrupti*.[13] State law is used to determine the substantive issues of trade secrets.[14]

The Uniform Trade Secrets Act (UTSA) has been promulgated by 26 states.[15] Each state may have modified the UTSA; therefore, it is necessary to check the language of a state's individual act.

RESOURCE: For current information on states incorporating the UTSA, contact:

National Conference of Commissioners on Uniform State Laws
676 North St. Clair Street, Suite 1700
Chicago, IL 60611
(312) 915-0195

In states that have not passed the UTSA, trade secrets have traditionally been protected under the principles of common law (the body of law our country inherited from Great Britain, which is not based upon statute but upon case-by-case determinations). Over the years a significant body of

---

[12] Capsonic Group, Inc. v. Plas-Met Corp., 46 Ill. App. 3d 436, 361 N.E.2d 41 (1977); Amoco Prod. Co. v. Lindley, 609 P.2d 733, 743 (Okla. 1980).

[13] Schiller, *Trade Secrets in the Roman Law; The Actio Servi Corrupti,* 30 Colum. L. Rev. 837 (1930).

[14] Kewanee Oil Co. v. Bicron Corp., 416 U.S. 470 (1974).

[15] Ark. Stat. Ann. §§ 70-1001 to 1007 (1981); Cal. Civil Code § 3246 (West Supp. 1986); Colo. Rev. Stat. § 7-74-101 (1986); Conn. Gen. Stat. Ann. § 35-50 (West 1983); Del. Code Ann. tit. 6, §§ 2001 to 2009 (1981); Idaho Code §§ 48-801 to 807 (1981); Ind. Code Ann. § 24-2-3-1 (West 1986); Kan. Stat. Ann. §§ 60-3320 to 3330 (1981); La. Rev. Stat. Ann. § 51:1431 (West 1981); Minn. Stat. Ann. § 325 C.01 (West Supp. 1987); Mont. Code Ann. § 30-14-401 (1985); N.C. Gen. Stat. §§ 77-152 to 162 (1981); N.D. Cent. Code § 47-25.1-01 (1983); Okla. Stat. Ann. tit. 78, § 85 (West Supp. 1987); R.I. Gen. Laws § 6-14-1 (1956); Va. Code Ann. § 59.1-336 (1950); Wash. Rev. Code Ann. § 19.108.010 (1986); W. Va. Code § 47-22-1 (1986); Wisc. Stat. Ann. § 134.90 (West Supp. 1986).

law has been developed by the courts in the area of trade secrets, based principally upon the *Restatement of Torts* definition. See § **1.2**. Protection of trade secrets exists under a variety of state laws and is based in the following legal theories:

Contract and implied in fact contract. For example, two parties agree in writing to protect trade secrets.[16]

Fiduciary and confidential relationships. For example, a director or officer of a corporation has a duty not to disclose trade secrets. However, after termination of a confidential relationship there is no fiduciary duty to refrain from developing or selling one's own apparatus.[17]

Unfair competition. An example is the enticement away from a competitor of employees knowing trade secrets.[18]

Civil misappropriation. This is the actual appropriation of trade secrets without authorization.

Most states have also passed criminal trade secret statutes precisely covering the situation of an employee stealing the company's trade secrets.[19] If a company suspects its trade secrets have been stolen, it should consider commencing criminal proceedings. Such actions are lower in cost than civil suits because attorneys' fees are incurred by the government; and also a criminal action will send a message to all employees that the company considers trade secret theft a punishable offense. Many district attorneys, however, do not consider such actions high priority in comparison to murder and drug trafficking. For example, NCR Corp. cooperated with the FBI in a spy sting operation that

---

[16] Stanley Aviation Corp. v. United States, 196 U.S.P.Q. (BNA) 612, 617 (D. Colo. 1977).

[17] Automated Sys., Inc. v. Service Bureau Corp., 401 F.2d 619, 159 U.S.P.Q. (BNA) 395 (10th Cir. 1968).

[18] See **Ch. 3**.

[19] Ark. Stat. Ann. § 41-2207 (1977); Cal. Penal Code § 499c (West Supp. 1986); Colo. Rev. Stat. § 18-4-408 (1986); Ga. Code Ann. § 16-18-13 (1984); Ill. Ann. Stat. ch. 38, para. 15 (Smith-Hurd Supp. 1986); Ind. Code Ann. § 35-43-4-2 (West 1986); Me. Rev. Stat. Ann. tit. 17A, § 351 (1986); Mass. Gen. Laws Ann. ch. 266, § 30 (West Supp. 1986); Mich. Comp. Laws Ann. §§ 752–772 (West Supp. 1987); Neb. Rev. Stat. § 28-509 (1985); N.H. Rev. Stat. Ann. § 637:2 (1986); N.J. Stat. Ann. § 2C:20-1 (West Supp. 1986); N.M. Stat. Ann. § 30-16-24 (1978); N.Y. Penal Law § 165.07 (McKinney 1977); Ohio Rev. Code Ann. § 1333.51 (Page 1979); Okla. Stat. Ann. tit. 21, § 1732 (West Supp. 1987); Pa. Stat. Ann. tit. 18, § 2930 (Purdon 1983); Tenn. Code Ann. § 39-3-1126 (1982); Tex. Penal Code Ann. § 31.05 (Vernon 1974); Wis. Stat. Ann. § 943.205 (West Supp. 1986).

resulted in the arrest of an NCR employee. The employee had attempted to sell the NCR technological specifications and marketing plans for its imaging technology to Unisys for $200,000. The employee now faces a 10-year sentence.[20]

The Federal Trade Secrets Act covers only the specific criminal acts of federal employees. This Act states in part:

> Whoever, being an officer or employee of the United States or of any department or agency thereof, publishes, divulges, discloses, or makes known in any manner or to any extent not authorized by law any information . . . which . . . concerns or relates to the trade secrets . . . of any person, firm, partnership, corporation or association . . . shall be fined not more than $1,000, or imprisoned not more than one year, or both, and shall be removed from office or employment.[21]

§ 1.7   Term of a Trade Secret

Trade secrets have an indeterminate term, which may be perpetual. Whether a trade secret is perpetual is determined by the inherent nature of the secret itself. If the trade secret is a new product idea for a simple mechanic's tool, the term of the trade secret is only as long as the corporation keeps it an internal secret. The day the tool is shown at a convention or sold to a member of the public, the world at large understands how to copy the tool, and the term of protection ends. In this case, the term of the trade secret from conception to the first demonstration or sale, although short, has been extremely valuable. A corporation keeps new product ideas secret during this time for the reason that it does not want its competitors to know what valuable new products are under consideration. This produces a significant marketing edge over competitors.

The term of a trade secret may be lengthy, as in the areas of organic materials. It is said that the trade secret for the soft drink Coca-Cola still has not entered the public domain despite the fact that the common ingredients of Coca-Cola are known. When a chemical composition falls within this category, it is a wise business decision to protect the chemical formulation as a trade secret and not publicly disclose it in an issued patent.

Electronics manufacturers have long sought to encapsulate or otherwise mask their electronic circuitry, integrated circuit chips, and the like. When they do this, they are availing themselves of self-help techniques to lengthen the terms of their trade secrets.

---

[20] Booker, *Spy Sting Nabs NCR Worker Trying to Pawn Image Goods,* Computer World, Dec. 18, 1989, at 1 & 89.

[21] 18 U.S.C. § 1905 (Supp. 1988).

Therefore, the term of a trade secret is indeterminate. The term is as long as it takes for the public or a competitor to figure out how to make the product and to ascertain the nature and identity of the trade secret.

From a practical point of view, a corporation should take whatever steps are necessary to lengthen the term of its trade secret. Engineers should be requested to find technical ways to hide the invention better in packaging, and thought should be given to how much technical information should be provided in operating manuals and technical specifications.

§ 1.8   Role of Reverse Engineering

For years, businesses have purchased competing products and have subjected such products to a full battery of tests and analysis. It is well recognized that trade secret law does not offer protection against discovery by such fair and honest means. This is simply the well-known *doctrine of reverse engineering,* that is, starting with a known product and working backward to understand its particular makeup and the competitor's trade secrets. For example, when a business visually inspected the paving machine of a competitor, it had the full legal right to copy the design which, in fact, it did. The competitor was able to come out with a competing paving machine in less than a year. No trade secret misappropriation occurred.[22] But watch out for patent infringement. See **Chapter 2**.

Keep in mind that reverse engineering must occur by "fair and honest means." If improper means such as gaining the information unfairly through breach of a confidential relationship occurs, the doctrine of reverse engineering will not provide a defense.[23]

Industrial espionage is undertaken not only by small corporations but by very large ones. A number of electronic devices are commercially available to ascertain whether phone lines are being tapped, conversations are being recorded, or other electronic bugging devices are present in offices and conference rooms. There are security firms specializing in this area, and it may be wise to retain their services to conduct a periodic electronic sweep of your premises to ascertain the existence of any such devices.

In certain situations such as software shrink wrap and end user agreements, some corporations are attempting to prevent reverse engineering contractually. For example, the standard form IBM agreement states that the "customer shall not reverse assemble or reverse compile the license programs in whole or in part." A legal concern of such contractual

---

[22] CMI Corp. v. Jakob, 209 U.S.P.Q. F. Supp. (BNA) 233 (W.D. Okla. 1980).

[23] Digital Dev. Corp. v. International Memory Sys., 185 U.S.P.Q. (BNA) 136, 141 (S.D. Cal. 1973).

waivers is whether they are constitutionally invalid as attempts to preempt federal patent law by means of state contract law.

RESOURCE: An important resource reference in this area is Laurie, "Protection of Trade Secrets in Object Form Software: The Case for Reverse Engineering," in *The Computer Lawyer,* Vol. 1, No. 6, pp. 1–11 (July 1984).

On the flip side of the coin, in order to successfully reverse engineer a competitor's product to gain information, it is important to carefully document the steps of reverse engineering. The following procedure should be considered:

1. Before conducting the reverse engineering, check employee files to ascertain whether you have recently hired employees from the competitor whose product is being reverse engineered. If so, carefully isolate those employees from the reverse engineering project.
2. Maintain documentation setting forth step-by-step procedures of the reverse engineering of the competitor's product, including the purchase invoice and all costs involved. For example, if a chemical analysis of material was performed, keep accurate records of who in the organization conducted the experiments, the time and costs, and the results.

In the event a competitor sues, this evidence can help establish "fair and honest" reverse engineering of the purchased product. Such objective evidence substantiates the step-by-step reverse engineering. Overkill and diligence in reverse engineering will be an evidentiary boon should litigation result. In the case of independent development of a new product (that is, without reverse engineering another's product), objective evidence of development is also important to defeat a future claim of trade secret theft.[24]

§ 1.9 Setting Up a Corporate Trade Secret Program

The more rigorously your business sets up its trade secret program, the more successful the program will be, and the easier it will be for a court of law to protect the trade secrets from misappropriation. **Sections 1.10**

---

[24] Eco-Separator Co. v. Shell Canada Ltd., 872 F.2d 427, 431, 12 U.S.P.Q. 2d (BNA) 1635, 1637 (9th Cir. 1989).

through **1.14** set forth the basics of a corporate trade secret program, including physically securing the plant, controlling entrance to the plant by suppliers and vendors, creating technological fingerprints, and properly marking and categorizing documents.

§ 1.10 —Physical Plant

Our firm once had a client who had just raised $5 million in a public offering. The company was flush with cash and had rented lavish office space. Capital was principally raised on the company's trade secret process for mining oil underground. We were called to the new office to review intellectual property matters with company officials. As we sat in their elegant conference room, we viewed diagrams and formulas setting forth the process of oil extraction carefully printed and drawn on the blackboard. These trade secrets were the corporate jewels, the actual heartbeat of the company.

In discussing plant security, we asked when the janitors came to clean the premises. We were told that between 6:00 and 7:00 p.m. every night the janitors came, opened the doors of each of the offices and proceeded to clean them.

Even as they explained this, the company officials were not aware of the terrible risk of a competitor coming into the premises with a camera to steal their trade secrets by photographing the blackboard. After we discussed this possibility with them, that office became much more secure. All cleaning from that day forward occurred during the last working hour of the day, while the employees were still present.

Physical plant security must be taken seriously. Technology is so sophisticated that laser beams can be bounced off glass windows of offices and conversations can be picked up and recorded from the reflected laser beams. Techniques presently exist to monitor, from several floors away, the activity of a personal computer on an executive's desk. Surveillance technology is quite sophisticated.

Resources may not be available to "totally secure" a business, but some rather obvious physical steps of protection can be taken.

Trash. More trade secrets physically leave a company's premises through its trash than from any other single leak. One case in which trade secrets were obtained by a competitor's ransacking a company's trash resulted in an award of $100,000 compensatory damages and $400,000 punitive damages.[25]

---

[25] Tennant Co. v. Advance Mach. Co., 355 N.W. 2d 720 (Minn. Ct. App. 1984).

At a minimum, a business should buy a heavy-duty shredder and make it standard office procedure to shred all documents. There is no need to train a clerk regarding what should or should not be shredded. Simply shred all work product that is thrown away. This most assuredly includes shredding all magnetic storage material, and it also means destroying typewriter ribbons, which contain a running diary of what has been typed.

Check into the nature and operation of the garbage hauling service. If trash is mingled with trash picked up from other offices in the building or industrial complex, the risk of theft is not as great as if it is not.

Employee access.   After normal business hours, doors should be secured and the premises protected with an effective burglar system. If employees must enter the premises after hours, let them log in and out under control of the burglar alarm company. Larger businesses will have full-time security guards who monitor this process.

Allowing employees to work on Saturdays or after hours or to take work home constitutes a substantial risk of misappropriation of trade secrets.

An employer's control over employees working at home is easily lost. Employees may be tempted to set up a competing business or to sell trade secret technology to a competitor. The employer's control is too remote and the temptations are too great.

Miscellaneous plant security.   Do not overlook the necessity for locked file cabinets and restricted areas within the physical plant so that, for example, factory workers in one area do not have access to engineering documents located in another area.

§ 1.11   —Visitors, Vendors, and Suppliers

A significant source of trade secret leaks is the disclosure of information to visitors. Most suppliers and vendors are honest and trustworthy; however, some may try to learn about trade secrets. They may then discuss this technology with a competitor, hoping that the competitor will also buy from them. Even if there is no evil intent on the part of vendors or suppliers, they can quickly pass on valuable trade secret information in idle conversation with competitors.

Here are some suggestions for dealing with visitors:[26]

Sign in/sign out sheet.   All visitors, including suppliers, vendors, and maintenance persons, must sign in, state the nature of their business,

---

[26] These suggestions are taken from SI Handling Sys., Inc. v. Heisley, 581 F. Supp. 1563, 222 U.S.P.Q. (BNA) 52 (M.D. Pa. 1989).

indicate with whom they are visiting, and sign out. A sample of an appropriate log is:

Form 1–1
VISITOR LOG IN

Date	Name	Company	Who Visiting	Purpose	Time In	Time Out

Repair and service personnel.   Separate logs should be established for repair and service personnel. Before admitting such personnel to the plant, it may be wise to set up an internal procedure either (1) to verify the service call with the person at the plant making the service request, or (2) to call the service company to verify the service person's credentials and the purpose of the visit. A suitable log, similar to the Sign In/Sign Out Sheet above, should be set up.

Agreement.   In highly sensitive areas, prudent businesses will ask visitors to sign the type of agreement to respect the company's trade secrets set forth in **§ 1.16, Form 1–6.** After signing, the visitor should be given a badge identifying her as a visitor and be met by or escorted to the person being visited.

Keeping quiet.   Employees should be instructed that when dealing with visitors, especially suppliers and vendors, they should never discuss any project as a whole. Employees must limit their conversation to only the specific needs and requirements of the individual vendor. For example, a vendor should know only that a particular engineer needs a brushless DC motor of a particular specification and tolerance. She should not know that the motor will go into a revolutionary optical disk memory. You must educate employees not to brag about the company's new product on which they are working.

After a meeting, a visitor should be escorted out and not be allowed to stroll from aisle to aisle or from office to office, even if the visitor simply wants to say "Hi" to some old chums. Once implemented, such a program of strict control will be easy to enforce.

For example, we were involved in a lawsuit in which an employee of the company, while working at home, had the complete schematics of the company's new electronic product spread all over the basement floor. The employee invited the vendor that had been supplying parts to the company to help convert the schematics over to a new logic family. The vendor willingly did this (after all, the vendor wanted the additional business). The employee then left the company and formed a new business. The vendor said nothing to the company about the theft of the schematics or his role in it until his deposition was taken in the ensuing lawsuit.

Plant tours.   When conducting plant tours, it is mandatory that trade secrets be secured and out of sight of persons touring the plant. The tour group should be carefully guided through the plant and not allowed to wander about. They should not be permitted to talk idly to company engineers or technicians.

Single access to plant.   All visitors to the plant should be directed through a single entrance, and such visitors should both enter and leave the plant through the same access.

§ 1.12   —File and Document Control

It is important to mark all internal memoranda, drawings, blueprints, schematics, software listings, and all other items that contain a business's secrets with a suitable confidentiality legend, such as:

Form 1–2
TRADE SECRET LEGEND

TRADE SECRET—DO NOT COPY. THIS MATERIAL IS CONFIDENTIAL AND PROPRIETARY, BEING EXCLUSIVELY OWNED BY POORHORSE CORPORATION, P.O. BOX 1022, SUREFIRE, COLORADO 80187. THE EXPRESSION OF THE INFORMATION CONTAINED HEREIN IS PROTECTED UNDER FEDERAL COPYRIGHT LAWS AND ALL COPYING IS PROHIBITED AND MAY BE SUBJECT TO CRIMINAL PENALTIES.

Two points are important. First, a clear statement that the material contains trade secrets should be made and, second, the particular document should be protected as a writing under the federal copyright laws. This is overlapping protection in that the ideas and concepts contained within the document are protected as trade secrets, and the expression (how they are written, drawn, and so forth) is protected under federal copyright law as an unpublished manuscript.

Of course, variations on this tough sounding legend can be made, but failure to use such legends may negate the existence of trade secrets.[27] Some companies simply use:

---

[27] Stanley Aviation Corp. v. United States, 196 U.S.P.Q. (BNA) 612, 620–22 (D. Colo. 1977).

Form 1-3

TRADE SECRET

or

COMPANY PROPRIETARY INFORMATION

Such legends should appear on each schematic, drawing, or blueprint. Typically they are incorporated in the box bearing the title of the document and authorship information. Such legends should also appear on floppy diskettes, tape cartridges, software listings, manuals, internal memos, and the like.

Some organizations assign trade secrets to sophisticated categories, thereby setting up caste systems for trade secrets. The most important trade secrets are separately categorized, carefully marked, and stored in file cabinets with locks that can be opened only by selected employees. At the other end of the spectrum, documents may be considered as not subject to trade secret protection and freely disseminated inside and outside the business. Hierarchies of secrecy should be well thought out initially and then continually monitored. This can be a difficult task for smaller businesses.

It is important not to put a TRADE SECRET legend on *all* company material—only on valued trade secrets. Some courts may find an overuse of such legends (such as placing TRADE SECRET on the company's food menu) to be evidence of no trade secret protection at all.

When trade secrets are no longer secret (for example, if they have been publicly disclosed in trade journals, conference presentations, or in product announcements and sales), what has been formally marked as trade secret within the company should be declassified. This is an important step, because it clearly establishes good faith and proper intent to the judge or jury in subsequent trade secret litigation.

Most businesses now make extensive use of computers. Computers, however, are quite vulnerable to theft. It is important to use the best technology to safeguard trade secrets in a computer system. Access not only by entities outside the company but also by unauthorized employees within the company must be carefully regulated. In other words, access to the computer database should be secured upon a need-to-know basis.

Techniques that can be used are:

1. Record all accesses to the computer (user, time, duration, purpose, and the like)
2. Use software access passwords

3. Only allow remote access from outside the plant to a computer inside the plant by having the computer call back to an authorized telephone number
4. Encrypt database and software
5. If accessing an outside network or bulletin board, install antiviral software to protect against software viruses and worms. See **Chapter 8**.

§ 1.13   —Technological Fingerprints

In trade secret litigation, valuable evidence of misappropriation or trade secret theft is found in the copying of intentional mistakes or buried "technological fingerprints" in the material. Consequently, engineers should be instructed to include these types of fingerprints. For example, a useless loop in a programming module can be significant evidence of trade secret misappropriation, as well as solid evidence of access in a copyright infringement lawsuit (see **Chapter 5**).

§ 1.14   —Customer Lists

Customer, supplier, prospective customer, vendor, manufacturer, and other comparable lists are important categories of business information that need protection as trade secrets. The United States Supreme Court in *Kewanee Oil Co. v. Bicron Corp.* stated:

> [I]t is hard to see how the public would be benefited by disclosure of customer lists or advertising campaigns; in fact, keeping such items secret encourages businesses to initiate new and individualized plans of operation, and constructive competition results. This, in turn, leads to a greater variety of business methods than would otherwise be the case if privately developed marketing and other data were passed illicitly among firms in the same enterprise.[28]

Unfortunately, courts across the United States grant customer lists varying degrees of protection. Everything that has been suggested in this chapter must be rigorously applied to these lists. Customer lists should be marked TRADE SECRET, their distribution restricted, and their use by employees monitored closely.

These lists are not protectable if they are generally available, for example, in industry directories; nor are they protectable if the employee

---

[28] 416 U.S. 470, 483 (1974).

appropriating the list brought with her the customer and client contacts when originally hired.[29]

The more detailed the information in a list, the more likely it is that a court will protect it from misappropriation. Therefore, it is important to establish detailed information (such as customer characteristics, merchandising data, prices, purchasing approval, and delivery addresses) in the customer database. Records should be internally preserved establishing the time, energy, and money expended to screen and develop the customer list.

§ 1.15   Employee Agreements

Exiting employees represent the highest degree of risk for trade secret theft. Every business must worry not only about one of its key employees leaving and setting up a competing business, but also about the departure of lower level employees. A set of floppy diskettes illegally taken by a disgruntled employee may contain tens or hundreds of thousands of dollars worth of valuable secrets. The protection of a business's trade secrets, therefore, constitutes an important part of the employee agreement.

The employee agreement varies in composition depending on the nature of the employee's duties and obligations. A contract for the employment of a president, CEO, or manager of a business may have not only substantial trade secret protection clauses, but also covenants not to compete. A technical clerk's agreement, on the other hand, may have no trade secret or confidentiality clauses. Usually, most middle level management, engineers, and technicians have employment agreements that protect the company's trade secrets.

Pre-employment clearance.   A company should be cautious when hiring employees away from its competitors. During the employment interview or at the point of job offer, it should be made crystal clear to a prospective employee that none of the trade secrets from any prior employments are to be used in the performance of their duties. Under no circumstances are another company's physical material, such as diskettes, technical specifications, drawings, and so forth, to be brought onto the premises of the company. A wise company will carefully assign new employees to areas that do not correspond to prior areas of employment, at least for a period of time.

---

[29] *See* Mid-America Nat'l Agency v. Albert H. Wohlers & Co., 8 U.S.P.Q.2d (BNA) 1780, 1781–82 (D. Kan. 1988) (holding list to be generally available); Nutmeg Technologies v. Mahshie, 12 U.S.P.Q.2d (BNA) 1469, 1472–73 (N.D.N.Y. 1989) (holding lists protectable and setting forth list of criteria to be met in establishing protection).

Common law duties. Employees are bound at common law, even in the absence of an agreement, not to use or disclose the employer's trade secrets. Yet an employee has the legal right upon termination to use the general skill and knowledge that was acquired during employment. This right has strong public policy arguments supporting it: freedom of competition, the freedom of the employee to practice and advance in a skill or profession, and the public's interest in labor mobility. In view of this strong public policy, it becomes important to mark and designate trade secrets in a business.[30]

Employee agreements. Although it is not necessary to protect trade secrets with a written contract, the written contract is a vehicle by which to maximize trade secret protection while minimizing legal risks. Such written agreements, however, must be reasonable in scope and must not be contrary to public policy. As mentioned, there is a clear public policy favoring the employee's right to use the general knowledge and skill obtained during the course of employment to freely compete with the former employer. There is a countervailing public policy to protect the employer's trade secrets in order to promote the progress of science and the useful arts.

RESOURCE: For a thorough, well-referenced treatise on employee restrictions, see McCarthy, J. Thomas, *Trademarks and Unfair Competition*, Ch. 29: "Competitive Restrictions on Employees" (Lawyers Cooperative Publishing Co., Aqueduct Bldg., Rochester, NY 14694) (2d ed. 1989).

An example of a suitable clause for an employee agreement regarding confidential information is set forth in **§ 1.16, Form 1–4.**

Employee education. It is important for a business to educate its employees at least twice a year to the importance of protecting a business's trade secrets. This meeting should not last more than one hour and should be accompanied by a written policy statement from upper management. An example of such an employee memorandum is set forth in **§ 1.16, Forms 1–5** and **1–6.**

   At the meeting the employees should be encouraged to ask questions, and actual examples of corporate trade secrets should be discussed. The purpose of the meeting is to educate, not intimidate.

---

[30] CVD, Inc. v. Raytheon Co., 769 F.2d 842, 850, 227 U.S.P.Q. (BNA) 7, 12 (1st Cir. 1985), *cert. denied,* 475 U.S. 1016 (1986).

Company bulletin boards.   Use of written trade secret notices placed on company bulletin boards is to be encouraged. These notices provide continued reminders to employees of the importance of keeping information secret. The notices should be changed periodically and can make effective use of cartoons, graphics, and colors.

Employee publications.   All employee publications, technical presentations, and software demonstrations should be carefully reviewed before they are used outside the company. Significant and valued trade secrets can be lost simply because an employee is overzealous in making a thorough and professional presentation.

Job assignments.   Although it is difficult because many companies prefer to have employees work in teams to solve a problem or to design a product, when possible it is a good idea to segregate particular trade secret information to only one or two key personnel who absolutely need to know. Other engineers or employees working on the project should not have access to the information.

Pumping of information.   Competitors may go to great lengths to garner volunteered information from your employees. This takes place under a number of guises. In a most common scenario, competitors may try to pump information concerning products or new products from a sales team at conventions.

For example, we were involved in a trade secret theft lawsuit and, in discovery, we found that our client had a large number of corporate internal files on the competition. It was a policy of our client to have its engineers attend conferences and trade shows and talk to distributors and representatives of its competitors. Later, through casual conversation usually over drinks, the engineers were to obtain as much information about new products, materials, and prices as they possibly could. After each meeting, the engineers would dictate memos according to corporate standards setting forth as much information as possible. These memos were then delivered to the director, who would summarize them on a per competitor basis. This information, in turn, went to the executive vice president in charge of the technological area.

Advise your employees to watch out for any type of information pumping.

Compensation.   When one of your key or valued employees leaves and sets up a competing business or works for a competitor, your company will incur substantial costs. One of the costs may be the great expense of bringing a trade secret misappropriation lawsuit against the key employee.

Another significant cost, of course, is the loss of the key employee and the impact it will have on your business. Such key employees are often basic entrepreneurs. Therefore, you should seriously consider providing a working environment and a compensation package that will encourage motivated individuals to stay with the company. If your competitors are willing to seek out and pay more money to such key employees, you should minimize this type of enticement by keeping them satisfied financially.

Termination.   Properly handling the termination of employees is becoming an art form. More and more often, employees leaving to work for a competitor or leaving to form a competing business may be under careful legal guidance. Sample documents related to termination of an employee are set out in **Forms 1–7, 1–8,** and **1–9** in § **1.16.**

In physically escorting the terminated employee out of the plant, inspect all materials being removed to verify that all items are personal to the employee and that there are no corporate items. A guard or a member of the personnel department should conduct the inspection.

§ 1.16   —Forms: Employee Agreements

Form 1–4
EMPLOYMENT AGREEMENT
REGARDING CONFIDENTIAL INFORMATION

I acknowledge that this Agreement concerns all confidential information relating to the intellectual property, trade secrets, confidential business and technical information, processes, applications, business practices and agreements, financial information, drawings, plans, methods, manufacturing information, engineering, research and development, and know-how imparted to me or learned or made by me in connection with my employment with Poorhorse Corp. As to this confidential information and any portions thereof, I agree:

   a.   to use it only in the performance of my *company* duties; and
   b.   to hold it in confidence and trust, using all reasonable precautions to assure that it is not disclosed to any unauthorized persons or used in an unauthorized manner or published either during or after my employment with Poorhorse Corp.

In the event I have some question as to whether certain information is covered by this paragraph, I agree to treat such information as falling under this paragraph until told otherwise in writing by Poorhorse Corp.

This clause is but part of an overall employment agreement. See **Chapter 2** for other clauses.

Form 1–5
MEMORANDUM TO EMPLOYEE FROM PRESIDENT

Poorhorse Corp. has a number of valuable trade secrets. These include customer, vendor, and supplier lists, research and development information for new products, and current product manufacturing techniques. This material is TRADE SECRET and MUST NOT be disclosed to persons outside of the corporation. Poorhorse Corp. has prepared the following manual for use by employees in protecting its trade secrets. Please read through it carefully. Should you have any questions, please contact me.

POORHORSE CORPORATION

_____

President

Form 1–6
EMPLOYEE MANUAL
What Are Trade Secrets?

What is a _trade secret,_ and what makes it a valuable property of Poorhorse Corp.? A trade secret is confidential information known only to the corporation and to those of its employees entrusted to use it. It is not necessary that the confidential information be patentable or copyrightable, although it may also be. Trade secrets give Poorhorse Corp. the opportunity to obtain an advantage over our competitors who do not have the information or don't know how to use it.

The following are examples of trade secrets owned by Poorhorse Corp.:

a.   Customer, supplier, and vendor lists
b.   Research and development information for new products
c.   All financial information pertaining to sales, profits, rebates, discounts, etc.
d.   Manufacturing processes, sources of materials, and inventories.

Why Protect Trade Secrets?

Trade secrets are legally protected as long as they are kept secret. If Poorhorse Corp. did not take the steps discussed in the following sections of this manual, it would lose valuable legal rights. An accidental publication in a journal or a careless statement made at a convention almost always results in significant loss to the corporation.

Common examples of trade secrets in the marketplace are the recipe for Coca-Cola, the seasonings for coating Kentucky Fried Chicken, and the compositions of certain paints and oils. Most products lose their trade secret status when sold, because anyone can buy the product and reverse engineer it. However, throughout research, development, and manufacture, until the point of market introduction, the product and its associated information are all treated as *trade secret*.

Trade secrets legally protect the company's investment in time, money, manpower, and materials in developing new products. Even our attempts and failures are trade secret; if our competitors knew of them, they could arrive at competing products in a shorter time and with less financial investment.

This manual sets forth the legal procedures for protecting these trade secrets.

How to Identify Trade Secrets

Trade secrets exist in many forms. Examples of documents which may contain trade secrets are internal memos, blueprints, schematics, engineering drawings, specifications, manuals, lists, etc. Trade secrets may also be contained in software, databases, software listings, etc. Some trade secrets may be orally discussed in engineering, marketing, sales, or brainstorming sessions.

Who Has Access?

Poorhorse Corp. is not a large corporation; consequently, almost every employee will have a need to use various trade secrets at one time or another. However, some trade secrets will be made available on a strict need-to-know basis to only certain employees. In the case of such need-to-know trade secrets, employees are not to disclose them to fellow employees unless specific authorization is given by the President.

Use of Trade Secret Legends

Poorhorse Corp. requests all employees to make frequent use of the following legends to mark its trade secrets. These legends are available on rubber stamps, preprinted on engineering drawings, etc.

a.   Internal/External (Subject to an Agreement):

TRADE SECRET—DO NOT COPY. THIS MATERIAL IS CONFIDENTIAL AND PROPRIETARY, BEING EXCLUSIVELY OWNED BY POORHORSE CORPORATION, P.O. BOX 1022, SUREFIRE, COLORADO 80187. THE EXPRESSION OF THE INFORMATION CONTAINED HEREIN IS PROTECTED UNDER FEDERAL COPYRIGHT LAWS, AND ALL COPYING IS PROHIBITED AND MAY BE SUBJECT TO CRIMINAL PENALTIES.

b.   Need-to-Know:

NEED-TO-KNOW TRADE SECRET. DO NOT COPY! DO NOT DISTRIBUTE!

How to File

Since trade secrets must be kept secret, stringent filing of documents containing trade secrets must be adhered to.

a. Never leave trade secret material lying open on your desk, especially after hours.

b. Always file trade secret material into your file cabinet or desk. Need-to-know trade secrets are to be filed in a locked file cabinet designated for such use.

c. Secure all computers containing trade secrets with suitable passwords, codes, and, if possible, use encryption software to encode the secret information.

Copies of documents not to be filed *are to be destroyed!* Several shredders are available in central locations. *All documents,* whether or not they contain trade secrets, are to be shredded.

How to Handle Visitors

Outside persons frequently visit Poorhorse. They include vendors, repair persons, suppliers, manufacturers' representatives, sales personnel, advertising agents, and outside support persons. All visits are to be strictly monitored.

a. Each visitor shall complete the *visitor log* at the reception desk. This will show the time of the visit, the person being visited, and the purpose of the visit.

b. Each visitor shall also sign the following agreement, which will be given and preserved by the receptionist:

Visitor's Pass

In consideration of permission to enter the premises of Poorhorse Corp., I agree neither to disclose to others nor to use any trade secret or confidential information disclosed by Poorhorse Corp. or derived by me during this visit. I verify that I have read and understood this document.

_____   _____

Date   Signature of Visitor

c. Each visitor shall wear a *visitor's badge* given by the receptionist while on the premises of Poorhorse Corp.

d. Visitors are not allowed to wander around the premises. An employee shall meet each visitor at the reception desk and guide the visitor to the employee's office or meeting room. After the visit, the employee will accompany the visitor back to the reception desk.

e. Employees shall not give any visitor more information than is necessary for purposes of the visit.

Form 1–7
EMPLOYEE EXIT INTERVIEW CHECKLIST

Employee _____   File Number _____

Interviewer _____   Date of Termination _____

Yes/No

_____ 1.   Did employee show up for interview?
           If yes, did employee act hostile or make any adverse comments?

           _____

           _____

           _____

_____ 2.   Were all secrecy provisions of the employment agreement and cor-
           porate trade secret policy reviewed?

           Any comments by employee?

           _____

           _____

           _____

_____ 3.   Does employee have any corporate documents, software, material,
           hardware, etc., at home or elsewhere away from the office?

           If yes, detail the items and how they will be returned.

           _____

           _____

           _____

_____ 4.   Did employee mention the name of any attorney or future employer?

           If so, please identify:

           _____

           _____

           _____

_____ 5.   Were the boxes of materials taken by the employee inspected?

           If yes, set forth all details on inspecting (i.e., what was taken from
           the premises, who inspected, the circumstances of the escort, and
           all other details).

           _____

           _____

           _____

___ 6. Obtain address to which any of employee's personal mail should be forwarded.

_____

_____

_____

_____	_____
Date	Signature of Inspector

_____	_____
Date	Signature of Interviewer

The exit interview can be touchy and should, under certain circumstances (e.g., the exit of key employees), be done under careful guidance of either in-house or outside counsel. Be advised that some exiting employees may also be under the careful guidance of their attorneys.

The exit interview provides the company an opportunity to remind the employee of the trade secret program and of the obligation to protect trade secrets even after termination; to inspect physically the materials being taken; and to record any adverse or hostile comments being made. Be watchful; be professional; respect the employee's right of privacy with respect to personal property; and be on guard for possible trade secret theft.

Form 1–8
ACKNOWLEDGMENT OF EXIT INTERVIEW

I acknowledge that the undersigned representative of Poorhorse Corp. has conducted an exit interview with me.

At this interview, my employment obligations to protect the trade secrets of Poorhorse Corp. as set forth in my employment agreement were reviewed.

I acknowledge that I have been privy to various trade secrets during my employment with Poorhorse Corp. and that if I have any doubt as to whether a particular item of information is considered by Poorhorse Corp. to be a trade secret, I will treat it as trade secret.

I further acknowledge that I have returned all trade secret material that I may have had at my home or elsewhere, including any and all copies thereof.

_____	_____
Date	Employee

_____	_____
Date	Representative of Poorhorse Corp.

The employee may resist signing this acknowledgement. Do not become forceful in obtaining the signature. If you do not get it, make note of this fact, carefully recording any comments the employee made.

Form 1–9
FOLLOW-UP LETTER AFTER TERMINATION

Dear _____:

The purpose of this letter is to discuss with you several remaining matters, as reviewed in your exit interview, following your departure from Poorhorse Corp.

Mail.   Please make immediate plans for transferring all personal mail to your new address. We will endeavor to forward all personal mail to you at the following address which you gave us during your exit interview:

_____

_____

_____

If this is incorrect, please call. All other mail will be opened in our normal course of business and, if determined to be personal, it will be forwarded to you. If not, it will be retained by Poorhorse Corp.

Corporation Property.   Please verify that you have taken no property owned by the corporation. This includes data, drawings, research information, software, hardware, memos, letters, and all other physical items of any nature whatsoever. If you have such property or if you subsequently find such property, please return it to Poorhorse Corp. at our full cost for transportation.

Trade Secrets.   All Poorhorse Corp. trade secrets are owned exclusively by Poorhorse Corp. As set forth in your employment agreement, you are not permitted after termination to use these secrets yourself or disclose them to others.

If you have any questions concerning the above, please give me a call.

Very truly yours,

Poorhorse Corp.

Date: _____   By: _____

Automatically send this letter by certified mail, return receipt requested, to all exiting employees. In addition to verifying the employee's forwarding address, you are reminding the employee to return any newly discovered corporation information.

§ 1.17   Covenants Not to Compete

Covenants not to compete are harsh restrictions on the future employment capabilities of a person. Therefore, it is not surprising that some states view them as unenforceable, and 15 states have specific statutes on these covenants.[31]

Business counsel must review covenant-not-to-compete law in the particular state of concern; the many variations among the states make it unwise to ignore this basic premise.

RESOURCES:

1. Valiulis, Anthony C., *Covenants Not to Compete* (John Wiley & Sons: New York, NY) (1988). This is an excellent reference that sets forth case law and breaks down reasonableness requirements in each state.

2. Aspelund, Donald J., *Employee Noncompetition Law* (Clark Boardman Co.: 375 Hudson St., New York, NY 10014) (1988).

3. Annotation, *Efficiency of Consideration for Employee's Covenant Not to Compete, Entered into after Inception of Employment,* 51 A.L.R. 3d 825 (1987).

4. Note, *Consideration for Employee Non-Competition Covenants in Employments-at-Will,* 54 Fordham L. Rev. 1123 (1986).

Most states, however, will enforce a covenant not to compete in an employment relationship (1) if it is reasonable and necessary to protect a business's trade secrets, (2) if the technical field of noncompetition is narrowly drafted, (3) if it is reasonable as to term (such as two to three years), (4) if it is geographically reasonable in territorial restrictions (such as a given state), and (5) if valuable consideration is given for the covenant.

For example, a five-year worldwide noncompetition clause in the field of computers for the vice president of a company that manufacturers WORM (write once, read many) computer data storage would be held unenforceable. The time is too long, the territory is too broad, and the field of noncompetition is overbroad. However, a one-year noncompetition clause restricted to the United States and limited to the technical area of WORM data storage devices may well be proper and enforceable.

---

[31] Ala. Code § 8-1 (1975); Cal. Bus. & Prof. Code § 16600 (West 1964); Colo. Rev. Stat. § 8-2-113(2) (1973); Fla. Stat. Ann. § 542.12 (West 1964 & Supp. 1980); Haw. Rev. Stat. § 480-4 (1976); La. Rev. Stat. Ann. § 23.921 (West 1964); Mont. Code Ann. § 13-807 (1967); N.C. Gen. Stat. § 75-2 (1975); N.D. Cent. Code § 9-08-06 (1975); Okla. Stat. tit. 15, § 217 (1971); Ore. Rev. Stat. § 653.295 (1977); Tex. Bus. & Com. Code Ann. §§ 15.03, 1505 (Vernon Supp. 1987); Wis. Stat. Ann. § 103.465 (West 1974).

An example of one type of covenant not-to-compete agreement is set forth in § **1.18, Form 1–10**.

§ 1.18   —Form: Covenant Not to Compete

Form 1–10
COVENANT NOT TO COMPETE

In consideration of my employment with Benji Corporation and its successors, assigns, or duly authorized representatives (hereinafter collectively referred to as the "Benji Corp.") and of $100, receipt of which is hereby expressly acknowledged and other valuable consideration paid for my services, I understand and specifically covenant:

1. That Benji Corp. is primarily engaged in the research, design, engineering, development, manufacture and sales of digital cuff-links, and is secondarily engaged in the research and development of new products and areas.

2. That employment by the Benji Corp. and the compensation paid to me by it are at least in part dependent upon earnings or profits which accrue to the Benji Corp. through its ownership of assets relating to know-how, trade secrets, inventions, patents, trademarks, and copyrights.

3. That this covenant not to compete is necessary because I will be employed in the professional staff of Benji Corp. reporting directly to executive and management personnel of Benji Corp. and in that employment I will have access to valuable trade secrets and proprietary information owned by Benji Corp.

4. That I will not, for a period of 18 months following termination of my employment for whatever reason or cause, either directly or indirectly as an employee, consultant, investor, or owner, associate myself with any other entity which directly competes with the Benji Corp. in the development, manufacture, sale, distribution, or servicing of products similar to the digital cuff-links of Benji Corp., nor will I divert or attempt to divert from the Benji Corp. any business whatsoever by influencing or attempting to influence any customers of the Benji Corp. I understand that the Benji Corp. does and its competitors do distribute their product nationwide and I therefore specifically consent to this restriction being within the United States of America and do not believe such restriction to be an unreasonable restraint on any future employment by me. I understand and agree that this covenant not to compete is necessary to provide Benji Corp. with protection for its aforesaid valuable trade secrets which it now has or may acquire during my term of employment.

5. That a breach of the obligations imposed on me in Paragraph 4 regarding competition with the Benji Corp. is not one which is capable of being easily measured by monetary damages, but that *this provision is an essential part of my employment with the Benji Corp.* Consequently,

I specifically agree that this covenant not to compete may be enforced by injunctive relief. Additionally, I specifically agree that, in addition to such injunctive relief, and not in lieu of it, the Benji Corporation may also bring suit for actual damages if such be incurred by the Benji Corp. as a result of a breach of my obligations under this covenant not to compete.

6. That in the event a court of competent jurisdiction finds any of the provisions of this Agreement to be so overbroad as to be unenforceable, it is my specific intent that such provision be reduced in scope by the court, but only to the extent deemed necessary by the court to render the provision reasonable and enforceable, keeping in mind that it is my present intention to give the Benji Corp. the broadest possible protection against harmful future competition.

7. That this agreement is executed and delivered within the State of Montana, and I agree that it shall be construed, interpreted and applied in accordance with the laws of that state except with regard to the conflict of law provisions of that state which shall not apply. The court and authorities of the State of Montana and the Federal District Court for the District of Montana shall have jurisdiction over all controversies which may arise with respect to the execution, interpretation and compliance with this agreement, and I hereby waive any other venue to which I may be entitled by virtue of domicile or otherwise. Further, should I initiate or bring a suit or action in any state other than the State of Montana, I agree that upon application by the Benji Corp. said suit shall be dismissed without prejudice and filed in a court in the State of Montana.

8. That for the noncompetition period of 18 months following my termination from the Benji Corp., I am prepared for the possibility that my standard of living may be reduced and I fully accept any risk associated therewith.

9. That this agreement shall be binding on my heirs, executors, administrators and legal representatives, and shall inure to the benefit of the Benji Corp., its assigns, and successors in interest.

10. That Benji Corp. has not forced, threatened, or by any means intimidated me to sign this agreement and that *I have been advised by Benji Corp. to contract an attorney of my choice in reviewing this covenant prior to my signing.*

_____

Date

_____

Signature of Employee

It may be important to pay the key employee upon employment a bonus (or more money) for the covenant not to compete. Sometimes it is important to advise the key employee that upon termination future earnings may be affected. Such a clause appears as **Paragraph 8.**

All contracts incorporating covenants not to compete must be carefully reviewed by corporate counsel.

§ 1.19   Freedom of Information Act

The Freedom of Information Act (FOIA) can either be a disaster or a boon to a corporation. On one hand, it can be beneficial because it may be a perfectly legal vehicle for a business to discover trade secret information about its competitors contained in government agency files. But it can be a disaster if the trade secret information being evaluated by competitors falls under the Freedom of Information Act. An exemption for trade secrets exists under the Freedom of Information Act. This exemption comprises: "trade secrets and commercial or financial information obtained from a person are privileged or confidential."[32] Hence, in submitting trade secret and confidential information to the government, proceed with caution. It is important to check the following resource materials for current procedures for submitting trade secret information to the government.

RESOURCE: McCarthy, Kevin R. & John W. Kornemeier, *Protecting the Confidentiality of Business Information Submitted to the Federal Government* (Matthew Bender: 1275 Broadway, Albany, NY 12201) (1988). An excellent reference, complete with addresses, forms, and practical pointers.

The starting point in the delivery of trade secret information to the government is to mark the material clearly with an appropriate legend, such as:

Form 1–11
FOIA TRADE SECRET LEGEND

This information is exempt from disclosure under the Freedom of Information Act as a TRADE SECRET by reason of Exemption (b)(4), as it contains privileged and confidential commercial or financial information.

Non-trade secret information should be separated out, should not be attached to the trade secret information, and should also be suitably marked as follows:

Form 1–12
FOIA NON-TRADE SECRET LEGEND

This document contains information which may be disclosed under the Freedom of Information Act.

Because government regulations vary from agency to agency and case law is forever changing in this area, it is important to review the current agency

---

[32] 5 U.S.C. § 552(b)(4) (1976).

regulations and case law before proceeding to disclose information to a government agency. Do not rely on promises from government agents, and keep in mind that written agreements with the government may or may not be enforced at a future date. Carefully research this issue before divulging your trade secrets to the federal government.

§ 1.20   Contractually Protecting Trade Secrets with Others

Most corporations will receive trade secret information of others pursuant to an executed trade secret agreement. Internal corporate procedures and policies for handling and processing such trade secret information should be established.

First, all such written agreements must be centrally reviewed by corporate counsel, and the material should be processed and evaluated according to a fixed internal process *and* according to the requirements of the trade secret contract.

At a minimum, when trade secret information is received from an outside source, stamp it with the following type of notice:

Form 1–13
SUBMITTED TRADE SECRETS LEGEND

THIS MATERIAL IS TRADE SECRET AND HAS BEEN DELIVERED TO POORHORSE CORPORATION PURSUANT TO A NON-DISCLOSURE AGREEMENT. DO NOT COPY.

You may even want to stamp numbers on each page by using a BATES stamp.

Date Received: _____

Owner: _____
                Name of Outside Company

Contract: _____
                Contract Identity

Use this legend on a rubber stamp to mark all incoming trade secret information. When you receive such information, limit it to only those persons having a need to know, and file it separately with restricted access. Most nondisclosure contracts have provisions that when such contracts terminate, the material (and all copies) must be returned. When this occurs, bundle up the materials and prepare the following type of receipt:

Form 1–14
RECEIPT FOR DELIVERY OF TRADE
SECRETS BACK TO SUBMITTOR

The undersigned hereby acknowledges receipt of the following material (identify specifically the material returned):

1.

2.

3.

all of which was delivered to Poorhorse Corp. according to a nondisclosure agreement (fully identify the date and the agreement) and returned.

Signed By: _____   _____
              Outside Company   Date

§ 1.21   —Treatment of Unsolicited Ideas

From time to time a company may receive unsolicited ideas for new products, marketing ideas, and the like. Large companies receive a substantial number of these unsolicited submissions. An internal procedure should be set up to handle these submissions. You may direct the submissions to officers, engineers, or marketing people. The submissions should then be immediately delivered to legal counsel for processing. Advise your employees in a written policy statement that they are not to read or analyze such submissions, and that they are to deliver them over immediately to the legal department for handling. Then send a letter to the person making the submission and enclose with the letter the type of disclosure agreement found in **Form 1–15.**

Form 1–15
DISCLOSURE AGREEMENT

I request that Surefire Corp. consider my idea relating to Mud Bullets described in the material submitted herewith and listed below. All additional disclosures relating to the idea submitted herewith shall be subject to the provisions of this Agreement.

I understand that no confidential relationship whatsoever is established by or is to be implied from this submission or consideration of the submitted material, and that such material is not submitted *in confidence.*

By this request and submission I do not grant Surefire Corp., or any of its subsidiaries, any right under any patents on the idea submitted. I agree that, except as this Agreement may be superseded by a subsequent agreement in writing, I will make no claim against Surefire Corp., or any of its subsidiaries, with respect to the idea here submitted except for patent infringement.

_____   _____
Date   Signature

Effective use of this agreement will defuse subsequent litigation should the submitter believe that your company has misappropriated her valuable trade secrets.

§ 1.22   —Trade Secret Nondisclosure Agreements

When your company deals with outside vendors, manufacturers, joint developers, and the like, you will need to include confidentiality clauses in a written agreement with the outside party. Without a written agreement, outside parties are not bound to any duties of confidentiality with you. Indeed, manufacturers may well become privy to your trade secret information and then peddle their manufacturing capabilities to competitors of yours. Always have outside parties sign an agreement like the one set forth in **§ 1.23, Forms 1–16** through **1–17. Form 1–16** is a long form agreement which provides comprehensive coverage. **Form 1–17** is a short form agreement which is more typically found in industry.

§ 1.23   —Form: Trade Secret
Nondisclosure Agreement

Form 1–16
TRADE SECRET NONDISCLOSURE AGREEMENT
(LONG FORM)

WHEREAS, Poorhorse Corp., P.O. Box 1022, Surefire, Colorado 80187 is the owner of valuable Trade Secrets relating to dog food;

WHEREAS, Boss-A-Matic, Inc., a New Jersey Corporation located at 11 Summit Peak, Gaspar, New Jersey 70111 (hereinafter referred to as _Recipient_) is desirous of reviewing Poorhorse Corp.'s Trade Secrets for the purpose of evaluating said Trade Secrets and the possibility of entering into further agreements regarding possible use of said Trade Secrets;

WHEREAS, the parties desire that such disclosure of said Trade Secrets not compromise any of Poorhorse Corp.'s rights in such Trade Secrets;

NOW THEREFORE, Poorhorse Corp. and Recipient agree as follows:

1. Recipient shall observe the strictest secrecy with respect to said Trade Secrets disclosed and all information generated therefrom including evaluations thereof, and shall take all affirmative steps necessary to maintain the trade secret status of said Trade Secrets, subject to the provisions of

Paragraph 3 herein. Recipient shall be responsible for any damages resulting from any breach of this Agreement, which includes the dissemination of said Trade Secrets to any third party who learned of such information through Recipient.

2. Recipient shall neither make use of, except for the purposes of evaluating the present invention, nor disclose to third parties, said Trade Secrets or the evaluation produced by Recipient, unless prior consent in writing is given by Poorhorse Corp. Should Recipient think that one or more of the exceptions to the restrictions set forth in Paragraph 3 applies and Recipient desires to disclose said Trade Secrets pursuant to Paragraph 3, then Poorhorse Corp. will not unreasonably withhold its consent to such release, provided Recipient produces clear and convincing evidence of the applicability of the exceptions to the restrictions set forth in Paragraph 3, and Recipient provides Poorhorse with sixty (60) days' prior written notice of its intent to disclose said Trade Secrets under Paragraph 3.

3. The restrictions on disclosure set forth herein shall not apply to any portion of said Trade Secrets which:

    a. at the time of disclosure to Recipient are generally available to the public or thereafter becomes generally available to the public, through no fault of Recipient, but only to the extent said Trade Secrets become available to the public;

    b. recipient has recorded in writing and has said writing in its possession prior to the time of disclosure of said Trade Secrets to Recipient by Poorhorse Corp., but only to the extent said Trade Secrets are included in said writing;

    c. recipient at any time lawfully obtains in writing from a third party not under any obligation of secrecy or confidentiality to Poorhorse Corp., under circumstances permitting disclosure or use by Recipient without restriction but only to the extent said Trade Secrets are disclosed; and

    d. Poorhorse Corp. hereafter discloses to a third party not under conditions of confidence but only to the extent said Trade Secrets are disclosed.

4. If Recipient determines that it must consult third parties other than direct employees of Recipient in order to perform the evaluation, all such third parties must enter into a separate agreement directly with Poorhorse Corp. prior to any disclosure of said Trade Secrets to said third parties by Recipient.

5. Recipient agrees to return all original materials provided by Poorhorse Corp. and all copies thereof within a period of sixty (60) days from the effective date of this Agreement, provided Recipient and Poorhorse Corp. have not entered into another written agreement regarding Recipient's future use of said Trade Secrets. Additionally, Recipient covenants:

    a. To return any written documentation generated by Recipient which pertains to said Trade Secrets within said sixty (60) day period;

b.   Not to use said Trade Secrets as a basis for any future research and development effort; and

c.   Not to use said Trade Secrets to improve upon any Poorhorse Corp. invention.

6.   Recipient agrees that this Agreement shall be binding upon Recipient's employees and that Recipient will not disclose said Trade Secrets or the subject matter of any evaluation produced by Recipient to anyone other than those employees of Recipient who have a need to know such information.

7.   Recipient warrants that all of Recipient's employees who come into contact with said Trade Secrets have signed or will sign agreements consistent with the terms and conditions of this Agreement before they are allowed to have any contact whatsoever with said Trade Secrets as set forth herein.

8.   Nothing herein shall constitute or otherwise be construed as granting to Recipient any interest or license under said Trade Secrets or any patent or patent application or any copyright heretofore or hereafter granted or filed in which Poorhorse Corp. now has or subsequently may obtain any right, title or interest.

9.   Recipient agrees that all rights to any inventions, copyrights, trademarks or trade secrets that arise or are developed as a result of disclosure of said Trade Secrets by Poorhorse Corp. pursuant to this Agreement are the sole property of Poorhorse Corp. Recipient and its employees agree to execute all documents necessary for Poorhorse Corp. to maintain rights in said inventions, copyrights, trademarks, and trade secrets.

10. Recipient represents to Poorhorse Corp. that it has not entered into any agreement (either oral or written) with, nor is it under any obligation to, any third parties which conflicts with any of the provisions of the Agreement, nor will Recipient disclose said Trade Secrets to others having obligations to third parties which conflict with any of the provisions of this Agreement.

11. Recipient recognizes that the unauthorized use or disclosure by Recipient of said Trade Secrets would cause irreparable injury to Poorhorse Corp. Recipient agrees that Poorhorse Corp. shall be entitled, in addition to any other remedies and damages available, to a temporary injunction (without necessity of posting or filing a bond or any other security) to restrain violation hereof by Recipient, its agents, servants, employers, employees, and all persons acting therefore.

12. This Agreement is executed and delivered within the State of Colorado, and Recipient agrees that it shall be construed, interpreted, and applied in accordance with the laws of that state. The court and authorities of the State of Colorado and the Federal District Court for the District of Colorado shall have the sole jurisdiction and venue over all controversies which may arise with respect to the execution, interpretation and compliance with this Agreement, and Recipient hereby waives any other jurisdiction and venue to which we may be entitled by virtue of domicile or

otherwise. Further, should Recipient initiate or bring a suit or action in any state other than the State of Colorado, Recipient admits and agrees that upon application by Poorhorse Corp. said suit shall be dismissed without prejudice and filed in a court in the State of Colorado.

13.   This Agreement, including this provision hereof, shall not be modified or changed in any manner except only in writing signed by all the parties hereto. In the event a court of competent jurisdiction finds any of the provisions of this Agreement to be so overbroad as to be unenforceable, such provisions may be reduced in scope by the court to the extent it deems necessary to render the provision reasonable and enforceable.

14.   This Agreement supercedes and replaces all other prior agreements between the parties.

Effective this _____ day of _____, 19____.

BOSS-A-MATIC, INC.   Poorhorse Corp.

By: _____   By: _____

Title: _____   Title: _____

Date: _____   Date: _____

Form 1–17
TRADE SECRET NONDISCLOSURE AGREEMENT
(Short Form)

WHEREAS, Poorhorse Corp. (hereinafter referred to as Owner) is the Owner of information relating to _____; and

WHEREAS, the Owner is desirous of disclosing said information to the undersigned (hereinafter referred to as "Recipient") for the purposes of _____; and

WHEREAS, the Owner wishes to maintain in confidence said information as trade secret; and

WHEREAS, the undersigned Recipient recognizes the necessity of maintaining the strictest confidence with respect to any trade secrets of the Owner.

Recipient hereby agrees as follows:

1.   Recipient shall observe the strictest secrecy with respect to all information presented by the Owner and Recipient's evaluation thereof and shall disclose such information only to persons authorized to receive same by the Owner. Recipient shall be responsible for any damage resulting from any breach of this Agreement by Recipient.

2.   Recipient shall neither make use of nor disclose to any third party during the period of this Agreement and thereafter any such trade secrets or evaluation thereof unless prior consent in writing is given by the Owner.

3.   This Agreement covers only information not previously known to Recipient from other sources or otherwise in the public domain. If Recipient has prior knowledge of any alleged trade secrets disclosed by Owner, Recipient

will notify the Owner of such knowledge within thirty (30) days, specifically identifying in writing the alleged trade secrets involved and the source of any such public information while maintaining confidence with regard to information owned by others.

4. At the completion of the services performed by Recipient, Recipient shall within thirty (30) days return all original materials provided by Owner and nay copies and notes or other documents which are in the Recipient's possession pertaining thereto.

5. This Agreement does not apply to any information reflecting any violation of law, nor does it apply to disclosure which might be required of Recipient by order of any court of law.

6. This Agreement shall be binding on all of the Owner's trade secrets but not those trade secrets which are made public through publication, product announcement by Owner, whichever shall be earlier.

7. Nothing herein shall be construed as granting to the Recipient any interest or license under the aforementioned trade secrets, nor under any patent, patent application or any copyright heretofore or hereafter granted or filed in which the Owner now has or subsequently obtains any right, title or interest.

8. This Agreement is executed and delivered within the State of Colorado, and it shall be construed, interpreted and applied in accordance with the laws of that State. The court and authorities of the State of Colorado and the Federal District Court for the District of Colorado shall have sole jurisdiction and venue over all controversies which may arise with respect to the execution, interpretation and compliance with this Agreement.

9. This Agreement, including this provision hereof, shall not be modified or changed in any manner except only by writing signed by all parties hereto.

Effective this _____ day of _____, 19 ____.

RECIPIENT: _____

On behalf of the Recipient and personally binding myself:

By: _____

Title: _____

_____
(Signature)

§ 1.24   Litigation

Because of the sense of urgency surrounding trade secret protection, litigation in this area is actively pursued. This is especially true when the owner is concerned that the unauthorized taking of the trade secret will result in a loss of the trade secret through public disclosure. Protective orders are customarily granted by courts in litigation to protect the confidentiality of trade secrets.[33]

Under the Uniform Trade Secrets Act, *misappropriation* must be established in order to obtain statutory remedies. Two areas of misappropriation are defined:

1. acquisition of a trade secret of another by a person who knows or has reason to know that the trade secret was acquired by improper means.[34] § 1(2)(i) "Improper means" includes theft, bribery, misrepresentation, breach or inducement of a breach of a duty to maintain secrecy, or espionage through electronic or other means.[35]

2. disclosure or use of a trade secret of another without express or implied consent by a person who:

   A. used improper means to acquire knowledge of a trade secret, or

   B. at the time of disclosure or use, knew or had reason to know that his knowledge of the trade secret was:

      (I) derived from or through a person who had utilized improper means to acquire it;

      (II) acquired under circumstances giving rise to a duty to maintain its secrecy or limit its use; or

      (III) derived from or through a person who owed a duty to the person seeking relief to maintain its secrecy or limit its use.

   C. Before a material change of his position, knew or had reason to know, that it was a trade secret and that knowledge of it had been acquired by accident or mistake.[36]

Injunctive relief.   Temporary and permanent injunctive relief is commonly sought in this area. Specifically, an application can be made to the court to enjoin the wrongdoer temporarily for 10 days or until a preliminary injunctive hearing occurs. At the preliminary injunctive hearing, the trade secret owner must specifically describe the acts or things to be enjoined. In order to prevail, the trade secret owner must show:

1. That it will suffer immediate irreparable injury if the preliminary injunction is not granted,[37]

2. That the trade secret owner has a likelihood of success at trial on the merits,[38] and

3. That in balancing the equities for both parties, the equities weigh in favor of the trade secret owner.[39]

Types of monetary recovery. Compensatory damages such as the trade secret owner's lost profits, investment into the research and development of the trade secret, loss of reputation in the community, or loss of the value of the trade secret if a public disclosure results can be recovered.[40] When a trade secret is deliberately misappropriated, the owner's damages are not limited by a lead time period (the head start rule).[41] See § **1.4.**

Accounting for the wrongdoer's profits is permitted. For example, an employee who profits from the information belonging to the business is required to disgorge his profits, and this is true even though the employee's profits deprive the employer of nothing.[42] The UTSA provides that damages may "include both the actual loss caused by misappropriation and the unjust enrichment that is not taken into account in computing actual loss."[43] In lieu of damages, some states permit a reasonable royalty to be granted.[44]

Exemplary damages such as punitive damages may be recovered. UTSA only provides punitive damages equal to twice the damage award.[45]

Attorneys' fees are generally not awarded to the prevailing trade secret owner.[46] Under UTSA, the court may discretionarily award attorneys' fees if plaintiff's claim was made in bad faith or if defendant's misappropriation was willful and malicious.[47]

Identifying trade secrets. At some time in the litigation process, the trade secrets taken must be specifically identified. Often, the trade secret owner does not know what was taken, and the actual identification of

---

[38] Bolt Assocs., Inc. v. Alpine Geophysical Assocs., Inc., 244 F. Supp. 458, 146 U.S.P.Q. (BNA) 536 (D.N.J. 1963).

[39] Midland-Ross Corp. v. Sunbeam Equip. Corp., 316 F. Supp. 171, 167 U.S.P.Q. (BNA) 460 (W.D. Pa.), *aff'd per curiam,* 435 F.2d 159, 167 U.S.P.Q. (BNA) 422 (3d Cir. 1970).

[40] Colgate-Palmolive Co. v. Carter Prods., 230 F.2d 855, 108 U.S.P.Q. (BNA) 383 (4th Cir. 1956).

[41] Killbarr Corp. v. Business Sys., Inc., 679 F. Supp. 411, 6 U.S.P.Q.2d (BNA) 1698 (D.N.J. 1988).

[42] Hunter v. Shell Oil Co., 198 F.2d 485 (5th Cir. 1952).

[43] Uniform Trade Secrets Act § 3(a) (1985), 14 U.L.A. 288 (Supp. 1987).

[44] *Id.*

[45] Uniform Trade Secrets Act § 3(b) (1985), 14 U.L.A. 288 (Supp. 1987).

[46] Forrest Labs, Inc. v. Pillsbury, 452 F.2d 621, 626, 171 U.S.P.Q. (BNA) 731, 735–36 (7th Cir. 1971).

[47] Uniform Trade Secrets Act § 4 (1985), 14 U.L.A. 288 (Supp. 1987).

the trade secret may occur only after full and complete discovery of the wrongdoer's material. At the outset, discovery should be conducted under protective orders issued by the court to preserve and protect the secrecy of the material. When full and complete discovery has occurred, then specific identification of the trade secrets can be made.

Attorney vigilance.   Do not make the mistake of filing the identified trade secrets in court without the required sealing of the material. One law firm forgot to stamp and seal its client's trade secrets when a pleading was filed. A trade journal monitoring the lawsuit then published the secrets.[48]

Failure to litigate.   In the event the trade secret owner knows of a wrongful use of its trade secrets and permits such use, it will not be allowed to proceed with a trade secret cause of action.[49]

---

[48] Bellew, *For Sale: Secret Papers of National Semiconductor ($6),* Wall St. J., Oct. 9, 1984 at _____, col. _____.

[49] Globe Ticket Co. v. International Ticket Co., 90 N.J. Eq. 605, 104 A. 92, 95 (1919).

CHAPTER 2

PROTECTING PATENTS

§ 2.1   Importance of Patents

Ancient civilizations often paid tribute to various gods of invention. For example, the ingenious and highly inventive ancient Egyptians worshiped Thoth, god of letters, invention, and wisdom. And while the first patent law was enacted in the city-state of Venice on March 19, 1474,[1] the practical beginnings of American patent law occurred during the sixteenth century reign of Queen Elizabeth I with the issuance of Letters Patent for Inventions by the Crown. Despite an extreme hatred of British monopolies by the colonies, the Madison-Pinckney proposals for the adoption of Letters Patents for Inventions in the United States were readily received by our founders as necessary for the public good. Indeed, Article I, Section 8 of the Constitution established a legal monopoly for patent holders by granting Congress the power "to promote the progress of Science in the useful Arts by Securing for limited times to Authors and Inventors the exclusive Right to their respective Writings and Discoveries."

To date, over 4.8 million patents have been issued by the United States Patent and Trademark Office (PTO) located in Washington, D.C. These patents are issued by the Government Printing Office in consecutive order, with the first patent having been issued in 1836.

---

[1] Patent Study No. 15, 85th Cong., 2d Sess. (1958).

Because patents have taken on new meaning and new power, this chapter is important reading for all businesses. Phenomenal damages are now being awarded in patent infringement cases. We are all familiar with Polaroid's victory over Kodak that resulted in the declaration that seven patents had been infringed; the withdrawal of Kodak's instant cameras from the market; and the possibility that final damage awards may be in the several billions of dollars. Pfizer sued International Rectifier Corp. for violation of Pfizer's patent on the antibiotic doxycycline, resulting in a $55.8 million award. In settlement, International Rectifier assigned its animal-health and feed additive divisions to Pfizer. On a victory roll, Pfizer sued American Hospital Supply for infringement of its blood oxygenators used in heart-lung machines. Pfizer obtained a $44.2 million damage award. Hughes Tool sued Smith International for infringement of a patent for an O-ring used to seal lubricant in oil drills. The patent was held valid, infringed, and the judgment amounted to about $205 million.[2]

Without question, patents have been resurrected from several decades of obsolescence and thrust into the forefront of modern business practice. Foreign companies, especially those in Japan, seek and obtain United States patents. About half of all United States patents are now being issued to foreign companies (in 1961–65 foreigners received only 17 percent of the issued United States patents). The Japanese aggressively seek United States patents, presently receiving approximately 20 percent of all issued United States patents. We have heard it rumored that each Japanese engineer is expected to file on three inventions per year. If this is true, United States businesses will have to rethink their patent policy and become much more aggressive in obtaining patents. Unfortunately, such rethinking may come too late to catch up with the foreign invasion.[3]

RESOURCE: Rosenberg, Peter D., *Patent Law Fundamentals* (Clark Boardman Co.: 375 Hudson St., New York, NY 10014) (1990). This two-volume set is an excellent beginning treatise on the subject of patents.

---

§ 2.2   Patent and Trademark Office

The Patent and Trademark Office (PTO) is part of the Commerce Department and consists of the Commissioner of Patents and Trademarks, the Board of Appeals (the administrative body that considers appeals of

---

[2] All of these cases are discussed in Perry, *The Surprising New Power of Patents,* Fortune, June 23, 1986, at 57.

[3] Barrett, *Lost In Paper,* Wall St. J., Feb. 24, 1989, at R5–R6; *"More U.S. Patents Going to Foreigners,"* (AP) Rocky Mountain News, Mar. 19, 1989, at 91.

rejected patent applications), and more than 1,500 assistant commissioners, examiners-in-chief, and patent examiners. The Patent Office maintains an extensive scientific library of about 29 million documents consisting of American and foreign patents, leading technical magazines, technical works, and patent applications on a variety of scientific subjects. The collection grows at the rate of 700,000 documents per year.[4]

Because the PTO has always experienced a substantial backlog of patent applications, it has a goal to become paperless in the near future. It is estimated that automating the PTO will cost $800 million to $1 billion.

RESOURCE: A copy of any American patent may be obtained by requesting the patent from Commissioner of Patents and Trademarks, Washington, D.C. 20231, (703) 557-3158. Each copy costs $1.50; copies of plant patents cost $6.00. Coupon books are also available from the PTO, and if your business orders a large number of patents, you may set up a deposit account number by calling the above number.

An important publication from the Patent and Trademark Office is the *Official Gazette of the United States Patent Office,* obtainable from the Superintendent of Documents, Government Printing Office, Washington, D.C. 20402. The annual subscription is $375.00. This publication comes out weekly and contains a synopsis of the 1,500 to 2,000 patents issued each week. The *Official Gazette* publishes the patents according to classifications, making it easy for a subscriber to follow the patents issued in classes of interest. In addition, alphabetical indexes of inventors and of the corporations the inventions are assigned to are also provided. This is valuable information that allows businesses to keep track of patents issued to competitors. An example of an entry in the *Official Gazette* is shown in **Figure 2–1**.

The PTO classifies the subject matter of inventions into some 400 classes of technical art, which are then divided into about 115,000 subclasses. Sometimes it is difficult to understand the logic or reasoning behind the classifications.

In addition to the collection at the PTO, libraries in 41 states are designated Patent Depository Libraries. All current issues of United States patents are sent to each of these libraries by the PTO. Some libraries have rather complete collections of patents going back in time and others do not. An on-line computer database called Classification and Search Support Information System (CASSIS) is available in each of the Patent Depository Libraries.

---

[4] American Intellectual Property Lawyer Assoc. Bulletin, p. 661 (Feb.–March 1989).

4,916,789
VALVE STEM CONSTRUCTION
Joseph H. Robinson, Alexander City, Ala., assignor to Robinson
Foundry, Inc., Alexander City, Ala.
Filed Apr. 13, 1989, Ser. No. 337,673
Int. Cl.⁴ F16K 1/02
U.S. Cl. 29—890.123   8 Claims

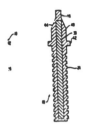

1. A method of constructing a valve stem comprising:
evaporative foam casting to at least near net shape an elongated member having an outside valve stem surface including a threaded portion and an engagement surface
turning portion, and with a rod member of substantially
the same length as and of a different material than that of
the elongated member cast in the elongated member.

4,916,790
BACKER-ROD INSTALLATION TOOL
John T. Vlahogeorge, Lafayette, Ind., assignor to Control Tool
Company, Inc., Lafayette, Ind.
Filed Jul. 20, 1989, Ser. No. 383,000
Int. Cl.⁴ B23P 19/02
U.S. Cl. 29—235   18 Claims

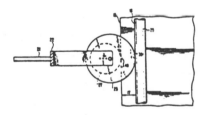

1. A tool for installing a sealant backer-rod to a desired
depth in a joint between building surfaces comprising:
a frame for a worker to hold;
a joint wheel rotatably mounted to said frame about a first
axis of rotation, said wheel having a width in the direction
of said axis sized to fit into said joint and further having an
outer circumferential surface to contact a sealant backer-
rod in said joint as said frame is moved along said joint;
backer-rod depth control means on said frame and adjacent
said wheel having a first contact surface spaced inwardly
from said outer circumferential surface a distance equal to
the desired depth of said backer-rod, said control means
with said first contact surface operable to contact and
move along one of said building surfaces limiting inward
movement of said wheel in said joint when said frame is
forced toward and along the length of said joint forcing
said backer-rod to said desired depth; and,
first adjustment means on said frame operable to adjust the
inward spacing between said first contact surface and said
outer circumferential surface equal to said desired depth.

4,916,791
BALL BEARING PULLER ATTACHMENT
Mary A. Clouse, 2249 E. Leland Rd., Apt. 238, Pittsburg, Calif.
94565, and David E. Voorhis, 815 Murray Ave., San Luis
Obispo, Calif. 93401
Filed Jul. 26, 1989, Ser. No. 385,073
Int. Cl.⁴ B23P 17/04
U.S. Cl. 29—261   18 Claims

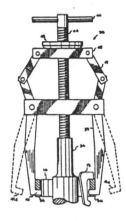

1. A ball bearing puller attachment for a standard ball bearing puller for removing a ball bearing assembly in an axial
direction from a shaft and a housing, said assembly having an
inner race and an outer race, each of said races having an
internal groove, comprising:
a ring having means including notches for pulling engagement in the axial direction with the standard ball bearing
puller; and
a linking means having means for pulling engagement in the
axial direction with the internal groove of the outer race,
said linking means having means for pulling engagement
with said ring in the axial direction, said linking means
axially engaging the groove only in the outer race for
pulling the assembly from the housing and shaft when
force is applied to the ring by the standard ball bearing
puller.

4,916,792
CLUTCH ALIGNMENT TOOL
Waldemar Haubus, 24 Federal Parade, Brookvale, New South
Wales, 2011, Australia
Continuation-in-part of Ser. No. 894,417, Aug. 8, 1986,
abandoned. This application May 6, 1988, Ser. No. 190,870
Int. Cl.⁴ B23P 19/04
U.S. Cl. 29—262   6 Claims
1. A tool for centering a clutch plate and a clutch pressure
plate having a spring diaphragm, comprising a tube having an
elongate bore extending therethrough; an axially slidable bolt
extending through said bore and having a draw nut at one end
and a head at its other end; the bore of said tube being stepped
along its length; an elongate hollow insert being provided
within said bore; said axially slidable bolt extending therethrough; said insert having a resiliently deformable enlargement at one end thereof; the other end of said insert being
adapted in use to be seated against a step in said bore; tighten-
ing of said draw nut causing the the head of said bolt to be
drawn into an interior region of said enlargement of said insert,
such as to hold an inner end of said insert against the step of
said bore and so as to radially expand said enlargement such
that the expanded enlargement is able to be brought into engagement with a splined hub of a clutch plate; adjustable
clamping means being engaged with an outer surface of said

Figure 2–1. Example of an entry in the *Official Gazette of the United States Patent Office.*

47

RESOURCE: Reference Collections of United States Patents Available for Public Use in Patent Depository Libraries.

STATE	NAME OF LIBRARY	TELEPHONE CONTACT
Alabama	Auburn Univ. Library	205-844-1747
	Birmingham Public Library	205-226-3680
Alaska	Z.J. Loussac Public Library, Anchorage	907-261-2916
Arizona	Noble Library, Ariz. State Univ., Tempe	602-965-7607
Arkansas	Ark. State Library, Little Rock	501-682-2053
California	Los Angeles Public Library	213-612-3273
	Calif. State Library, Sacramento	916-322-4572
	San Diego Public Library	619-236-5813
	Sunnyvale Patent Clearinghouse	408-730-7290
Colorado	Denver Public Library	303-571-2347
Connecticut	Science Park Library, New Haven	203-786-5447
Delaware	Univ. of Delaware Library, Newark	302-451-2965
District of Columbia	Howard Univ. Libraries	202-636-5060
Florida	Broward County Main Library, Fort Lauderdale	305-357-7444
	Miami-Dade Public Library	305-375-2665
	Univ. of Central Florida Library, Orlando	407-275-2562
Georgia	Price Gilbert Memorial Library, Georgia Inst. of Technology, Atlanta	404-894-4508
Idaho	Univ. of Idaho Library, Moscow	208-885-6235
Illinois	Chicago Public Library	312-269-2865
	Illinois State Library, Springfield	217-782-5430
Indiana	Marion County Public Library, Indianapolis	317-269-1741
Iowa	State Library of Iowa, Des Moines	515-281-4118
Kentucky	Louisville Free Public Library	502-561-8617
Louisiana	Troy H. Middleton Library, Louisiana State Univ., Baton Rouge	504-388-2570
Maryland	Engineering & Physical Sciences Library, Univ. of Maryland, College Park	301-454-3037
Massachusetts	Physical Science Library, Univ. of Mass., Amherst	413-545-1370
	Boston Public Library	617-536-5400, Ext. 265

STATE	NAME OF LIBRARY	TELEPHONE CONTACT
Michigan	Engineering Transportation Library, Univ. of Michigan, Ann Arbor	313-764-7494
	Detroit Public Library	313-833-1450
Minnesota	Minneapolis Public Library & Information Center	612-372-6570
Missouri	Linda Hall Library, Kansas City	816-363-4600
	St. Louis Public Library	314-241-2288, Ext. 376
Montana	Montana College of Mineral Science & Technology Library, Butte	406-496-4281
Nebraska	Engineering Library, Univ. of Nebraska-Lincoln	402-472-3411
Nevada	Univ. of Nevada-Reno Library	702-784-6579
New Hampshire	Univ. of New Hampshire Library, Durham	603-862-1777
New Jersey	Newark Public Library	201-733-7782
	Lib. of Science & Medicine, Rutgers Univ., Piscataway	201-932-2895
New Mexico	Univ. of New Mexico General Library, Albuquerque	505-277-4412
New York	New York State Library, Albany	518-473-4636
	Buffalo & Erie County Public Library	716-858-7101
	New York Public Library (The Research Libraries)	212-714-8529
North Carolina	D.H. Hill Library, North Carolina State Univ., Raleigh	919-737-3280
Ohio	Cincinnati & Hamilton County Public Library	513-369-6936
	Cleveland Public Library	216-623-2870
	Ohio State Univ. Libraries, Columbus	614-292-6175
	Toledo/Lucas County Public Library	419-259-5212
Oklahoma	Oklahoma State Univ. Library, Stillwater	405-744-7086
Oregon	Oregon State Univ., Salem	503-378-4239
Pennsylvania	The Free Library of Philadelphia	215-686-5331
	Carnegie Library of Pittsburgh	412-622-3138
	Pattee Library, Penn. State Univ., Univ. Park	814-865-4861
Rhode Island	Providence Public Library	401-455-8027
South Carolina	Medical Univ. of South Carolina Library, Charleston	803-792-2371

STATE	NAME OF LIBRARY	TELEPHONE CONTACT
Tennessee	Memphis & Shelby County Public Library & Info. Center	901-725-8876
	Stevenson Science Library, Vanderbilt Univ., Nashville	615-322-2775
Texas	McKinney Engineering Library, Univ. of Texas at Austin	512-471-1610
	Sterling C. Evans Library, Texas A&M Univ., College Station	409-845-2551
	Dallas Public Library	214-670-1468
	The Fondren Library, Rice Univ., Houston	713-572-8101, Ext. 2587
Utah	Marriott Library, Univ. of Utah, Salt Lake City	801-581-8394
Virginia	Virginia Commonwealth Univ. Library, Richmond	804-367-1104
Washington	Engineering Library, Univ. of Washington, Seattle	206-543-0740
Wisconsin	Kurt F. Wendt Library, Univ. of Wisconsin-Madison	608-262-6845
	Milwaukee Public Library	414-278-3247

It is important for businesses, especially those with research and development efforts, to keep abreast of the patents being issued in their areas of specialty. This can be done by surveying the patents issued each week in the *Official Gazette* or by subscribing to a computerized service in a specific area of interest. For example, we regularly advise our larger corporate clients to maintain internal libraries of recent patents issued to their competitors. The PTO automatically sends subscribers patents issued in their technical areas of interest. To subscribe to this service, you will need to know the class and subclass of the technical area.

RESOURCES: Several computerized patent databases are available:

1. *World Patents Index,* available from Derwent Publications, Ltd., Rochdale House, 128 Theobolds Road, London WCIX8RP, Telephone (01) 242-5823 (about 4,000,000 foreign patents).
2. *CLAIMS,* available from IFI/Plenum Data Corp., 302 Swann Ave., Alexandria, Virginia 22301, Telephone 800-368-3093 (about 1.8 million United States patents).

3. *INPADOC,* available from International Patent Document Center, Moellwaldplatz 4, A-1040 Vienna, Postfach 163, Austria, Telephone (431) 50155, Ext. 77 (about 15 million patent documents).

These databases above allow a business to search for patents (1) assigned to a competing company, (2) issued to a particular individual, or (3) in a particular technological area based upon key words or classification.

RESOURCE: Inexpensive publications available from the Superintendent of Documents, United States Government Printing Office, Washington, D.C. 20402, include:

1. *Index of Patents*—an annual two-volume index containing the patentee and subject matter index for the patents issued during the preceding year.
2. *Manual of Classification*—a looseleaf book containing a list of all classes and subclasses of inventions used by the PTO.
3. *Title 37 Code of Federal Regulations*—the rules of patent practice.
4. *Directory of Registered Patent Attorneys and Agents Arranged by States and Country.*
5. *Manual of Patent Examining Procedure*—the rules for filing and prosecuting patent applications.
6. *The Story of the United States Patent Office.*

---

§ 2.3   Basic Patent Principles

The land under your corporate headquarters is legally termed *real property.* The corporate cars, computers, and desks are legally termed *personal property.* Patents are also classified legally as personal property. However, whereas the corporate car is entirely tangible, a patent is legally *intangible personal property.* This intangible personal property carries with it the right to exclude others from making, using, or selling the patented invention. In *Kewanee Oil Co. v. Bicron Corp.,*[5] the United States Supreme Court summarized the nature of patents as follows:

> The stated objective of the Constitution in granting the power to Congress to legislate in the area of intellectual property is to "promote the Progress of Science and useful Arts." The patent laws promote this progress by offering

---

[5] 416 U.S. 470 (1974).

a right of exclusion for a limited period as an incentive for inventors to risk the often enormous costs in terms of time, research, and development. The productive effort thereby fostered will have a positive effect on society through the introduction of new products and processes of manufacture into the economy and the emanations by way of increased employment and better lives for our citizens. In return for the right of exclusion—this "reward for inventions,"—the patent laws impose upon the inventor a requirement of disclosure. To insure adequate and full disclosure so that upon the expiration of the 17-year period "the knowledge of the invention inures to the people, who are thus enabled without restriction to practice it and profit by its use," the patent laws require that the patent application shall include a full and clear description of the invention and "of the manner and process of making and using it" so that any person skilled in the art may make and use the invention. When a patent is granted and the information contained in it is circulated to the general public and those especially skilled in the trade, such additions to the general store of knowledge are of such importance to the public wealth that the Federal Government is willing to pay the high price of 17 years of exclusive use for its disclosure, which disclosure, it is assumed, will stimulate ideas and the eventual development of further significant advances on the art.[6]

A patent, therefore, is a right granted by the federal government to the inventor entitling the inventor, for a limited time, to exclude all others from making, using, and selling the patented process or article throughout the United States. This patent monopoly is a negative legal right giving the patent owner the right of exclusion. This negative right is intangible personal property that may be bought, sold, licensed, assigned, used as collateral to secure a loan, enforced in lawsuits, and so forth.

Of course, what the government gives, the government can take away. The patent monopoly is not an absolute right. If the patent owner misuses this property right, the privilege may be lost under various antitrust and patent misuse laws. This is especially true if the patents are used to restrain trade unreasonably or otherwise hurt the public interest.

§ 2.4 Types of Patents

Three types of *Letters Patents* are available for issuance by the PTO: the plant patent, the design patent, and the utility patent.

Plant patents are granted for newly discovered asexually reproduced plants. These patents represent a limited area of interest, with only slightly more than 6,500 having been granted to date.

---

[6] *Id.* at 480–81.

§ 2.5 —Design Patents

The second type of patent is the design patent. Traditionally, businesses have considered design patents meaningless, primarily because they are easy to design around and because the product life is usually shorter than the time it takes for issuance of the patent. This is changing. Companies are now taking a new look at design patent protection for original product designs. For example, Reebok International, Ltd., obtained a design patent on a new line of running shoes in nine months and sued and obtained an injunction against L.A. Gear from selling similarly designed shoes.[7]

The relevant section on design patents of the United States Code states that "whoever invents any new, original and ornamental design for an article of manufacture may obtain a patent therefor . . . ."[8] Common examples of design patents are set forth in **Figure 2–2**.

Design patents are utilized to protect the ornamental, not the functional characteristics of a product. In fact, if the design is entirely functional, a design patent, even if mistakenly issued, is actually invalid. In the examples shown in **Figure 2–2**, each functional idea can be expressed in a number of different ornamental or aesthetic appearances. Design patents are especially valuable in businesses to protect molded plastic parts, extrusions, and product and container configurations against identical copying. Some states have passed mold protection statutes prohibiting a person from copying a molded product. The United States Supreme Court in *Bonito Boats, Inc. v. Thunder Craft Boats, Inc.*[9] has now invalidated such state statutes as being preempted by federal design patent law.

In litigation of design patents, most judges and juries are capable of easily determining if infringement exists because the legal test is the "ordinary eyeball examination." In other words, the alleged infringing design is placed next to the design shown in the issued patent and is visually compared. If the product design is highly original, greater design patent protection will be accorded it. In those situations, infringement will be found even though the designs are not identical. For the most part, however, especially in the crowded areas of computer peripherals, watch faces, magwheels, and silverware, the scope of design patent protection will most likely be limited to the identical design found in the issued patent.

Design patents are relatively inexpensive to obtain. The filing fee is $150, the issue fee is $220 (large entity), and there are no additional

---

[7] MacDonald, *A New Legal Hope for Design Patents,* Wall St. J., Sept. 27, 1988, 2, at 37, col. 1. *See* AVIA Group Int'l, Inc. v. L.A. Gear Cal., Inc., 853 F.2d 1557, 4 U.S.P.Q.2d 1016 (Fed. Cir. 1988).

[8] 35 U.S.C. § 171 (1953).

[9] 489 U.S. 141, 109 S. Ct. 971, 9 U.S.P.Q.2d (BNA) 1847 (1989).

304,747
DOLL
Steven K. Dunlap, and Richard A. Jurczyk, both of Memphis,
Tenn., assignors to I.O.O.H., Inc., Memphis, Tenn.
Filed Jan. 26, 1989, Ser. No. 302,723
Term of patent 14 years
U.S. Cl. D21—171

304,266
SOFA
Richard Frinier, Long Beach, Calif., assignor to Brown Jordan
Company, El Monte, Calif.
Filed Jul. 3, 1985, Ser. No. 752,240
The portion of the term of this patent subsequent to Jul. 5, 2002,
has been disclaimed.
Term of patent 14 years
U.S. Cl. D6—381

304,407
BEVERAGE DISPENSER
Gregory Fossella, Boston, Mass., assignor to Jet Spray Corp.,
Norwood, Mass.
Filed Jun. 12, 1986, Ser. No. 873,338
Term of patent 14 years
U.S. Cl. D7—308

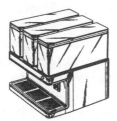

304,445
VIDEO DISPLAY
Lawrence M. Kuba, Nashua, N.H., assignor to Wang Laborato-
ries, Inc., Lowell, Mass.
Filed Nov. 10, 1986, Ser. No. 929,136
Term of patent 14 years
U.S. Cl. D14—113

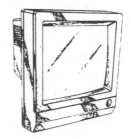

Figure 2–2. Examples of design patents in the *Official Gazette of the United States Patent Office.*

maintenance fees after issuance. The term of design patents is 14 years from the date of issuance by the Government Printing Office.

§ 2.6 —Utility Patents

The third type of patent is the utility patent. Without doubt, utility patents compose the bulk of all patents issued. During the first week of 1989, for example, 1,634 utility patents were issued. (During the same period of time, only 99 design patents and 16 plant patents were issued.) The remainder of this chapter is principally directed toward how to obtain

Table 2–1

Fees Associated with Utility Patents

	Small Entity ($)	Large Entity ($)
Filing	185	370
Issue Fee	310	620
1st Maintenance (3½ Years)	245	490
2nd Maintenance (7½ Years)	495	990
3rd Maintenance (11½ Years)	740	1,480

and protect utility patents. This is the type of patent used by most businesses to protect the fruits of their expensive R&D efforts.

Utility patents are issued for a term of 17 years from the date printed by the Government Printing Office and are not renewable. In the case of inventions requiring FDA approval, the patent law has been amended to extend the term of the patent by the amount of time the FDA takes to review the invention.[10] Utility patent fees are shown in **Table 2–1**.

A small entity has fewer than 500 employees; a large entity is anything greater. The PTO aggressively levies these fees and other fees as part of its goal that its operations be totally self-funded. An example of a utility patient is shown in **Figure 2–3**.

The front page of the short utility patent in **Figure 2–3** shows that the patent was issued to an individual. Important information can be ascertained from this page. The invention has been assigned to a corporation, Electropore, Inc. The 17-year monopoly commences with the Date of Patent, July 18, 1989, and terminates on July 18, 2006. This invention is related to other applications that are fully identified in the section of the patent entitled "Related U.S. Application Data." The international classification (Int. Cl.) is set forth in part 51, the United States Classification (U.S. Cl.) is found in part 52, and the classification searched by the examiner is set forth in part 58. The PTO then specifically lists all references considered by the examiner in part 56. The names of the primary examiner, the assistant examiner, and the patent law firm are fully identified. A short abstract follows. Twenty-four claims were issued for this patent.

---

[10] 35 U.S.C. § 156 (1953).

United States Patent [19]

Marshall, III

[11] Patent Number: **4,849,089**

[45] Date of Patent: **Jul. 18, 1989**

[54] **DISPOSABLE ELECTROMANIPULATION CHAMBER**

[75] Inventor: **John Marshall, III,** Boulder, Colo.

[73] Assignee: **Electropore, Inc.,** Boulder, Colo.

[21] Appl. No.: **313,169**

[22] Filed: **Feb. 21, 1989**

Related U.S. Application Data

[63] Continuation-in-part of Ser. No. 283,215, Dec. 12, 1988, which is a continuation-in-part of Ser. No. 47,208, May 8, 1987, which is a continuation-in-part of Ser. No. 861,534, May 9, 1986, abandoned.

[51] **Int. Cl.**^{4} **C12N 13/00; C12N 15/00**
[52] **U.S. Cl.** .... **204/299 R;** 204/183.1; 204/180.1; 935/52; 935/85; 935/93; 435/287; 435/173; 435/172.2; 435/172.3
[58] **Field of Search** .... 204/299 R, 183.1, 180.1; 435/287, 289, 173, 172.2, 172.1, 172.3; 935/52, 53, 93, 89

[56] **References Cited**

U.S. PATENT DOCUMENTS

3,095,359	6/1963	Heller	195/78
4,634,665	1/1987	Axel et al.	435/68

FOREIGN PATENT DOCUMENTS

WPB01J/24-
76 404   9/1984   German Democratic Rep. .

OTHER PUBLICATIONS

"Introduction and Expression of DNA Molecules in Eukaryotic Cells by Electroporation"—Andreason & Evans, BioTechniques—vol. 6, No. 7 (1988).
"Hemolysis of Human Erythrocytes by a Transient Electric Field"—Kinosita and Tsong—Proc. Natl. Acad. Sc. U.S.A., vol. 74, No. 5, pp. 1923–1927, May 1977, Biochemistry.

Primary Examiner—John F. Niebling
Assistant Examiner—John S. Starsiak, Jr.
Attorney, Agent, or Firm—Dorr, Carson, Sloan & Peterson

[57]   **ABSTRACT**

An electromanipulation chamber for selectively holding a suspension of vesicles is disclosed having a one-piece holder molded from dielectric material wherein the holder comprises an outer cylindrically-shaped collar and an inner circular-shaped ring having a formed annular region centrally located therein. A passageway is formed through the ring and the collar and a pair of electrodes having a diameter slightly greater than the inner diameter of the collar is mounted on opposing sides of the annular region. The pair of electrodes and the annular region form the electromanipulation chamber and a positive fluid-tight seal is formed aournd the edges of the annular region with electrodes to contain the suspension with the vesicles.

24 Claims, 2 Drawing Sheets

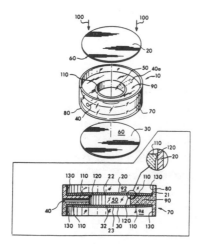

Figure 2–3. Example of a utility patent.

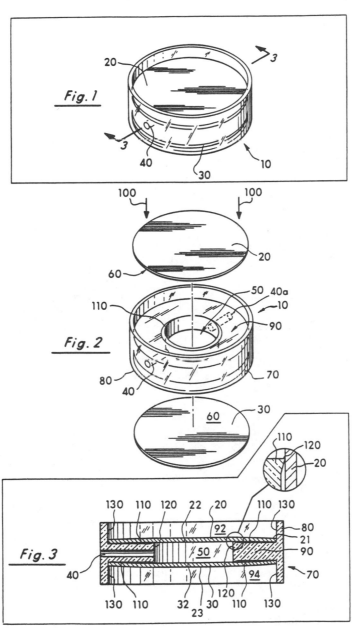

Figure 2–3. *(Continued)*

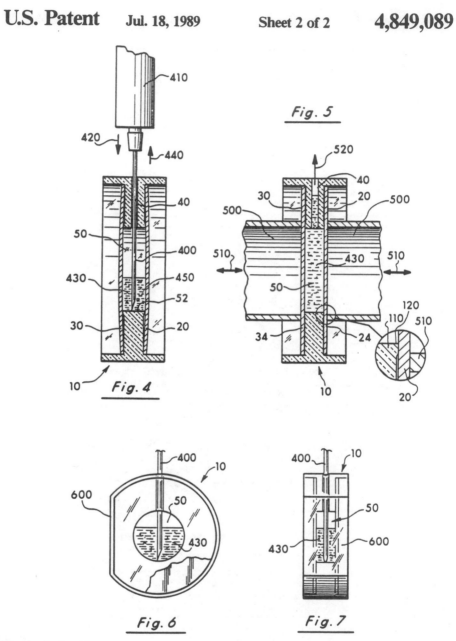

Fig. 5

Fig. 4

Fig. 6

Fig. 7

Figure 2–3. *(Continued)*

4,849,089

1

DISPOSABLE ELECTROMANIPULATION CHAMBER

BACKGROUND OF THE INVENTION

1. Related Applications

This is a continuation-in-part of application Ser. No. 07/283,215 filed Dec. 12, 1988, now pending, entitled "Improved Impedance Matching for Cell Membrane Alteration Instrumentation" which is a continuation-in-part of application Ser. No. 07/047,208, filed May 8, 1987, now pending, entitled "High Speed, High Power Apparatus for Vesicle Prealignment, Poration, Loading and fusion in Uniform Electric Fields and Method Therefor" which is a continuation-in-part of Ser. No. 06/861,534, filed May 9, 1986, now abandoned.

2. Field of the Invention

The present invention is related to a chamber for the electromanipulation of vesicles in liquid suspension. Vesicle is herein defined as a body which resembles a bladder especially in constituting a small thin-walled cavity such as (a) a plant or animal structure (e.g., a cyst, vacuole, or cell) or (b) a non-biological structure (e.g., as a liposome or microsphere) having the general form of a membranous cavity such as a thin sac and especially when filled with fluid. Cells are generally defined as microscopic masses of protoplasm bounded externally by a semi-permeable membrane. More particularly, this invention relates to the electromanipulation of vesicles in a uniform electric field produced by a disposable apparatus having a chamber formed between two parallel plate electrodes and a dielectric holder.

Statement of the Problem

It is well known that vesicular structures can be altered through the application of electric fields (i.e., electroporation). For example, electroporation is a type of electromanipulation of a biological membrane such that a style of permeability is induced in the membrane which acts like small holes or "pores." This process establishes a semi-stable membrane state such that molecules and macromolecules may cross the otherwise impermeable membrane barrier. This semistable state may be reversed and repaired upon warming the membrane in question. If stored at low temperatures, however, the semi-stable membrane state can exist for hours or days. Electroporation has been successfully utilized to create semi-stable membrane states in a number of different cell types such as cultured cell lines, mammalian primary cell cultures, mammalian and embryonic stem cells, isolated intracellular vesicles, dicot and monocot plant protoplasts, protists and bacteria. Electroporation has been used to introduce DNA molecules, to load cells with dyes and other molecules, and to extract molecules from cells without requiring cell lysis. See "Introduction and Expression of DNA Molecules in Eukaryotic Cells by Electroporation", Volume 6, No. 7, BIOTECHNIQUES (1988), Page 6750. The use of electric fields to transfer biological macromolecules such as genetic material (DNA), RNA, and protein into cells is well know. Another form of electromanipulation is fusion. Fusion is defined as the merger or coalescence of at least two vesicles to form a single vesicular entity.

The prior approach of Heller as set forth in U.S. Pat. No. 3,095,359 shows the use of a reaction chamber having an open top formed within a rectangular vessel preferably of glass or other high dielectric material. The electrodes of Heller are flat metal plates mounted on the

2

outside of the vessel and out of direct contact with the material in the chamber being treated. The volume of the chamber shown in Heller is not disclosed. Both Stolley (German Democratic Republic Pat. No. WP B 01 J/2476 404, Sept. 12, 1984) and Kinosita & Tsong ("Hemolysis of Human Erythrocytes by a Transient Electric Field, Proc. Natl. Acad. Sc. USA, Vol. 74, No. 5, pp. 1923–1927, May 1977, Biochemistry) discuss the use of parallel electrodes. Stolley discloses the use of two plate electrodes arranged parallel to each other in a container holding vesicles but no specific structure is shown. Kinosita and Tsong illustrate the use of a cylindrical cavity enclosed by a pair of stainless steel electrodes and a plexiglass cell.

In "Introduction and Expression of DNA Molecules in Eukaryotic Cells by Electroporation+, by Andreason and Evans, 650 Biotechniques, Volume 6, No. 7 (1988) the authors disclose a rectangular reusable parallel stainless steel electromanipulation chamber utilizing disposable one milliliter spectrophotometer curvettes.

A need exists in the field of treating solutions containing particles, vesicles and cells for a disposable chamber capable of treating large volumes of solutions such as one milliliter or greater.

Solution to the Problem

The present invention is also discussed in the Andreason, et al. article and provides a solution to the problem in the industry stated above of providing a fully disposable chamber capable of holding large quantities such as 1.0 milliliters of suspension. The suspension carrying the vesicles is selectively inserted and removed through a small hole in the side of the chamber.

SUMMARY OF THE INVENTION

The electromanipulation chamber of the present invention comprises a central holder having a cylindrically shaped collar with an integral centrally disposed ring. The ring has a central cavity which defines the sides of the chamber. The collar and the ring are made from a dielectric material which is nonbinding to protein. A ridge is formed around the cavity on each of the upper and lower surfaces of the ring. A hole is formed through the collar and the ring to provide a fluid pathway from the cavity to the atmosphere. A pair of disk-shaped electrodes press-fittingly engage the opposite ends of the collar and engage the formed ridge on each side of the ring to form a fluid seal. The electrodes define the top of the fluid-tight chamber. Each of the electrodes are comprised of conductive material coated with an inert noble metal.

DESCRIPTION OF THE DRAWING

FIG. 1 is a perspective view of the electromanipulation chamber of the present invention;

FIG. 2 is an exploded perspective view showing the components of the electromanipulation chamber of FIG. 1;

FIG. 3 is a cross-sectional view through the center of the chamber of FIG. 1;

FIG. 4 is an illustration showing a syringe injecting a solution into the electromanipulation chamber of FIG. 1 viewed in cross-section;

FIG. 5 is a cross-sectional illustration of the electromanipulation chamber of FIG. 1 mounted in a fixture to discharge electrodes;

Figure 2–3. *(Continued)*

FIG. 6 is a second embodiment of the present invention making use of an optical viewing window; and

FIG. 7 is a side view of the alternate embodiment of the FIG. 6.

DETAILED DESCRIPTION OF THE PRESENT INVENTION

In FIG. 1 the electromanipulation chamber 10 of the present invention is shown. The chamber 10 has two opposing electrodes 20 and 30 and a small formed hole 40. As shown in FIG. 2, the chamber 10 has a formed annular region or cavity 50 which comprises the sides of the electromanipulation chamber as will be discussed.

1. Electrodes—In FIG. 2, each of the electrodes 20 and 30 are identical and are formed of conductive material such as copper, brass, or steel. Each electrode 20 and 30 is plated on all sides with an inert noble metal such as gold or platinum so as not to react chemically with the solution before, during, or after electromanipulation. Each electrode is formed in the shape of a thin disk having a diameter of about 2⅜ inches and a thickness of about 1/16 inch.

It is to be expressly understood that different conductive metals, plating material, geometric shapes other than circular (such as square) and dimensions could be utilized under the teachings of the present invention for different suspensions and applications.

2. Holder—The chamber 10 also incorporates a holder 70 which comprises an outer cylindrically-shaped collar 80 and an inner circular ring 90. The outer edge of the ring 90 is integral, in the preferred embodiment with the central area of the inside surface of the collar 80 and is made from a one-piece polycarbonate material or from any suitable dielectric material which is non-binding with protein such as plastic, ceramic, or glass. The ring 90 splits the collar 80 into upper and lower regions 92 and 94 which are substantially equal in volume. The cavity 50 has a diameter of about ⅜ inch and a height of about ⅛ inches to obtain a volume of at least 1 ml.

Under the teachings of the present invention, the holder 70 may be of one piece construction or with the ring 90 and collar 80 separately manufactured and connected together. The upper and lower regions 92 and 94 may in certain applications be of unequal volume, the volume of the cavity 50 may be varied to meet design requirements, and different geometric shapes other than cylindrical may be utilized.

3. Chamber 50—Each electrode 20, 30 is designed, as shown in FIG. 3, to press-fittingly engage the inner surface 100 of the collar 80 as the electrode is pushed with a suitable tool, not shown, in the direction of arrows 100 causing the edge of the collar to move slightly outward. The diameter of each electrode is slightly greater than the inside diameter of the collar 80 such as by 0.002 inch. When press-fittingly engaged with the holder 70, the electrodes 20, 30 abut the formed V-shaped ridge 110 outer surfaces 110 of the ring 90 and press-fittingly engage the inner surface of the collar at the juncture of the ring. The electrodes 20, 30, as shown in FIG. 3, are spherically deformed with the edges 21 being held lower by the inner surfaces 130 of the collar 80 than the center 23 of the electrodes which abut the ridges 110. Ridges 110 are each circular in shape and comprise a right triangle shaped configuration having a height of about 0.015 inches and a base about 0.100 inches. The knife edge 120 abuts against the electrode 20, 30. This forms an electromanipulation chamber 50

between the inner surfaces 22 and 32 of electrodes 20 and 30 respectively and the inner surface 120 of the ring 90 defining a volume of at least 1 ml. Hence, vesicles, can now be suspended in a solution inserted in cavity 50. The electrodes engage the edges 120 under tension due to the aforesaid spherical deformation thereby creating a fluid-tight seal.

It is to be expressly understood that the use of a ridge of triangular cross-section represents a preferred approach to sealing the chamber 50 and that other suitable cross-sections and approaches could be utilized to achieve the desired fluid-tight seal.

4. Insertion of Suspension—In FIG. 3, a passageway or hole 40 is formed through the collar 80 and the ring 90 to provide access by means of a needle 400 connected to a syringe 410 as shown in FIG. 4 to the cavity 50.

In FIG. 4, a syringe 410 bearing a solution 430 such as HEPES buffered saline is injected into the cavity 50. The solution 430 contains the vesicles (illustrated as 450) which are to be electrically treated. In a preferred use, the chamber 10 is held vertically, as shown, and the needle 400 is inserted until it hits the end 52 of the cavity 50 opposing the hole 40. The solution 430 is carefully injected into the cavity to avoid the creation of bubbles in the solution. The operator can observe the insertion through the transparent sides of the holder 70. If bubbles are present when in solution 430 when electromanipulation occurs substantial damage could result or inaccurate electromanipulation could be obtained due to the electric field distortions caused by the bubbles. After injection, the needle 400 is removed.

In FIGS. 6 and 7 an alternative embodiment shows the use of a flat optical viewing port 600 to better view the operation of fluid injection. In the embodiment of FIG. 1, the plastic of the holder 70 is sufficiently optically transparent to view the injection, but the use of a flat surface 600 enhances the viewing.

5. Electromanipulation—In FIG. 5, the chamber 10 is vertically mounted between two ring-shaped discharge electrodes or electrical contacts 500 and 510 which selectively engage or disengage the chamber by moving the contacts in the direction of arrows 510. The discharge contacts 500 firmly engage the electrodes 20, 30 with sufficient force to deform the knife edge 120 of the ridge 110 by partially flattening the knife edge. This also causes some of the solution to move upwardly through the hole 40 which pushes out any remaining bubbles of air in the solution 430. When the contacts 500 properly engage the outer surfaces 24, 34 of electrdes 20, 30, an electromanipulation pulse or pulses are applied to the chamber 50. Treatment of the vesicles now occurs. It is to be noted that the size of the formed hole 40 is such that the solution, because of the surface tension of the solution, does not normally leave the chamber 50 except as described above.

After treatment, the suspension 430 can be removed by means of the syringe 410 and needle 400 as shown in FIG. 4 by withdrawing the solution in the direction of arrow 440 through the needle 400. The needle 400 is inserted until it hits the opposing wall. After use, the cylinder may be disposed of.

6. Summary—What has been set forth in FIGS. 1 through 5 is a disposable electromanipulation chamber that utilizes a pair of opposing electrodes 20 and 30 mounted in a holder above an electromanipulation chamber. The chamber is low cost in manufacture in that the holder 70 can be quickly manufactured from a

Figure 2–3. *(Continued)*

5

single-piece polycarbonate material. The hole **40** can be drilled and then the parallel opposing plates **20** and **30** can be inserted. The upstanding collar **80** forms a guide for positioning the plates **20** and **30** above the inner ring **90** as well as providing a convenient lip **130** for the upper and lower regions for holding and carrying the chamber **10** by the user. In addition, the raised collar on both sides of the chamber serves the function of guiding the discharge electrodes **500** in their engagement onto the outer surfaces of the electrodes **20** and **30**. In the preferred embodiment, the ring-shaped discharge electrodes are greater in diameter than the diameter of the electromanipulation chamber **50**.

Finally, as shown in FIG. **3**, the chamber **10** is symmetrical above and below the formed hole **40** which is designed to access the electromanipulation chamber at its center.

The chamber of the present invention is designed as a non-flow through chamber. However, it is expressly understood that a second formed hole **40a** in the inner ring **1290** opposing the first hole **1240** could be inserted and that fluid could be pumped into and out from the chamber.

While preferred embodiments of the present invention have been shown, it is to be expressly understood that modifications and changes may be made thereto and that the present invention is set forth in the following claims.

I CLAIM:

1. An apparatus having an electromanipulation chamber selectively holding a suspension, said apparatus comprising:

a holder comprising:

(a) an outer collar,

(b) an inner ring having a formed annular region centrally located therein, said ring dividing said collar into upper and lower regions,

(c) a passageway formed through of said ring and said collar,

a pair of thin electrodes made from conductive material having a diameter slightly greater that the inner diameter of said collar, each said electrode press-fittingly engaging one of said upper or lower regions, the outer edge of each said electrode press-fittingly engaging the inner surface of said collar at the junction of said ring with said collar,

means on the outer surface of said ring for providing a fluid-tight seal between each of said electrodes and said ring, and

said pair of electrodes and said annular region of said ring forming said chamber, said formed passageway providing means for the delivery of said suspension into and out from said chamber, said diameter of said passageway being small enough so that the surface tension of said suspension prevents the flow of said suspension from said chamber.

2. The apparatus of claim **1** wherein said collar extends above said engaged electrodes to provide a lip around said upper and lower regions.

3. The apparatus of claim **1** wherein said holder is of one-piece cylindrical construction and is made from dielectric material which is nonbinding to protein.

4. The apparatus of claim **1** wherein said holder is made from optically transparent material for viewing the insertion of said suspension into said chamber.

5. The apparatus of claim **4** wherein one side of said collar is formed with a flat surface in order to provide a viewing port for said chamber.

6

6. The apparatus of claim **1** wherein said electrodes are circular disks plated with an inert noble metal.

7. The apparatus of claim **1** wherein said providing means are opposing formed circular ridges.

8. The apparatus of claim **1** wherein said apparatus further comprises a pair of opposing electrical contacts selectively abutting the outer surfaces of said electrodes with sufficient force to push a portion of said suspension in said chamber into said passageway in order to remove any air bubbles in said chamber.

9. The apparatus of claim **8** wherein each said electrical contact is ring-shaped with a diameter greater than the diameter of said chamber.

10. An apparatus having an electromanipulation chamber selectively holding a suspension, said apparatus comprising:

a holder molded from dielectric material, said holder comprising:

(a) an outer cylindrically-shaped collar,

(b) an inner circular-shaped ring having a formed annular region centrally located therein, said ring dividing said collar into upper and lower regions, said ring having its outer edge engaging the inside surface of said collar, said ring further having a pair of opposing formed circular ridges on the upper and lower edges of said annular region,

(c) a passageway formed through of said ring and said collar,

a pair of electrodes made from conductive material having a diameter slightly greater that the inner diameter of said collar, each said electrode press-fittingly engaging one of said upper or lower regions, the outer circular edge of each said electrode press-fittingly engaging the inner surface of said collar at the junction of said ring with said collar and abutting said ridge of said ring so that said each said electrode is spherically deformed, and

said pair of electrodes and said formed annular region forming said chamber, said formed passageway providing means for the delivery of said suspension into and out from said chamber, said diameter of said passageway being small enough so that the surface tension of said suspension prevents the flow of said suspension from said chamber.

11. An apparatus having an electromanipulation chamber selectively holding a suspension, said electromanipulation chamber comprising:

a one-piece holder molded from dielectric material, said holder comprising:

(a) an outer cylindrically-shaped collar,

(b) an inner circular-shaped ring having a formed annular region centrally located therein, said ring dividing said collar into upper and lower regions, said ring having its outer edge integral with the inside surface of said collar,

(c) a passageway formed through said ring and said collar,

a pair of electrodes made from conductive material having a diameter slightly greater that the inner diameter of said collar, each said electrode press-fittingly engaging one of said upper or lower regions, the outer circular edge of each said electrode press-fittingly engaging the inner surface of said collar at the junction of said ring with said collar, and

said pair of electrodes and said formed annular region forming said chamber, said formed passageway providing means for the delivery of said suspension

Figure 2–3. *(Continued)*

4,849,089

7 8

into and out from said chamber, said diameter of said passageway being small enough so that the surface tension of said suspension prevents the flow of said suspension from said chamber.

12. An apparatus having an electromanipulation chamber selectively holding a suspension, said electromanipulation chamber comprising:
a one-piece holder molded from dielectric material, said holder comprising:
(a) an outer cylindrically-shaped collar,
(b) an inner circular-shaped ring having a formed annular region centrally located therein, said ring dividing said collar into upper and lower regions, said ring having its outer edge integral with the inside surface of said collar, said ring further having a pair of opposing formed circular ridges on the upper and lower edges of said annular region, each of said ridges terminating in a knife edge,
(c) a passageway formed through said ring and said collar,
a pair of electrodes made from conductive material having a diameter slightly greater that the inner diameter of said collar, each said electrode press-fittingly engaging one of said upper or lower regions, the outer circular edge of each said electrode press-fittingly engaging the inner surface of said collar at the junction of said ring with said collar and abutting said circular knife edge of said ring so that said each said electrode is spherically deformed, and
said pair of electrodes and said formed annular region forming said chamber, said formed passageway providing means for the delivery of said suspension into and out from said chamber, said diameter of said passageway being small enough so that the surface tension of said suspension prevents the flow of said suspension from said chamber.

13. The apparatus of claim 12 wherein said knife edge of said ridge further deforms under force applied to said electrodes during said electromanipulation in order to remove any air bubbles in said suspension out through said passageway.

14. A system having an electromanipulation chamber selectively holding a suspension and electrical contacts for applying electromanipulation pulses, said electromanipulation chamber comprising:
a one-piece holder molded from dielectric material which is nonbinding with protein, said holder comprising:
(a) an outer cylindrically-shaped collar,
(b) an inner circular-shaped ring having a formed annular region centrally located therein, said ring dividing said collar into equal upper and lower regions, said ring having its outer edge integral with the central area of the inside surface of said collar, said ring further having a pair of opposing formed circular ridges on the upper and lower edges of said annular region, each of said ridges being substantially triangular in cross-section and terminating in a knife edge,
(c) a passageway formed through the center of said ring and said collar, said passageway lying in a plane parallel to said ring,
a pair of electrodes made from conductive material having a diameter slightly greater that the inner diameter of said collar, each of said electrodes being plated with an inert noble metal and formed in the shape of a disk, each said electrode press-fit-

tingly engaging one of said upper or lower regions, the outer circular edge of each said electrode press-fittingly engaging the inner surface of said collar at the junction of said ring with said collar and abutting said circular knife edge of said ring so that said each said electrode is spherically deformed, and said electrical contacts abutting the outer surfaces of said electrodes with aforesaid force, and

said pair of electrodes and said formed annular region forming said chamber, said formed passageway providing means for the delivery of said suspension into and out from said chamber, said diameter of said passageway being large enough to receive a syringe needle but small enough so that the surface tension of said suspension prevents the flow of said suspension from said chamber.

15. The system of claim 14 wherein each of said electrical contact are ring-shaped with a diameter greater than the diameter of said annular region.

16. A method for electromanipulation of vesicles suspended in a solution, said method comprising the steps of:
inserting the needle of the syringe containing said solution into a passageway formed in an electromanipulation chamber,
said chamber having a pair of opposing conductive electrodes over a cavity formed from dielectric material, delivering said solution from said syringe into said chamber,
removing said needle of said syringe from said chamber,
applying electrical contacts to the outer surface of said opposing electrodes with sufficient force to provide a fluid seal between said electrodes and said cavity,
electro-pulsing the electrical contacts and electrodes in order to electromanipulation the vesicles in said solution contained in said cavity,
removing said electrical contacts from said electrodes,
inserting said needle of said syringe in said formed passageway of said chamber and removing said solution from said chamber, and
removing said needle of said syringe from said chamber.

17. The method of claim 16 wherein the steps of inserting said needle into said chamber occurs with said needle being inserted into said chamber until the end of said needle hits the inner wall of said chamber.

18. The method of claim 16 wherein the step of applying said electrical contacts further includes the step of removing air bubbles from said chamber by forcing said solution from said chamber into said formed passageway.

19. An electromanipulation chamber comprising:
a central holder made from transparent dielectric material, said central holder comprising:
a. a collar,
b. a ring centrally disposed in said collar, said ring having a centrally located formed cavity, said cavity being at least 1 ml in volume,
c. a ridge formed around said cavity on each of the upper and lower surfaces of said ring, each said ridge being located at the edge of said ring at said cavity, and
d. a passageway formed through said collar and said ring, said passageway extending from the outer surface of said collar to said cavity,

Figure 2–3. *(Continued)*

4,849,089

9

a pair of electrodes, said electrodes press-fittingly engaging opposing ends of said collar, each of said electrodes abutting the ridge on said ring closest to said electrode in order to seal said cavity thereby making said cavity fluid tight.

20. The electromanipulation chamber of claim 19 in which said ring is integral with said collar.

21. The electromanipulation chamber of claim 19 wherein said ring is composed of polycarbonate.

10

22. The electromanipulation chamber of claim 19 wherein said ring is composed of material which is non-binding to protein.

23. The electromanipulation chamber of claim 19 wherein said electrodes are composed of a conductive material coated with an inert noble metal.

24. The electromanipulation chamber of claim 19 wherein said collar is cylindrically-shaped, said ring is circular, and said electrodes are each formed in the shape of a thin disc.

* * * * *

Figure 2–3. *(Continued)*

§ 2.7   Subject Matter for Utility Patents

The Patent Act expressly provides that "whoever invents or discovers any new and useful process, machine, manufacture, or composition of matter, or any new or useful improvement thereof, may obtain a patent. . . ."[11] The following are examples of proper subject matter for issuance of utility patents:

1. New and useful process. For example, the processes for making fertilizer and insecticides, for inserting shoe polish and hair spray into containers, and for fabricating pellets of nuclear fuel.
2. New and useful machine. For example, the manufacturing machines for making wine glasses, for forming aluminum extrusions, and for producing campaign buttons.
3. New and useful manufacture. For example, the actual product itself such as a typewriter, a digital calculator, an adjustable wrench, and a transmission.
4. New and useful compositions of matter. For example, the formulations for toothpaste, medical drugs, adhesives, and plastics.
5. New and useful improvements. For example, improvements to any of the above.

It is rare that an inventor discovers a "pioneer" invention. But it does happen, as witnessed by the discovery of xerography, instant photography, the transistor, and the laser. Most companies and individuals file for and obtain patents in the last category of "useful improvements." For example, the invention of the lead pencil represented a pioneer patent. The subsequent invention of the eraser at the end of the lead pencil represented an improvement which resulted in the issuance of an improvement patent (an equally valuable patent).

Unfortunately, many businesses fail to recognize the importance of obtaining improvement patents. Without doubt, from a cost-benefit point of view, the first patents to be filed must cover the pioneer approaches of your company. Do not overlook however, the importance of improvement patents, not only for your products but the products of your competitors. For example, if you invent a new feature for your competitor's product, you may want to file a patent application on this improvement in the hope that when it is issued, you will be in a position to block your competitor from using the improved feature, or you will be able to extract a favorable license agreement from your competitor. Later in this chapter (§ 2.32) we

---

[11] 35 U.S.C. § 101 (1953).

discuss the importance of obtaining a portfolio of improvement patents around your product lines.

What is proper subject matter for utility patents? The United States Supreme Court in *Diamond v. Diehr* has stated that "anything under the sun that is made by man" may well be proper subject matter.[12] Despite such a broad statement, there is clearly a cutting edge of what is and what is not proper subject matter for patents.

The Supreme Court in *Funk Bros. Seed Co. v. Kalo Inoculant Co.* has also determined that improper subject matter for a utility patent includes mathematical formulas, methods of doing business, principles or laws of nature, and printed matter.[13]

For a number of years it was hotly debated if software was proper subject matter for utility patents. Such patents are now available and they are aggressively sought. This issue is discussed in greater depth in **Chapter 8** on software protection.

The Merrill Lynch case[14] represents an important turning point for obtaining a patent on a computer system involving a method of doing business. In that case, Merrill Lynch received a patent on its cash management account (CMA) system, which Paine Webber sought to invalidate based on the belief that it "merely describe[d] a series of manipulated steps which could be performed by hand with the aid of paper, pencil and telephone." The trial court held Merrill Lynch's patent to be valid and with respect to the "method of doing business argument" stated:

> This court has carefully examined the claims in this case and is unable to find any direct or indirect recitation of a procedure of resolving a mathematical problem. Rather, the patent allegedly claims a methodology to effectuate a highly efficient business system and does not restate a mathematical formula. . . .[15]

Although this case was settled before appeal, it is an important case because it represents an area of creative patenting pertaining to computerization of methods of doing business. In Merrill Lynch's cash management account system, the computer would take an individual's charge accounts, certificates of deposit, and bank accounts, even if information pertaining to those accounts was located outside of Merrill Lynch, and automatically centralize all such information in order to provide the customer with a monthly summary of account. Businesses involved in the computerization

---

[12] Diamond v. Diehr, 450 U.S. 175, 182, 209 U.S.P.Q. (BNA) 1, 6 (1981).

[13] Funk Bros. Seed Co. v. Kalo Inoculant Co., 333 U.S. 127, 76 U.S.P.Q. (BNA) 280 (1948).

[14] Paine, Webber, Jackson & Curtis, Inc. v. Merrill Lynch, Pierce, Fenner & Smith, Inc., 564 F. Supp. 1358, 218 U.S.P.Q. (BNA) 212 (D. Del. 1983).

[15] *Id.* at 1358, 218 U.S.P.Q. at 220.

of traditional areas and methods of doing business, such as inventory control and collection of accounts, may want to aggressively consider whether a utility patent will enhance their competitive position.

In the famous *Diamond v. Chakrabarty*[16] case, the United States Supreme Court upheld the patentability of living, genetically modified microorganisms that were essentially designed to function as little "PAC MEN" to gobble up oil spills on the surface of water. Even though this product did not become commercially successful, General Electric Corp. made patent history by being the first company to patent a new form of life. This case has opened the doors to patenting non-naturally occurring, nonhuman, multicellular living organisms, including animals.[17]

It has been humorously stated that Harvard now has patented a mouse that chases a Yale cat. What Harvard did patent was a genetically new mouse that is susceptible to cancer.[18] In this cutting edge area, a lot of activity is presently taking place. The PTO is being criticized for its delay in processing biotechnology patent applications. More than 7,000 of these applications are in backlog, and it is estimated that it will take five to six years to resolve the backlog.[19]

§ 2.8   Statutory Requirements

Whether an invention is patentable is primarily determined in the sole discretion of the assigned patent examiner. From a statistical point of view, it has been said that approximately 65 percent of all patent applications are eventually allowed. Obviously, the statistical odds are in favor of allowance. The Japanese, who are aggressive businessmen, tend to file on minor technological advances as well as the major advances. In contrast, engineers in most American businesses honestly believe that what they are doing is the result of their engineering skill and is not patentable. This is a widespread belief; unfortunately for American businesses, it constitutes narrow and possibly deadly thinking. Some corporations institute patent compensation programs to spur their engineers to think "inventive."

Sections 2.9 through **2.11** set forth the essentials of the legal requirements necessary to obtain a patent. The patent examiner must adhere to the statutory requirements set forth in the Patent Act. These requirements are nonobviousness, novelty, and usefulness.

---

[16] 447 U.S. 303, 206 U.S.P.Q. (BNA) 193 (1980).

[17] Notice, April 7, 1987 by Donald J. Quigg, Assistant Secretary and Comm'r of Patents & Trademarks, 1059 Official Gazette 27.

[18] Leder and Stewart, "Transgenic Non-Human Mammals," U.S. Patent No. 4,736,866 (Apr. 12, 1988).

[19] Naj, *Clouds Gather over the Biotech Industry,* Wall St. J., Jan. 30, 1989, at B1.

Before discussing these three requirements, it is necessary to understand the term *prior art*. Prior art is defined as knowledge in certain statutorily defined categories which predates the invention.[20] Such prior art categories include patents of any country, printed publications throughout the world, and a public use in this country by anyone, including the inventor, more than one year before the filing date of the application. The term prior art implies public disclosure.

§ 2.9   —Nonobviousness

The Patent Act mandates that a patent may not be obtained if "the differences between the subject matter sought to be patented and the prior art are such that the subject matter as a whole would have been obvious at the time the invention was made to a person having ordinary skill in the art to which said subject matter pertains."[21]

In the *Graham v. John Deere* case, the Supreme Court set forth the following standard, which is frequently quoted by the courts for determining obviousness:

Under § 103, the scope and content of the prior art are to be determined; differences between the prior art and the claims at issue are to be ascertained; and the level of ordinary skill in the pertinent art resolved. Against this background, the obviousness or nonobviousness of the subject matter is determined. Such secondary considerations as commercial success, long felt but unsolved need, failure of others, etc., might be utilized to give light to the circumstances surrounding the origin of the subject matter sought to be patented. As indicia of obviousness or nonobviousness, these inquiries may have relevancy.[22]

There are three essential elements necessary for a finding of nonobviousness; they are (1) the idea was not obvious (2) at the time of the invention (3) to one having ordinary skill in the art.[23]

At this time, we should combine the meaning of prior art with the concept of obviousness. The inventor is charged with a mythical standard of knowledge, which is stated as knowledge worldwide and at any time. For example, the term *ordinary skill in the art* has different meanings in different technological areas. At one end of the spectrum, assume that the invention is a simple household utensil such as a nutcracker. The level of

---

[20] 35 U.S.C. §§ 101–103 (1953).

[21] 35 U.S.C. § 103 (1953).

[22] Graham v. John Deere Co., 383 U.S. 1, 148 U.S.P.Q. (BNA) 459, 467 (1966).

[23] Swift Agricultural Chems. Corp. v. Farmland Indus. Inc., 674 F.2d 1351, 1356, 213 U.S.P.Q. (BNA) 930, 934 (10th Cir. 1982).

skill in the art may well include millions of people across the world who are familiar with the use and design of nutcrackers. At the other end of the spectrum, assume that the invention pertains to the detection of a vitamin K analog in blood. Only four or five people worldwide may have ordinary skill in the art of vitamin K blood chemistry. Hence, the level of skill significantly varies from invention to invention.

The wide discretion that a court has in going back in time and interpreting what is meant by "level of skill in the art" is illustrated by the case of the "column-spanning hammers for high-speed, on-the-fly printers."[24] In litigation concerning this patent, the court rendered the issued patent invalid because it would have been obvious for one skilled in the art of printing mechanisms to modify a very old "printing telegraph" as described in an 1887 patent to arrive at the alleged nonobvious modern high-speed printer. Many consider the reliance on such an old patent ludicrous.

This example also illustrates another important concept. The standard of obviousness is encountered at least twice (as are the other legal requirements for patents). The Patent Office examiner utilizes this standard in the allowance or denial of a patent, and if the patent issues, the patent owner is once again faced with the possibility of an obviousness counterattack by an alleged infringer in court.

Although examiners are usually individuals trained in science and technology in the area of their specialty, the federal courts most frequently have rudimentary or no technical experience whatsoever. How is it possible for such courts or juries (usually composed of nonscientifically trained people) to decide complex questions such as patent infringement, obviousness, and the like? To deal with this problem, the courts have incorporated additional subtests to the definition of nonobviousness.

The following areas of practical inquiry set forth by the Supreme Court in *Graham v. John Deere*[25] are almost always considered by the courts:

1. Long-felt but unresolved need. A problem existed in industry for a long time, and the invention provided a practical solution to the problem.

2. Failure by others. Unsuccessful attempts were made by competitors to arrive at a solution.

3. Commercial success. Once on the market, the invention enjoyed significant acclaim, success in sales, and product recognition.

4. Imitation by others. Competitors immediately recognized the value of the invention and decided to copy it.

---

[24] Potter Instrument Co. v. ODEC Computer Sys., Inc., 499 F.2d 209, 211, 182 U.S.P.Q. (BNA) 386, 387 (1974).

[25] Graham v. John Deere Co., 383 U.S. 1, 148 U.S.P.Q. (BNA) 459 (1966).

Evidence under these four factors is extremely probative and is entitled to great weight in patent litigation.[26] From a business point of view then, marketing departments should work closely with patent lawyers and market products by emphasizing attributes of inventions that demonstrate these factors. Marketing departments should also solicit favorable product reviews, customer praises, and product comparisons.

There is no doubt that the obviousness standard is the great patent killer. It is under this standard that 60 percent of all patents historically litigated have been held invalid.[27] This statistic, however, needs to be placed in proper perspective. Only a small number (one-half to one percent) of issued patents have ever been litigated, and these patents were weak patents to begin with, that is, there is doubt whether they should have been issued in the first place. More importantly, approximately 90 percent, if not more, of threatened patent litigation is settled before trial.

The story of the Weed Eater illustrates an important point.[28] The inventor of the Weed Eater, George C. Ballas, washed his car at a local car wash. One day while watching the swirling brushes whip around to clean the car, he came up with the concept of whipping a fiber around to cut grass and weeds, and thus the invention known as the Weed Eater was conceived. The inventor went to a patent firm, which presumably did a thorough patent search and advised the inventor that his new invention was patentable. Patent applications were applied for. The examiner in the Patent Office also did a patent search and concluded that the invention was patentable and issued three patents. Subsequently, the product became commercially successful.

A competitor, Toro, came out with a similar product and Ballas sued. In the resulting patent litigation, the Weed Eater patent was held to be invalid under a French patent. The court held the Weed Eater patent to be obvious based upon the teachings of the French patent. (Patents do "teach." Although they contain technological descriptions, what is "taught" is more important to the advancement of science than what is "contained.") Quite clearly, once in litigation, Toro expended a considerably larger amount of money in doing a worldwide prior art search in the hope of invalidating the Weed Eater patent than the inventor expended at the outset during the initial patentability search.

A business cannot afford to spend $50,000 or $100,000 in a search to evaluate (or attempt to evaluate) all the prior art before filing for a patent.

---

[26] *See* Simmons Fastener Corp. v. Illinois Tool Works, Inc., 739 F.2d 1573, 222 U.S.P.Q. (BNA) 744 (Fed. Cir. 1984).

[27] *See* Horn & Epstein, *The Federal Courts' View of Patents—A Different View,* 55 J. Pat. Off. Soc. 134, 139 (1973).

[28] Ballas Liquidating Co. v. Allied Indus. of Kan., Inc., 205 U.S.P.Q. (BNA) 331 (D. Kan. 1979).

A clear assumption of risk must be made. Once in litigation, money apparently becomes no object, and hundreds of thousands of dollars can be expended in attorneys' fees and in searches in an attempt to invalidate or render a patented invention obvious.

Businesses must understand that the standard of obviousness varies significantly with the discretion of each examiner, with each court, and with each jury. The only consistency is that all patent cases are now appealable to the Court of Appeals for the Federal Circuit. The change in appellate procedure is important, because the new Court of Appeals for the Federal Circuit is said to be upholding the validity of 80 percent of all litigated patents. This is a surprising turnabout, because only 10 years ago only 40 percent of such patents were upheld.

§ 2.10   —Novelty

The second requirement for patentability is novelty. This is a relatively easy standard to meet. If the patent is found in identical form, that is, it exists element-for-element in a prior art reference, then a new patent should not be issued. Lack of novelty is defined in the Patent Act simply as, "the invention was known or used by others in this country, or patented or described in a printed publication in this or a foreign country before the invention thereof by the applicant for patent."[29]

We once had a dentist as a client who had invented and sketched out an interesting medical appliance. We conducted a patentability search on this appliance in Washington, D.C., and uncovered a United States patent issued to a German inventor. When we saw the patent, we firmly believed that our client had seen the German product and had copied it. The drawings were uncannily close. Under the novelty standard, our client was not entitled to apply for a patent. As it turned out, the client was able to obtain the exclusive rights under the United States patent from the German inventor at a cost that was less than obtaining his own patent. This resulted in a win-win situation, even though it provided an excellent example of an invention failing to meet the novelty requirement. We have a number of foreign clients who come into our office seeking to obtain a United States patent on a product they have already seen in their own country. This simply cannot be done.

§ 2.11   —Usefulness

An invention, to be patentable, must also be useful. Historically, usefulness was dependent upon moral and social values. A gambling machine

---

[29] 35 U.S.C. § 102(a) (1970).

100 years ago simply was not useful in the moral or social sense and therefore not patentable. The requirement of usefulness is primarily of importance today in the areas of new chemical inventions. Often a new chemical process is not useful within the requirements of patentability until some practical use for it has been discovered. The Supreme Court held in *Brenner v. Manson*[30] that a "patent is not a hunting license. It is not a reward for the search, but compensation for its successful conclusion."[31] Further, the Court held that until the chemical "process claim has been reduced to production of a product shown to be useful, the metes and bounds of that monopoly are not capable of precise delineation."[32]

§ 2.12   Statutory Bars

Statutory bars are an area of key importance to all businesses. United States patent law provides the inventor with a "grace period" of one year in which to file a patent application after the date of public use or offer for sale. Most foreign countries do not provide such a grace period. By treaty, the United States application must be on file before any public use or on-sale date, and the foreign filing date relates back to the United States filing date. These two concepts are discussed in **§ 2.13**. For businesses that need foreign patents, it is imperative that the patent application be on file before any public disclosure, use, or sale.

§ 2.13   —On-Sale and Public Use Bar

The Patent Act provides that a patent will not issue if "the invention was patented or described in a printed publication in this or a foreign country or in public use or on-sale in this country, more than one year prior to the date of the application for the patent in the United States."[33]

In the early days of patent law, *on-sale* simply meant that the product was placed in the store window and advertised to the public as being for sale. Today, the law defining on-sale is complex and frequently litigated. The best legal advice for any business is to avoid this hotbed of complexity by planning for and actually filing patent applications before any possible on-sale or public use date.

One rather humorous story of a prior public use invalidating a patent occurred in 1881. At that time, a grace period of two years was enacted into the patent laws. In the United States Supreme Court case of *Egbert v.*

---

[30] 383 U.S. 519, 148 U.S.P.Q. (BNA) 689 (1966).

[31] *Id.* at 536, 148 U.S.P.Q. (BNA) at 696.

[32] *Id.* at 534, 148 U.S.P.Q. (BNA) at 695.

[33] 35 U.S.C. § 102(b) (1970).

Lippmann,[34] 11 years before filing for a patent application, the inventor gave his fiancee a pair of corset springs which she subsequently wore. By its very nature, the invention comprising a new and improved set of corset springs was never exposed for public viewing. The results, however, were viewed by the public, and the court found the use by the fiancee to be a public use, thereby invalidating the inventor's patent.

The present filing period is one year; after one year has elapsed, and if a filing for a patent has not occurred, the invention is given to the public and a patent can never be obtained. The start of the one-year period is determined by the on-sale, offer of sale, and public use considerations. Many issued patents are held invalid by a court for violating this one-year rule.

Businesses often believe that if an idea is still experimental, it is exempt from the on-sale doctrine because there is no public use. The Federal Circuit has clearly stated that experimental use is not an exception but is one of the factors to be considered in determining whether an on-sale or public use has occurred. The Federal Circuit has stated that public use:

> must be determined by considering the totality of circumstances. Factors to be considered in deciding whether there is a public use include, for example, the length of the test period, whether any payment has been made for the device, whether there is a secrecy obligation on the part of the user, whether progress records were kept, whether persons other than the inventor conducted the asserted experiments, how many tests were conducted, and how long the testing period was in relationship to tests of other similar devices.[35]

There is strong public policy favoring a prompt and widespread disclosure of inventions to the public, while at the same time giving the inventor a reasonable amount of time to determine whether a patent is worthwhile.[36]

A recent public use case involved a new type of corn planter developed by the John Deere Co.[37] The planter prepared the soil, carefully placed the seed, and covered the seed with a predetermined degree of firmness and thickness. Because of this precise control over the planting process, all of the seeds would sprout and emerge from the ground at about the same time. John Deere enjoyed substantial commercial success in the marketplace with this planter. A patent infringement lawsuit arose, and all five of the John Deere patents covering the planter were invalidated. One of the

---

[34] 104 U.S. 333 (1881).

[35] Hycor Corp. v. Schulueter Co., 740 F.2d 1529, 1535, 222 U.S.P.Q. (BNA) 553, 557 (Fed. Cir. 1984).

[36] *See* Western Marine Elec., Inc. v. Furuno Elec. Co. Ltd., 764 F.2d 840, 845, 226 U.S.P.Q. (BNA) 334, 337 (Fed. Cir. 1985).

[37] Kinzenbaw v. Deere & Co., 222 U.S.P.Q. (BNA) 929 (Fed. Cir. 1984).

patents was invalidated under the on-sale doctrine, because more than one year before filing for the patent, John Deere had placed the planter in farmers' fields to evaluate the planters and had, in fact, planted 40,000 acres. The court found that the purpose of John Deere's evaluation was commercial. Because of this, the court found the use to be a public use, and John Deere lost valuable patent rights.

This area of the law is complex. For example, the three-dimensional puzzle concept capable of rotational movement underlying the Rubik's Cube was actually invented first by a United States inventor. The United States inventor obtained a patent on his invention and proceeded to sue the distributors of the Rubik's Cube puzzle for patent infringement. The owners of Rubik's Cube countered with a defense stating that the inventor's patent was invalid because the inventor had made a disclosure of his invention to friends, to colleagues, and to his employer at work. The inventor had placed his prototype on his desk. If anyone came into his office, he would demonstrate the operation of the puzzle to them. In fact, the inventor had explained the puzzle to the president of an outside company who had then contacted Parker Bros. The disclosure to Parker Bros., however, did not set forth how the puzzle operated. The court held that a public disclosure had not occurred, thereby maintaining the validity of the patent.[38]

A business must clearly establish the first date that an invention is disclosed to a member of the public outside the corporation, then take all steps necessary to file the patent application before that date.

§ 2.14   —Beta-Test Sites

Beta-test is a common phrase used to describe taking software or a system into a real-life environment like the one found at a customer's place of business. During the critical beta-test period, it is important that there be no offer for sale or public use of an invention. If so, it can affect foreign filing rights. With respect to United States filing rights, an inventor has a year after a public disclosure in which to file a United States application. Most industrialized foreign countries, however, have an absolute novelty rule; consequently United States patent applications must be on file before any sale or public use.

For beta-site testing, we recommend the following:

1. Obtain a confidential agreement
2. Allow no purchases or payments from the beta user back to you

---

[38] Moleculon Research Corp. v. CBS, Inc., 793 F.2d 1261, 229 U.S.P.Q. (BNA) 805 (Fed. Cir. 1986).

3. Maintain a complete set of progress reports and records
4. Have the inventor(s) conduct the testing
5. Make sure you have complete control over the test.

With respect to any offers for sale, clearly there cannot be any freely circulated sales literature on the product, nor can there be any demonstrations of the product or software to prospective customers in order to obtain a sale.

§ 2.15 —Submission of Papers for Publication

It is not surprising that what constitutes a "publication" is open to litigation and varying judicial interpretations. For example, in one case the distribution of papers at various technological conferences in Europe constituted printed publication which served as a bar against issuance of United States patents.[39] On the other hand, distribution of a paper to a limited group with a requirement of secrecy is not a publication.

The difficult cases are those cases constituting a limited distribution beyond a single company where there is no express or implied requirement of secrecy. In one case[40] 25 copies of a United States government research report marked "Unclassified" were circulated to various government individuals and agencies. This was held not to be a publication, because each government official received a copy in his official capacity. On the other hand, a deposit of even a single copy of the document in a library or other depository has been held to constitute a publication. Thus, a doctoral thesis deposited in the library constitutes a printed publication.[41]

Businesses are constantly faced with the problem of inventor publishing. In one case[42] the plaintiff submitted papers to the IEEE (a professional organization of electrical and electronic engineers) for consideration for presentation at the International Solid State Circuits Conference. The papers were submitted in October of 1973 and presented in February of 1974. The court held the submission to the technical committee not to constitute a publication.

---

[39] Deep Welding, Inc. v. Sciaky Bros., Inc., 417 F.2d 1227, 163 U.S.P.Q. (BNA) 144 (7th Cir. 1969).

[40] Ex parte Suozzi, 125 U.S.P.Q. (BNA) 445 (Pat. & Trademark App. Bd. 1959).

[41] In re Hall, 781 F.2d 897, 899–900, 228 U.S.P.Q. (BNA) 453, 456 (Fed. Cir. 1986).

[42] National Semiconductor Corp. v. Linear Technology Corp., 703 F. Supp. 897, 8 U.S.P.Q.2d (BNA) 1359 (N.D. Cal. 1988).

In submitting articles, the following procedure should be adhered to by your inventors:

1. Ascertain the editorial policy of the publication or association, that is, does it treat submissions as privileged or confidential?
2. Clearly mark all submissions as follows: PRIVILEGED: This article is being submitted for consideration for possible publication and is not to be disclosed to others before publication. No one with access to this article under review shall make any inappropriate use of the special knowledge contained herein. (This language is a paraphrase of the IEEE policy approved by the court.)
3. Provide in-house counsel with a copy of all submitted articles.

§ 2.16 —Foreign Patents

Preserving foreign rights is an extremely important patent consideration, especially in today's marketplace where the worldwide market is opening up. The laws of almost all foreign countries do not allow any grace period. Therefore, any sale or public disclosure of an invention constitutes an absolute bar. If foreign patents are a consideration, the inventor must not make a sale or public disclosure of the invention until after the United States patent application is on file. Then, by treaty with foreign countries, the foreign patent when filed is accorded the United States filing date. To take advantage of this treaty provision, the foreign patent application must be made within one year of the United States filing date, and the foreign filing date will relate back to the United States filing date. The United States filing preserves your right to actually file a foreign patent in the 30-month time frame after the filing date of the United States patent application.

§ 2.17 Invention Protection

Certain activities are of particular importance to the inventor prior to applying for a patent, while obtaining the patent, and after the patent is issued. In §§ 2.18 through 2.24, practical guidelines for maximizing invention protection during these three stages are set forth.

§ 2.18 —Maintaining Running Records

Record-keeping is especially disliked by engineers and scientists; most would rather go to the dentist and have teeth pulled! An inventor, however, must be counseled to maintain a running record of all of his activities, and it is important for companies to constantly request, supervise, and maintain neat and complete records of such inventive activities. From a patent protection viewpoint, the keeping of an engineering notebook, an engineering diary, and a running record of the invention may be crucial. This type of running record is important because, at least in the United States, the first to invent is entitled to the patent.

The running record should be kept in bound notebooks with each entry signed and dated by the inventor. A disinterested, technically minded third party who understands the invention should periodically read through the notebook and sign it. The following is an example of what should appear at the bottom of each page of this notebook:

Witnessed and Understood

| _____ | _____ |
| Date | Signature |

Notebooks not properly witnessed or signed only by the inventor do not constitute independent corroborating evidence and will not be admitted into evidence, so it is important for the employer to make sure proper procedure is being followed. The witness cannot be a spouse, a co-inventor, or anyone related to the inventor.[43]

The running record should contain the following chronological sequence of events: (1) when the invention was first conceived; (2) when, where, and to whom it was disclosed; (3) success and failure each step of the way; (4) when the first working model was constructed and who witnessed it working; and (5) all contacts with a patent attorney or agent in preparing the application for the patent.

The inventor should include photographs and/or drawings of various aspects of the invention, as well as any other literature pertaining to it. The inventor should never erase entries within the notebook, but should take care to line out wrong information while still maintaining the legibility of the lined out information. All entries should be entered in indelible ink.

With the use of engineering work stations, personal computers, and mainframes, it is becoming increasingly difficult to get engineers to maintain handwritten diaries. There is a simple solution. Periodically, such as every two or four weeks, have each engineer "dump" the data from memory. This freezes in time the status of the engineering development. This dump should produce both a printout and a floppy disc or tape of the engineering file and should be preserved in at least two locations. One copy should be preserved on premises; the second copy should be preserved off premises, preferably in a vault. A secretary or technical clerk

---

[43] Dentsply Research & Dev. Corp. v. Cadco Dental Prods., Inc., 14 U.S.P.Q.2d (BNA) 1039 (C.D. Cal. 1989).

should be responsible for binding the computer listings and setting forth statements on the bound listings that they were dumped and bound on certain dates. In addition, a witness should review the material and sign and date it.

From a practical standpoint, the date of conception is simply the date the idea is first disclosed to someone who technically understands it and who can reduce it to practice.[44] Conception occurs when an idea becomes a useful result that can be achieved in some specific manner. Therein lies the importance of having third parties witness the progress of the invention in a carefully kept running record.

When two or more inventors file patent applications claiming the same invention, the importance of a running record becomes paramount. When the PTO receives two patent applications on the same invention, it initiates an interference proceeding. Indeed, if a patent is issued and another party believes that he was the first inventor of the invention, he can immediately file an application copying the claims of the issued patent, thereby forcing the commencement of an interference proceeding in the PTO. The interference proceeding is a miniature lawsuit that can be both costly and time-consuming.

§ 2.19   —Reduction to Practice

After conceiving the invention, the inventor must be diligent in reducing the invention to practice.[45] **Figure 2–4** illustrates the importance of this concept. If inventor X fails to perform any work on the invention for a period of time, for example, five to six months (that is, a period of no diligence), and then proceeds to construct his first working model, X may lose priority in an interference proceeding. Suppose, for example, that a second inventor, Y, conceived the same idea three months after X's date of conception, but Y diligently reduced it to practice within a month. The results of the interference proceeding between X and Y would result in the patent being awarded to Y on the basis that X was not diligent in pursuing his idea toward a reduction to practice. In **Figure 2–4**, the period of "no diligence" is clearly illustrated. Hence, even though inventor X is first in time of conception, through X's lack of diligence, Y is awarded the patent.

Under the general rule, actual reduction to practice is established when the invention is tested under actual working conditions.[46] Again, this illustrates the importance of having good records. Actual reduction to practice

---

[44] Hiatt v. Ziegler & Kilgour, 179 U.S.P.Q. (BNA) 757 (Pat. Off. Bd. Pat. Interferences 1973).

[45] Harrington Mfg. Co. v. White, 475 F.2d 788, 177 U.S.P.Q. (BNA) 289 (5th Cir. 1973).

[46] Laminex, Inc. v. Fritz, 389 F. Supp. 369, 183 U.S.P.Q. (BNA) 215 (N.D. Ill. 1974).

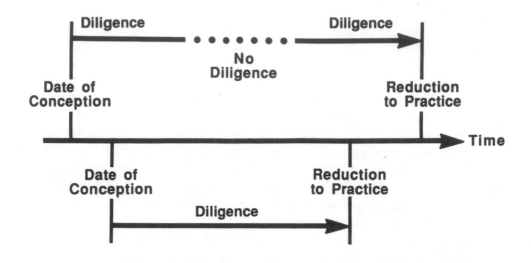

Figure 2–4. Importance of reducing the invention to practice promptly.

cannot be based upon the uncorroborated testimony of the inventor. This surprises most inventors and their employers. The inventor's own testimony with respect to the invention and reduction to practice has been held to constitute a self-serving declaration.[47]

Operability is a primary characteristic of an actual reduction to practice. In the early days of the PTO, submission of a working model of the invention, usually carefully constructed from wood, was a mandatory requirement for the issuance of a patent. Today, the requirement is not mandatory. However, the PTO may request a working model.[48] Even if the invention was not truly operable at the time of actual reduction to practice, if it could have been made operable by a person ordinarily skilled in the art, then a sufficient reduction to practice has been made under the law.[49] The reduction to practice must occur, for interference proceeding purposes, in the United States.[50]

---

[47] *Id.*

[48] 35 U.S.C. § 114 (1970).

[49] Bennett v. Halahan, Aronson & Lyon, 285 F.2d 807, 128 U.S.P.Q. (BNA) 398 (CCPA 1961).

[50] Shurie v. Richmond, 699 F.2d 1156, 216 U.S.P.Q. (BNA) 1042 (Fed. Cir. 1983).

Patent applications are often filed even though the invention itself has not been actually reduced to practice. The filing of a patent application on the invention is a *constructive reduction to practice.*

§ 2.20   —Patent Search

The purpose of a patent search is to find out what prior patents and other literature exist on file in the PTO or elsewhere that relate to the invention. The results of a patent search can be helpful in deciding whether the application is novel and nonobvious and, if so, whether a patent application should be filed. It is estimated that over 29 million references are on file in the PTO. It is not surprising that a patent search can be quite expensive.

Some corporations simply do not conduct patentability searches. They believe that their engineers are already on the cutting edge of technology and, therefore, there is no need to go to the time and expense of a patentability search. The risk, of course, is that a patent or paper that substantially discloses the invention exists, thereby knocking out the expensive patent application.

Most companies, however, do conduct patentability searches, but try to keep the costs down. There are two types of patentability searches that can be performed. One search can be performed on a computer database, examples of which were given in § 2.2. Computer databases are thorough because they permit access to information on all available issued patents and printed publications. The problem with computer searching, however, is the selection of the proper key search words. If the proper key words are not selected, the search may miss the important references. The second type of search is conducted by a professional patent searcher, usually in Washington, D.C. Such searches take several weeks to perform. The problem with professional searches that utilize the PTO files is that, at any given time, approximately seven percent of the patents are missing from the Patent Office files. They may be missing because they are gone, are misfiled, are bad copies, or are in the process of being used.[51]

It is the advice of the authors that a computerized search be performed on at least essential key terms and, most definitely, on patents issued to competitors who manufacture the same or similar products. Such a computerized search should, at a minimum, include not only United States patents but all available foreign patents and engineering articles and dissertations.

---

[51] American Intellectual Property Lawyers Ass'n Bulletin 661 (Jan.–March 1989).

§ 2.21 —Application for Patent

From the date of the application to the issuance of a patent, on the average two years will elapse. The PTO has set 18 months as a goal. During this time, the PTO keeps the application a secret.

There are a number of ways to speed up the application process. If the inventor is over 65, if the invention relates to energy, or if the application is based on the results of a professional search, then the PTO will give the application priority. In such situations, it may only take six to twelve months for a patent to issue. If it is important for a business to have a patent issue immediately (for example, in the case of a start-up company raising capital, or in the case of a product with a short market life), having a professional search performed is worth the investment.

The first office action from the Patent Office is generally negative. All or most of the claims are rejected. Inventors are often dismayed at the pessimistic attitude displayed by the examiner and the numerous and various grounds upon which the rejection is made. Inventors generally believe that what they filed was truly novel and nonobvious. Each inventor should carefully read through the office action and if he has any questions, contact his patent attorney. The most important contribution the inventor can make at this time is to distinguish his invention technically from the references relied on by the examiner. This will be invaluable information for the patent attorney.

In the chart featured in **Figure 2–5**, a typical time sequence for a non-priority patent application is set forth. Typically two office actions occur. Likewise, two amendments are filed. What takes place in the PTO is similar to what happens when a buyer negotiates the price of a used car with a used car salesman. The inventor submits broad claims on his invention, and in the first office action, the examiner rejects those claims. Your response to the examiner's rejection is usually a set of amendments to the orginally submitted claims. Usually after the second office action and the second response, the patent attorney and the Patent Office examiner have mutually arrived at language sufficiently limiting the scope of the claims and distinguishing the invention over approaches that have existed before. If the examiner had allowed all the claims at the time of the first office action, the inventor might not have obtained the broadest possible legal coverage that he was entitled to.

The office actions and the amended applications are called the period of prosecution of the patent with the PTO. **Figure 2–5** shows that you have three months in which to respond to each office action. Statutorily you are allowed up to six months in which to respond; up to three months of *extensions* can be purchased for a fee from the Patent office for each office action.

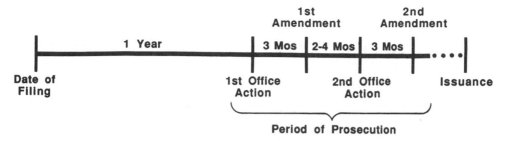

Figure 2–5. Typical time sequence for a patent application.

If you disagree with the examiner's conclusion concerning your invention, you have the right to appeal the decision to the Patent Office Board of Appeals. If you disagree with the Patent Office Board of Appeals, you can appeal its decision out of the Patent Office and into a federal court. Occasionally such appeals are necessary, and there is no doubt that the resulting court decisions improve the quality of the examining process in the PTO.

Often, inventors want to add to or change the originally filed patent application. The introduction of new material into the patent application will be rejected as "new matter." At the time of filing, the technical disclosure is "frozen" and cannot be added to. The claims at the end of the application most assuredly can be changed, because they affect the scope and coverage of the invention and are the very heart of the examining process. However, the drawings and the technical disclosure cannot be changed if the change involves new matter.

§ 2.22   —Continuation-in-Part Application

Procedures exist whereby improvements to a basic invention can be presented to the PTO in a separate application called a continuation-in-part application. Suppose, for example, an inventor has developed a new feedback circuit for an invention which he filed a patent application for last year. The inventor believes the feedback circuit to be a significant cost savings approach and one that substantially increases feedback control. That circuit can be added to the existing patent application through the addition of new drawings and new discussion; thus, this new *in-part* portion, along with all the other material from the original application, constitutes a new patent application that has two separate filing dates. The first filing date relates to the original material, and the second filing date relates to the added or in-part material.

§ 2.23   —Continuation Application

A second type of patent application is called a continuation patent application. This type of application simply continues an application filed earlier. Continuations are made for a number of reasons. Most commonly, a new type of invention that was not originally claimed but exists in the earlier application is being claimed. Continuation applications always relate back to the filing date of the original or parent patent application.

§ 2.24   —Secrecy Order

If an application relates to national security, the PTO may disclose it to the appropriate agency (for example, the Department of Energy), which may order that the invention be kept secret and a patent withheld "for such period as the national interest requires."[52] If this occurs, the inventor has a right to compensation for damages due to the secrecy order and the use of the invention by the government.[53]

§ 2.25   Post Issuance Matters

After issuance of the patent by the Government Printing Office, the PTO loses jurisdiction except in two limited areas, which are discussed in §§ 2.26 and 2.27.

§ 2.26   —Reexamination

Reexamination of a patent by the PTO occurs when prior art prints and publications raise "a substantial new question of patentability."[54] Any person (including competitors) may request reexamination of an issued patent by the PTO upon payment of a fee.

A few years ago, we represented a client who was quite excited that a patent had been issued. The excitement was based upon the fact that at least three companies had already infringed upon the issued claims. Indeed, during pendency of the patent application, we drafted narrow claims exactly covering the products of these three competitors. As soon as the patent issued, cease and desist letters were mailed to each of these three competitors. One company caved in and changed its design. One

---

[52] 35 U.S.C. § 181 (1982).
[53] 35 U.S.C. § 183 (1982).
[54] 35 U.S.C. § 301 (1980).

company sent back a list of several references that they maintained would have barred our patent in the first place, had the patent examiner evaluated them. The third company filed a lawsuit seeking a declaratory judgment that our client's patent was invalid. A decision had to be made with respect to reexamination of the patent.

In the lawsuit, we requested that our opponents provide all references which allegedly invalidated the issued patent. They did so. We then moved that the court stay the lawsuit until the reexamination process was completed. We filed the reexamination request and submitted all the prior art references provided by the two companies. The PTO denied our petition for reexamination, concluding that the additional references were all simply accumulative and contained no new teachings not already considered. With the petition denied, the second company, which provided the references, stopped making the infringing product, and the third company, which brought the lawsuit, settled by entering into a license to the issued patent.

The purpose of the reexamination procedure after the issuance of the patent is to save the tremendous cost of patent litigation and the delays associated with it. Our experience, as related above, illustrated the working of this procedure in actual practice.

§ 2.27   —Reissuance

The reissue procedure allows the PTO to reissue an issued patent which is deemed wholly or partly inoperative or invalid because the inventor claims more or less than the patent as originally issued allows.[55] For example, if the inventor believes that the patent attorney did not accurately represent the scope of the invention through mistake or inadvertence, then the inventor has the right within two years after the patent has issued to seek broader (or narrower) claim coverage.

§ 2.28   Notice Requirements

After the patent has been formally applied for, and during pendency, the words *patent applied for, patent pending, application pending, or pat. pend.* may be placed on the invention as a means of warning the public that the inventor is applying for a patent and, upon the issuance thereof, has the right to prosecute anyone who commits infringement. It must be understood that such notices do not provide patent protection under these notices. This is a common misconception in the public. *Patent pending*

---

[55] 35 U.S.C. § 251 (1982).

simply serves notice to third persons that a patent may be awarded sometime in the future.

As a practical matter, the words *patent pending* may have substantial psychological or marketing value. It is much like a game of poker. A company is selling a product with the words *patent pending* on it, and its competitor cannot ascertain the filing date of the patent application or any information about it. Prudent competitors wait until the patent issues before deciding whether to copy, closely copy, or design around such a product.

In addition, marketing studies have shown that, in certain industries, people like to buy products marked *patent pending*. In the golf, skiing, and motorcycle industries, for example, *patent pending* prominently placed on new accessory products attract purchasers (such as spouses and parents) because they believe the patent pending product represents a new product that would make a good gift. From time to time in our practice, we have clients who file for patent applications, knowing it may be very difficult to obtain a patent, in order to make full marketing use of the words *patent pending* not only to scare away competitors, but as a means to enhance sales.

If the words *patent pending* or the like are used when in fact no patent has been applied for, the party falsely marking its product has violated the Patent Act and is subject to penalties.[56]

The Patent Act provides the following guidance as to notice after issuance of the patent:

> Patentees, and persons making or selling any patented article for or under them, may give notice to the public that the same is patented, either by affixing thereon the word "patent" or the abbreviation "pat.", together with the number of the patent, or when, from the character of the article, this cannot be done, by fixing to it, or to the package wherein one or more of them is contained, a label containing a like notice.[57]

In accordance with the above law, after receiving his patent the inventor should mark his invention in a manner such as:

Patent 4,111,013

or

Pat. 4,111,013

---

[56] 35 U.S.C. § 292 (1952).
[57] 35 U.S.C. § 287 (1952).

If a person falsely marks his product with issued patent notices, that person has violated the Patent Act and is subject to penalties of $500 per article. Private parties may sue to recover one-half of such penalties.[58]

Failure to provide an issued patent notice is failure to inform the public that the product has received a constitutionally protected patent. Therefore the public, including competitors, may unknowingly infringe upon the patent. An inventor who fails to give notice cannot sue for damages. Notice may be given by mailing a letter to or filing a lawsuit against an alleged infringer. That type of notice, however, does not commence until the date the letter is received or the lawsuit is filed.

§ 2.29   Assignment of Inventions

Employers must always obtain written agreements from their employees in order to secure rights to inventions. Absent a written agreement, the general rule as stated by the United States Supreme Court is that the employee owns the inventions made in the course of his employment.[59] A sample long form invention agreement, assigning inventions from the employee to the employer, is set forth in **Form 2–1.**

A short form invention agreement is set forth in **Form 2–2.** In essence, these agreements not only assign inventions from the employee to the employer, but they also require the employee to cooperate in the signing of all necessary papers and the keeping of all records of inventions, not only during employment but after termination of employment.

Form 2–1
**EMPLOYEE INVENTION PROVISIONS
(Long Form)**

I agree:

1.   To disclose promptly and fully in writing to Poorhorse Corp. all inventions, improvements, or discoveries of whatever kind or description made, conceived, developed, or first reduced to practice by me, either solely or in collaboration with others, during the period of my employment by Poorhorse Corp. and within 12 months thereafter, which relate (a) to any products, research, or business of Poorhorse Corp. or to tasks assigned to me by or on behalf of Poorhorse Corp.; (b) to any process, method, apparatus, or article useful in connection with the manufacture or development of such products or in the prosecution of such work or business; (c) to anything done upon the time or with the facilities of Poorhorse Corp.; or (d) to any invention and

---

[58] 35 U.S.C. § 292 (1952).
[59] United States v. Dubilier Condenser Corp., 289 U.S. 178 (1938).

discovery which relates directly or indirectly to the present or prospective business of Poorhorse Corp.

2.   To sign and deliver all writings to Poorhorse Corp., at the request and expense of Poorhorse Corp., and to do all other things as may be required to vest in Poorhorse Corp. as its absolute and exclusive property my entire right, title, and interest in and to all inventions, improvements, or discoveries referred to in paragraph 1 above; and, at the election of Poorhorse Corp. and at its expense, to do all such acts which its counsel may specify or which it may otherwise reasonably require or request for or in connection with making application for Letters Patent in the United States, or in any country throughout the world, on the aforesaid inventions, improvements, or discoveries and for the purpose of procuring the issue, reissue, division, continuation, continuation-in-part, or renewal of any patent application(s) or patent(s) thereon for the sole benefit of Poorhorse Corp. and in any name designated by it. Unless so requested or otherwise permitted in writing by Poorhorse Corp., I will not, either during or after my employment with Poorhorse Corp., apply for any patents, domestic or foreign, on any such inventions, improvements, or discoveries. I further agree to assist and cooperate (at the expense of Poorhorse Corp.) with Poorhorse Corp. in any controversy or legal or administrative proceedings involving or relating to such inventions, improvements, or discoveries, or patents which may be issued thereon.

3.   To keep and maintain, or assist in keeping and maintaining, such records as will show the conception, reduction to practice, and operation of all of the aforesaid inventions, improvements, or discoveries, as well as such other records as Poorhorse Corp. may request, which records shall be and remain the property of, and available to, Poorhorse Corp.

4.   Not to reveal to any person, unless authorized in writing by Poorhorse Corp., any information concerning its inventions, improvements, or discoveries.

5.   That, except as otherwise noted on the attachment hereto, (a) there are at present no inventions, improvements, or discoveries that have been made, conceived, or first reduced to practice by me, whether solely or in collaboration with others, which I desire to remove from the operation of this agreement; and (b) I hereby release Poorhorse Corp. and hold Poorhorse Corp. harmless from, and agree to pay any attorneys' fees incurred by Poorhorse Corp. in connection with, any and all claims by me by reason of any use by it of any inventions, improvements, or discoveries which may have been heretofore made, conceived, or first reduced to practice by me, either solely or in collaboration with others.

6.   To disclose and to submit to Poorhorse Corp. any particular invention or discovery I may make during the period of time set forth in Paragraph 1, even if I am unsure whether the invention or discovery relates to Paragraph 1 (a),

(b), (c), or (d). I agree that Poorhorse Corp. shall have the sole right to determine whether or not any such particular invention or discovery falls within the contemplation of the present agreement and that, if and when Poorhorse Corp. subsequently determines that it has no interest in the particular invention or discovery, then such invention or discovery shall be released back or reassigned to me.

Form 2–2
EMPLOYEE INVENTION PROVISIONS
(Short Form)

I agree as follows:

1.   (A) That this agreement concerns inventions, improvements, any works of authorship, ideas, data, processes, computer software programs, and discoveries (hereafter called intellectual property) that are conceived or developed by me alone or with others while I am employed with Poorhorse Corp. and for one (1) year thereafter and that relate to the actual or anticipated business, research, or development of Poorhorse Corp. Such intellectual property is the sole property of Poorhorse Corp. and I agree, without charge to the Poorhorse Corp., that during my employment with Poorhorse Corp. and for one (1) year thereafter:

   (i)   to disclose all intellectual property fully and promptly to my supervisor or to the president of Poorhorse Corp.;

   (ii)   to assign all my right, title and interest in and to all intellectual property to Poorhorse Corp.; and

   (iii)   to execute all documents and do all things necessary to assist Poorhorse Corp., at its expense, in obtaining protection therefor including patent, trademark, copyright, maskwork, and trade secret protection or other form of protection throughout the world.

   (B) That, except as expressly set forth in the attached exhibit, (i) there is no existing intellectual property prior to my employment with the Poorhorse Corp. that I desire to remove from the operation of this Agreement, and (ii) I hereby release Poorhorse Corp. from any and all claims by me by reason of any use by it of such intellectual property.

These employment agreements must be reasonable in time and scope. In **Form 2–1,** the agreement assigns over to the company any inventions that relate to any of the products, research, or business of the corporation or to tasks assigned to the employee by the corporation. It also relates to any process, method, apparatus, or article useful in connection with the manufacture or development of the products or in the prosecution of such work or business. It further relates to anything done on the time or with the facilities of the corporation. And it broadly relates to any invention or discovery directly or indirectly related to the present and prospective business of the corporation. This latter provision may be somewhat broad, and some states have passed protective statutes restricting the employer's ownership of the employee's patent to job related inventions and to inventions made during working hours. Since this varies from state to state, it is important to check applicable state law. States that have passed protective statutes are California, Minnesota, North Carolina, Washington, and Illinois.[60]

Absent written invention assignment clauses in an employment contract, the employer obtains, by operation of law, a personal, nontransferable, royalty-free, nonexclusive license to the patent, only if the employer's time, materials, or facilities were used.[61] This has been commonly referred to as a *shop right*. The employee, however, still *owns* the invention.

The following story highlights the importance of the written agreement. A manufacturing company entered into written invention assignment agreements with its engineering staff. It did not have such agreements with its supervisory shop personnel. An engineer came up with a new product that was favorably received by management. The product was delivered over to the shop for manufacturing. The shop supervisor, as is frequently done, improved upon the engineer's idea to make the product less costly to manufacture by enhancing certain features of the invention. A patent application was filed in the names of both parties as co-inventors.

The shop supervisor refused to sign the papers to assign the invention over to the company. A dispute arose and the shop supervisor voluntarily terminated his employment. He then sold the invention to a Hong Kong competitor of the company for a substantial figure. A lawsuit arose, but the court held in favor of the supervisor. Absent the written agreement, as a co-inventor of the invention, the supervisor was a co-owner of the invention and had the full right to sell or license the invention to whomever he pleased without restriction and without sharing in the profits. Companies can easily avoid this situation through use of written assignments.

When the patent application is filed, a formal assignment of the invention from the employee to the corporation occurs. This assignment, of which **Form 2–3** is an example, is required under the Patent Act[62] and is filed in the PTO.

---

[60] Cal. Lab. Code §§ 2780–2782 (Supp. 1989); Minn. Stat. § 181.78 (West 1977 & Supp. 1989); N.C. Gen. Stat. § 66-57.1 (1981); Wash. Rev. Code Ann. § 49.44.140; 49.44.150 (West 1979 & Supp. 1989); Ill. Rev. Ch. 140 § 302(2) (1983).

[61] Mechmetals Corp. v. Telex Computer Prods., Inc., 709 F.2d 1287, 219 U.S.P.Q. (BNA) 20 (9th Cir. 1983).

[62] 35 U.S.C. § 261 (1982).

Form 2–3
PATENT ASSIGNMENT

WHEREAS, we, Thomas H. Smith whose residence address is 4121 West 35th Avenue, Aurora, Colorado 80211 and Susan P. House whose residence address is 4110 25th Street, Boulder, Colorado 80302 (the assignors), have invented a certain new and useful invention for a very unusual dog house, for which we are about to make application for Letters Patent of the United States, said application being identified as Docket No. 7923 in the law offices of Dorr, Carson, Sloan & Peterson, 3010 East 6th Avenue, Denver, Colorado 80206; and

WHEREAS, Poorhorse Corp., a Colorado corporation, whose post office address is 5789 West 6th Street, Boulder, Colorado 80301, (the assignee) is desirous of acquiring the entire right, title, and interest in and to the aforesaid invention and application for Letters Patent in the United States and in any and all foreign countries;

NOW, THEREFORE, in consideration of the sum of ten dollars ($10.00) in hand paid to the assignors by the assignee, and other good and valuable consideration, receipt whereof is hereby expressly acknowledged, we the assignors hereby sell, transfer, and set over to the assignee, its successors, legal representatives, and assigns, the entire right, title, and interest in and to the aforesaid invention and the aforesaid patent application, for the territory of the United States of America and for all foreign countries, and to all Letters Patents, divisions, continuations, continuations-in-part, substitutions, reissues, reexaminations, and extensions to be obtained therefor; and we further agree to cooperate with the assignee hereunder in the obtaining and the sustaining of any or all such Letters Patent, but at the expense of the assignee.

The Commissioner of Patents is hereby authorized and requested to issue the Letters Patent solely, in accordance with this assignment, to the assignee, its successors, legal representatives and assigns, as the assignee of the entire right, title and interest therein.

Further, we agree that we will communicate to the assignee or its representatives any facts known to us respecting said invention, and testify in any legal proceedings, sign all lawful papers, execute all division, continuation, continuation-in-part, substitution, reissue, reexamination, and extension applications, execute all necessary assignment papers to cause any and all of said Letters Patent to be issued to the assignee, make all rightful oaths and generally do everything necessary or desirable to aid the assignee, its successors, and assigns, to obtain and enforce proper protection for said invention in the United States and in any and all foreign countries.

This assignment is to be effective as of the date of signing set forth below.

_____   _____

Date   Assignor

_____   _____

Date   Assignor

§ 2.30   Inventions Received from Third Parties

Corporations frequently receive invention submittals from third parties. Management and the legal department should establish routine procedures that can be handled by clerical or secretarial staff to deal with invention submissions. At the outset, corporate policy must be determined. Because most corporations do not want to receive ideas from the outside, they establish a procedure that causes all submitted inventions and ideas to be delivered immediately to a single person, usually in the legal department, who will then use a standard form letter to mail the submission back, along with a disclosure agreement. **Form 2–4** sets forth an example of a disclosure agreement.

The disclosure agreement clarifies the relationship between the submitter and the corporation. By signing the disclosure agreement, the submitter agrees that no confidential relationship is established and that any rights of the submitter will be set forth in any issued patent or copyright. Such an agreement formalizes the relationship between the corporation and the submitter.

Form 2–4
DISCLOSURE AGREEMENT

I request that Surefire Corp. consider my idea relating to mud bullets described in the material submitted herewith and listed below. All additional disclosures relating to the idea submitted herewith shall be subject to the provisions of this agreement.

I understand that no confidential relationship is established by or is to be implied from this submission or from Surefire Corp.'s consideration of the submitted material, and declare that such material is not submitted in confidence.

By this request and submission I do not grant Surefire Corp. or any of its subsidiaries any right under any patents on the idea submitted. I agree that, except as this agreement may be superseded by a subsequent agreement in writing, I will make no claim against Surefire Corp. or any of its subsidiaries with respect to the idea here submitted except for patent infringement.

The foregoing may not be changed or waived except in writing signed by an officer of Surefire Corp.

_____   _____
          Date   Signature of Submitter

From a practical point of view, submitters should wait until the patent has been issued and then submit to the corporation the actual patent, complete with any prototypes, test results, and demonstrations.

Smaller corporations generally do not have the extensive research and engineering staffs necessary to come up continually with new product ideas; consequently, they should be more receptive to ideas from the outside. Rather than using disclosure agreements, smaller corporations should consider signing trade secret nondisclosure agreements.

§ 2.31   Patents and Competition

What is a company's goal in obtaining patents? Some companies obtain patents to block competition. Other companies obtain patents to fund extensive programs designed to acquire royalties, set standards, and obtain the benefits of other technology through cross-licensing arrangements. Still other companies (Sun) do not place much emphasis on patents, but rather seek to make their technology available in the hopes of setting standards so that other companies can come out with peripheral products, thereby insuring success in the marketplace. Each business should carefully analyze its philosophy regarding patents.

§ 2.32   —Using Patents Offensively

Aggressive patent filings can have a positive effect in raising capital through the Small Business Administration, through public offerings, or from venture capitalists. Start-up companies may wish to file as many different patent applications as they can think of on the product in question to take advantage of this positive effect.

Aggressive filing can also be a definite plus when it comes time to sell your business. Having an extensive patent portfolio may well return many times over the cost of obtaining the patents. Aggressive use of patents may also foreclose competitors. Specifically, anticipating the trends of product development and basing patent applications on those trends can provide a company significant advantages in the future, thereby foreclosing its competitors from entering these trend areas.

Aggressive use of patents may also entail building a patent thicket. A business is wise not to rely on the one or two initial patents it received on the product at its inception. Rather, it should aggressively seek patents on any and all improvements. By combining the trend patents with the improvement patents, a business can build a formidable thicket of patents with which to foreclose competition.

Please keep in mind that being too successful in the aggressive use of patents can lead to antitrust problems. The goal is to obtain a legal patent thicket without running the risk of antitrust violations.

Conversely, if you believe that you are a competitive victim of another company's thicket of patents, you should contact the Antitrust Division of the Justice Department. The Division's eight field offices are located in

Atlanta, Chicago, Cleveland, Dallas, Los Angeles, New York, Philadelphia, and San Francisco. You should specifically contact the Patent Section. There are no formal procedure and no form to file to make a complaint to the Division regarding suspected patent antitrust violations. However, written complaints are preferred to telephone complaints, and any written memorandum should be as thorough as possible.[63]

§ 2.33   —Using Patents Defensively

Patents provide insurance against being shut out of the market. Obtaining patents insures a corporation the right to make the products itself without being foreclosed in the future. In the past, when antitrust charges were more prevalent, large corporations were more concerned about having the right to make the patented products rather than foreclosing their competition.

As part and parcel of such an insurance program, some large companies also engage in aggressive public disclosure of large numbers of ideas which are not patented. For years IBM has published a technical disclosure bulletin wherein a large number of ideas are set forth in a publicly available document. This insures that no other party can patent any of the ideas.

Along with this insurance philosophy, large corporations will often make their patents available through cross-licensing arrangements in order to obtain technology from their competitors. Again, this insures corporations the right to make their products without worry of being foreclosed.

§ 2.34   Licensing Considerations

Patents can either be exclusively or nonexclusively licensed. Exclusive licenses are akin to actual assignments and, in some cases, an exclusive license may constitute an actual assignment of the invention. Exclusive licenses demand higher royalties or payments. Nonexclusive licenses are generally issued to a number of different entities and, therefore, command lower payments or royalties. Whether a business should license its invention exclusively or nonexclusively must be carefully considered.

Practically speaking, exclusive licenses give the highest return, yet it may take longer for the return to be realized. Granting nonexclusive licenses to a number of entities generally enables the product to be marketed faster. Hence, if the product is a faddish type of product, serious consideration should be given to granting nonexclusive licenses to a number of businesses so that the product can quickly enter the marketplace.

---

[63] Stern, *How to Obtain the Antitrust Division's Assistance in Preventing or Remedying Violations of Federal Law,* 1977 Patent Law Annual 121, 134.

RESOURCES:

1. Nordhaus, Raymond C., *Patent License Agreements* (Jurst Publishing Co.: 7122 North Clark St., Chicago, IL 60626) (1990). This excellent reference provides a discussion of each of the various types of licensing clauses, sample clauses, and pertinent case law.
2. Mayers, Harry R. and Brian G. Brunsvold, *Drafting Patent License Agreements* (BNA: 1231 25th St., N.W., Washington, D.C. 20037) (1984). This is an excellent reference that details all aspects of patent license agreements.

§ 2.35 —Payment

In a patent license agreement, payment can be in the form of a lump sum, a royalty, installments, or a combination of all three. Payments can also be tied to a number of factors such as manufacturing quantity, sales to wholesalers, or retail sales. The United States Supreme Court in *Zenith Radio Corp. v. Hazeltine Research Inc.*[64] has even permitted royalties to be based upon a percentage of the licensee's total sales, provided that it is only for the convenience of the parties and if not insisted upon by the licensor.

One royalty scheme which shares the risk for both licensor and licensee in the marketing of a new product is the *sliding royalty*. **Table 2–2** below shows that as the sales increase, the royalty slides up.

In **Table 2–2** below, both parties are sharing the risk of market introduction. The licensor is not receiving royalties during the initial marketing stages, whereas the licensee is using all of its initial investment monies for research development and marketing. However, as sales of the product take off, the licensee recoups its initial investment and the licensor's share of the royalties increases.

Table 2–2

Sliding-up Royalty Scheme

Sales Quantity	Royalty (%)
0– 99	0
100– 499	3
500– 999	5
1,000–9,999	7
10,000 and more	10

[64] 395 U.S. 100, 161 U.S.P.Q. (BNA) 577 (1969).

Table 2–3

Sliding-down Royalty Scheme

Sales Quantity	Royalty (%)
0– 999	10
1,000– 9,999	9
10,000–49,999	8
50,000 and more	7

Conversely, in certain product lines, a sliding-down royalty should be considered, as illustrated in **Table 2–3**.

In the arrangement shown in **Table 2–3**, the product is being offered to the public at a high price because the product is so unique and novel that a certain percentage of the public will pay a higher price for the product. As sales increase, the licensee starts dropping the price of its product, not only to appeal to a larger market segment, but also to frustrate possible competitors coming out with similar products. In this situation, as price is lowered and quantities increase, the licensor's royalty drops. The licensor is not suffering, because greater and greater quantities of the product are being sold.

§ 2.36 —Length of Payment

The payment of royalties under a license agreement must stop when the patent expires and the technology goes into the public domain. If trade secrets or know-how are also licensed with the patent, then a separate royalty can continue to be paid, even if the patent expires or is invalidated by a court of law. This is an important principal for a business to understand fully and was thoroughly discussed by the Supreme Court in *Aronson v. Quick Point Pencil Co.*[65]

In *Aronson*, the inventor filed a patent application on a new form of key holder. While the patent application was pending, the inventor entered into an agreement with Quick Point, which desired to manufacture and sell the key holder. Quick Point received an exclusive license and agreed to pay the inventor five percent of the selling price. As part of the agreement, if the patent application did not mature into an issued patent, then Quick Point would only have to pay two and one-half percent of the sales price as long as it continued to sell the key holder. The patent never issued and Quick Point commenced to pay royalties at the rate of two and one-half percent, continuing to do so for 14 years. By 1975, Quick Point had

---

[65] 440 U.S. 257, 201 U.S.P.Q. (BNA) 1 (1979).

sold $7 million worth of key holders and paid the inventor approximately $200,000 in royalties.

Once competitors came on the scene, Quick Point's share of the inventor's key holder market began to decline. Quick Point commenced a lawsuit against the inventor on the premise that the key holder was in the public domain and was not patented; therefore Quick Point should not have to continue to pay royalties. The Supreme Court disagreed and enforced the original agreement, requiring Quick Point to pay two and one-half percent royalties as long as it sold the key holder. From a business point of view, therefore, it is important in patent license agreements to separate royalty payments for patent rights, know-how rights, or trade secret rights. When a patent does not issue, or when an issued patent expires, then the agreement should specify that royalties drop to a lower value based upon licensing of know-how or trade secrets.

§ 2.37   —Guidelines for Licensor

The following guidelines for the licensor and the licensee are by no means complete. The reader should refer to the resource material in § 2.34 or consult with an attorney experienced in this area. However, here is practical advice for the licensor:

1. Prior to negotiation, thoroughly study who the licensee is:
    (a)   What are the financial history and current assets of licensee?
    (b)   Has the licensee been involved in litigation?
    (c)   Are the press reports favorable?
    (d)   Is there any other pertinent information? Meet with the prospective licensee as frequently as possible, and evaluate the licensee and its business based upon your own personal experience.
2. Set the stage early with a professional presentation of the subject matter that is being licensed. If it is the patent, set forth the results of the patent search and the copy of the patent application, as well as any office actions and art cited by the examiner.
3. Thoroughly evaluate the market and analyze how the licensee fits into the marketplace and your goals.
4. With patent licensing, exclusive geographical territories are possible. Therefore, determine the licensee's geographical territories.
5. Deal only with representatives of the licensee who have authority to negotiate.
6. Carefully summarize all oral negotiation points in follow-up letters, and preserve all correspondence in a "letter-book" devoted to that set of negotiations. (We have one client that binds together letters regarding each round of negotiations resulting in a new draft agreement.)

7. The licensor may be wise to seek a sizable down payment in return for a partial reduction in the royalty rate. That way, even if the licensee fails to sell the invention, the licensor is fairly compensated.

8. The licensor should obtain all lump sum payments in certified funds at the time of signing the agreement.

9. Every possible inducement should be given to the licensee to accelerate product introduction.

10. The licensor should obtain a clear statement that the licensee will use its best efforts to perform the agreement, and those best efforts should be tied into a benchmark that can be measured, for example:

    (a) A minimum production quantity per month (or year)

    (b) A minimum payment of royalties per month

    (c) A minimum number of sales per month

    (d) A minimum advertising budget.

11. The licensee should be penalized for failure to exploit the market early, such as by the conversion of the exclusive license into a nonexclusive one.

12. The licensor should, at least initially, supervise the quality of performance of the licensee.

13. The licensor should require that all future improvements be done by the licensor and that the licensor be responsible for the engineering, research, and development of such improvements.

14. The licensor should require the licensee to report immediately all problems encountered with customers. Standardized forms should be set up for this purpose.

15. The licensor should require the licensee to notify it of any possible infringements or new competing products.

16. The licensor should require the licensee to mark the units appropriately with *patent pending* or the patent numbers.

17. The licensor should require the licensee to escrow royalty payments if the licensee disputes the validity of the patent.

§ 2.38   —Guidelines for Licensee

The licensee under a patent license should consider doing the following:

1. Conduct a patentability search and an infringement search of its own before entering into a written contract for the product.

2. Have a patent attorney thoroughly analyze the results of the search and the entire PTO file of the patent, legally called the "file wrapper" or "prosecution history."

3. Have the licensor warrant that it is the inventor and that it owns the United States patent and patent application. There should be a hold harmless agreement in this warranty.

4. Analyze the product from a products liability viewpoint.

5. Obtain a clear definition of terms from the licensor, including the market, the territory, and the specifications of this product.

6. Carefully review all payment obligations and be sure to provide enough time for the licensee to comply procedurally. Use a statement such as, "Royalties are to be based upon total sales for each month, and payment for a given month is to be made on or before forty-five (45) days after the end of the month."

§ 2.39   —Arbitration Clause

The Patent Act was amended in 1982 to make arbitration of patent disputes mandatory, providing both parties agree in writing.[66] The goal of this amendment to the Patent Act is to reduce the enormous costs associated with federal district court patent litigation.

RESOURCE: Creel, Thomas L., *Guide to Patent Arbitration* (BNA: 1231 25th St., N.W., Washington, D.C. 20037) (1987). This current and authoritative source includes the American Arbitration Association rules, sample arbitration clauses, and a checklist for drafting patent arbitration agreements.

Great care should be taken by a business in selecting for the license agreement the rules of arbitration, where the arbitration is to take place, what issues are to be arbitrated, and who the arbitrator(s) should be.

It is anticipated that the use of arbitration to settle patent disputes will grow for two primary reasons. First, arbitration was successfully used in the settlement of a copyright suit between IBM and Fujitsu, in which an award of approximately $833 million was made.[67] Second, federal district court litigation is significantly slowing down due to the priority of criminal cases over civil cases. Businesses in general need a faster resolution of such intellectual property disputes than afforded to them by the federal district courts.

---

[66] 35 U.S.C. § 294 (1983).

[67] Santo, *IBM Corp. v. Fujitsu Ltd.,* 37 Pat., Trademark & Copyright J. (BNA) 130 (1988).

§ 2.40   Infringement

Once a business has received a patent on its product, the business enjoys a constitutionally protected monopoly which Congress has decreed will last 17 years. It is estimated that the cost of patent litigation to enforce these monopolies is $800 million per year,[68] not an insubstantial expense for business. The infringement of a patent may be deliberate, or it may be completely innocent. Even if the act of infringement is innocent, the Patent Act specifically allows the inventor to enjoin all infringing activities and to collect all damages.

§ 2.41   —Direct Infringement

The owner of a patent may sue to enforce the patent against infringers who wrongly make, use, or sell the invention covered by the patent. The concepts of *make, use,* and *sell* need to be explained.

Assume that your company has a patent on a product in the United States. Three scenarios can arise. First, assume that another company infringes your patent by manufacturing the product, distributing the product to United States retailers and to consumers who buy the product from the retailers for their personal use. Under the Patent Act you can sue the manufacturer (who *makes*), the retailer (who *sells*), and the consumer (who *uses*). As a practical matter, you will sue the manufacturer and perhaps one or two of the large retailers.

Under the second scenario, a foreign company manufactures an infringing product and sells it to a retailer in the United States, who in turn sells it to consumers. You are not able to sue the manufacturer, because the manufacturer is out of the country and your United States patent is territorially limited. You may be able to stop the manufacturer from importing the product into the United States by appealing to the United States International Trade Commission.[69] You are able, of course, to sue the retailer (who sells) and the consumers (who use). This may be a viable route if the product is expensive and is limited to a narrow vertical marketplace (for example, CAT scanners for hospitals).

In the third scenario, the infringing product is both made and sold outside of the United States to a consumer who brings it back into the United States for use. Clearly, you are able to bring a lawsuit against the consumer in the United States under the Patent Act.

An important amendment to the federal patent law was made in 1989. If a product is made outside of the United States, but according to a

---

[68] Patent & Trademark Office, Quality Reinforcement Program 3 (Feb. 1987).

[69] 19 U.S.C. § 1337 (1988).

process covered by a United States patent, then is imported for use or sale in the United States, patent infringement has occurred.[70] Under this amendment a competitor has the right to request that a manufacturer disclose all of its process patents on a particular product.

RESOURCE: Rubin, James S., *HOW: Working With the NEW Process Patent Law* (National Association of Manufacturers: 1331 Pennsylvania Ave., N.W., Suite 1500, North Lobby, Washington D.C. 20004-1703) (1989). Every manufacturer and retailer should obtain this inexpensive but valuable 24-page monograph complete with forms and practical guidance.

---

§ 2.42   —Contributory and Inducing Infringements

Providing a material component that goes into a product that infringes another's patent may be an act of contributory infringement actionable under the patent laws. It is contributory infringement if the component is especially made for the product and is not a staple component which is used for non-infringing products. Likewise, a person who actively induces infringement of a patent by encouraging or aiding an infringer is also liable.[71]

§ 2.43   —Statute of Limitations

The statute of limitations for patent infringement is six years.[72] The clock starts ticking when the patent holder obtains actual or constructive knowledge of the alleged infringing activity.

§ 2.44   —Damages

This is the era of massive damage awards. Multimillion dollar awards are becoming rather common for patent infringement cases. For example, Pfizer has received an award of $55.8 million from International Rectifier.[73] Hughes Tool has received an award of $134 million from Smith International plus $70 million in interest.[74] With such large damage

---

[70] 35 U.S.C. § 154 (1988).

[71] 35 U.S.C. § 271 (1956). *See* Oak Indus. Inc. v. Zenith Elec. Corp., 697 F. Supp. 988, 9 U.S.P.Q.2d (BNA) 1138 (N.D. Ill. 1988).

[72] 35 U.S.C. § 286 (1982).

[73] Pfizer Inc. v. International Rectifier Corp., 218 U.S.P.Q. (BNA) 586 (C.D. Cal. 1983).

[74] Smith Int'l, Inc. v. Hughes Tool Co., 229 U.S.P.Q. (BNA) 81 (C.D. Cal. 1986), *appeal dismissed as moot,* 839 F.2d 663, 5 U.S.P.Q.2d (BNA) 1686 (Fed. Cir. 1988).

awards, businesses are wise to take steps to minimize exposure to litigation. In a traditional sense, damages are the lost profits that the patent holder would have been entitled to but for the infringing product.[75] The courts may also award the infringer's own profits as a damage award.[76] Reasonable royalties have also been awarded as damages. Reasonable royalty rates have varied from one percent to 30 percent and are entirely dependent upon the facts of each individual infringement.[77]

§ 2.45   —Treble Damages

In the event of willful infringement, the court has the power to increase the damages to up to three times the amount of the actual damages. Usually in trebling damages, attorneys' fees and prejudgment interest are also awarded, so that what could have been a $200,000 or $300,000 damage award can amount to $1 million.

It is important for corporate counsel and business executives to seek the opinion of outside patent counsel concerning infringement. The United States Court of Appeals for the Federal Circuit has stated that a business has an affirmative duty to obtain a validity and an infringement opinion from outside counsel before initiating a potentially infringing activity, and that a failure to do so may result in the assessment of treble damages.[78]

§ 2.46   —Attorneys' Fees

In exceptional cases such as those involving willful infringement, the courts tend to award attorneys' fees. Thus a company may not only lose a patent infringement lawsuit, but then be required to subsidize the winning side through payment of their attorneys' fees.

An interesting case involved the Johns-Manville Corp.[79] Johns-Manville had spent several years trying to develop a satisfactory indirect lighting fixture for fluorescent lighting. A small competitor, Lam, Inc., had developed a successful HID fixture for which it obtained a patent. Working from a Lam brochure, one of Johns-Manville's engineers designed an infringing

---

[75] Lam, Inc. v. Johns-Manville, 668 F.2d 462, 213 U.S.P.Q. (BNA) 1061 (10th Cir. 1982).

[76] Del Mar Avionics, Inc. v. Quinton Instrument Co., 836 F.2d 1320, 1326–28, 5 U.S.P.Q.2d (BNA) 1255, 1260–61 (Fed. Cir. 1987).

[77] Deere & Co. v. International Harvester Co., 710 F.2d 1551, 218 U.S.P.Q. (BNA) 481 (Fed. Cir. 1983).

[78] Underwater Devices, Inc. v. Morrison-Knudsen Co., 717 F.2d 1380, 1388, 219 U.S.P.Q. (BNA) 569, 576 (Fed. Cir. 1983).

[79] Lam, Inc. v. Johns-Manville, 668 F.2d 462, 213 U.S.P.Q. (BNA) 1061 (10th Cir. 1982).

Table 2–4

Damages Awarded in Johns-Manville Case

Lost profits (trebled)	$ 267,927.00
Prejudgment Interest	61,200.00
Reduced profits (trebled)	13,752.00
Prejudgment interest	2,330.00
Projected lost profits (trebled)	862,500.00
Attorneys' fees and expenses	432,115.21
	$1,639,824.21

fixture virtually identical to Lam's in a single day. The court awarded damages as shown in **Table 2–4**.

It is important for businesses to avoid a finding of willful infringement, and an investment in the time and costs of outside patent counsel can pay off handsomely in this area.

§ 2.47   —Injunctions

Under patent law, injunctions are granted in accordance with principles of equity. Affirmative injunctions are available.[80] In everyday terms, an *injunction* is an order to cease all infringing activity. The Patent Act, however, also provides for *affirmative injunctions,* which require the performance of a specified act. For example, Polaroid obtained an affirmative injunction against Kodak requiring Kodak to recall its instant cameras.

There are various stages of injunctive relief. The patent holder may obtain an *ex parte* temporary restraining order (in which the other side is not informed of the lawsuit and the judge issues an injunction on the strength of the allegations of just one side), a temporary restraining order (in which both parties are present and the issue is whether an immediate injunction should be put into place); a preliminary injunction (in which both parties are present and the issue is whether the alleged infringer should be enjoined during the pendency of litigation); or a permanent injunction (in which the infringing party is permanently enjoined after a trial).

Historically, temporary and preliminary injunctions were infrequently granted in the patent context. This has now changed and they are granted much more often. It is a sobering experience for a business to be restrained immediately from the sales of its product line.

---

[80] 35 U.S.C. § 283 (1982).

CHAPTER 3

UNFAIR COMPETITION

§ 3.1   Introduction

The tort of unfair competition was recognized as early as the eighteenth century in England. A 1706 English case involved a farmer named Keeble who owned a pond that was visited frequently by ducks and geese. Keeble trapped the fowl and made a living selling them. Keeble had a neighbor who mimicked Keeble's small business and, in order to secure a competitive advantage in the sale of the birds, went to Keeble's pond on three different occasions and discharged firearms to frighten the fowl away from Keeble's farm. The court awarded Keeble twenty pounds, saying that ". . . he that hinders another in his trade or livelihood is liable to an action for so hindering him."[1]

Modern law of unfair competition is intended to resolve the natural conflict between the need for competition in the commercial arena and the opposing need for reasonable restraints on methods of competition. The threshold question is whether legal protection from competition is available in the first place, and once that obstacle is overcome, the issue becomes the particular offending deeds of a competitor are actionable. The resolution of the latter question depends on various factors, including recognition of the product or service by the public, length of time the product or service has been on the market, the distinctiveness of identification of the product or service, the sophistication of the sector of the public interested in the product or service, the good faith of the parties, the investment of the parties, and the likelihood of confusion on the part of the public.

§ 3.2   Types of Unfair Competition

Unfair competition in today's business world takes many forms, including passing off, pirating, false advertising, disparagement, misappropriation, dilution, and torts related to rights of publicity.

§ 3.3   —Passing Off

Passing off occurs when a competitor's trade name, trade dress, or trademark is fraudulently imitated in an attempt to foist off another's product or service. For example, in *National Lampoon, Inc. v. American Broadcasting Cos.,* the court ruled that the defendant ABC was attempting to "pass off its goods as those of the plaintiff's" when it used the word

---

[1] Keeble v. Hickeringill [1558–1774] All E.R. Rep. 286 (Q.B. 1706).

"lampoon" in the title of a television series. ABC produced the series after unsuccessfully attempting to negotiate production of a television show with the publisher of the *National Lampoon* magazine, and the court held that the use of the word lampoon was an attempt to exploit the publisher's name and reputation.[2]

It is important to note that passing off in its purest form requires actual substitution, not simply copying, of another's goods.[3] The line that courts draw between copying and actual substitution, however, is an indistinct one. In *Feltman-Langer, Inc. v. Orient Trading Co.,*[4] for example, a competing company that copied a big-bottomed coffee mug, distinguished by different labels and logos, was enjoined by a California district court for trade dress infringement. The exact physical object was substituted for the Feltman-Langer mug, and the substitution itself was the basis for the action, that is, the copying of the trade dress would tend to deceive and mislead the consumer, and so would meet the test of passing off. However, in *Colonel W.F. Cody Historical Picture Co. v. Colonial Amusement Co.,*[5] the Colorado Federal District Court refused to enjoin a rival motion picture company from using the phrase *In the Days of Buffalo Bill* in its advertisements for a motion picture. The court defined this sort of unfair competition as passing off the goods and services of one party as those of another, the gist of which would be deception practiced by the party seeking to succeed in the passing off. It refused to decree an injunction, or to find any passing off in these circumstances however, because the advertisements also announced the names of the actors and producers of the rival motion picture, and nowhere indicated any connection of W.F. Cody with the defendant's film. The plaintiff's previous film, in which W.F. Cody played a leading role, was found not to have achieved such notoriety as would support likelihood of deception of the public.

People who have either spent some time in New York City or have watched vintage films on late night television are acquainted with Murphy beds that fold up by day into a closet concealed by a door. Even though the term "Murphy bed" has become generic to describe a bed that folds into a closet, a company passing off its own version of a Murphy bed as the genuine item has been held liable to the Murphy Door Bed Company for disgorgement of its profit on all its sales as compensatory damages.[6]

---

[2] National Lampoon, Inc. v. American Broadcasting Co., 376 F. Supp. 733, 182 U.S.P.Q. (BNA) 24 (S.D.N.Y. 1974), *affirmed,* 497 F.2d 1343, 182 U.S.P.Q. (BNA) 6 (2d Cir. 1974).

[3] *In re* Certain Caulking Guns 223 U.S.P.Q. (BNA) 338 (U.S. Int'l Trade Comm'n 1984).

[4] 223 U.S.P.Q. (BNA) 336 (C.D. Cal. 1983).

[5] 284 Fed. 873 (D. Colo. 1922).

[6] Murphy Door Bed Co. v. Interior Sleep Sys., Inc., 874 F.2d 95, 10 U.S.P.Q. 2d (BNA) 7383 (2d Cir. 1974).

The unfair business practice of passing off may also be proved by implication arising from the conduct of the one accused of passing off. For example, slavishly copying a merchant price list and utilizing it as one's own, even changing the color of the paper on which the list is printed every time the first user changes color, constitutes conduct proving the intention to pass off the second price list as the price list of the first user.[7]

One final word on the term *passing off* and its near synonym, *pawning off*. These terms are not always used to describe the same type of activity. The terms were apparently used in the earlier cases only to describe substitution of a second supplier's brand for the first supplier's brand. Later cases seem to broaden the use of the terms to include the intentional misleading of buyers short of substitution, and still later cases have broadened the coverage of the terms to encompass activities simply giving rise to a likelihood of confusion.

§ 3.4 —Pirating

Trading on the goodwill and reputation of a competitor is known as *pirating*. This type of unfair competition often involves an attempt to deceive the public. In *Thomas A. Edison, Inc. v. Shotkin*,[8] the defendant used the phrase "certified by Edison" in advertising his products, but his business was not connected with the Edison corporation. The court held that the defendant's actions "constituted a direct attempt to deceive the public." The fact that Edison had selectively prosecuted pirates of its name in the past was also a factor acknowledged by the court in granting Edison relief.

§ 3.5 —False Advertising

The generally accepted definition of *false advertising* is contained in the *Restatement of Torts:*

> One who diverts from a competitor by fraudulently representing that the goods which he markets have ingredients or qualities which in fact they do not have but which the goods of the competitor do have is liable to the competitor for the harm so caused, if (a) when making the representation

---

[7] Surgical Supply Serv., Inc. v. Adler, 321 F.2d 536, 138 U.S.P.Q. (BNA) 263 (E.D. Pa. 1962).

[8] 69 F. Supp. 176, 72 U.S.P.Q. (BNA) 329 (D. Colo. 1946), *appeal dismissed*, 163 F.2d 1020, 76 U.S.P.Q. (BNA) 8 (10th Cir.), *cert. denied*, 332 U.S. 813 (1947).

he intends that it should or knows or should know that it is likely to divert trade from the competitor, and (b) the competitor is not marketing his goods with material fraudulent misrepresentations about them.[9]

Cases that fall within this definition include those involving deceptive advertising and bait-and-switch tactics. In *People ex rel. Dunbar v. Gym of America, Inc.,*[10] a case brought under the current Colorado Consumer Protection Act, a health club was found to have advertised falsely when it failed to comply with the terms of its advertised offers. Similarly, salesmen in a 1948 Colorado case[11] were found to have mislead customers by claiming that a book entitled *Fighting Men of Colorado* was sponsored by the Colorado Historical Society or the VFW when in fact it was not. Under Colorado law at the time, however, the salesmen's conduct constituted only a misdemeanor.

False advertising may also be the subject of suits by the Federal Trade Commission. Recently a travel and vacation firm was enjoined from advertising a $29 certificate redeemable for round-trip airfare to Hawaii when a minimum of eight days' hotel accommodations were booked through the agency. The agency had been adding the actual airfare to the normal hotel room price and it also kept the $29.[12]

§ 3.6   —Disparagement

Disparagement is a frivolous falsehood that injures a competitor, such as a bait-and-switch advertisement that lures away another's potential customers,[13] or untrue statements about flaws or shortcomings in a competitor's services or goods. A common bait-and-switch operation by some unscrupulous carpet cleaners is to advertise a very low price for cleaning a given number of rooms. Then, once engaged, they find the rug either "too dirty" or the dirt too ground in, rendering additional services and solvents necessary for that particular rug at, of course, an increased price. Many of the cases in the disparagement area involve disgruntled former employees or unsuccessful competitors who make false and frivolous statements to persuade a business's actual and potential customers not to do business with that establishment.[14]

---

[9] Restatement of Torts § 761 (1939).

[10] 177 Colo. 97, 493 P.2d 660, 50 A.L.R. 3d 992 (1972).

[11] People v. Byrnes, 117 Colo. 528, 190 P.2d 584 (1948).

[12] Federal Trade Comm'n v. World Travel Vacation Brokers, Inc., 861 F.2d 1020 (7th Cir. 1988).

[13] People *ex rel.* Dunbar v. Gym of Am., Inc., 177 Colo. 97, 493 P.2d 660, 50 A.L.R. 3d 992 (1972).

[14] *E.g.,* Diehl & Sons, Inc. v. International Harvester Co., 445 F. Supp. 282 (1978).

§ 3.7 —Misappropriation

Misappropriation consists of three basic elements:

1. The plaintiff has made a substantial investment of time, effort, and money to create a thing misappropriated
2. The defendant has appropriated the thing at little or no cost
3. The defendant has injured the plaintiff by the misappropriation.

Examples of misappropriation acknowledged by the courts include: a news service that sent observers to note and later report the major news items listed in a competitor's news bulletin room;[15] and an American firm, licensed by an Italian firm to distribute a medicinal preparation, that began marketing its own preparation using similar trade dress after the licensing agreement terminated.[16]

Suits claiming misappropriation that have been denied by the courts include a 1984 Wisconsin suit brought when an ambitious salesman legally changed his name to "Count Copy Fuller" and, in bizarre costumes, went door-to-door selling presold Fuller products from a Fuller brush catalog with his own label on it.[17] Count Copy Fuller's activities were entirely honest. The goods of another that he sold were clearly identified as such; consequently his actions involved neither disparagement nor misappropriation. In a Ninth Circuit case, copying carpet samples in a display folder, although they did not qualify as an original work of art under copyright law, was held to constitute unfair competition. The court ruled that because preemption of state law by the Federal Copyright Act, that is, the federal law, did not displace state law under these circumstances, did not apply, the common law of unfair competition did.[18]

A recent case updating the doctrine of misappropriation is *Zacchin v. Scripps-Howard Broadcasting Co.*[19] This case, which was remanded to the Ohio courts, involved a news broadcast of Mr. Zacchin's entire performance of being shot from a cannon into a net. The plaintiff was third generation in a family that made its living by performing this stunt at various carnivals and other events throughout the country. The amount of time consumed in the performance was quite minimal, but the Court ruled that the unauthorized broadcast of the entire performance was not justifiable

---

[15] International News Serv. v. Associated Press, 248 U.S. 215, 39 S. Ct. 68, 2 A.L.R. 293 (1918).

[16] Distillerie Filli Ramazzoti S.P.A. v. Banfi Prods. Corp., 52 Misc. 2d 593, 276 N.Y.S.2d 413, 151 U.S.P.Q. (BNA) 551 (1966), *aff'd*, 595 F. Supp. 1088, 27 A.D.2d 905, 280 N.Y.S.2d 892 (1967).

[17] Fuller v. Fuller Brush Co., 224 U.S.P.Q. (BNA) 575 (1984).

[18] Fabrica, Inc. v. Eldorado Corp., 697 F.2d 890 (9th Cir. 1983).

[19] 433 U.S. 562, 97 S. Ct. 2849, 205 U.S.P.Q. (BNA) 741 (1977).

on the basis of public interest in news events and, therefore, constituted an unlawful misappropriation of Mr. Zacchin's commercial rights.

§ 3.8   —Dilution

Dilution occurs when a merchant's name or symbol identifying his goods or services is used by another without his permission in connection with noncompeting goods or services. In order to avoid confusion of the public, parties may charge that such dilution is unfairly competitive.

For example, in 1983 when the NAACP and the NAACP Legal Defense and Education Fund, Inc. ceased to operate in conjunction with one another, the NAACP initially successfully enjoined the Legal Defense and Education Fund from using its initials. But the case was reversed on appeal on the ground of laches because of the lapse of 13 years and no negotiations prior to bringing suit.[20]

Dilution claims typically fail when the names or symbols in question are not confusingly similar, or when the plaintiff's name or symbol is not particularly well known. In *Ye Olde Tavern Cheese Products, Inc. v. Planters Peanuts Division,*[21] the defendant's use of the term "Planters Tavern Nuts" on a label was ruled dissimilar enough from the plaintiff's trademarked label, "Ye Olde Tavern Nuts" because the borders, script, size of letters, and coloring were not confusingly similar. Because the plaintiff did not originate the word tavern and the labels were dissimilar, the Illinois federal district court denied the plaintiff's claim for relief.

Similarly, in *Toho Co., Ltd. v. Sears, Roebuck & Co.,*[22] the plaintiff owned the rights to the movie monster "Godzilla" and Sears made a strong plastic garbage bag called "Bagzilla," with a picture of a reptilian creature and the phrase "Monstrously Strong Bags" on the boxes. The court ruled in favor of Sears that there was no possibility of confusion as to the source nor was there a reasonable implication of an endorsement by Toho of the garbage bags.

§ 3.9   —Right of Publicity

The *right of publicity* is essentially the exclusive right to commercial exploitation of one's likeness or one's name.

---

[20] NAACP v. NAACP Legal Defense Fund, Inc., 559 F. Supp. 1337, 222 U.S.P.Q. (BNA) 128 (D.D.C. 1983), *rev'd,* 753 F.2d 136, 225 U.S.P.Q. (BNA) 264 (D.C. Cir. 1985) *cert. denied,* 472 U.S. 1021 (1985).

[21] 261 F. Supp. 200, 1510 U.S.P.Q. (BNA) 244 (N.D. Ill. 1966), *aff'd,* F.2d 833, 155 U.S.P.Q. (BNA) 481 (7th Cir. 1967).

[22] 645 F.2d 788, 210 U.S.P.Q. (BNA) 547 (9th Cir. 1981).

While some authorities classify the right of publicity as simply another category under the long-recognized area of right of privacy, recent developments focusing exclusively on the right of publicity would seem to place it squarely in the area of unfair competition. The nature of this cause of action is, in effect, the misappropriation of valuable commercial rights linked to specific public figures in entertainment or sports. For example, the right of privacy was clearly distinguished from the right of publicity in a case involving the commercial use of the names and likenesses of Laurel and Hardy. The right of publicity in that situation was categorized as property which could descend to the heirs of Laurel and Hardy.[23]

§ 3.10   Law of Unfair Competition: What Is Protected?

The law of unfair competition attempts to encourage and support vigorous trade and commerce by inhibiting certain harmful interferences by a competitor with the business activities and reputation of another. The emphasis is on honesty and good faith. The law recognizes the value of goodwill and investment in customer acceptance and satisfaction, but not at the diminution of strong commercial competition, which may in fact diminish or even destroy one's business.

§ 3.11   —Trade Names

Trade names are protected by the law of unfair competition when the public is likely to be confused by the similarity of competitors' names. In *National Lampoon, Inc. v. American Broadcasting Cos.,*[24] the name "Lampoon" was protected against the defendant ABC's use of it in the title of a television series (See § 3.3). In a 1974 case, the Colorado Court of Appeals held that the public was likely to be confused between the plaintiff's "Wood Bros Homes, Inc." and the defendant's "Wood's Homes, Inc."[25]

§ 3.12   —Trade Dress

Trade dress is a nonfunctional aspect of a useful item that may likewise be protected. In *Distillerie Filli Ramazzoti S.P.A. v. Banfi Products,*

---

[23] Price v. Roach, 400 F. Supp. 836 (S.D.N.Y. 1975).

[24] 376 F. Supp. 733, 182 U.S.P.Q. (BNA) 24 (S.D.N.Y.), *aff'd,* 497 F.2d 1343 (2d Cir. 1974).

[25] Wood v. Wood's Homes, Inc., 33 Colo. App. 285, 519 P.2d 1212, 181 U.S.P.Q. (BNA) 787, 72 A.L.R. 3d 1 (1974).

Corp.,[26] an American company began marketing a medicinal preparation using trade dress similar to that of an Italian firm. The shape of the bottle, format and color scheme of the label, and arrangement of the wording were held to be protected.

§ 3.13   —Trademarks

Trademark infringement is also a branch of unfair competition. For example, in *Thomas A. Edison, Inc. v. Shotkin,*[27] the trademark "Edison" was protected against the defendant's use of the words "certified by Edison" when in fact the defendant's products were not at all connected with Thomas Edison.

§ 3.14   —Goodwill

The goodwill of a business is similarly protected from misappropriation. In *Hobart Manufacturing Co. v. Kitchen Aid Service, Inc.,*[28] a district court in New York ruled that the goodwill of a dishwasher manufacturer, Kitchen Aid, was injured when an inferior repair service adopted the name Kitchen Aid. An unfair competition count was similarly ruled potentially valid in *Cytanovich Reading Center v. Reading Game,*[29] in which the plaintiff reading clinic had heavily advertised its identity via the clinic telephone number, 321-7233, which it advertised as 321-READ.

When the defendant reading clinic opened a block away, using the same "READ" series for its telephone number with a different prefix, the plaintiff clinic claimed that this practice constituted unfair competition. The suit failed, with the court ruling that the plaintiff did not prove that the public specifically identified the "READ" gimmick with the first user; but the court did agree that the defendant's use of the gimmick could have been the basis of a successful unfair competition claim.

§ 3.15   —Trade Secrets

Trade secrets, discussed in Chapter 1, are also protected from unfair competition. In brief, any improper method used to obtain a competitor's trade secret is an infringement and is subject to injunction and damages.

---

[26] 52 Misc. 2d 593, 276 N.Y.S.2d 413, 151 U.S.P.Q. (BNA) 551 (1966), *aff'd,* 27 A.D.2d 905, 280 N.Y.S.2d 892 (1967).

[27] 69 F. Supp. 176 (D. Colo. 1946), *appeal dismissed,* 163 F.2d 1020, 76 U.S.P.Q. (BNA) 8 (10th Cir.), *cert. denied,* 332 U.S. 813 (1947).

[28] 260 F. Supp. 559, 151 U.S.P.Q. (BNA) 325 (E.D.N.Y. 1966).

[29] 126 Cal. App. 3d 109, 208 Cal. Rptr. 412, 225 U.S.P.Q. (BNA) 588 (1984).

§ 3.16 —False Advertising

False advertising is now considered a form of unfair competition, and in addition to its inclusion in the Uniform Deceptive Trade Practices Act (see § 3.29), false advertising is also a common law cause of action.[30]

§ 3.17 —Right of Publicity

A right of publicity is now recognized in some states in order to protect a celebrity's right to publicity from various forms of unfair competition.[31] For example, in *Gautier v. Pro Football, Inc.,*[32] (the first baseball card case), the first contractee was awarded not only a release right in using the ball player's photograph, but also the right sounding in property to enjoin other subsequent contractees from using the photograph in promoting chewing gum sales.

Courts also distinguish between the use of a public figure's likeness in a news item and in a commercial setting; the use of a likeness in a news report does not permit subsequent use of the likeness in a commercial setting. This right of publicity is generally limited, however, as it was in *Paulsen v. Personality Posters, Inc.,* to unauthorized use for advertising purposes in connection with the sale of a commodity.[33]

Similarly, commercialization without permission won the bout for Muhammad Ali in *Ali v. Playgirl, Inc.,*[34] where an offensive drawing of Ali was enjoined despite previous gratuitous "surrenders of privacy" by Ali.

It should be noted that the "use during lifetime dilemma" arises when the right of publicity is exploited, or is claimed to have been exploited, during the lifetime of the celebrity in question, thus giving an assignee exclusive right to publicity after the celebrity's death. In *Factors Etc., Inc. v. Pro Arts Inc.,*[35] for example, the assignment and commercial exploitation of Elvis Presley's likeness during his lifetime established a right of publicity

---

[30] Electronics Corp. of Am. v. Honeywell, Inc., 428 F.2d 191 (1st Cir. 1970) (defendant used descriptive material for use of its products in plaintiff's system, and the brochure misled purchasers to believe easy installation was possible).

[31] Haelen Laboratories, Inc. v. Tops Chewing Gum, Inc., 202 F.2d 866 (2d Cir.), *cert. denied,* 346 U.S. 816, 74 S. Ct. 26 (1953).

[32] 304 N.Y. 354, 105 N.E.2d 485 (1952).

[33] 59 Misc. 2d 44, 229 N.Y.S.2d 501, 505 (1968).

[34] 447 F. Supp. 723, 206 U.S.P.Q. (BNA) 1021 (S.D.N.Y. 1978).

[35] 579 F.2d 215, 205 U.S.P.Q. (BNA) 751 (2d Cir. 1978), *cert. denied,* 440 U.S. 908 (1979), *remanded,* 496 F. Supp. 1090, 208 U.S.P.Q. (BNA) 529 (S.D.N.Y. 1980), *rev'd,* 625 F.2d 278, 211 U.S.P.Q. (BNA) 1 (2d Cir. 1981), *cert. denied,* 456 U.S. 927 (1982), *remanded,* 541 F. Supp. 231 (S.D.N.Y. 1982), *vacated,* 562 F. Supp. 304 (S.D.N.Y. 1983), *reh'g denied,* 701 F.2d 11 (2d Cir. 1983).

under New York law, thus giving Presley's assignee the right to enjoin the sale of "In Memory" posters depicting a likeness taken from a news photo after Presley's death. The Second Circuit Court of Appeals affirmed, applying New York law.

This was contrary to the conclusion reached by the Sixth Circuit Court of Appeals in *Memphis Development Foundation v. Factors, Inc.*[36] In that case the court held that the right of publicity did not descend as property to the heirs of the deceased artist under Tennessee law. On appeal from remand, the Second Circuit reversed itself on the basis that it should have applied Tennessee law (applied in the *Memphis Development* case) instead of New York law.

Similarly, in *Lugosi v. Universal Pictures,*[37] a California court decided that the contractual grant by Bella Lugosi to Universal during his lifetime to use his likeness in promotion of the film *Dracula* was not an exploitation of the right of publicity during the life of the artist. The court therefore held that the right of publicity expired with the artist.

A recent case that strengthened the right of publicity cause of action involved the famous *Johnny Carson* in a case captioned *Carson v. Here's Johnny Portable Toilets.*[38] The defendant sold or rented portable toilets and adopted the name "Here's Johnny," along with the slogan "The World's Foremost Commodian." He said he thought that taken together they would "make a good play on a phrase."

The trial court held for the defendant, but on appeal the Sixth Circuit held that the defendant's acts violated the plaintiff's right of publicity, and the second opinion on appeal enjoined the manufacturer of the portable toilet from exploiting the phrase in any state. The original holding was that the use violated Johnny Carson's right of publicity under Michigan law, but the injunction was extended to all states, even though it was uncertain that other states would even recognize the entertainer's right of publicity.

Two examples of cases falling short of success are *T.J. Hooker v. Columbia Pictures Industries, Inc.*[39] and *Rogers v. Grimaldi, MGM/UA Entertainment Co.*[40] In the former case a woodcarver named T.J. Hooker sought unfair competition relief, both under common law principles and the Deceptive Practices Act, for the defendant's use of his name in connection with the television drama series. Mr. Hooker failed to show (1) a likelihood

---

[36] 626 F.2d 986, 205 U.S.P.Q. (BNA) 784 (6th Cir. 1980).

[37] 25 Cal. 3d 813, 603 P.2d 425, 160 Cal. Rptr. 323, 205 U.S.P.Q. (BNA) 1090 (1979).

[38] 698 F.2d 831, 218 U.S.P.Q. (BNA) 1 (6th Cir. 1986), *after remand,* 810 F.2d 104, 1 U.S.P.Q. 2d (BNA) 2007 (6th Cir. 1987).

[39] 551 F. Supp. 1060 (N.D. Ill. 1982).

[40] 695 F. Supp. 112, 8 U.S.P.Q.2d (BNA) 1502 (S.D.N.Y.), *aff'd,* 875 F.2d 794, 10 U.S.P.Q.2d (BNA) 1829 (2d Cir. 1988).

of confusion with any possibility of harm to his business, (2) any right of publicity stemming from public recognition of his name or (3) any misuse of the name by the defendant. In the *Rogers* case, the holding was that the title of the movie *Ginger and Fred* did not explicitly claim endorsement or participation in the film by Ginger Rogers, and that the title was adopted in good faith and bore a close connection to the story line of the movie.

Finally, a very interesting case in the right of publicity area involved the unauthorized selling by the defendant of buttons containing the plaintiff's likeness.[41] The court held not only that the plaintiff's right of publicity was infringed, but that the nature of the infringement and the nature of the cause of action under the right of publicity resembled a cause of action for infringement of copyright rights. The court therefore awarded damages analogous to the *in lieu* (statutory) damages provided by the Copyright Act as fair compensation for violation of the right of publicity. However, whether there is general consensus on the viability of the right of publicity, its recognition as an unfair business practice is growing in popularity.

§ 3.18   Law of Unfair Competition: How Is One Protected?

Federal statutes having an impact on the field of unfair competition include those discussed in §§ 3.19 through 3.22.

§ 3.19   —Sherman Antitrust Act

The Sherman Antitrust Act provides that "every contract, combination in the form of trust or otherwise, or conspiracy, in restraint of trade or commerce among the several states, or with foreign nations is declared illegal."[42] A companion act, the Clayton Act,[43] deals specifically with price discrimination but also covers other topics in the field of unfair competition.

§ 3.20   —Federal Trade Commission Act

A far-reaching act, the Federal Trade Commission Act provides in § 45 that "unfair methods of competition in or affecting commerce, and unfair or deceptive acts or practices in or affecting commerce are declared

---

[41] Bi-rite Co. v. Button Master, 578 F. Supp. 59 (S.D.N.Y. 1983).

[42] Sherman Antitrust Act, 15 U.S.C. § 1.

[43] Clayton Act, 15 U.S.C. § 12.

unlawful."[44] At least one case decided under that Act is revealing, because the Supreme Court recognized that the phrase "unfair methods of competition" has no precise meaning and that its meaning and application must be arrived at by the gradual process of judicial inclusion and exclusion.[45]

§ 3.21   —Unfair Practices in Import Trade Act

The federal government also regulates unfair trade practices in the import trade. The Unfair Practices in Import Trade Act provides:

> Unfair methods of competition and unfair acts in the importation of articles into the United States, or in their sale by the owner, importer, consignee, or agent or either, the effect or tendency of which is to destroy or substantially injure an industry, efficiently and economically operated, in the United States, or to prevent the establishment of such an industry, or to restrain or monopolize trade and commerce in the United States, are declared unlawful, and when found by the Commission to exist shall be dealt with, in addition to any other provisions of law, as provided in this section.[46]

§ 3.22   —Lanham Act

The Lanham Act, discussed in **Chapter 4**, provides that:

> Any person who shall . . . use in connection with any goods or services a false designation of origin, or any false description or representation, including words or other symbols tending falsely to describe or represent the same, and shall cause such goods or services to enter into commerce . . . shall be liable to a civil action by any person doing business in the locality falsely indicated as that of origin or in the region in which said locality is situated, or by any person who believes that he is or is likely to be damaged by the use of any such false description or representation.[47]

The two-pronged impact of the Lanham Act on unfair competition centers on false designation of origin or any false description of the goods. Therefore, even though trade dress is not protectable by registration of a federal trademark on the principal register, it is and has been the subject of successful federal litigation as a Lanham Act infringement under the false advertising or false designation section.

---

[44] 15 U.S.C. § 11.

[45] Federal Trade Comm'n v. Raladum Co., 283 U.S. 643, 51 S. Ct. 587, 79 A.L.R. 1191 (1931).

[46] Unfair Practices in Import Trade Act, 19 U.S.C. § 1337.

[47] Lanham Act, 15 U.S.C. § 1125(a).

The tests for determining the strength of the first user's trade dress have generally been described as (1) distinctiveness, (2) secondary meaning, and (3) functionality serving to identify either the goods or source.

Infringement under the Lanham Act is a relatively simple test involving the likelihood of confusion. This in turn takes into consideration the sophistication of the consumers and any prominent markings or symbols that would tend to avoid likelihood of confusion.

An ancillary consideration present in many Lanham Act cases focuses on whether a secondary meaning attaching to the packaging or products of the first user is established, which, of course, directly relates to likelihood of confusion in the event secondary meaning is present.

Secondary meaning becomes important in determining whether the words or symbols used are common and in the public domain or are merely descriptive. Another important element in the area of determining likelihood of confusion is the similarity of goods or services of the two users, that is, how closely they are related.

The word "sage" was the center of attention in a dispute between *Sage Realty Corp. v. Sage Group, Inc.*[48] The realty corporation managed New York improved real estate, whereas the Sage Group was a construction company. The Sage Realty Corp. had used the name for about 50 years. The court felt that the close similarity of the services would result in a likelihood of confusion.

In contrast, closely copying medical carts utilized in hospital surgeries and recovery rooms, including closely copying the colors, was held not to create likelihood of confusion, considering, among other things, the sophistication of the buyers constituting the public likely to be confused, as well as a very prominent label on the allegedly offending carts identifying their true source, name, and manufacturer.[49]

The importance of secondary meaning attached to a poster depicting a Daytona Beach scene utilized in advertising to attract travel for students during spring break was highlighted in *Echo Travel, Inc. v. Travel Associates.*[50] The facts involved an innocent use of a photograph furnished by the Daytona Chamber of Commerce to promote spring break and other Chamber of Commerce goals. The prior use of the photo by Echo Travel was held insufficient to acquire a secondary meaning and was therefore not sufficiently distinctive. Several hundred other posters had been distributed by the Chamber of Commerce that contained the same scene or very similar beach scenes.

---

[48] 711 F. Supp. 134 (S.D.N.Y. 1989).

[49] Blue Bell Bio-Medical v. Cin-Bad, Inc., 864 F.2d 1253 (5th Cir. 1989).

[50] 870 F.2d 126, 10 U.S.P.Q. 2d (BNA) 1368 (7th Cir. 1989).

§ 3.23   —Common Law and State Statutes

Much broader protection from unfair competition exists in the common law, and of course each of the 50 states varies slightly in its approach to the causes of action of unfair competition recognized under its own common law.

Of great importance in a given state is the statutory law announcing the state's policy with respect to unfair competition. Perhaps the most familiar statute is the Uniform Deceptive Trade Practices Act, reproduced in its entirety in § 3.29. Individual states may somewhat alter the uniform law, so inspection of the law of the jurisdiction in which the unfair business practice has occurred is necessary in order to determine the exact coverage in a given state.

In addition, many states have versions of a consumer protection Act, which commonly incorporate into the statutory scheme the common law causes of action of passing off, false representations of source, sponsorship, or approval, false representations with respect to affiliation or certification, geographic origin, composition of goods or services, bait-and-switch, disparagement, and other statutory versions of the common law forms of unfair competition discussed earlier.

The statutes ordinarily provide specific remedies that may either expand or duplicate the remedies we find at common law, as discussed in §§ 3.24 through 3.28.

§ 3.24   Remedies Against Unfair Competition

Most of the remedies against unfair competition simply parallel the remedies available for infringement in other areas of the law of intellectual property.

§ 3.25   —Temporary Restraining
Order and Injunction

The temporary restraining order and the injunction are commonly the most effective and sometimes the only remedies available to alleviate the harm of unfair competition. Examples of the sweeping relief that may result from the granting of an injunction are those bestowed upon an Italian licensor to prevent the misappropriation of its goodwill for its product in the United States by a former American licensee of the product.[51] And

---

[51] Distillerie Filli Ramazzoti S.P.A. v. Banfi Prods. Corp., 52 Misc. 2d 593, 276 N.Y.S.2d 413, 151 U.S.P.Q. (BNA) 551 (1966), *aff'd,* 27 A.D.2d 905, 280 N.Y.S.2d 892 (1967).

in a different situation, an injunction was granted requiring a defendant cigarette company to white out on all existing billboard advertisements the phrase "NOW the lowest tar of all cigarettes."[52]

§ 3.26   —Accounting for Profits

We have seen earlier that accounting for or disgorgement of profits is another common remedy for losses accrued because of someone else's unfair competition. This remedy is particularly appropriate when the products or services are in direct competition. The implication is that profits made unfairly by a competitor should belong to the innocent party as a rational measure of damages.

In the rather narrow field of cuticle cutting instruments, Revlon, Inc., tried unsuccessfully to buy out a competitor's cuticle cutting instrument that was federally registered under the trademark "TRIM."[53] Revlon then tried to register its own mark "CUTI-TRIM." It was unsuccessful, but sold its cuticle cutting implements under the name "CUTI-TRIM" anyway. The proper remedy, said the court, was an accounting of the defendant's profits; otherwise the defendant would have been unjustly enriched.

§ 3.27   —Compensatory and Punitive Damages

Naturally, ordinary compensatory and punitive damages are also available to the victim of unfair competition, because unfair competition is a tort. These damages (when compensatory and punitive damages are combined) are frequently overwhelming. In a case in which a national tire company willfully infringed a local company's common law trademark, "Big Foot," it was required to pay almost $5 million in punitive and compensatory damages.[54]

§ 3.28   —Criminal Penalties

In the statutes of many states and in federal law, criminal penalties for unfair competition may also be provided. For example, the Sherman

---

[52] American Brands, Inc. v. R.J. Reynolds Tobacco Co., 413 F. Supp. 1352, 1360 (S.D.N.Y. 1976).

[53] W.E. Bassett Co. v. Revlon Inc., 473 F.2d 656 (2d Cir. 1970).

[54] Big O Tire Dealers, Inc. v. Goodyear Tire & Rubber Co., 408 F. Supp. 1219, 189 U.S.P.Q. (BNA) 17 (D. Colo. 1976), *modified,* 561 F.2d 1365, 195 U.S.P.Q. (BNA) 417 (10th Cir. 1977), *cert. dismissed,* 434 U.S. 1052 (1978).

Antitrust Act[55] provides criminal penalties of imprisonment of up to three years or a $100,000 fine or both. If the felon is a corporation, it may be fined up to $1 million.

§ 3.29   Uniform Deceptive Trade Practices Act

Uniform Deceptive Trade Practices Act

§ 1. Definitions.—As used in this Act, unless the context otherwise requires:

(1) "article" means a product as distinguished from its trademark, label, or distinctive dress in packaging;

(2) "certification mark" means a mark used in connection with the goods or services of a person other than the certifier to indicate geographic origin, material, mode of manufacture, quality, accuracy, or other characteristics of the goods or services or to indicate that the work or labor on the goods or services was performed by members of a union or other organization;

(3) "collective mark" means a mark used by members of a cooperative, association, or other collective group or organization to identify goods or services and distinguish them from those of others, or to indicate membership in the collective group or organization;

(4) "mark" means a word, name, symbol, device, or any combination of the foregoing in any form or arrangement;

(5) "person" means an individual, corporation, government, or governmental subdivision or agency, business trust, estate, trust, partnership, unincorporated association, two or more of any of the foregoing having a joint or common interest, or any other legal or commercial entity;

(6) "service mark" means a mark used by a person to identify services and to distinguish them from the services of others;

(7) "trademark" means a mark used by a person to identify goods and to distinguish them from the goods of others;

(8) "trade name" means a word, name, symbol, device, or any combination of the foregoing in any form or arrangement used by a person to identify his business, vocation, or occupation and distinguish it from the business, vocation, or occupation of others.

§ 2. Deceptive Trade Practices.—

(a) A person engages in a deceptive trade practice when, in the course of his business, vocation, or occupation, he:

(1)   passes off goods or services as those of another;

(2)   causes likelihood of confusion or of misunderstanding as to the source, sponsorship, approval, or certification of goods or services;

---

[55] Sherman Antitrust Act, 15 U.S.C. § 52.

(3) causes likelihood of confusion or of misunderstanding as to affiliation, connection, or association with, or certification by, another;

(4) uses deceptive representations or designations of geographic origin in connection with goods or services;

(5) represents that goods or services have sponsorship, approval, characteristics, ingredients, uses, benefits, or quantities that they do not have or that a person has a sponsorship, approval, status, affiliation, or connection that he does not have;

(6) represents that goods are original or new if they are deteriorated, altered, reconditioned, reclaimed, used, or secondhand;

(7) represents that goods or services are of a particular standard, quality, or grade, or that goods are of a particular style or model, if they are of another;

(8) disparages the goods, services, or business of another by false or misleading representation of fact;

(9) advertises goods or services with intent not to sell them as advertised;

(10) advertises goods or services with intent not to supply reasonably expectable public demand, unless the advertisement discloses a limitation of quantity;

(11) makes false or misleading statements of fact concerning the reasons for, existence of, or amounts of price reductions; or

(12) engages in any other conduct which similarly creates a likelihood of confusion or of misunderstanding.

(b) In order to prevail in an action under this Act, a complainant need not prove competition between the parties or actual confusion or misunderstanding.

(c) This section does not affect unfair trade practices otherwise actionable at common law or under other statutes of this state.

§ 3. Remedies.—

(a) A person likely to be damaged by a deceptive trade practice of another may be granted an injunction against it under the principles of equity and on terms that the court considers reasonable. Proof of monetary damage, loss of profits, or intent to deceive is not required. Relief granted for the copying of an article shall be limited to the prevention of confusion or misunderstanding as to source.

(b) Costs shall be allowed to the prevailing party unless the court otherwise directs. The court [in its discretion] may award attorneys' fees to the prevailing party of (1) the party complaining of a deceptive trade practice has brought an action which he knew to be groundless or (2) the party charged with a deceptive trade practice has willfully engaged in the trade practice knowing it to be deceptive.*

(c) The relief provided in this section is in addition to remedies otherwise available against the same conduct under the common law or other statutes of this state.

§ 4. Application.—

(a) This Act does not apply to:

(1)   conduct in compliance with the orders or rules of, or a statute administered by, a federal, state, or local governmental agency;

(2)   publishers, broadcasters, printers, or other persons engaged in the dissemination of information or reproduction of printed or pictorial matters who publish, broadcast, or reproduce material without knowledge of its deceptive character; or

(3)   actions or appeals pending on the effective date of this Act.

(b) Subsections 2(a)(2) and 2(a)(3) do not apply to the use of a service mark, trademark, certification mark, collective mark, trade name, or other trade identification that was used and not abandoned before the effective date of this Act, if the use was in good faith and is otherwise lawful except for this Act.

§ 5. Uniformity of Interpretation.—This Act shall be construed to effectuate its general purpose to make uniform the law of those states which enact it.

§ 6. Short Title.—This Act may be cited as the Uniform Deceptive Trade Practices Act.

§ 7. Severability.—If any provision of this Act or the application thereof to any person or circumstance is held invalid, the invalidity does not affect other provisions or applications of the Act which can be given effect without the invalid provision or application, and to this end the provisions of this Act are severable.

§ 8. Repeals.—The following acts or parts of acts are repealed:

(1)

(2)

(3)

§ 9. Time of Taking Effect.—This Act takes effect . . . .

CHAPTER 4

PROTECTING TRADEMARKS

§ 4.1 Introduction

Of all the intellectual property assets owned by a business, the most important are its trademarks. Indeed, the simple mention of the following trademarks brings forth immediate good or bad connotations: Smurfs, Edsel, McDonald's, and Exxon. A healthy trademark serves as a mental mind-grabber, representing the quintessence of the goodwill of a business. Successful trademarks are the result of a long effort involving research and development, years of product sales in the marketplace, and all the goodwill that a business has so diligently worked to earn. There is no question that if we were to take all of the physical assets of a company such as the Coca-Cola Co. and eliminate them from the face of the earth,

Coca-Cola could still acquire new capital and obtain billions of dollars worth of new financing simply on the goodwill represented by the two words "Coca-Cola."

This is an important chapter for any company. It covers the proper selection of a trademark, the clearance of the selected trademark, the grammatical use of the trademark, the policing of the trademark, and the enforcing of the trademark. These are crucial steps and must be implemented by businesses as a matter of course.

A trademark is the only intellectual property asset that is protected by three separate bodies of law. There are approximately 800,000 federally registered marks, and each state has provisions for the state registration of a mark. In addition, trademarks are protected at common law. This chapter discusses the interplay among these three bodies of law. The Federal Trademark Revision Act of 1988, which became effective on November 16, 1989, made many fundamental changes to American trademark law. This chapter also discusses those changes in detail.

RESOURCES:

1. McCarthy, J. Thomas, *Trademarks and Unfair Competition* (Lawyers Co-operative Publishing Co.: Aqueduct Bldg., Rochester, NY 14694) (2d ed. 1988). Without question, Professor McCarthy is the premier authority on this topic.

2. Kane, Siegrun D., *Trademark Law—A Practitioner's Guide* (Practicing Law Institute: 810 7th Ave., New York, NY 10019) (1987). This hands-on book is invaluable for corporate and general practice counsel.

3. The United States Trademark Association (USTA), 6 East 45th Street, New York, NY 10017, (212) 986-5880, has as members more than 1,900 corporations, law firms, and other organizations and individuals involved with trademarks. The USTA also publishes a journal, *The Trademark Reporter*.

---

§ 4.2   —Functions of Trademarks

Trademarks are used to identify and distinguish goods or services in the marketplace. Occasionally, despite extensive name selection and market study, chosen trademarks do not fare well with the public. For example, the name Edsel brings to mind one of the most significant failures of new car introduction in the United States. Datsun enjoyed high public recognition, so when the cars began to be called Nissan, a lot of goodwill and name recognition was lost.

If a company's products are sold abroad, great care must be taken to find out the connotations of the trademark in foreign languages. For example, Nova in Spanish means *won't go*. The term Bimbo has a negative connotation in the United States, but in Spain Bimbo is a market leader for high quality premium bakery products. Bimbo is owned by Anheuser Busch.

§ 4.3   —United States Patent and Trademark Office

Federal trademark protection is administered by the United States Patent and Trademark Office (PTO) whose address is: Commissioner of Patents & Trademarks, Washington, DC 20231, (703) 557-3080. The following may be obtained from the PTO:

1. Copies of issued trademarks ($1.50 each)
2. *General Information Concerning Trademarks*
3. *Questions and Answers about Trademarks: Answers to Questions Frequently Asked about Trademarks*

The following may be obtained from the United States Government Printing Office, Superintendent of Documents, Washington, DC 20402:

1. *Patents and Trademarks* (SB–21) (free)
2. *Official Gazette: Trademarks*
3. *Index of Trademarks*

§ 4.4   Types of Trademarks

Theoretically, a trademark can be anything that identifies a single source for a product or a service. Legally, a trademark for federal registration is defined as:

> any word, name, symbol, or device or any combination thereof (1) used by a person, or (2) which a person has a bona fide intention to use in commerce and applies to register on the principal register established by this Act, to identify and distinguish his or her goods, including a unique product, from those manufactured or sold by others and to indicate the source of the goods, even if that source is unknown.[1]

---

[1] 15 U.S.C. § 1127 (1988)—definition of Trademark.

Words constitute the most common form of trademark. A simple word such as Apple for computers is an excellent example. Stylized logos, artistic designs, and graphic symbols constitute a second category of commonly used trademarks. The five interlocking rings designating the Olympics fall into this classification. Color may function as a trademark. The multi-colored striping on pharmaceutical drugs are commonplace trademarks. Even the single color pink for fiberglass insulation has been held to be exclusively owned by Owens Corning.[2] Sound may function as a trademark. For example, the theme song of the "Heartbeat of America" campaign is a trademark owned by General Motors. A slogan may also be a trademark; one example is Clairol's use of the words "color so natural only her hairdresser knows for sure."

While the above represent some rather obvious and important types of trademarks, the shape of the product, a configuration on a product, and the container of a product may also constitute valuable trademarks. For example, a few years ago 7-Up had trademark rights to the image of an upside down Coca-Cola glass. This was part of their "Un-Cola" campaign. Indeed, the shape of a franchise unit building and the interior design of a restaurant can both function as protectable trade dress, which is a form of trademark eligible for protection. The five-sided shape of Bose speakers and the pebbled silver, blue, and white wrapper of a Klondike bar have been held protectable.[3]

Figure 4–1 reproduces five trademarks that were published for opposition in the *Official Gazette*. From top left, they illustrate: a graphic design; a common animal; a perfume container; a common word; and three colors.

It is not surprising, therefore, that a single product and the marketing of that product can involve a number of different trademarks. The McDonald's trademarks provide an interesting illustration. The physical device of the golden arches has become one of the first symbols learned by a young child, one readily recognized worldwide. Yet, Mcdonald's uses many more trademarks to protect its rights, including the name McDonald's, the roof design of its franchise units, the names of its various products such as McD.L.T., the shape of its containers (such as the container for the McD.L.T.), and so on. The next time you visit a McDonald's, look at the napkins, the cups, the containers, and the wrappings for the food products; you will be amazed at all of the visual trademarks found in a McDonald's unit.

---

[2] *In re* Owens Corning Fiberglass Corp., 774 F.2d 1116, 227 U.S.P.Q. (BNA) 417 (Fed. Cir. 1985).

[3] *In re* Bose Corp., 772 F.2d 866, 227 U.S.P.Q. (BNA) 1 (Fed. Cir. 1985); Isaly Co. v. Kraft Inc., 619 F. Supp. 983, 226 U.S.P.Q. (BNA) 801 (M.D. Fla. 1985), *aff'd in part*, 812 F.2d 1531, 1 U.S.P.Q.2d (BNA) 1161 (11th Cir. 1986).

SN 73-801,543. CHARTER GOLF, INC., CARLSBAD, CA. FILED 5-22-1989.

FOR MEN'S GOLF APPAREL, NAMELY MEN'S SHIRTS, SLACKS, SHORTS AND SWEATSUITS (U.S. CL. 39).
FIRST USE 12-1-1987; IN COMMERCE 12-1-1987.

SN 74-007,335. H. ALPERT & COMPANY, INC., LOS AN-GELES, CA. FILED 12-4-1989.

FOR COLOGNE AND PERFUME (U.S. CL. 51).
FIRST USE 11-8-1988; IN COMMERCE 11-8-1988.

SN 74-007,003. GLASSER, KEITH, BROOKLINE, MA. FILED 12-1-1989.

THE STIPPLING SHOWN IN THE DRAWING IS FOR SHADING PURPOSES ONLY AND IS NOT INDICATE COLOR.
FOR MEN'S, WOMEN'S AND CHILDREN'S CLOTHING - NAMELY, T-SHIRTS, PANTS, SHIRTS, TANK TOPS, SHORTS, COATS, JACKETS, SOCKS AND HATS (U.S. CL. 39).

SN 73-839,658. MARS, INCORPORATED, MCLEAN, VA. FILED 11-15-1989.

DOVE

OWNER OF U.S. REG. NO. 1,415,202 AND OTHERS.
FOR ICE MILK FROZEN CONFECTIONS (U.S. CL. 46).
FIRST USE 2-24-1989; IN COMMERCE 2-24-1989.

SN 73-729,971. ALEXANDER JULIAN, INC., NEW YORK, NY. FILED 5-23-1988.

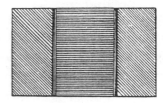

OWNER OF U.S. REG. NO. 1,486,167.
THE MARK IS LINED FOR THE COLORS BLUE, RED AND GREEN.
THE MARK CONSISTS OF THE BACKGROUND DESIGN FOR A LABEL.
FOR LUGGAGE (U.S. CL. 3).
FIRST USE 4-0-1988; IN COMMERCE 4-0-1988.

Figure 4–1. Trademarks published for opposition in *Official Gazette of the United States Patent Office.*

§ 4.5 —Trade Names Distinguished

A trade name is the name of a business and is not generally a trademark. Local governments require the filing of a trade name affidavit at the county level or the state level or both. These requirements vary from jurisdiction to jurisdiction. The purpose of trade name registration is to provide a means for the creditors of a business to find out who the real party in interest is for purposes of debt collection. The trade name of the company that markets Coca-Cola is Coca-Cola Co. The trade name of the company that markets the famous Monopoly game is Parker Brothers, Inc.

§ 4.6 —Service Marks

Trademarks are for products. I Can't Believe It's Butter is a trademark for a food product. Safeway is a service mark for a retail grocery store that sells food products. Wendy's can function both as a trademark and a service mark, because it is used on hamburger products and on a retail business that sells fast food items. Throughout the remainder of the chapter, everything discussed with respect to trademarks also applies to service marks. The federal Lanham Act, discussed in detail in **§ 4.22**, defines service marks as those used to "identify and distinguish the services of one person, including a unique service, from the services of others and to indicate the source of the services, even if that source is unknown. Titles, character names and other distinctive features of radio or television programs may be registered as service marks notwithstanding that they, or the programs, may advertise the goods of the sponsor."[4]

§ 4.7 —Certification Marks

Federal certification marks are those used to "certify regional or other origin, material, mode of manufacture, quality, accuracy, or other characteristics of such person's goods or services or that the work or labor on the goods or services was performed by members of a union or other organization."[5] A good example of a certification mark is the UL symbol from Underwriters Laboratory. The Good Housekeeping Seal of Approval is another example.

---

[4] 15 U.S.C. § 1127 (1988)—definition of Service Mark.
[5] 15 U.S.C. § 1127 (1988)—definition of Certification Mark.

§ 4.8 —Collective Marks

The federal Lanham Act defines these marks as being "used by the members of a cooperative, an association or other collective group or organization . . . and includes marks indicating membership in a union, an association or other organization."[6] For example, a famous collective mark is AFL-CIO for a particular labor union.

§ 4.9 —State Trademarks

Most businesses are involved in the interstate sales of goods and services; therefore they are principally concerned with obtaining federal trademark rights. Some businesses, however, are solely located within the confines of a particular state and may prefer to seek only state trademark protection. Each state has its own set of unique requirements for obtaining state trademark protection.

RESOURCE: *United States Trademark Association, State Trademark and Unfair Competition Law* (Clark Boardman Company, Ltd.; 375 Hudson St., New York, NY 10014) (1989). This valuable book sets forth the trademark procedures for all 50 states, and lists the addresses and phone numbers of the applicable state governing bodies.

---

§ 4.10 —Common Law Trademarks

Trademarks are protected at common law everywhere in the United States. To have common law trademark protection, a business must simply *adopt* the mark and *affix* it to a product or service and *use it* in commerce. Placing a label or hang-tag onto the product constitutes affixation. Common law trademarks provide exclusivity only in the physical territories of actual use. For example, if a business uses the mark Poorhorse for dog food in Havre, Montana only, it will be protected, at common law, only in an area around Havre, Montana. The extent of the area will be dependent upon how far the influence of the mark exists from Havre, Montana. Because of this geographic limitation, reliance on common law trademark protection is a fallback position, and all businesses should file for state or federal protection.

---

[6] 15 U.S.C. § 1127 (1988)—definition of Collective Mark.

§ 4.11   Duration of Trademarks

In the past, federal trademarks received a 20-year registration that could be renewed forever.[7] This changed with the Trademark Revision Act of 1988, and federal trademarks now receive only a 10-year duration but can still be renewed forever. The Revision Act seeks to clear the registers of marks no longer used. State trademark registrations are typically 10 years and also can be renewed forever. At common law, there is no specific duration. Duration at common law continues for as long as the mark continues to be used. Whether a mark is protected federally, at the state level, or at common law, when a company stops using the trademark it is at definite risk that it may have abandoned its trademark and, therefore, the duration of exclusivity has come to an end. It is not surprising that what constitutes abandonment is heavily litigated.

When does trademark protection commence? It commences federally when a federal registration number is issued. At the state level it commences when a certificate from the state is issued. At common law, it commences when a company starts sale of the product in commerce with the mark affixed to the product.

Another hotly litigated area is the fuzzy concept of *preparation to use a trademark*. Having a graphics shop draw up a trademark, filing papers using the trademark with government officials (for example, filing plans in a country for a real estate development), or putting a sign up on a business without opening the business (such as a restaurant prior to opening) may constitute simple preparation to use and may not lead to any exclusive trademark rights of ownership.

It is not surprising that some businesses, especially large companies, carefully guard as a trade secret new product names before the date of product introduction. As discussed in **§ 4.21**, the Trademark Revision Act provides a great deal of comfort in that corporations can now reserve new product trademarks in advance of use.[8]

§ 4.12   Trademark Distinctiveness

The distinctiveness of a trademark is an important factor in the legal strength of the trademark. It is a goal of all businesses to select and use highly distinctive, legally strong trademarks. By doing so, they greatly minimize their trademark infringement legal exposure and greatly maximize their right to stop infringing uses.

---

[7] 15 U.S.C. § 1059(a) (1988).

[8] 15 U.S.C. § 1127 (1988).

§ 4.13   —Fanciful Trademarks

Fanciful trademarks are words created and coined to function as trademarks.[9] Such words never existed before. Examples are Kodak for cameras, Polaroid for cameras, Exxon for oil and gas products, and Advil for headache and pain reliever medicine. Fanciful marks are legally the strongest trademarks, because each one has been created to function as an exclusive property right. Fanciful trademarks are protectable at the outset without the need for proof of secondary meaning. See § **4.16**.

§ 4.14   —Arbitrary Trademarks

Arbitrary trademarks are well-known words arbitrarily used.[10] For example, the word Apple is commonly used and is also arbitrarily applied to computers. Fox is arbitrarily applied to photos and Camel is arbitrarily applied to cigarettes. In choosing an arbitrary trademark, a business tries to pick a mark that will aid in the sale of the product. For example, the word "apple" has traditional significance in the educational industry. "An apple for a good student" and "Bring an apple to the teacher" are both well-known usages in the educational context. A significant part of the Apple computer business relates to the educational marketplace.

The arbitrary words Coyote and Weasel could not be as successfully used in the photo finishing business as Fox because they have negative connotations. Most people think of foxes as clean, quick, and intelligent, all positive attributes. Likewise, the word "camel" suggests a Turkish blend of tobacco.

Legally, arbitrary trademarks may be either strong or weak. The strength of such marks depends upon how frequently they are used by others as trademarks. For example, the term Mustang is used in the vehicle industry by a number of different companies (for example, Mustang for tires and for batteries). Hence, although the mark is arbitrary, its legal strength is weak, and each owner of the word "mustang" has rights of exclusivity narrowly limited to its particular product or product line. The mark Apple was not previously being used in the computer industry; hence its selection, adoption, and use have been legally strong enough to foreclose other companies from using it on related products.

In selecting an arbitrary mark, it is important to research it thoroughly to make sure that the legal strengths of the mark will be high and that it is not in common use as a trademark by others. Arbitrary marks are

---

[9] Tisch Hotels, Inc. v. Americana Inn, Inc., 350 F.2d 609, 146 U.S.P.Q. (BNA) 566 (7th Cir. 1965).

[10] Standard Brands, Inc. v. Smidler, 151 F.2d 34 (2d Cir. 1945).

inherently distinctive and are registerable and legally protected from the outset. Proof of secondary meaning is not necessary. See § **4.16.**

§ 4.15 —Suggestive Trademarks

Suggestive marks are words that suggest but do not describe the product.[11] Computerworld for the retail stores selling computers, Coppertone suntan oil, Hula-Hoop plastic toy hoops, and Stronghold threaded nails are all examples of suggestive marks. Suggestive marks are legally distinctive and therefore protectable from the outset without the need for proof of secondary meaning.[12] See § **4.16.** However, such marks are not legally as strong as fanciful and arbitrary trademarks. Suggestive marks are not given as broad a legal scope of protection in infringement situations as that given to arbitrary and fanciful marks.

Courts use several tests to evaluate the degree of inventiveness, imaginativeness, remoteness, and subtlety of suggestive trademarks.[13] For example, the mark Skinvisible for transparent medical adhesive tape was held to be protectable as a suggestive mark, because the suggestion made by the mark is remote and subtle. The term "skinvisible" does not need to be used by competitors in describing their products.[14] The mark The Equalizer for software that placed the user "on equal footing with stock market professionals" was held to be suggestive based on imaginativeness.[15]

§ 4.16 —Merely Descriptive Trademarks

Merely descriptive trademarks describe the quality, ingredients, or characteristics of the product. If a term describes the intended purpose, function, or use of the goods, it is merely descriptive. For example, Bed and Breakfast Registry was held to be merely descriptive.[16] If the term describes the size of the goods, it is merely descriptive. For example, Baby Brie has been

---

[11] Inc. Publishing Corp. v. Manhattan Magazine, 616 F. Supp. 370, 227 U.S.P.Q. (BNA) 257 (S.D.N.Y. 1985), *aff'd,* 788 F.2d 3 (2d Cir. 1986).

[12] Watkins Prods., Inc. v. Sunway Fruit Prods., Inc., 311 F.2d 496 (7th Cir. 1962), *cert. denied,* 373 U.S. 904 (1963).

[13] Stix Prods., Inc. v. United Merchants & Mfrs., Inc., 295 F. Supp. 479, 160 U.S.P.Q. (BNA) 777 (S.D.N.Y. 1968). Restatement of Torts § 721 comment a (1939).

[14] Minnesota Mining & Mfg. Co. v. Johnson & Johnson, 454 F.2d 1179, 172 U.S.P.Q. (BNA) 491 (C.C.P.A. 1972).

[15] Charles Schwab & Co. v. Hibernia Bank, 665 F. Supp. 800, 805, 3 U.S.P.Q.2d (BNA) 1561, 1565 (N.D. Cal. 1987).

[16] *In re* Bed & Breakfast Registry, 791 F.2d 157, 229 U.S.P.Q. (BNA) 818 (Fed. Cir. 1986).

held to be merely descriptive of small pieces of brie cheese.[17] When the term describes the end effect upon the user, it is merely descriptive. For example, Saporita (Italian for *tasty*) has been held to be merely descriptive for sausages.[18] When the term designates a geographic designation, it is merely descriptive. Appalachia Log Homes, for example, has been held to be geographically descriptive.[19]

For example, to aid practical application, it has been suggested that if one were to take a product to Australia and attempt to explain it to an aborigine (that is, to someone who has never seen it and doesn't know what it is), all the words used to describe the product would most likely be merely descriptive terms and, therefore, would fall within this category of trademarks.[20]

It is important to understand that merely descriptive trademarks are not protectable from the outset. Rather, evidence of *secondary meaning* must be established. The doctrine of secondary meaning is easy to apply. Secondary meaning is found when a significant number of people readily understand the name as referring to a product from a single source or origin.[21] For example, when we see golden arches, all of us instantly recognize the single source to be McDonald's. The United States Supreme Court, in *Armstrong Paint & Varnish Works v. Nu-Enamel Corp.*,[22] stated:

> Here we have a secondary meaning to the descriptive term "Nu-Enamel." This establishes . . . the common law right of the Nu-Enamel Corporation to be free from the competitive use of these words as a trademark or trade name. . . . The right arises . . . from the fact that "Nu-Enamel" has come to indicate that the goods in connection with which it is used are the goods manufactured by the respondent. When a name is endowed with this quality, it becomes a mark, entitled to protection.[23]

An interesting set of three cases involves the term Chocolate Fudge for diet soft drinks containing no chocolate.[24] One court held the term

---

[17] *In re* Bongrain Int'l Corp., 229 U.S.P.Q. (BNA) 818 (T.T.A.B. 1985).

[18] *In re* Geo. A. Hormel Co., 227 U.S.P.Q. (BNA) 813 (T.T.A.B. 1985).

[19] Burke-Parsons-Bowlby Corp. v. Appalachian Log Homes, Inc., 871 F.2d 590, 10 U.S.P.Q.2d (BNA) 1443 (6th Cir. 1989).

[20] Stix Prods., Inc. v. United Merchants & Mfrs., Inc., 295 F. Supp. 479, 160 U.S.P.Q. (BNA) 777, 784 (S.D.N.Y. 1968).

[21] *See* Union Carbide Corp. v. Ever-Ready, 531 F.2d 366, 188 U.S.P.Q. (BNA) 623 (7th Cir. 1976); President & Trustees of Colby College v. Colby College—New Hampshire, 508 F.2d 804, 185 U.S.P.Q. (BNA) 65 (1st Cir. 1975).

[22] 305 U.S. 315 (1938), *reh'g denied,* 305 U.S. 675 (1938).

[23] Armstrong Paint & Varnish Works v. Nu-Enamel Corp., 305 U.S. 315, 335 (1938), *reh'g denied,* 305 U.S. 675 (1938).

[24] A.J. Canfield Co. v. Vess Beverages, Inc., 796 F.2d 903, 230 U.S.P.Q. (BNA) 441 (2d Cir. 1986), *later proceeding,* 674 F. Supp. 642, 5 U.S.P.Q.2d (BNA) 1672, *vacated,* 859 F.2d

Chocolate Fudge to be descriptive but protectable, because secondary meaning had been established. A second court held the term to be descriptive but with no secondary meaning established. A third court held that Chocolate Fudge was the name of a well-recognized (that is, generic) taste (see § 4.17) to which no party had exclusive rights. These cases illustrate the importance of selecting marks that are not merely descriptive.

It is not surprising that merely descriptive trademarks are legally weak. First, such trademarks are not legally protected without evidence of secondary meaning. Producing evidence of secondary meaning can be quite expensive for a business. For example, a costly survey of the consuming public may be required to prove secondary meaning. Even if secondary meaning is established, the trademark protection is weak, and, as shown by the above Chocolate Fudge trio of cases, a court's decision finding protectability may be attacked by later courts.

§ 4.17   —Generic Words

Generic words can never function as trademarks. They are not trademarks and are not legally protectable. Generic words have been defined as "referring to a particular genus or class of which an individual article or service is but a member."[25]

Nobody can take the word gas and use it as a trademark for a service station dispensing gasoline fuel products. The word "gas" is generic and all competitors in the business are entitled to utilize that word. Tollhouse for cookies was used by Nestle for many years. A court has held tollhouse to be generic, because the word can be found in three separate dictionaries defining a type of cookie.[26] Bundt has been held to be generic for a ring cake mix.[27] The word "team" in Team Xerox has been held to be generic because it is being used in its common dictionary sense.[28]

36, 8 U.S.P.Q.2d (BNA) 1626 (7th Cir. 1988). *See also* A.J. Canfield Co. v. Honickman, 629 F. Supp. 200, 228 U.S.P.Q. (BNA) 429 (E.D. Pa. 1985), *aff'd*, 808 F.2d 291, 1 U.S.P.Q.2d (BNA) 1364 (3d Cir. 1988); and Yoo-Moo Chocolate Beverages v. A.J. Canfield Co., 229 U.S.P.Q. (BNA) 653 (D.N.J. 1985).

[25] Beer Nuts v. Clover Club Foods, 711 F.2d 934, 221 U.S.P.Q. (BNA) 60 (10th Cir. 1983).

[26] Nestle Co. v. Chester's Market, Inc., 571 F. Supp. 763, 219 U.S.P.Q. (BNA) 298 (D. Conn. 1983).

[27] *In re* Northland Aluminum Prods., 777 F.2d 1556, 227 U.S.P.Q. (BNA) 961 (Fed. Cir. 1985).

[28] Team Central, Inc. v. Xerox Corp., 606 F. Supp. 1408, 226 U.S.P.Q. (BNA) 929 (D. Minn. 1985).

Occasionally, fanciful trademarks become generic. The fanciful mark aspirin for a pain relieving medicine was held to become generic through common use by the public. Aspirin is still a valid trademark in parts of the world outside the United States. Thermos is generic in the United States but still a registered trademark in Canada. The common words "kleenex," "escalator," "brassiere," "cellophane," "corn flakes," "dry ice," "harmonica," "lanolin," "malted milk," "trampoline," and "yo-yo" were all valued trademarks but are now generic through common use by the public.

Some companies actively police the media to ensure that their extremely valuable trademarks do not fall into the generic trap. Xerox Corp. expends substantial amounts of money insisting on proper use of its famous Xerox trademark. If actors state on television, "Go get a xerox of this page," Xerox Corp. will send a letter requesting that its mark be used only as a trademark and not as a common word in the English language. The owners of the famous Formica trademark are also concerned that it not become a generic and common word. When a company thinks that its trademark may become generic, it may use the word *brand,* for example: Jello brand gelatin dessert, Band-Aid brand adhesive bandages, Formica brand countertops.

§ 4.18   Selection of a Trademark

The first step in the selection of a trademark is to pick an arbitrary or fanciful name. These two classes of trademarks are protectable from the outset. If an arbitrary mark is chosen, care must be taken to be sure it is not frequently used by others. It is important to maximize the legal strength of the trademark being selected.

As a practical matter, the public does not like lengthy trademarks. It is not surprising that most famous trademarks, for example, Exxon, Kodak, Charmin, and Fox, have only one or two syllables. Harsh enunciations are frequently used, such as Kodak and Exxon. The product itself may dictate soft enunciations, such as Charmin and Puffs for tissue products.

In the computer field, there is a glut of the following prefixes: *soft-, compu-, micro-, hard-,* and *mini-.* Likewise, frequently used suffixes are: *-tech, -onics, -data,* and *-tron.* These should all be avoided. As an extreme example, almost 2,600 corporations in the United States incorporate the word *data* into their name or trademark.[29]

---

[29] *See Electronic Firms Often Find Picking a Name Can Be a Tough Assignment,* Los Angeles Times, Feb. 7, 1982.

§ 4.19   —Prescreening

Some businesses select their own trademark, whereas others use the professional services of an advertising agency. Whether the mark is selected in-house or by an agency, the first step in trademark clearance is prescreening, which involves searching for the selected mark in competitors' literature, trade directories, and catalogs. If the company has salesmen or distributors, it should circulate the selected mark to them and ask whether they are aware of the same or similar mark being used by others.

Remember that it is important to look not only for the identical mark on identical products but also to expand the search by looking for similar marks on related products.

§ 4.20   —Professional Search

When the trademark has been selected and prescreened, a professional search must be done. Several computer databases are available on which relatively inexpensive trademark clearance searches can be performed. Two of these are Trademarkscan by Thomson & Thomson, and Compu-Mark.

RESOURCES:

1. Trademarkscan (Federal and State), Thomson & Thomson, 500 Victory Road, North Quincy, MA 02171-1545, telephone 1-800-692-8833.
2. Compu-Mark, 1333 F Street, N.W., Washington, DC 20004, telephone 202-737-7900.

An example of a Thomson & Thomson record is shown in **Figure 4–2**. Notice that graphics are available.

Although the state trademark databases contain the trademarks in all 50 states, and although the federal database contains some 800,000 federally registered trademarks, do not rely solely on these sources. In conducting computerized searches, you may wish to search not only the trademark databases but also the other available databases, such as the Electronic Yellow Pages and Dun & Bradstreet. If software is involved, you may wish to search the International Software Menu and similar sources. You should search all pertinent databases for use of your mark. For example, we took the mark Poorhorse through the USCO cross-index search for businesses on DIALOG; the results are shown in **Figure 4–3**. Note the cost of this search. It does not cost that much extra to go through several (or many) millions of database records.

SAMPLE RECORD
TRADEMARKSCAN®FEDERAL DATABASE

FLIGHT   and Design
     US CLASS   :   003 (Baggage, Animal Equipment, Purses, and Portfolios)
                         039 (Clothing)
     INTL CLASS :   018 (Leather Goods)
                         025 (Clothing)
     STATUS : Pending; (Intent To Use)
     GOODS/SERVICES : (INT. CL. 18) BAGS (INT. CL. 25) FOOTWEAR AND
      CLOTHING
     SERIES CODE : 74   SERIAL NO. : 000759
     FILED : November 16, 1989
     DATE OF FIRST USE : No date available
     ORIGINAL OWNER : NIKE, INC. (OREGON CORPORATION) ; BEAVERTON,OR
     EXTRA STATUS DATA : INTENT TO USE APPLICATION

Figure 4–2. Sample record from TRADEMARKSCAN database. Reprinted with permission of Thomson & Thomson.

File 226:TRADEMARKSCAN OG:05/22/90 AP:04/04/90
　　(Copr. 1990 Thomson & Thomson)
File 246:TRADEMARKSCAN STATE DATABASE
　　(Copr. 1990 Thomson & Thomson)
File 515:DUNS Electronic Yellow Pages - 03/90
　　(Copr. 1990 D&B)

　Set Items Description
　--- ----- -----------
?ss poorhorse? or poor(w)horse?

　　S1　　0 POORHORSE?
　　S2　900 POOR
　　S3　12050 IIORSE?
　　S4　　1 POOR(W)HORSE?
　　S5　　1 POORHORSE? OR POOR(W)HORSE?

　5/2/1　　(Item 1 from file: 515)
02611516　　　　　　　　DMI RECORD AVAILABLE IN FILE 516
HIDDEN VALLEY RANCH INC
POOR HORSEMEN'S TACK SHOP
OLD GREENFIELD RD
FRANCESTOWN, NH　03043

TELEPHONE: 603-547-3351
COUNTY: HILLSBOROUGH
INDUSTRY GROUP: RETAIL
PRIMARY SIC:
　5941　　SPORTING GOODS AND BICYCLE SHOPS, NSK

SECONDARY SIC(S):
　0752　　ANIMAL SPECIALTY SERVICES
　7999　　AMUSEMENT AND RECREATION, NEC, NSK

D-U-N-S NUMBER:　　　09-205-9229
NUMBER OF EMPLOYEES:　B (1-4)
CITY POPULATION:　　　0 (UNDER 1,000)
?logoff

　　　13jun90 09:10:57 User031170 Session A484.2
　　　　　$1.17　0.009 Hrs File226
　　　$1.17 Estimated cost File226
　　　　　$0.39　0.003 Hrs File246
　　　$0.39 Estimated cost File246
　　　　　$1.50　0.020 Hrs File515
　　　　　　$0.35 1 Type(s) in Format 2
　　　　　$0.35 1 Types
　　　$1.85 Estimated cost File515
　　　　　OneSearch, 3 files, 0.033 Hrs FileOS
　　　$0.33 Dialnet
　　　$3.74 Estimated cost this search
　　　$4.14 Estimated total session cost   0.033 Hrs.

Figure 4–3. Poorhorse cross-index search for businesses on
DIALOG.

In addition, play games with spelling and phonetic variations for the mark. Look for the singular. Look for the plural. Try spelling variations. For example, for the ending *-tech,* try also *-tek, -teck,* and *-tec.* Try one- or two-word spellings, as we did for Poorhorse and Poor Horse.

Remember, computer searching, which costs several hundred dollars, is relatively inexpensive. Some of the professional software for the trademark databases, such as Trademarkscan and Compu-Mark, use a searching software with artificial intelligence that automatically looks for variations. However, do not rely solely on the software's ability to look for variations. Use your own intuition.

When the mark has been cleared by both the client and the computer search, we highly recommend that a company use the services of a professional searching company.

RESOURCES:

1. Thomson & Thomson, 500 E Street, S.W., #970, Washington, DC 20024-2710, telephone 1-800-356-8630.
2. Compu-Mark, 1333 F Street, N.W., Washington, DC 20004, telephone 202-737-7900.

A professional search will serve as a double check for all that has been done before. Searches are usually available on a 24-hour or 48-hour expedited basis. In addition, these organizations are capable of doing an international search on the mark.

We highly recommend doing both a United States and an international search on a mark. All it takes is one lawsuit to convince a business of the importance of thoroughly (and we mean thoroughly) clearing the mark beforehand. Spending several thousand dollars in initial trademark clearance activity pales in comparison to the tens of thousands of dollars that the business may spend in trademark litigation. Add to those dollars the possibility that a business may have to stop using the mark because it infringes another's mark, and the money paid for computer, professional, and preclearance searches is well invested.

For example, the value of clearance is highlighted by the following story. A young couple came into our office who, three years earlier, had commenced the manufacture and sale of an expensive line of products. It was the type of product they could make with high-quality materials and sell for a high price. The business was located in one of the major ski resort areas in the Rocky Mountains. After three years of steadily watching their sales skyrocket, they exhibited in a booth at their first national convention. At the same convention they discovered a Fortune 100 company using the identical trademark on a similar product line.

When they came home, in the mail was a letter from this company, demanding immediate cessation of all use of its trademark. Sadly, we had to advise this young couple to change over and to obtain a new mark. The Fortune 100 mark was federally registered, incontestable, and had been in use for a number of years (although it did not represent a major product line for the company).

Had the young couple expended a few hundred dollars in a simple trademark clearance search in a computer database, they would have uncovered the larger company's trademark. They did not, nor were they advised to do so by their corporate attorney. After three years, at the peak of their success, they had to change. Unfortunately, the name change dealt a death blow to the business. The couple had recently borrowed capital to meet their expanding business needs, and they had established substantial goodwill in a small, expensive product. With the name change, all of the positive name recognition evaporated.

§ 4.21   Trademark Ownership

The Trademark Revision Act of 1988 opened up a whole new aspect of trademark ownership. Prior to this Act, ownership was acquired only upon affixation and use of a mark. At common law, the exclusive trademark rights are territorially limited. Under state law, such rights exist throughout the state, even though the mark is not physically used throughout the state. Under prior federal law, registration granted exclusive rights throughout the United States providing there is an interstate use of the mark. These three time-honored and traditional ways of acquiring trademark ownership still exist and are still legally valid. The Trademark Revision Act of 1988, however, has now given tentative ownership to marks selected and intended to be used, that is, based on *constructive use,* rather than actual use.

§ 4.22   —Intent-to-Use Application

The Trademark Revision Act of 1988, which took effect on November 16, 1989, permits the filing of an *intent-to-use* application.[30] No specimens are required. The Revision Act requires that the application be based upon a "bona fide intention, under circumstances showing the good faith of such person, to use a trademark in commerce."[31] What constitutes *bona fide* intent and *good faith circumstances* will be the subject of future litigation:

---

[30] Trademark Law Revision Act of 1988, Pub. L. No. 100–667, 102 Stat. 3935 (enacted Nov. 16, 1988, effective Nov. 16, 1989).

[31] 15 U.S.C. § 1051(2)(b).

A statement of intent to use a mark on specifically identified products in the future may be sufficient. An applicant may safely make this statement in its original application without having taken concrete steps to create and introduce a new product provided that in fact it intends to use the mark.[32]

What constitutes a lack of bona fide intent may involve the filing of "numerous intent-to-use applications to register the same mark for many more new products than are contemplated" or "numerous intent-to-use applications for a variety of desirable trademarks intended to be used on a single new product."[33]

The filing of an intent-to-use application is a *constructive use* of the mark. It is as if the applicant actually used the mark in all 50 states on the date of filing. This is truly a race to file. An intent-to-use application is set forth as **Form 4–1**. Note that the same form is used for the principal registration of a trademark (§ **4.37**).

The intent-to-use application will not be registered until a statement of use is timely filed (**Form 4–2**). However, the PTO will examine the application in a manner similar to existing practice, reject it or approve it and pass it for publication for opposition by issuing a notice of publication. Once published, a standard opposition proceeding can be filed by any member of the public. If no opposition occurs, a notice of allowance is issued. At any time prior to the issuance of the notice of publication, the application can be amended to actual use, thereby converting it to a normal application. During the time between notice of publication and notice of allowance no amendments based upon actual use will be permitted.

RESOURCE: The final rules regarding the filing of trademark intent-to-use applications were approved on September 9, 1988. Such forms are available from Office of Trademark Procedures at 703-557-3268.

The applicant has six months to file a statement of use with specimens showing actual use of the mark in commerce. The examiner performs a minor reexamination to verify that all formalities have been complied with and the mark is registered. The applicant may obtain an automatic six-month extension to file his statement of use and, upon a showing of good cause, the applicant may obtain up to two additional years in six-month increments. A request for an extension of time appears as **Form 4–3**.

Essentially, the Trademark Revision Act provides three years after the notice of allowance in which to file the statement of use. This is a considerable period of time to reserve a trademark.

---

[32] S. Rep. No. 515, 102d Cong., 2d Sess. 23 (1989).
[33] *Id.*

TRADEMARK/SERVICE MARK APPLICATION, PRINCIPAL REGISTER, WITH DECLARATION	MARK (Identify the mark) FROGWARE
	CLASS NO. (if known) 42

TO THE ASSISTANT SECRETARY AND COMMISSIONER OF PATENTS AND TRADEMARKS:

APPLICANT NAME:
Frogware, Inc.

APPLICANT BUSINESS ADDRESS:
2100 E. Flyville, Muddy Pond, Colorado 80116

APPLICANT ENTITY: (Check one and supply requested information)

☐ Individual - Citizenship: (Country) _____

☐ Partnership - Partnership Domicile: (State and Country) _____
Names and Citizenship (Country) of General Partners: _____

☒ Corporation - State (Country, if appropriate) of Incorporation: ___Colorado___

☐ Other: (Specify Nature of Entity and Domicile) _____

GOODS AND/OR SERVICES:

Applicant requests registration of the above-identified trademark/service mark shown in the accompanying drawing in the United States Patent and Trademark Office on the Principal Register established by the Act of July 5, 1946 (15 U.S.C. 1051 et. seq., as amended.) for the following goods/services: ___Fly Detection Software___

BASIS FOR APPLICATION: (Check one or more, but NOT both the first AND second boxes, and supply requested information)

☐ Applicant is using the mark in commerce or in connection with the above identified goods/services. (15 U.S.C. 1051(a), as amended.) Three specimens showing the mark as used in commerce are submitted with this application.
• Date of first use of the mark anywhere: _____
• Date of first use of the mark in commerce which the U.S. Congress may regulate:_____
• Specify the type of commerce: _____
   (e.g., interstate, between the U.S. and a specified foreign country)
• Specify manner or mode of use of mark on or in connection with the goods/services:_____
   (e.g., trademark is applied to labels, service mark is used in advertisements)

☒ Applicant has a bona fide intention to use the mark in commerce on or in connection with the above identified goods/services. (15 U.S.C. 1051(b), as amended.)
• Specify intended manner or mode of use of mark on or in connection with the goods/services:_____
   Labels
   (e.g., trademark will be applied to labels, service mark will be used in advertisements)

☐ Applicant has a bona fide intention to use the mark in commerce on or in connection with the above identified goods/services, and asserts a claim of priority based upon a foreign application in accordance with 15 U.S.C. 1126(d), as amended.
• Country of foreign filing: _____ • Date of foreign filing: _____

☐ Applicant has a bona fide intention to use the mark in commerce on or in connection with the above identified goods/services and, accompanying this application, submits a certification or certified copy of a foreign registration in accordance with 15 U.S.C. 1126(e), as amended.
• Country of registration:_____ • Registration number: _____

Note: Declaration, on Reverse Side, MUST be Signed

PTO Form 1478 (REV. 9/89)
OMB No. 06510009
Exp. 5-31-91

U.S. DEPARTMENT OF COMMERCE/Patent and Trademark Office

Form 4–1. Intent-to-use application.

DECLARATION

The undersigned being hereby warned that willful false statements and the like so made are punishable by fine or imprisonment, or both, under 18 U.S.C. 1001, and that such willful false statements may jeopardize the validity of the application or any resulting registration, declares that he/she is properly authorized to execute this application on behalf of the applicant; he/she believes the applicant to be the owner of the trademark/service mark sought to be registered, or, if the application is being filed under 15 U.S.C. 1051(b), he/she believes applicant to be entitled to use such mark in commerce; to the best of his/her knowledge and belief no other person, firm, corporation, or association has the right to use the above identified mark in commerce, either in the identical form thereof or in such near resemblance thereto as to be likely, when used on or in connection with the goods/services of such other person, to cause confusion, or to cause mistake, or to deceive; and that all statements made of his/her own knowledge are true and all statements made on information and belief are believed to be true.

_____   _____
Date   Signature

_____   _____
Telephone Number   Print or Type Name and Position

INSTRUCTIONS AND INFORMATION FOR APPLICANT

To receive a filing date, the application must be completed and **signed by the applicant** and submitted along with:

1. The prescribed fee for each class of goods/services listed in the application;
2. A drawing of the mark in conformance with 37 CFR 2.52;
3. If the application is based on use of the mark in commerce, three (3) specimens (evidence) of the mark as used in commerce for each class of goods/services listed in the application. All three specimens may be the same and may be in the nature of: (a) labels showing the mark which are placed on the goods; (b) a photograph of the mark as it appears on the goods, (c) brochures or advertisements showing the mark as used in connection with the services.

Verification of the application - The application must be signed in order for the application to receive a filing date. Only the following person may sign the verification (Declaration) for the application, depending on the applicant's legal entity: (1) the individual applicant; (b) an officer of the corporate applicant; (c) one general partner of a partnership applicant; (d) all joint applicants.

Additional information concerning the requirements for filing an application are available in a booklet entitled **Basic Facts about Trademarks,** which may be obtained by writing:

U.S. DEPARTMENT OF COMMERCE
Patent and Trademark Office
Washington, D.C. 20231

Or by calling: (703) 557-INFO

This form is estimated to take 15 minutes to complete. Time will vary depending upon the needs of the individual case. Any comments on the amount of time you require to complete this form should be sent to the Office of Management and Organization, U.S. Patent and Trademark Office, U.S. Department of Commerce, Washington D.C., 20231, and to the Office of Information and Regulatory Affairs, Office of Management and Budget, Washington, D.C. 20503.

Form 4-1. *(Continued)*

STATEMENT OF USE UNDER 37 CFR 2.88, WITH DECLARATION	MARK (Identify the mark) FROGWARE
	SERIAL NO. #007

TO THE ASSISTANT SECRETARY AND COMMISSIONER OF PATENTS AND TRADEMARKS:

APPLICANT NAME:
Frogware, Inc.

NOTICE OF ALLOWANCE ISSUE DATE:
June 15, 1990

Applicant requests registration of the above-identified trademark/service mark in the United States Patent and Trademark Office on the Principal Register established by the Act of July 5, 1946 (15 U.S.C. 1051 et. seq., as amended). Three (3) specimens showing the mark as used in commerce are submitted with this statement.

☐　Check here only if a Request to Divide under 37 CFR 2.87 is being submitted with this Statement.

Applicant is using the mark in commerce on or in connection with the following goods/services: (Check One)

☒　Those goods/services identified in the Notice of Allowance in this application.

☐　Those goods/services identified in the Notice of Allowance in this application except: (Identify goods/services to be deleted from application) _____

_____

Date of first use of mark anywhere: _____ January 1, 1991 _____

Date of first use of mark in commerce which the U.S. Congress may regulate: _____ January 1, 1991 _____

Specify type of commerce: (e.g., interstate, between the U.S. and a specified foreign country) _____
_____ Interstate _____

Specify manner or mode of use of mark on or in connection with the goods/services: (e.g., trademark is applied to labels, service mark is used in advertisements) _____ Labels _____

The undersigned being hereby warned that willful false statements and the like so made are punishable by fine or imprisonment, or both, under 18 U.S.C. 1001, and that such willful false statements may jeopardize the validity of the application or any resulting registration, declares that he/she is properly authorized to execute this Statement of Use on behalf of the applicant; he/she believes the applicant to be the owner of the trademark/service mark sought to be registered; the trademark/service mark is now in use in commerce; and all statements made of his/her own knowledge are true and all statements made on information and belief are believed to be true.

March 15, 1991
Date

1-303-333-3010
Telephone Number

I. M. Froggy
Signature

I.M. Froggy, President
Print or Type Name and Position

PTO Form 1580 (REV. 9/89)
OMB No. 06510023
Exp. 6-30-92

U.S. DEPARTMENT OF COMMERCE/Patent and Trademark Office

Form 4–2. Statement of use.

INSTRUCTIONS AND INFORMATION FOR APPLICANT

In an application based upon a bona fide intention to use a mark in commerce, applicant must use its mark in commerce before a registration will be issued. After use begins, the applicant must submit, along with evidence of use (specimens) and the prescribed fee(s), **either:**

> (1) an Amendment to Allege Use under 37 CFR 2.76, or
> (2) a Statement of Use under 37 CFR 2.88.

The difference between these two filings is the timing of the filing. Applicant may file an Amendment to Allege Use before approval of the mark for publication for opposition in the **Official Gazette**, or, if a final refusal has been issued, prior to the expiration of the six month response period. Otherwise, applicant must file a Statement of Use after the Office issues a Notice of Allowance. The Notice of Allowance will issue after the opposition period is completed if no successful opposition is filed. Neither Amendment to Allege Use or Statement of Use papers will be accepted by the Office during the period of time between approval of the mark for publication for opposition in the **Official Gazette** and the issuance of the Notice of Allowance.

Applicant may call (703) 557-5249 to determine whether the mark has been approved for publication for opposition in the **Official Gazette.**

Before filing an Amendment to Allege Use or a Statement of Use, applicant must use the mark in commerce on or in connection with **all** of the goods/services for which applicant will seek registration, **unless** applicant submits with the papers, a request to divide out from the application the goods or services to which the Amendment to Allege Use or Statement of Use pertains. (See: 37 CFR 2.87, Dividing an application)

Applicant **must** submit with an Amendment to Allege Use or a Statement of Use:

> (1) the appropriate fee of $100 per class of goods/services listed in the Amendment to Allege Use or the Statement of Use, and

> (2) three (3) specimens or facsimiles of the mark as used in commerce for each class of goods/services asserted (e.g., photograph of mark as it appears on goods, label containing mark which is placed on goods, or brochure or advertisement showing mark as used in connection with services).

Cautions/Notes concerning completion of this Statement of Use form:

> (1) The goods/services identified in the Statement of Use must be identical to the goods/services identified in the Notice of Allowance. Applicant may delete goods/services. Deleted goods/services may not be reinstated in the application at a later time.

> (2) Applicant may list dates of use for only one item in each class of goods/services identified in the Statement of Use. However, applicant must have used the mark in commerce on all the goods/services in the class. Applicant must identify the particular item to which the dates apply.

> (3) Only the following person may sign the verification of the Statement of Use, depending on the applicant's legal entity: (a) the individual applicant; (b) an officer of corporate applicant; (c) one general partner of partnership applicant; (d) all joint applicants.

This form is estimated to take 15 minutes to complete. Time will vary depending upon the needs of the individual case. Any comments on the amount of time you require to complete this form should be sent to the Office of Management and Organization, U.S. Patent and Trademark Office, U.S. Department of Commerce, Washington D.C., 20231, and to the Office of Information and Regulatory Affairs, Office of Management and Budget, Washington, D.C. 20503.

Form 4–2. *(Continued)*

REQUEST FOR EXTENSION OF TIME UNDER 37 CFR 2.89 TO FILE A STATEMENT OF USE, WITH DECLARATION	MARK (Identify the mark) FROGWARE
	SERIAL NO. #007

TO THE ASSISTANT SECRETARY AND COMMISSIONER OF PATENTS AND TRADEMARKS:

APPLICANT NAME:
Frogware, Inc.

NOTICE OF ALLOWANCE MAILING DATE:
June 15, 1990

Applicant requests a six-month extension of time to file the Statement of Use under 37 CFR 2.88 in this application.

☐ Check here if a Request to Divide under 37 CFR 2.87 is being submitted with this request.

Applicant has a continued bona fide intention to use the mark in commerce in connection with the following goods/services: (Check one below)

☒ Those goods/services identified in the Notice of Allowance in this application.

☐ Those goods/services identified in the Notice of Allowance in this application except: (Identify goods/services to be **deleted** from application) _____

_____

This is the ___1st___ request for an Extension of Time following mailing of the Notice of Allowance.
(Specify first - fifth)

If this is not the first request for an Extension of Time, check one box below. If the first box is checked, explain the circumstance(s) of the non-use in the space provided:

☐ Applicant has not used the mark in commerce yet on all goods/services specified in the Notice of Allowance; however, applicant has made the following ongoing efforts to use the mark in commerce on or in connection with each of the goods/services specified above:

_____

_____
If additional space is needed, please attach a separate sheet to this form

☐ Applicant believes that it has made valid use of the mark in commerce, as evidenced by the Statement of Use submitted with this request; however, if the Statement of Use is found by the Patent and Trademark Office to be fatally defective, applicant will need additional time in which to file a new statement.

The undersigned being hereby warned that willful false statements and the like so made are punishable by fine or imprisonment, or both, under 18 U.S.C. 1001, and that such willful false statements may jeopardize the validity of the application or any resulting registration, declares that he/she is properly authorized to execute this Request for Extension of Time to File a Statement of Use on behalf of the applicant; he/she believes the applicant to be the owner of the trademark/service mark sought to be registered; and all statements made of his/her own knowledge are true and all statements made on information and belief are believed to be true.

November 15, 1990	*I. M. Froggy*
Date	Signature
1-303-333-3010	I.M. Froggy, President
Telephone Number	Print or Type Name and Position

PTO Form 1581 (REV. 9/89)
OMB No. 06510023
Exp. 6-30-92

U.S. DEPARTMENT OF COMMERCE/Patent and Trademark Office

Form 4–3. Request for extension of time.

INSTRUCTIONS AND INFORMATION FOR APPLICANT

Applicant must file a Statement of Use within six months after the mailing of the Notice of Allowance in an application based upon a bona fide intention to use a mark in commerce, UNLESS, within that same period, applicant submits a request for a six-month extension of time to file the Statement of Use. The request **must**:

(1) be in writing,
(2) include applicant's verified statement of continued bona fide intention to use the mark in commerce,
(3) specify the goods/services to which the request pertains as they are identified in the Notice of Allowance, and
(4) include a fee of $100 for each class of goods/services.

Applicant may request four further six-month extensions of time. No extension may extend beyond 36 months from the issue date of the Notice of Allowance. Each request must be filed within the previously granted six-month extension period and must include, in addition to the above requirements, a showing of **GOOD CAUSE**. This good cause showing must include:

(1) applicant's statement that the mark has not been used in commerce yet on all the goods or services specified in the Notice of Allowance with which applicant has a continued bona fide intention to use the mark in commerce, **and**

(2) applicant's statement of ongoing efforts to make such use, which may include the following: (a) product or service research or development, (b) market research, (c) promotional activities, (d) steps to acquire distributors, (e) steps to obtain required governmental approval, or (f) similar specified activity .

Applicant may submit one additional six-month extension request during the existing period in which applicant files the Statement of Use, unless the granting of this request would extend beyond 36 months from the issue date of the Notice of Allowance. As a showing of good cause, applicant should state its belief that applicant has made valid use of the mark in commerce, as evidenced by the submitted Statement of Use, but that if the Statement is found by the PTO to be defective, applicant will need additional time in which to file a new statement of use.

Only the following person may sign the verification of the Request for Extentsion of Time, depending on the applicant's legal entity: (a) the individual applicant; (b) an officer of corporate applicant; (c) one general partner of partnership applicant; (d) all joint applicants.

This form is estimated to take 15 minutes to complete. Time will vary depending upon the needs of the individual case. Any comments on the amount of time you require to complete this form should be sent to the Office of Management and Organization, U.S. Patent and Trademark Office, U.S. Department of Commerce, Washington D.C., 20231, and to the Office of Information and Regulatory Affairs, Office of Management and Budget, Washington, D.C. 20503.

Form 4–3. *(Continued)*

RESOURCE: "The Trademark Revision Act of 1988," *The Trademark Reporter,* Vol. 79, No. 3 (United States Trademark Association) (May-June 1989). This is one of the first publications to analyze the new act.

§ 4.23   —Actual Use

To acquire ownership based on actual use, the trademark must be affixed to the product and used in commerce.[34] The first person to so appropriate and use the mark becomes the exclusive owner of the mark, at common law, in the territory of use. For federal protection, the use has to be in interstate commerce, and the actual use can either be a sale or transport across a state line.[35] States require a use in commerce within the state, and common law requires use within the territory of protection.

A great deal of case law exists as to what is a *bona fide* first use of a trademark. Clearly, there has to be a bona fide sale of the product with the mark followed by continued use. Some companies make token sales of the product with the trademark simply to establish the basis for common law, or for state or federal trademark rights. In the past, courts were liberal in supporting such token sales as long as they were not shams. The $3.60 sale of one case of soft drinks, however, with no other sales for several years has been held insufficient and representing a sham sale.[36] On the other hand, the single sale of a $1 million computerized fingerprint system followed by a period of sales solicitations but no actual sales, although token, has been held sufficient.[37]

A goal of the intent-to-use system of the Trademark Revision Act is to eliminate token use. With the right to file an intent-to-use application, there is no need to use the fiction of token sales to reserve marks as was previously done. It is anticipated that in the future the courts will not be as liberal as they were in the past. It is important that actual use constitute genuine business sales. The Revision Act requires that the use be in *the ordinary course of trade.* Without doubt, future litigation will hone the meaning of this definition.

A second requirement after the bona fide sale is the continuous use of the mark. The doctrines of bona fide first sale and continuous use are important doctrines since at common law "the first in time wins the territory."

---

[34] Blisscraft of Hollywood v. United Plastics Co., 294 F.2d 694, 131 U.S.P.Q. (BNA) 55 (2d Cir. 1961).

[35] *See* J. Thomas McCarthy, Trademarks and Unfair Competition § 19:37 at 962 (1984) (2d ed. 1988).

[36] CPC Int'l, Inc. v. Seven-Up Co., 218 U.S.P.Q. (BNA) 379 (T.T.A.B. 1983).

[37] Department of Justice v. Calspon Corp., 578 F.2d 295, 198 U.S.P.Q. (BNA) 147 (C.C.P.A. 1978).

It is not uncommon for competitors to be locked in a deadly battle based upon only a few months between first use dates. For example, in the landmark *Goodyear v. Big O* trademark battle in which a jury held Goodyear liable for $19.6 million, only five months separated Big O's first use date of the mark Bigfoot and Goodyear's first use date of Bigfoot.[38]

§ 4.24 —Purchase

A third way to acquire ownership of a trademark is to purchase it. This commonly occurs in the acquisition of a business or a product line. Sometimes a business will purchase a trademark simply to remove it as a source of potential infringement litigation, or to prevent it from infringing the business's existing trademark. Whatever the reason, the purchase of a trademark is legally straightforward. All that is needed is a simple assignment of the type set forth in **Form 4–4**. This form covers the three situations of common law, state, and federal registrations.

Form 4–4

ASSIGNMENT OF TRADEMARK

WHEREAS, Poorhorse Corp., a Colorado corporation whose principal place of business is 2320 S. Mustang, Muddy Falls, Colorado, warrants that it has adopted, used, and is using a trademark "Poorhorse" for dog food which is also registered in the Colorado Secretary of State's Office; and

WHEREAS, Good Food Corp., a Colorado corporation located and doing business at 660 Grocery Way, #200, Denver, Colorado, is desirous of acquiring the aforesaid trademark, its goodwill, and the Colorado registration thereof;

NOW THEREFORE, for valuable consideration, receipt of which is hereby acknowledged, Poorhorse Corp. grants and assigns unto Good Food Corp., all right, title, and interest in the trademark "Poorhorse" for dog food and the said Colorado registration No. 751632 of that mark, together with the goodwill symbolized by the trademark and the right to sue for past infringement.

This assignment is executed at Denver, Colorado, this 4th day of November 1989.

Poorhorse Corp.

By: _____   Date: _____

Title: _____

---

[38] Big O Tire Dealers, Inc. v. Goodyear Tire & Rubber Co., 408 F. Supp. 1219, 189 U.S.P.Q. (BNA) 17 (D. Colo. 1976) *aff'd and modified,* 561 F.2d 1365, 195 U.S.P.Q. (BNA) 417 (10th Cir. 1977), *cert. dismissed,* 434 U.S. 1052 (1978).

The Trademark Revision Act limits the assignability of intent-to-use applications to successors of the applicant's business.

While the assignment is straightforward, it is surprising how many trademark purchase situations are legally incomplete, thereby failing to transfer the trademark. A valid assignment conveying the mark must include the following key elements:

1. The transfer of all right, title and interest in the trademark
2. The transfer of the goodwill of the business associated with or symbolized by the mark
3. All common law rights and all state and federal registrations
4. The right to sue for past infringement.

Finally, if the mark has been registered either at the state level or the federal level, the assignment must be recorded. The fee for recording an assignment federally is $8.00, and the assignment should be mailed to: Commissioner of Patents & Trademarks, Washington, DC 20231, telephone (703) 557-3080.

§ 4.25   Trademark Grammar

The principles of trademark grammar are reminiscent of sixth-grade grammar. While boringly simple, they are drastically important principles, and ones that are often ignored by advertising agencies and businesses in general. Large companies with portfolios of trademarks publish small booklets that very precisely set forth the proper and improper use of corporate trademarks. One of the benefits of belonging to the United States Trademark Association is that members usually receive free copies of these booklets published by other members.

Maxim No. 1.   Never use a trademark as a noun.
   Improper Use: Buy your Poorhorse here.
   Proper Use: Buy your Poorhorse dog food here.

Maxim No. 2.   Never use a trademark as a verb.
   Improper Use: Poorhorse your dog with the finest dog food available.
   Proper Use: Buy Poorhorse dog food for your dog—the finest dog food available.

Maxim No. 3.   Never use a trademark as a plural.
   Improper Use: Buy Poorhorses for your kennel.
   Proper Use: Buy Poorhorse dog food for your kennel.

Maxim No. 4.   Never use a trademark as a possessive.
   Improper Use: Poorhorse's unique formula provides high quality nutrition.
   Proper Use: Poorhorse dog food's unique formula provides high quality nutrition.

Maxim No. 5.   Never use a trademark in other than the designated form.
   The integrity of the trademark should always be maintained. Abbreviations or spelling changes of the trademark should not be permitted; random insertion or deletion of hyphens must always be avoided; and a trademark that is normally two words should never be used as one word or vice versa.

Maxim No. 6.   Always use the trademark as an adjective.
   Improper Use: Try Poorhorse.
   Proper Use: Try Poorhorse dog food.
                 Try Poorhorse brand dog food.

Maxim No. 7.   Always use a trademark distinctively.
   The trademark is a valuable business asset. Raise the flag! Sound the horn! Set forth the trademark in all capital letters, or at least capitalize the first letter. In printed company materials make the trademark stand out from the rest of the words in the text: POORHORSE dog food is better than Poorhorse dog food.

   These maxims should be thoroughly discussed with internal marketing personnel and with external advertising agencies. In addition, standards should be set for lettering style, coloring, size, and the like.
   The proper grammatical use of trademarks is important. Improper use, as seen in the extensive list of former marks that are now generic words (aspirin, cellophane, etc.) can lead to loss of protection. In addition, improper trademark use can be used as evidence of *descriptiveness* of the mark in litigation. For example, a plaintiff suing to enforce its trademark Continuous Progress was found by a court to have used the term *continuous progress* in the ordinary sense to describe the educational concepts present in its products.[39] **Figures 4–4** and **4–5** illustrate the importance of proper trademark grammar.
   Trademark counsel must review all advertising in the proof stage to verify that trademarks are being used in the proper fashion. While this may seem to be an expensive loop in the process of advertising, it is not. The review by trademark counsel should only take a matter of minutes and through use of fax transmissions, quick turnaround can be obtained.

---

[39] Educational Dev. Corp. v. Economy Co., 562 F.2d 26, 195 U.S.P.Q. (BNA) 482 (10th Cir. 1977).

WE'RE TOUGH ABOUT TRADEMARKS!

Our products are champions. We've worked hard to earn our titles, and we don't want imitations in the ring.

Our lawyers say: "It is trademark infringement and unfair competition to manufacture, distribute, sell or advertise unauthorized merchandise featuring the trademarks or simulations of the trademarks of The Coca-Cola Company." Sound serious? It is. Those who disregard the law can wind up facing heavyweights in court.

How can you tell the real "Coca-Cola" or "Coke" brand merchandise from the pretenders? Look for our "Authorized Product" seal. It's on all authorized retail items bearing any of our trademarks. Ask your supplier for this proof. If you don't get it, don't buy the goods. And if **you** have been using our trademarks without permission, now's the time to stop.

We'd rather shake hands than deliver a knockout punch, but we **will** defend our trademarks. If your supplier can't give satisfactory proof of authorization, or if you want more information, please write:

Manager, Merchandise Licensing Department
The Coca-Cola Company
P.O. Drawer 1734
Atlanta, Georgia 30301
(404) 676-2737

Figure 4–4. Coca-Cola Company advertisement about proper trademark. Reprinted with permission.

XEROX

Once a trademark, not always a trademark.

They were once proud trademarks, now they're just names. They failed to take precautions that would have helped them have a long and prosperous life.

We need your help to stay out of there. Whenever you use our name, please use it as a proper adjective in conjunction with our products and services: e.g., Xerox

copiers or Xerox financial services. And never as a verb: "to Xerox" in place of "to copy," or as a noun: "Xeroxes" in place of "copies."

With your help and a precaution or two on our part, it's "Once the Xerox trademark, always the Xerox trademark."

Team Xerox. We document the world.

Figure 4–5. Xerox Corporation advertisement about the importance of trademark. Reprinted with permission.

§ 4.26   —Common Law Trademark Marking

Actually, there is no legal requirement at common law to mark your trademark. By convention, the abbreviations *TM* (trademark) and *SM* (service-mark) on the upper righthand corner of the trademark are used to identify trade or service marks :

POORHORSE™

Occasionally an asterisk is used, followed by a footnote at the bottom of the page:

POORHORSE*

*A trademark of Poorhorse Corp., Pueblo, Colorado.

The use of the abbreviations TM or SM is a self-help practice. Many trademarks have been protected at common law without the use of these markings. Clearly, use of such markings is helpful because it informs the consuming public and competitors to stand clear.

§ 4.27   —State Law Trademark Marking

Most states do not require the marking of trademarks registered in their state. Indeed, most owners of state registered trademarks simply follow the common law marking conventions set forth in **§ 4.26**. However, the following may be used:

POORHORSE*

*Registered Colorado Trademark

§ 4.28   —Federal Trademark Marking

The Lanham Act requires federally registered marks to be suitably marked. Failure to provide notice of federal registration precludes an award of damages and disgorgement of profits from an infringer unless the infringer had actual notice of the registration.[40] Likewise, if a company has not obtained federal registration and intentionally uses the federal marking, the federal Patent and Trademark Office may refuse to

---

[40] 15 U.S.C. § 1111 (1988).

register the mark and a court may render the mark unenforceable against an infringer.[41]

Three separate markings may be used to indicate federal registration:

1. POORHORSE®
2. POORHORSE*
   *Registered in U.S. Patent and Trademark Office
3. POORHORSE*
   *Reg. U.S. Pat. & Tm. Off.

Many clients question whether each appearance of the trademark in a page of advertising needs to be so marked. This becomes a question of discretion, aesthetics, and business practice. Clearly, if the mark is in danger of becoming generic, the encircled *R* notation should always be used. From a practical point of view, however, such religious marking is overkill and only the prominent uses of the trademark on the advertising page need to be marked. Please keep in mind that it is essential that all labels appearing on the product bear the encircled *R* notation.

A *house mark* is the overall mark used by a company. When a trademark also functions as a house mark, a combination of markings may be used effectively.

McDonald's® McD.L.T.® hamburgers
IBM™ Series II™ personal computers

§ 4.29   Policing Trademark Use

The use of a trademark style guide is important in controlling use of the trademark inside the company, as well as externally by licensees, suppliers, and customers. The trademark style guide performs an important educational function for a business. This is especially true in a franchise environment, because the franchisor must constantly control and supervise the use of the trademark by its franchisees. A franchisee must never be allowed to use the trademark in other than a strictly approved manner.

Large businesses also police and monitor the use of their trademarks by members of the public. For example, during the Watergate investigation when Senator Sam Irwin publicly stated that something was a bad "xerox" of a document, the Xerox Corp. quickly sent a polite letter to the senator reminding him that Xerox is a registered trademark and that it would be better to use the term "photocopy."

---

[41] Gear, Inc. v. L.A. Gear Cal., Inc., 670 F. Supp. 508, 4 U.S.P.Q.2d (BNA) 1192 (S.D.N.Y. 1987).

§ 4.30   Territorial Considerations

Territorial considerations involving the interplay of common law, state, and federal trademark rights are complex areas of the law. There are several basic concepts that corporate counsel and businesses should be familiar with.

§ 4.31   —Senior User of Trademark

Trademark law protects the senior user of a trademark in the territory of actual use. One of the most famous cases in this area is the Mattoon Burger King case.[42] As Burger King expanded its national franchise, it bumped into a small Burger King business in Mattoon, Illinois. Mattoon is located near the Champagne-Urbana campus of the University of Illinois. Because of the importance of the market area, a lawsuit was commenced, with the court ultimately holding that the senior user (the small Mattoon business) had exclusive rights in Mattoon, Illinois, and within a radius of 20 miles. These types of cases will always come up because, despite extensive clearance activity on the part of the trademark owner, it is simply impossible to uncover each and every use of a mark throughout the United States. The more extensive the trademark clearance search conducted, the smaller this type of risk will be.

If the clearance search does uncover a possible senior user of the trademark, any use of the mark makes the defense of an *innocent junior user* unavailable. The adoption of a trademark with knowledge of the senior use opens the door to an accounting for profits and/or punitive damages, as well as attorneys' fees.[43] This is a high risk area, and it is the duty of the junior user of the trademark to respect the senior user's exclusivity in its territory of use.

§ 4.32   —Innocent Junior Use of Trademark

A fundamental principle under the common law of trademarks is to allow two innocent entities to use the same trademark on the same product in remotely separate geographic areas. This was decided early by the United

---

[42] Burger King, Inc. v. Hoots, 403 F.2d 904, 159 U.S.P.Q. (BNA) 706 (7th Cir. 1968).

[43] Big O Tire Dealers, Inc. v. Goodyear Tire & Rubber Co., 408 F. Supp. 1219, 189 U.S.P.Q. (BNA) 17 (D. Colo. 1976), *aff'd and modified,* 561 F.2d 1365, 195 U.S.P.Q. (BNA) 417 (10th Cir. 1977), *cert. dismissed,* 434 U.S. 1052 (1978). *See also* 15 U.S.C. § 1117 (1988).

States Supreme Court in *Hanover Star Milling Co. v. Metcalf.*[44] This doctrine is still important today and there are many businesses that must use different trademarks in different geographic areas for their products.

Unfortunately, this judicial concept led to *"balkanizing"* and to the passage of the federal Lanham Act (see § **3.22**). The key factual inquiry in cases tried under the Lanham Act is that the junior user must be innocent; that is, the junior user must not have had knowledge of the senior use. Likewise, the two uses must not overlap geographically. As an extension of this doctrine, the Supreme Court in *United Drug Co. v. Theodore Rectanus Co.*[45] enjoined the senior user from entering into the geographical territory of the innocent junior user. Similarly, in the Mattoon case, even though Mattoon was the senior user and fully protected, it could not expand its territory outside of the protected area.[46]

§ 4.33   —Expansion by Senior User

At common law, it is incumbent upon the senior user of a trademark to achieve a national reputation for its trademark. When a national reputation is obtained, the junior user of the mark is no longer innocent and the senior user is able to expand throughout the United States. Without a national reputation, however, the senior user has to rely upon the *zone of natural expansion* doctrine and is required to use the following criteria to determine the extent of its zone of natural expansion:

1. How far is the senior user's actual location from a point on the perimeter of the zone of expansion?
2. What is the nature of the business and what is the actual market penetration?
3. Does the senior user's past expansion show a likelihood of continued expansion?
4. Is the alleged expansion as logical a step as those previously taken by the senior user?[47]

When a mark is federally registered, the registration constitutes *constructive notice* to all. This legally cuts off, as of the date of federal registration, the defense of an innocent junior user. Whether or not the junior user had actual knowledge, the federal registration supplies constructive

---

[44] 240 U.S. 403 (1916).

[45] 248 U.S. 90 (1918).

[46] *See* Food Fair Stores, Inc. v. Square Deal Mkt. Co., 206 F.2d 482, 98 U.S.P.Q. (BNA) 65 (D.C. Cir. 1953), *cert. denied,* 346 U.S. 937, 100 U.S.P.Q. (BNA) 447 (1954).

[47] J. Thomas McCarthy, *Trademarks and Unfair Competition,* § 27.10 at 220–21 (1988).

knowledge and thus has an important substantive advantage over common law.

In litigation, the date of federal registration is important. Prior to that date, a junior user can rely upon innocence and good faith and will be accorded all common law territories that it has acquired up until the date of federal registration. From that date forward, even though the senior user has not yet entered a territory, the federal registration forecloses the right of the junior user to enter into that territory. Simply stated, until the date of federal registration, the decision as to who owns what territory is dependent upon common law rules. This amounts to a land grab. After the date of federal registration, the registration itself serves as constructive notice and provides the right of the federal trademark owner to expand at a future date.

§ 4.34   —Constructive Use

Filing an intent-to-use application constitutes *constructive use*. This significantly affects the territorial considerations under common law as discussed in § 4.33. Look at the following examples. Assume that both parties are using the same mark on the same type of product.

Example 1:

June 1, 1990	Plaintiff files intent-to-use
Nov. 1, 1990	Defendant commences actual use
Feb. 1, 1991	Plaintiff commences actual use
Plaintiff wins:	*If* its application for intent-to-use is allowed;
	If it files a timely declaration of use; and
	If it is issued a principal registration.

Comment.   Plaintiff's constructive use date is June 1, 1990, and predates defendant's actual use date of November 1, 1990.

Example 2:

April 1, 1990	Defendant commences actual use
June 1, 1990	Plaintiff files intent-to-use
Feb. 1, 1991	Plaintiff commences actual use
Dec. 1, 1991	Plaintiff is issued principal registration

Defendant prevails in all territory prior to June 1, 1990; plaintiff is concurrent user in all territory after June 1, 1990.

Comment.   Plaintiff's constructive use date is June 1, 1990, and serves to establish rights for plaintiff in all geographic areas not accorded to defendant prior to June 1, 1990.

Example 3:

June 1, 1990	Plaintiff files intent-to-use
Dec. 1, 1991	Principal registration issues to plaintiff
Jan. 1, 1992	Defendant commences actual use

Plaintiff wins.

§ 4.35   Product Considerations

An equally complex doctrine relates to the actual determination of the scope of goods and services. A federal registration specifically recites the goods or services covered by the registration. If a good or service is not listed, a trademark owner cannot willy-nilly extend federal trademark protection to cover goods or services not listed therein.[48]

If the goods are noncompeting, the trademark owner may extend the trademark coverage to them based upon the following factors:

1.   What is the propensity of the company owning the trademark to expand into new products?[49]
2.   Does the mark have secondary meaning?[50]
3.   How famous is the mark?[51]
4.   What is the propensity of the owner company not to use differing trademarks on its various products?[52]

After receiving federal registration for a trademark, a company should review the federal registration at least once a year to see whether new goods or services are being offered or will be offered under the trademark. If so, it should give prime consideration to obtaining a new federal registration to cover the new goods or services. After a time, a portfolio of federal registrations in which the same trademark is registered for different goods and services will provide the company an important umbrella of protection for the trademark.

---

[48] Key Chems., Inc. v. Kelite Chems. Corp., 464 F.2d 1040, 175 U.S.P.Q. (BNA) 99 (C.C.P.A. 1972).

[49] W.E. Bassett Co. v. Revlon, Inc., 354 F.2d 868, 148 U.S.P.Q. (BNA) 170 (2d Cir. 1966).

[50] Id. at 872, 148 U.S.P.Q. (BNA) at 175 (2d Cir. 1966).

[51] Magnavox Co. v. Multivox Corp., 341 F.2d 139, 144 U.S.P.Q. (BNA) 501 (C.C.P.A. 1965).

[52] King Research, Inc. v. Shulton, Inc., 454 F.2d 66, 172 U.S.P.Q. (BNA) 321 (2d Cir. 1972).

§ 4.36   Federal Registration

The discussion in §§ **4.37** through **4.39** addresses, step-by-step, how to obtain a federal registration. Federal registration may be in the Principal or Supplemental Register and, other than filing an intent-to-use application, usually takes less than a year. The federal filing fee is $175 per class. Five identical specimens must accompany the application. **Table 4–1** sets forth the international classes.

Table 4–1

International Classes of Trademarks

CLASS	PRODUCTS
1	Chemicals
2	Paints
3	Cosmetics and Cleaning Preparations
4	Lubricants and Fuels
5	Pharmaceuticals
6	Metal Goods
7	Machinery
8	Hand Tools
9	Electrical and Scientific Apparatus
10	Medical Apparatus
11	Environmental Control Apparatus
12	Vehicles
13	Firearms
14	Jewelry
15	Musical Instruments
16	Paper Goods and Printed Matter
17	Rubber Goods
18	Leather Goods
19	Non-metallic Building Materials
20	Furniture and Articles Not Otherwise Classified
21	Housewares and Glass
22	Cordage and Fibers
23	Yarns and Threads
24	Fabrics
25	Clothing
26	Fancy Goods
27	Floor Coverings
28	Toys and Sporting Goods
29	Meats and Processed Foods
30	Staple Foods
31	Natural Agricultural Products
32	Light Beverages
33	Wines and Spirits
34	Smokers, Articles

Table 4–1 *(Continued)*

CLASS	SERVICES
35	Advertising and Business
36	Insurance and Financial
37	Construction and Repair
38	Communication
39	Transportation and Storage
40	Material Treatment
41	Education and Entertainment
42	Miscellaneous
200	Collective Membership
A	Certification Marks—Goods
B	Certification Marks—Services

RESOURCES:

1. Hawes, James E., *Trademark Registration Practice* (Clark Boardman, Ltd.: 375 Hudson St., New York, NY 10014) (1987) and Kramer, Barry and Allen D. Brufsky, *Trademark Law Practice Forms* (Clark Boardman, Ltd.: 375 Hudson St., New York, NY 10014) (1988) are two excellent sources for trademark registration practice and forms.

2. Pinckney, Francis, *Products Comparison Manual for Trademark Users* (Bureau of National Affairs, Inc.: Washington, DC 20037) (1988). This book provides information for properly categorizing goods and services.

§ 4.37 —Principal Register

Form 4–5 is used to apply for principal registration of a federal trademark in a single class. The form is filled in with the example of the Poorhorse mark for dog food. (This is the same form used for an intent-to-use application discussed in **§ 4.22**.)

Although the trademark application process appears to be simple, the application is carefully examined by a trademark examiner. The trademark examining section of the PTO is highly efficient and highly computerized. When the application is received, it is assigned to an examiner who does a thorough computer search of federally registered trademarks. If the examiner believes the mark is descriptive, the

TRADEMARK/SERVICE MARK APPLICATION, PRINCIPAL REGISTER, WITH DECLARATION	MARK (Identify the mark) POORHORSE
	CLASS NO. (If known) 31

TO THE ASSISTANT SECRETARY AND COMMISSIONER OF PATENTS AND TRADEMARKS:

APPLICANT NAME:
Joe Gill

APPLICANT BUSINESS ADDRESS:
2320 S. Mustang, Muddy Falls, Colorado 80116

APPLICANT ENTITY: (Check one and supply requested information)

[X] Individual - Citizenship: (Country) ____U.S.A._____

[ ] Partnership - Partnership Domicile: (State and Country) _____
Names and Citizenship (Country) of General Partners: _____

[ ] Corporation - State (Country, if appropriate) of Incorporation:_____

[ ] Other: (Specify Nature of Entity and Domicile) _____

GOODS AND/OR SERVICES:

Applicant requests registration of the above-identified trademark/service mark shown in the accompanying drawing in the United States Patent and Trademark Office on the Principal Register established by the Act of July 5, 1946 (15 U.S.C. 1051 et. seq., as amended.) for the following goods/services: Dog Food

BASIS FOR APPLICATION: (Check one or more, but NOT both the first AND second boxes, and supply requested information)

[X] Applicant is using the mark in commerce or in connection with the above identified goods/services. (15 U.S.C. 1051(a), as amended.) Three specimens showing the mark as used in commerce are submitted with this application.
* Date of first use of the mark anywhere: ___November 21, 1982___
* Date of first use of the mark in commerce which the U.S. Congress may regulate: _Nov. 21, 1982_
* Specify the type of commerce: _____Interstate_____
  (e.g., interstate, between the U.S. and a specified foreign country)
* Specify manner or mode of use of mark on or in connection with the goods/services:_____
  _____Labels_____
  (e.g., trademark is applied to labels, service mark is used in advertisements)

[ ] Applicant has a bona fide intention to use the mark in commerce on or in connection with the above identified goods/services. (15 U.S.C. 1051(b), as amended.)
* Specify intended manner or mode of use of mark on or in connection with the goods/services:_____

  (e.g., trademark will be applied to labels, service mark will be used in advertisements)

[ ] Applicant has a bona fide intention to use the mark in commerce on or in connection with the above identified goods/services, and asserts a claim of priority based upon a foreign application in accordance with 15 U.S.C. 1126(d), as amended.
* Country of foreign filing: _____   * Date of foreign filing: _____

[ ] Applicant has a bona fide intention to use the mark in commerce on or in connection with the above identified goods/services and, accompanying this application, submits a certification or certified copy of a foreign registration in accordance with 15 U.S.C. 1126(e), as amended.
* Country of registration:_____   * Registration number: _____

> **Note: Declaration, on Reverse Side, MUST be Signed**

PTO Form 1478 (REV. 9/89)
OMB No. 06510009
Exp. 5-31-91

U.S. DEPARTMENT OF COMMERCE/Patent and Trademark Office

Form 4–5. Application for principal register.

DECLARATION

The undersigned being hereby warned that willful false statements and the like so made are punishable by fine or imprisonment, or both, under 18 U.S.C. 1001, and that such willful false statements may jeopardize the validity of the application or any resulting registration, declares that he/she is properly authorized to execute this application on behalf of the applicant; he/she believes the applicant to be the owner of the trademark/service mark sought to be registered, or, if the application is being filed under 15 U.S.C. 1051(b), he/she believes applicant to be entitled to use such mark in commerce; to the best of his/her knowledge and belief no other person, firm, corporation, or association has the right to use the above identified mark in commerce, either in the identical form thereof or in such near resemblance thereto as to be likely, when used on or in connection with the goods/services of such other person, to cause confusion, or to cause mistake, or to deceive; and that all statements made of his/her own knowledge are true and all statements made on information and belief are believed to be true.

1-7-91	
Date	Signature
1-303-333-3010	Joe Gill, President
Telephone Number	Print or Type Name and Position

INSTRUCTIONS AND INFORMATION FOR APPLICANT

To receive a filing date, the application must be completed and **signed by the applicant** and submitted along with:

1. The prescribed fee for each class of goods/services listed in the application;
2. A drawing of the mark in conformance with 37 CFR 2.52;
3. If the application is based on use of the mark in commerce, three (3) specimens (evidence) of the mark as used in commerce for each class of goods/services listed in the application. All three specimens may be the same and may be in the nature of: (a) labels showing the mark which are placed on the goods; (b) a photograph of the mark as it appears on the goods, (c) brochures or advertisements showing the mark as used in connection with the services.

Verification of the application - The application must be signed in order for the application to receive a filing date. Only the following person may sign the verification (Declaration) for the application, depending on the applicant's legal entity: (1) the individual applicant; (b) an officer of the corporate applicant; (c) one general partner of a partnership applicant; (d) all joint applicants.

Additional information concerning the requirements for filing an application are available in a booklet entitled **Basic Facts about Trademarks**, which may be obtained by writing:

U.S. DEPARTMENT OF COMMERCE
Patent and Trademark Office
Washington, D.C. 20231

Or by calling: (703) 557-INFO

This form is estimated to take 15 minutes to complete. Time will vary depending upon the needs of the individual case. Any comments on the amount of time you require to complete this form should be sent to the Office of Management and Organization, U.S. Patent and Trademark Office, U.S. Department of Commerce, Washington D.C., 20231, and to the Office of Information and Regulatory Affairs, Office of Management and Budget, Washington, D.C. 20503.

Form 4–5. *(Continued)*

examiner also does a NEXIS search of newspaper articles and magazines to determine how descriptive the mark is. After conducting the searches, the examiner responds with an office action. The trademark applicant then has six months from the date of the office action in which to respond. Typically, a single response is all that is necessary to put the application in condition for allowance. If allowed by the examiner, the mark is published for opposition in the *Official Gazette*. An example is shown in **Figure 4–6**.

Any member of the public who believes she would be injured upon registration of the trademark has the right to file a notice of opposition with the Trademark Trial and Appeal Board (T.T.A.B.). An opposition proceeding is a miniature lawsuit conducted between the trademark applicant and the person alleging injury. Trademark watching services are available for monitoring marks published for opposition.

RESOURCES:

1. Thomson & Thomson, 500 E Street, S.W., #970, Washington, DC 20024-2710, telephone 1-800-356-8630, provides an excellent trademark watching service.
2. "Trademarks," *Official Gazette* (Superintendent of Documents, Government Printing Office: Washington, DC 20402); published weekly.

If no opposition is filed, the mark will be registered by the Patent and Trademark Office.

When the mark is registered, a listing such as the one shown in **Figure 4–7** will be made in the *Official Gazette*.

Once the mark has been federally registered, the owner has the exclusive right to use the mark throughout the United States. As mentioned in **§ 4.11**, the term of trademarks registered federally prior to November 16, 1989, is 20 years, whereas those marks registered after November 16, 1989, have a 10-year term.

After five years, the federal registrant must file a Section 8 and 15 Affidavit setting forth continuing use of the trademark. If the mark is no longer being used, there is no need to file this affidavit. If the affidavit of continued use is not filed, the mark will be cancelled from the federal rolls. However, if the mark is, in fact, in continuous use, filing the Section 8 and 15 Affidavit allows the registration to continue in force for the remainder of the term.

SN 73-824,237. AMERICAN OPTICAL CORPORATION, SOUTHBRIDGE, MA. FILED 9-8-1989.

PERMALITE

OWNER OF U.S. REG. NO. 907,984.
FOR OPTICAL LENSES (U.S. CL. 26).
FIRST USE 12-20-1980; IN COMMERCE 12-20-1980.

SN 73-824,940. SUBTLE CORPORATION, THE, BERKELEY, CA. FILED 9-11-1989.

FOR FASHION ACCESSORIES, NAMELY DECORATIVE SPECTACLE CORDS (U.S. CL. 26).
FIRST USE 8-5-1989; IN COMMERCE 8-5-1989.

SN 73-825,432. SORENSEN, THOMAS C., DBA TECHNEQUIP, ROSWELL, GA. FILED 9-14-1989.

HALOGUARD

FOR GAS LEAK MONITORS (U.S. CL. 21).
FIRST USE 7-26-1989; IN COMMERCE 7-26-1989.

SN 73-825,793. BABTECH ENTERPRISE COMPANY, INC., SAN JOSE, CA. FILED 9-18-1989.

FOR COMPUTER COMPONENTS, NAMELY, MOTHER BOARDS, INTERFACE CARDS, CONTROLLER CARDS, VIDEO CARDS, AND INPUT-OUTPUT (I-O) CONTROL CARDS (U.S. CL. 26).
FIRST USE 9-1-1989; IN COMMERCE 9-1-1989.

SN 73-826,117. LUCIDITY INSTITUTE, INC., THE, STANFORD, CA. FILED 9-18-1989.

DreamLight

FOR COMPUTERIZED BIOFEEDBACK APPARATUS CAPABLE OF FACILITATING LUCID DREAMS (U.S. CL. 26).
FIRST USE 9-1-1987; IN COMMERCE 1-17-1988.

Figure 4-6. Examples of trademarks published for opposition in *Official Gazette of the United States Patent Office.*

1,599,243. MULTI-CELL (STYLIZED). REPUBLIC STORAGE SYSTEMS COMPANY, INC., (U.S. CL. 23). SN 73–838,463. PUB. 3–13–1990. FILED 11–13–1989.

CLASS 8—HAND TOOLS

1,599,054 (See Class 1 for this trademark).
1,599,198 (See Class 6 for this trademark).
1,599,244. CHEFMASTER. CONAGRA, INC., MULTIPLE CLASS, (INT. CLS. 8 AND 21), (U.S. CLS. 13, 23 AND 50). SN 73–760,688. PUB. 12–5–1989. FILED 10–31–1988.
1,599,245. ANTOINE. ODABACH, ANTOINE, DBA ANTOINE DE PARIS, (U.S. CLS. 23 AND 44). SN 73–780,170. PUB. 3–13–1990. FILED 2–13–1989.
1,599,246. MISCELLANEOUS DESIGN. REED, D.L. WHITNEY, DBA DUALCO, (U.S. CL. 23). SN 73–802,029. PUB. 3–13–1990. FILED 5–18–1989.
1,599,247. MAINE SQUEEZE AND DESIGN. SCHOENERMARK, ERIK VON, DBA MAINE SQUEEZE COMPANY AND TA ERICK LLOYD, (U.S. CL. 23). SN 73–822,137. PUB. 3–13–1990. FILED 8–29–1989.
1,599,248. BIG SHOT. MINNESOTA MINING AND MANUFACTURING COMPANY, AKA 3M, (U.S. CL. 23). SN 73–832,624. PUB. 3–13–1990. FILED 10–20–1989.
1,599,249. BEACON. TOPCO ASSOCIATES, INC., (U.S. CL. 23). SN 73–836,532. PUB. 3–13–1990. FILED 11–6–1989.

CLASS 9—ELECTRICAL AND SCIENTIFIC APPARATUS

1,599,054 (See Class 1 for this trademark).
1,599,057 (See Class 1 for this trademark).
1,599,065 (See Class 1 for this trademark).
1,599,198 (See Class 6 for this trademark).
1,599,215 (See Class 7 for this trademark).
1,599,229 (See Class 7 for this trademark).
1,599,250. PROPER. SZAMITASTECHNIKAI KUTATO INTEZET ES INNOVACIOS KOZPONT, BY CHANGE OF NAME FROM SZAMITASTECHNIKAI KOORDINACIOS INTEZET, MULTIPLE CLASS, (INT. CLS. 9, 38 AND 42), (U.S. CLS. 21, 26, 100, 101 AND 104). SN 73–541,903. PUB. 5–24–1988. FILED 6–7–1985.
1,599,251. ASTEC INTERNATIONAL. ASTEC INTERNATIONAL LIMITED, (U.S. CL. 21). SN 73–594,090. PUB. 8–12–1986. FILED 4–18–1986.
1,599,252. COMPUTERPREP. COMPUTERPREP, INC., MULTIPLE CLASS, (INT. CLS. 9, 16 AND 41), (U.S. CLS. 38 AND 107). SN 73–596,571. PUB. 3–13–1990. FILED 5–2–1986.
1,599,253. CORREX EASI-PACK. AMCOR LIMITED, TA AUSTRALIAN PAPER MANUFACTURERS LTD., (U.S. CL. 38). SN 73–618,729. PUB. 3–13–1990. FILED 9–8–1986.
1,599,254. WILLIAMS AND DESIGN. WILLIAMS SIGN SUPPLIES LTD., (U.S. CLS. 21 AND 26). SN 73–640,236. PUB. 3–13–1990. FILED 1–16–1987.
1,599,255. NITON. NITON CORPORATION, (U.S. CL. 26). SN 73–651,154. PUB. 3–8–1988. FILED 3–24–1987.
1,599,256. PROPRINTER. INTERNATIONAL BUSINESS MACHINES CORPORATION, (U.S. CLS. 11 AND 26). SN 73–656,254. PUB. 3–13–1990. FILED 4–20–1987.
1,599,257. ROYAL BASE. VALHALL DATA AB, MULTIPLE CLASS, (INT. CLS. 9 AND 16), (U.S. CL. 38). SN 73–667,148. PUB. 3–13–1990. FILED 6–16–1987.
1,599,258. SCANET (STYLIZED). SKANDINAVISK DATACO A/S, MULTIPLE CLASS, (INT. CLS. 9 AND 42), (U.S. CLS. 26, 38, 100 AND 101). SN 73–679,246. PUB. 3–13–1990. FILED 8–18–1987.
1,599,259. NAZARENO CORSINI (STYLIZED). DEMENEGO OCCHIALI - LENTI OFTALMICHE S.R.L., (U.S. CL. 26). SN 73–693,070. PUB. 3–13–1990. FILED 11–2–1987.
1,599,260. LECO AND DESIGN. LECO CORPORATION, (U.S. CL. 26). SN 73–696,605. PUB. 9–19–1989. FILED 11–20–1987.

1,599,261. BIONAIRE H20 AND DESIGN. BIONAIRE INC., BY CHANGE OF NAME FROM BIOTECH ELECTRONICS LTD., MULTIPLE CLASS, (INT. CLS. 9 AND 11), (U.S. CLS. 26 AND 31). SN 73–711,212. PUB. 1–16–1990. FILED 2–16–1988.
1,599,262. AUTOSWING. BROOKES AND GATEHOUSE LIMITED, DBA B&G, (U.S. CL. 26). SN 73–728,108. PUB. 3–13–1990. FILED 5–13–1988.
1,599,263. SDM (STYLIZED). SCIENTIFIC DATA MANAGEMENT, INC., (U.S. CL. 38). SN 73–730,149. PUB. 3–13–1990. FILED 5–23–1988.
1,599,264. DISK MANAGER-N. ONTRACK COMPUTER SYSTEMS, INC., (U.S. CL. 38). SN 73–731,492. PUB. 8–1–1989. FILED 5–31–1988.
1,599,265. NYTALK. HUMMINGBIRD COMMUNICATIONS LTD., (U.S. CLS. 21 AND 38). SN 73–734,651. PUB. 3–13–1990. FILED 6–16–1988.
1,599,266. KNOWLEDGE FINDER (STYLIZED). ARIES SYSTEMS CORPORATION, (U.S. CL. 38). SN 73–738,525. PUB. 12–13–1988. FILED 7–1–1988.
1,599,267. THE PSYCHOLOGICAL CORPORATION. PSYCHOLOGICAL CORPORATION, THE, MULTIPLE CLASS, (INT. CLS. 9, 16, 41 AND 42), (U.S. CLS. 21, 36, 37, 38, 100 AND 107). SN 73–741,709. PUB. 3–13–1990. FILED 7–22–1988.
1,599,268. TOPCAD (STYLIZED). GRAPHISOFT SZAMITASTECHNIKAI GMK., (U.S. CL. 38). SN 73–755,218. PUB. 11–28–1989. FILED 9–30–1988.
1,599,269. JKSIMMET. UNIQUEST LIMITED, (U.S. CL. 38). SN 73–756,554. PUB. 3–13–1990. FILED 10–7–1988.
1,599,270. REKEY (STYLIZED). INFORMATION CONCEPTS, INC., (U.S. CL. 38). SN 73–757,264. PUB. 3–13–1990. FILED 10–12–1988.
1,599,271. REMOTETALK. DATASPACE CORPORATION. (U.S. CL. 38). SN 73–757,707. PUB. 3–13–1990. FILED 10–14–1988.
1,599,272. CPS CAPSCO PALLM SYSTEMS (STYLIZED). CAPSCO PALLM SYSTEMS, INC., (U.S. CL. 38). SN 73–758,273. PUB. 3–13–1990. FILED 10–17–1988.
1,599,273. DH (STYLIZED). MODA SOLARIS S.P.A., (U.S. CL. 26). SN 73–758,855. PUB. 3–13–1990. FILED 10–14–1988.
1,599,274. FONBLOK L. GUARDIAN MONITOR, INC., (U.S. CL. 21). SN 73–759,646. PUB. 3–13–1990. FILED 10–24–1988.
1,599,275. T AND DESIGN. TELEPANEL INC., (U.S. CLS. 21, 26 AND 38). SN 73–759,796. PUB. 3–13–1990. FILED 10–25–1988.
1,599,276. HARDPAC. ARISTOTLE INDUSTRIES INC., (U.S. CL. 26). SN 73–759,920. PUB. 3–13–1990. FILED 10–26–1988.
1,599,277. STD. STD COMPUTER INC., (U.S. CL. 26). SN 73–760,104. PUB. 3–13–1990. FILED 10–27–1988.
1,599,278. WORK-A-DOGS. GANEW IDEAS, MULTIPLE CLASS, (INT. CLS. 9 AND 16), (U.S. CLS. 14, 37 AND 38). SN 73–762,610. PUB. 3–13–1990. FILED 11–8–1988.
1,599,279. UNIFRAME. COMPAGNIE EUROPEENNE DES TECHNIQUES DE L'INGENIERIE ASSISTEE, (U.S. CL. 26). SN 73–766,288. PUB. 3–13–1990. FILED 11–29–1988.
1,599,280. EXPRESS 850. MOTOROLA, INC., (U.S. CL. 21). SN 73–766,614. PUB. 3–13–1990. FILED 12–1–1988.
1,599,281. HUBER + SUHNER. HUBER + SUHNER AG, MULTIPLE CLASS, (INT. CLS. 9 AND 17), (U.S. CLS. 16 AND 21). SN 73–768,479. PUB. 6–20–1989. FILED 12–9–1988.
1,599,282. RX 17. SUTPHEN, RICHARD, (U.S. CL. 36). SN 73–768,931. PUB. 3–13–1990. FILED 12–12–1988.
1,599,283. ADL/SF AND DESIGN. SAN FRANCISCO NEWSPAPER PRINTING CO., INC., DBA SAN FRANCISCO NEWSPAPER AGENCY, (U.S. CL. 38). SN 73–769,418. PUB. 5–9–1989. FILED 12–14–1988.
1,599,284. FLOTATION TECHNOLOGIES AND DESIGN. FLOTATION TECHNOLOGIES, INC., (U.S. CL. 26). SN 73–771,671. PUB. 3–13–1990. FILED 12–27–1988.
1,599,285. CENTRAL POINT SOFTWARE INCORPORATED (STYLIZED). CENTRAL POINT SOFTWARE, INC., (U.S. CL. 38). SN 73–772,063. PUB. 3–13–1990. FILED 12–28–1988.

Figure 4–7. *Official Gazette of the United States Patent Office* listing of registered trademarks.

§ 4.38 —Advantages of Principal Registration

Federal registration in the Principal Register enables the recovery of profits, damages, and costs. It further provides the possibility of treble damages and, in exceptional cases, the recovery of attorneys' fees.[53] The federal registration itself is prima facie evidence of ownership and the exclusive right to use the mark on the goods listed in the registration.[54] Registration is also prima facie evidence of continued usage of the mark from at least as early as the filing date of the application for registration,[55] provided that the mark is not confusingly similar to other marks,[56] has been used in interstate commerce,[57] and is valid.[58]

After five years of continuous use and upon the acceptance of the Section 8 and 15 Affidavit, the registration becomes *incontestable,*[59] that is, it provides conclusive evidence of the registrant's right to use the mark. It is important to note that a distinction exists between *prima facie* and *conclusive* evidence. In litigation, prima facie evidence may be rebutted and overcome by the opposing party. However, conclusive evidence is simply that—it is conclusive and cannot be rebutted. While incontestable marks are quite formidable, they are not completely free from attack. In fact, the Lanham Act delineates seven specific defenses that can be raised by an alleged infringer in trademark litigation cases.[60] These defenses are:

1. The mark was obtained through fraud.
2. The mark was abandoned.
3. The source of the goods or services of the trademark was misrepresented.
4. The trademark is an individual's name, is descriptive of the product, or is geographically descriptive of the product.
5. The alleged infringer is actually a senior user of the mark.

---

[53] 15 U.S.C. § 1117 (1988).

[54] 15 U.S.C. §§ 1057(b), 1115(a) (1988).

[55] J.C. Hall Co. v. Hallmark Cards, Inc., 340 F.2d 960, 144 U.S.P.Q. (BNA) 435 (C.C.P.A. 1965).

[56] Liberty Mutual Ins. Co. v. Liberty Ins. Co., 185 F. Supp. 895, 127 U.S.P.Q. (BNA) 312 (E.D. Ark. 1960).

[57] Maternally Yours, Inc. v. Your Maternity Shop, 234 F.2d 538, 110 U.S.P.Q. (BNA) 462 (2d Cir. 1956).

[58] Aluminum Fabricating Co. v. Season-All Window Corp., 259 F.2d 314, 119 U.S.P.Q. (BNA) 61 (2d Cir. 1958).

[59] 15 U.S.C. § 1121 (1988). *See also* Union Carbide Corp. v. Ever-Ready, Inc., 531 F.2d 366, 188 U.S.P.Q. (BNA) 623 (7th Cir. 1976), *cert. denied,* 429 U.S. 830 (1976).

[60] 15 U.S.C. § 1115(b) (1988).

6. The alleged infringer's mark was registered and used prior to the registration.

7. The mark is being used to violate antitrust laws.

All owners of federally registered marks must be careful to timely file the Section 8 and 15 Affidavit at five years and to timely renew the federal registration at either 10 or 20 years. The equitable defenses of laches, estoppel, and acquiescence are available to attack an incontestable registration.[61]

§ 4.39   —Supplemental Register

The Supplemental Register is a separate register in the PTO and registers *merely descriptive* marks. To qualify for registration on the Supplemental Register, marks registered prior to the Trademark Revision Act of 1988 (see § 4.11) must have been in use for at least one year.[62] After five years on the Supplemental Register, the registrant can transfer the mark to the Principal Register.[63] Typically, if the examiner of a trademark application for registration on the Principal Register believes the mark is too descriptive, the examiner will suggest registration on the Supplemental Register. Whenever the examiner rejects the mark as being merely descriptive, the applicant should consider transfer to the Supplemental Register.

Supplemental registration confers no substantive rights whatsoever. The advantage of registering on the Supplemental Register is to foreclose other registrations. In other words, the mark becomes part of the pool of marks for the examiner to use in rejecting the same or similar marks submitted by others in the future.

Under the Trademark Revision Act, the requirement that the trademark be in use for at least one year prior to filing for supplemental registration is no longer required. It is important to note that an intent-to-use application cannot be filed in the Supplemental Register. Registration in the Supplemental Register does not mean that the mark is not distinctive.[64]

---

[61] *Id.*

[62] 15 U.S.C. § 1091 (1988).

[63] *See In re* Wampole Ltd., 227 U.S.P.Q. (BNA) 74 (T.T.A.B. 1985); *In re* Research & Trading Corp., 793 F.2d 1276, 230 U.S.P.Q. (BNA) 49 (Fed. Cir. 1986). *See also* 15 U.S.C. § 1052(f) (1988); 15 U.S.C. § 1091(4)(c) (1988).

[64] *See* 15 U.S.C. § 1095 (1988); California Cooler, Inc. v. Loretto Winery, Ltd., 774 F.2d 1451, 1454, 227 U.S.P.Q. (BNA) 808, 809–10 (9th Cir. 1985).

§ 4.40   Licensing Trademarks

In licensing trademarks, the control of quality by the licensor over the licensee is paramount. Licensing of trademarks and quality control are the foundation of modern franchising. Without doubt, whether you walk into a Wendy's in Los Angeles or in Boise, the quality of the atmosphere, the food, and the service is substantially the same. The licensor, however, cannot exercise the type of control that constitutes a violation of the antitrust laws. For example, the Chicken Delight franchisor could not require its franchisees to buy specific brands of commonplace articles, because to do so would violate the antitrust laws.[65] On the other hand, the Baskin-Robbins franchisor was allowed to require its franchisees to purchase their ice cream from designated sources in order to maintain the quality of the ice cream product to the consuming public.[66] Quality control is also important in the merchandising of a trademark. For example, the National Football League has an extensive licensing program for its various trademarks. Again, the quality of the final product to the consuming public is of concern and the licensor, in the agreement, seeks to maintain this quality.

An example of a licensing agreement maintaining quality control of the product sold by the licensee is set forth in **Form 4-6**.

Form 4-6
EXCLUSIVE TRADEMARK LICENSE

Poorhorse Corp., a Montana corporation located and doing business at 100 Hardy Avenue, Havre, Montana, is the owner of the trademark "Poorhorse" and trademark application Serial No. 1,011,011 filed thereon; and

Abacus, Inc., located and doing business at Gorilla Lakes, Florida, is desirous of using the trademark on dog food; and

The parties agree as follows:

Poorhorse Corp. hereby grants an exclusive license to Abacus, Inc., to use the trademark "Poorhorse" on dog food.

Abacus, Inc., agrees that it will pay to Poorhorse Corp. as royalty the sum of $1,000 dollars upon the signing of this agreement and 10 percent (10%) of the net selling price of each item sold bearing the trademark "Poorhorse." Net selling price shall mean gross price less trade discounts, allowances, and returns. Such payments shall be made annually.

It is expressly agreed between the parties that Poorhorse Corp. retains full ownership of the trademark "Poorhorse" and application Serial No. 1,011,011 and any registration granted thereon. This license shall extend only to any registration granted on said application but not to any others.

---

[65] Siegel v. Chicken Delight, Inc., 448 F.2d 43, 171 U.S.P.Q. (BNA) 269 (9th Cir. 1971), *cert. denied,* 405 U.S. 955 (1972).

[66] Krehl v. Baskin-Robbins Ice Cream Co., 664 F.2d 1348 (9th Cir. 1982).

Abacus, Inc., agrees to maintain the quality of goods sold under the trademark "Poorhorse" according to the quality standards set forth by Poorhorse Corp. and attached herewith. Poorhorse Corp. reserves the right to inspect the quality of the goods sold under the trademark to ensure that the quality is as above required.

This license shall be effective as of _____, 19____.

                                        Poorhorse Corp.

_____   By: _____
Date   (Name and Title)

                                        Abacus, Inc.

_____   By: _____
Date   (Name and Title)

Whether a franchise program is embarked upon, a merchandising program is created, or the mark is simply licensed to another, the Lanham Act places a clear duty upon the licensor to take reasonable measures to protect and prevent misleading uses of its mark.[67]

Failure by the licensee to adhere to the quality control requirements of the license agreement constitutes a breach of the license and trademark infringement.[68] Failure by the licensor to control the quality of the licensee's products constitutes *naked licensing.* Courts consider naked licensing to be a fraud on the public that results in cancellation of the licensor's trademark.[69]

The Revision Act specifically permits trademark rights to be acquired by the licensor, even though the first use of the mark is made by a licensee or a related company.[70]

§ 4.41 Loss of Trademark Rights

The law imposes a number of duties on the owner of a trademark. Failure to perform these duties may well result in the loss of all trademark rights. For example, not using a trademark may result in its abandonment. Ten years of nonuse of the trademark Century 21 constituted abandonment by

---

[67] Dawn Donut Co. v. Hart's Food Stores, Inc., 267 F.2d 358, 121 U.S.P.Q. (BNA) 430 (2d Cir. 1959).

[68] Joseph Bancroft & Sons Co. v. Shelley Knitting Mills, Inc., 212 F. Supp.715 (E.D. Pa. 1962).

[69] Yamamoto & Co. (Am.), Inc. v. Victor United, Inc., 219 U.S.P.Q. (BNA) 968 (C.D. Cal. 1982).

[70] 15 U.S.C. § 1055 (1988).

a local company, allowing the national franchise to expand into Wisconsin.[71] Abandonment can also be intentional.[72]

Assigning a trademark without assigning goodwill is an assignment in gross and results in the loss of trademark rights.[73] If a mark is improperly used by others and becomes part of the common language, then the mark may become generic. Discontinued, sporadic, or lack of use of a trademark may constitute abandonment. The Lanham Act specifically holds that nonuse in two consecutive years shall be prima facie abandonment.[74]

§ 4.42   Security Interests

Security interests in trademarks are usually obtained by financial institutions and others under the Uniform Commercial Code (UCC).[75] A trademark is a general intangible in which a security interest can be perfected by filing. To do so, the secured party should ascertain the status of title to the trademark by first doing a trademark search.

It is important for the security agreement to be accompanied by an assignment of the trademark and its associated goodwill, plus a certain minimum of assets necessary for the creation or sale of the product or service. The collateral assignment should also include an assignment of the right to maintain suits for past infringement.

RESOURCE: Bahrick, "Security Interests in Intellectual Property," *AIPLA Quarterly Journal,* Vol. 15, pp. 30–49 (1987).

The perfection of a security interest in other general intangibles includes filing a UCC-1 filing statement with the appropriate state governmental office. Because the Lanham Act requires mandatory filing of trademark assignments, such security interests are usually also filed with the PTO. However, the security interest is perfected according to state procedures (such as filing a UCC financing statement) and not by filing with the PTO.[76]

---

[71] Century 21 Real Estate Co. v. Live Say & Mohrs, 26 Pat. Trademark & Copyright J. 280 (BNA) (1983).

[72] Intrawest Fin. Corp. v. Western Nat'l Bank, 610 F. Supp. 950, 227 U.S.P.Q. (BNA) 27 (D. Colo. 1985).

[73] Schneider Brewing Co. v. Century Distilling Co., 107 F.2d 699, 43 U.S.P.Q. (BNA) 262 (10th Cir. 1939).

[74] 15 U.S.C. § 1127 (1988).

[75] U.C.C. § 9-106 (1987).

[76] *In re* Roman Cleanser Co., 43 Bankr. 940, 225 U.S.P.Q. (BNA) 140 (Bankr. E.D. Mich. 1984), *aff'd,* 802 F.2d 207, 231 U.S.P.Q. (BNA) 301 (6th Cir. 1986).

§ 4.43   Infringement

Trademark infringement represents an area of high emotion—and perhaps significant legal fees. Usually the defendant being asked to change its trademark reacts as if being asked to change its personal name. The plaintiff, especially if it is a larger corporation, views the defendant's infringement as an attempt to ride on the plaintiff's fine reputation. Both sides may become emotionally charged. Trademark litigation can be prolonged, in some cases costing several million dollars in attorneys' fees, and the judge, acting as the protector of the public, has to make the final decision. In §§ **4.44** through **4.54**, the elements of trademark infringement lawsuits are discussed, as well as the available remedies. One of the purposes of this chapter is to minimize the risk of trademark infringement litigation. By thoroughly searching out the trademark and by seeking a distinctive mark rather than a descriptive mark, the risk of infringement litigation will be minimized.

What about bringing an infringement action based upon an intent-to-use application? In the Trademark Revision Act, no remedy is expressly provided. It is unclear whether any relief exists, although it is speculated that a creative remedy under the new Section 43(a) may be available.[77]

§ 4.44   —Likelihood of Confusion

Trademark infringement involves the determination of a *likelihood of confusion* between two marks by members of the consuming public. The likelihood of confusion test is also used by the PTO in determining whether to allow a trademark application or an intent-to-use application. In evaluating the likelihood of confusion, it is not proper to make a side-by-side comparison of the two marks.[78] The *Restatement of Torts* sets forth a sight, sound, and meaning test.[79]

The first subtest involves the *similarity of appearance.* When the visual appearance of a rearing horse and rider logo, for example, was compared to the visual appearance of a fighting buffaloes logo for oil and gas service stations, a likelihood of confusion was found.[80] In another case in which the plaintiff's and defendant's marks were only one millimeter across, the court found a visual likelihood of confusion.[81]

---

[77] Leeds, *Intent to Use—Its Time Has Come,* 79 Trademark Rep. 269, 284 (1989). *See* 15 U.S.C.S. § 1125b (Law. Co-op. 1988).

[78] Beer Nuts v. Clover Club, 711 F.2d 934, 221 U.S.P.Q. (BNA) 209 (10th Cir. 1983).

[79] Restatement of Torts, § 729 (1938). *See also* Dawn Donut Co. v. Day, 450 F.2d 332, 171 U.S.P.Q. (BNA) 453 (10th Cir. 1971).

[80] Blue Bell Co. v. Frontier Ref. Co., 215 F.2d 354, 101 U.S.P.Q. (BNA) 360 (10th Cir. 1954).

[81] Franklin Mint Corp. v. Master Mfg. Co., 212 U.S.P.Q. (BNA) 233 (C.C.P.A. 1981).

Phonetic similarity is the second subtest. For example, *Seiko* and *Seycos,* both used for watches, were found to be phonetically similar.[82]

The third subtest, *similarity of meaning,* is best represented by the following example. The use of Tornado on wire fencing was found to be confusingly similar to Cyclone on wire fencing.[83]

In light of these subtests and the examples illustrating them, the entire system of trademark protection seems questionable. Who would think to do a trademark clearance search for fighting buffaloes when the logo involves a horse and rider? Who would think to do a clearance search on Cyclone when the mark is Tornado? These are good questions, but not easy to answer. Trademark clearance searches can be no more than best guesses based upon the available information.

In addition to the sight, sound, and meaning subtests set forth in the *Restatement,* other subtests are also used by the courts to evaluate the likelihood of confusion.

The *channels of trade* subtest is often applied. If the channels of trade in which the two products are sold are separate and different, it is not likely that the buyers would be confused. For example, no confusion was found between Bigfoot for snowmobile track belts and Bigfoot for automobile tires.[84] But confusion was found between Nutra-Sweet for artificial sweeteners and Nutra Salt for table salt.[85]

Another subtest relates to how *directly competitive* the two products are with each other. According to the Supreme Court in *United States v. E.I. Du Pont de Nemours & Co.,*[86] competitive goods are those goods that are reasonably interchangeable by buyers for the same purposes. In this case, cellophane was held to be competitive with other types of wrapping materials. Even if the goods themselves are not directly competitive, a likelihood of confusion may still be found.[87]

The *degree of care* employed by the consumer constitutes another subtest.[88] This is determined by how casual the purchase is, how much the product costs, and the education and sophistication of the purchaser.[89]

---

[82] Kabushiki Kaisha Hattori Tokeiten v. Scuotto, 228 U.S.P.Q. (BNA) 461 (T.T.A.B. 1985).

[83] Hancock v. American Steel & Wire Co., 203 F.2d 737, 97 U.S.P.Q. (BNA) 330 (C.C.P.A. 1953).

[84] Big O Tire Dealers, Inc. v. Goodyear Tire & Rubber Co., 408 F. Supp. 1219, 189 U.S.P.Q. 17 (D. Colo. 1976), *aff'd and modified,* 561 F.2d 1365, 195 U.S.P.Q. 417 (10th Cir. 1977), *cert. dismissed,* 434 U.S. 1052 (1978).

[85] NutraSweet Co. v. K&S Foods, Inc., 4 U.S.P.Q.2d (BNA) 1964 (T.T.A.B. 1987).

[86] 351 U.S. 377 (1956).

[87] J.C. Penney Co. v. Artic Enters., Inc., 375 F. Supp. 913, 183 U.S.P.Q. (BNA) 342 (D. Minn. 1974).

[88] *Id.*

[89] Educational Dev. Corp. v. Economy Co., 562 F.2d 26, 195 U.S.P.Q. (BNA) 482 (10th Cir. 1977).

For example, the court may be more prone to find a likelihood of confusion between two trademarks involving a price of less than $10 or between two products found at a local convenience store. A higher standard for finding a likelihood of confusion would be used by the court when the purchase involves a $50,000 luxury car.[90]

The *strength of a famous mark* may be given consideration. Famous and well-known trademarks are accorded broader trademark protection than less famous ones. For example, the use of Seiko for tennis rackets infringes the use of Seiko for watches.[91] It is not uncommon for a single trademark infringement case to involve a consideration of all of the above factors and subtests. An example was the finding of no likelihood of confusion between Wuvs and Love's.[92]

It may be difficult to prove a "likelihood of confusion" in certain cases. The presence and importance of "actual confusion" should not be overlooked. Evidence of "actual confusion" may be vital in winning a trademark infringement case. It is prudent for a business (especially a franchise or a company having many distributors) to monitor for the presence of "actual confusion" as found in **Form 4–7**.

Form 4-7
DOCUMENTATION FOR CONFUSION OVER TRADEMARKS

Dear Distributor:

Occasionally, situations arise in dealing with members of the public wherein persons become confused between our trademark POORHORSE and the name or trademark of another product because the trademarks are so similar. Because POORHORSE is a federally registered trademark and because it is one of our most valuable assets, these instances of confusion must be carefully documented.

The sources of confusion may take on many forms. It may, for example, be misdirected mail or misplaced phone calls. It may be the result of a person calling in for information. It may be the delivery of goods to the wrong party. Or, it may take other forms not mentioned.

However, whenever such an instance of actual confusion is encountered, our attorneys advised us that the following must be done:

1. Record the time and date.
2. Ascertain the name, address and telephone number of the person confused.

---

[90] *Id.*

[91] Seiko Sporting Goods USA, Inc. v. Kabushiki Kaisha Hattori Tokeiten, 545 F. Supp. 221, 216 U.S.P.Q. (BNA) 129 (S.D.N.Y.), *aff'd,* 697 F.2d 276 (2d Cir. 1982).

[92] Wuv's Int'l, Inc. v. Love's Enters., Inc., 208 U.S.P.Q. (BNA) 736 (D. Colo. 1980).

3.   Set forth the details of the instance of confusion (e.g., they called in for information concerning dog food).

4.   Set forth what was done in response to the actual confusion (e.g., mail returned to post office, person directed to proper phone number, etc.).

5.   Make copies of documents, if any, showing the confusion (e.g., copy of the mail envelope).

6.   If possible, all of the above should be filled out on a form such as the attached sheet and notarized by a notary public.

Poorhorse, Inc., is only interested in instances of confusion concerning one of its valuable trademarks and not other situations—such as a misdialed phone number.

Please advise all personnel in your offices of this procedure. Thank you for your cooperation in this matter.

_____

Signature

(Attach the following affidavit to the above letter.)

AFFIDAVIT OF ACTUAL CONFUSION

DATE: _____TIME: _____

NAME, ADDRESS & PHONE NUMBER OF PERSON FILLING OUT THIS FORM:

_____

_____

_____

Relation to Poorhorse, Inc.: _____

NAME, ADDRESS & PHONE NUMBER OF CONFUSED PERSON:

_____

_____

_____

Relation, if any, to Poorhorse, Inc.: _____

TIME, DATE & DETAILS OF INSTANCE OF CONFUSION:

(e.g., misdirected mail or phone call, name of actual party the person was trying to contact, why and how a person thought POORHORSE was somehow associated with POORHORSE dog food, the name or mark causing the confusion)

_____

_____

_____

MY RESPONSE TO THE CONFUSED PARTY:

(e.g., directed the person to phone book or telephone operator, gave the person the current telephone number and/or address of desired party, returned or forwarded mail to any other party and advised the party of the difference in spelling between the two trademarks)

_____

_____

_____

_____

HAVE YOU ATTACHED COPIES OF DOCUMENTS SHOWING CONFUSION?

_____ YES_____ NO

If yes, please describe:

_____

_____

_____

(Signature of Person Filling out Form)

STATE OF:

  : ss.

COUNTY OF:

Before me, a Notary Public in and for the said County and State, personally appeared _____ known to me to be the person whose name is subscribed to the foregoing instrument, and acknowledges to me that he executed the same for the purposes and considerations therein expressed.

Given under my hand and seal of office this _____ day of _____, 19 ____.

My commission expires: _____

_____

Notary Public

_____

Address

§ 4.45 —Effect of Intentional Infringement

Courts often take a shortcut in evaluating all of the likelihood of confusion factors delineated in § **4.44** when a party willfully appropriates and uses the trademark of another. In such a case it is presumed that confusion will occur.[93] If the alleged infringer had earlier unsuccessfully requested permission to use the trademark, that party is estopped or precluded from claiming that it is an innocent user of the trademark for the goods involved.[94]

§ 4.46 —Use of Another's Trademark

Use of another's trademark is discussed more thoroughly in **Chapter 7.** At this point we will simply state that it is permissible to make truthful references to a competitor's trademark pursuant to the First Amendment (sometimes called *free commercial speech*). However, great care should be taken in doing so, because even truthful references may result in a finding of infringement.[95]

§ 4.47 —Parody and Satire

The First Amendment also protects parody and satire, and these First Amendment rights usually overshadow trademark rights. For example, L.L. Bean was unable to stop publication of "L.L. Bean's Back To School Sex Catalog" section in the magazine *High Society.* The court stated: "Denying parodists the opportunity to poke fun at symbols and names which have become woven into the fabric of our daily life would constitute a serious curtailment of a protected form of expression."[96] Likewise, Lardashe with a "pig pocket" was held to be a noninfringing parody of Jordache,[97] and Miami Mice, featuring two casually clad mice, did not infringe on Miami Vice.[98]

---

[93] Mortellito v. Nina of Cal., Inc., 335 F. Supp. 1288, 173 U.S.P.Q. (BNA) 346 (S.D.N.Y. 1972).

[94] Boston Professional Hockey Ass'n, Inc. v. Dallas Cap & Emblem Mfg., Inc., 501 F.2d 1004, 185 U.S.P.Q. (BNA) 364 (5th Cir. 1965).

[95] Invicta Plastics (USA) Ltd. v. Mego Corp., 523 F. Supp. 619, 214 U.S.P.Q. (BNA) 650 (S.D.N.Y. 1981).

[96] L.L. Bean, Inc. v. Drake Publishers, 811 F.2d 26, 1 U.S.P.Q.2d (BNA) 1753 (1st Cir. 1987), *cert. denied,* 483 U.S. 1013 (1987).

[97] Jordache Enters., Inc. v. Hogg Wyld, Ltd., 625 F. Supp. 48, 227 U.S.P.Q. (BNA) 794 (D.N.M. 1985), *aff'd,* 828 F.2d 1482, 4 U.S.P.Q.2d (BNA) 1216 (10th Cir. 1987).

[98] Universal City Studios, Inc. v. Casey & Casey, 622 F. Supp. 201, 228 U.S.P.Q. (BNA) 195 (S.D. Fla. 1985), *aff'd,* 792 F.2d 1125 (11th Cir. 1986).

§ 4.48   —Counterfeit Products

Billions of dollars are lost worldwide by United States manufacturers to counterfeiters. Counterfeit products range from bogus Rolex watches to fake Reeboks to copied Ford automotive parts. In the United States, the Trademark Counterfeiting Act of 1984 provides substantial legal remedies against such counterfeiters.[99]

§ 4.49   —Dilution

Some states have enacted antidilution statutes[100] or included antidilution provisions in their trademark statutes. These provisions protect the distinctive quality of a mark against dilution even though direct competition does not exist. Famous marks are good candidates for protection. For example, Ringling Bros.—Barnum & Bailey owns the famous trademark The Greatest Show on Earth. Under the Illinois Antidilution statute, Ringling Bros. successfully stopped an Illinois car dealership from using The Greatest Used Car Show on Earth. Ringling Bros. had spent more than $10 million promoting The Greatest Show on Earth in one year alone.[101] Likewise, Anheuser-Busch, which owns "Where there's life . . . there's Bud," stopped a Florida company from using "Where there's life . . . there's bugs" on a combined floor wax/insecticide product.[102] The rule of thumb for a business is: Do not use a famous trademark owned by another!

§ 4.50   Remedies

The traditional remedies of injunctive relief and monetary recovery are available for trademark infringement. Other unique remedies involve

---

[99] Trademark Counterfeiting Act of 1984, Pub. Law 98–473, 98 Stat. 1837, enacted Oct. 12, 1984.

[100] *See* Ala. Code § 8-12-17 (1988); Ark. Stat. Ann. § 4-71-113 (1967); Conn. Gen. Stat. § 35-11 (1963); Del. Code. Ann. tit. 6, § 3313 (1988); Fla. Stat. § 495.151 (1988); Ga. Code Ann. § 10-1-451 (1984); Idaho Code § 48-512 (1988); Ill. Rev. Stat. ch. 140, para. 22 (1987); Iowa Code § 548.11 (1989); La. Rev. Stat. Ann. § 51:223.1 (West 1986); Me. Rev. Stat. Ann. tit. 10, § 1530 (1988); Mo. Rev. Stat. § 417.061 (1973); Mont. Code. Ann. § 30-13-334 (1979); Neb. Rev. Stat. § 87-122 (1967); N.M. Stat. Ann. § 57-3-10 (1969); N.Y. Gen. Bus. Law § 368-d (Consol. 1989); Or. Rev. Stat. § 647.107 (1971); Pa. Cons. Stat. § 1124 (1987); R.I. Gen. Laws § 6-2-12 (1975); Tenn. Code Ann. § 47-25-512 (1982).

[101] Ringling Bros.-Barnum & Bailey Combined Shows, Inc. v. Celozzi-Ettelson Chevrolet, Inc., 6 U.S.P.Q.2d (BNA) 1300 (N.D. Ill. 1987), *aff'd,* 855 F.2d 480, 8 U.S.P.Q.2d (BNA) 1972 (7th Cir. 1988).

[102] Chemical Corp. of Am. v. Anheuser-Busch, Inc., 306 F.2d 433, 134 U.S.P.Q. (BNA) 524 (5th Cir. 1962), *cert. denied,* 372 U.S. 965 (1963).

cancelling a trademark registration, preventing importation of goods, and certain criminal penalties. In §§ **4.51** and **4.52**, the traditional remedies of injunctive relief and monetary recovery are discussed.

In a typical trademark dispute situation, a threatening letter is delivered to the alleged infringing party. Such a letter results in a high probability that the dispute will be settled without litigation. An example is set forth as **Form 4–8**.

Form 4-8
EXAMPLE OF NOTICE TO INFRINGING PARTY

Dog Products
28 Lincoln Drive
Firewood, Montana 86511

Dear Dog Products:

Our firm represents Poorhorse, Inc., which is the owner of the federally registered trademark POORHORSE. A copy of our federal registration is attached for your review (Exhibit B). Poorhorse, Inc., also owns extensive common law trademark rights to POORHORSE.

We have become aware of your use of POORHORSE on dog food as set forth in the attached Exhibit B. Your use is without authorization and represents a direct infringement of my client's POORHORSE trademark.

It is immediately demanded that you cease and desist from all use of the trademark POORHORSE, that you account for all quantities of dog food bearing the POORHORSE trademark that have already been delivered and sold, that you immediately destroy all remaining inventory of the POORHORSE advertising and that you set forth all profits that you have obtained from the first sale of POORHORSE dog food.

You are to comply with these demands immediately and if you have not fully complied within ten days, we shall proceed with the necessary litigation to protect our valuable trademark rights.

This is especially true if the owner of the exclusive rights to the trademark is willing to help the infringing party with trademark changeover costs. Such changeover costs could include the cost of a trademark search, the cost of filing a new trademark application, and the cost of changing stationery, business cards, signs, and the like. In addition to changeover costs, it is not uncommon to give a period of time such as three months, six months, or nine months in which to change over to a new mark. This allows the alleged infringer time to use up existing inventory and make a graceful changeover. It is certainly worthwhile to be creative in structuring and negotiating a suitable settlement that accommodates the alleged infringer. The cost of bringing a lawsuit is usually far greater than the cost of a structured settlement.

§ 4.51 —Injunctive Relief

Without question, injunctive relief constitutes the most frequent remedy sought in trademark litigation cases. The Lanham Act permits courts to grant injunctions according to the principles of equity and upon such terms as the court deems reasonable.[103] Under this rather broad statutory mandate, temporary restraining orders, preliminary injunctions, permanent injunctions, and permanent injunctions involving affirmative acts are awarded. Examples of injunctions involving affirmative acts are:

1. Correcting advertising by ordering the infringer to publish an ad properly informing the public[104]
2. Recalling and destroying the infringing material[105]
3. Placing a telephone number on an intercept, that is, having an operator intercept the calls.[106]

Temporary restraining orders are frequently granted in the seizure of counterfeit merchandise. Such orders are also granted in cases involving merchandise for sale at rock concerts, National Football League games, and the like.

More typically, if a trademark infringement lawsuit is filed, a preliminary injunction is sought. A preliminary injunction simply enjoins the alleged infringing party until a full trial on the merits is had. If the preliminary injunction is granted, a suitable bond must be posted. In trademark infringement cases, preliminary injunctions are frequently granted; therefore, strong consideration should be given to seeking one. The following factors are generally considered in awarding a preliminary injunction:

1. Probability of success at trial
2. Profitability that irreparable injury will occur if the preliminary injunction is not granted

---

[103] 15 U.S.C. § 1116 (1988).

[104] Thomas Nelson, Inc. v. Cherish Books, Ltd., 595 F. Supp. 989, 224 U.S.P.Q. (BNA) 104, 571 (S.D.N.Y. 1984).

[105] *Id.*

[106] Moore Business Forms, Inc. v. Seidenburg, 619 F. Supp. 1173, 229 U.S.P.Q. (BNA) 821 (W.D.La. 1985).

3. Preservation of the status quo
4. Balance of hardships in favor of the plaintiff
5. Protection of third parties such as the consuming public.[107]

§ 4.52   —Monetary Awards

The Lanham Act specifically allows the disgorgement of defendant's profits, award of damages sustained by the plaintiff, and award of litigation costs.[108] The award of damages in Lanham Act trademark infringement is subject to principles of equity; if the court believes that an injunction is sufficient, no monetary award will be made.[109] The Lanham Act allows the damage award to be increased by three times and allows the award of reasonable attorneys' fees in exceptional cases. The Act does not permit the recovery of punitive damages.[110]

The United States Supreme Court in *Hamilton-Brown Shoe Co. v. Wolf Bros. & Co.*[111] held that if the infringement was willful, the court should consider an award based upon an accounting of the infringer's profits. It is the duty of the plaintiff to show the infringer's profits, but then it is the duty of the infringer to apportion the profits properly to the infringing item.[112] However, because of the equitable nature of this award, a court has the right to deny the infringer's apportionment.[113] Finally, a court is permitted to treble the award of profits.[114]

Likewise, the plaintiff is entitled to recover the damages that it can prove. This award is in addition to any award for the infringer's profits. The plaintiff can base its damages upon its own lost profits.[115] The damage award may be based on the cost of correctional advertising. For example, U-Haul expended $13.6 million on a correctional advertising campaign to combat Jartran's original false advertising campaign. The court awarded the $13.6 million, even though Jartran spent only

---

[107] Dorr & Duft, *Trademark Preliminary Injunction Relief,* 62 J. Pat. Off. Soc'y 3 (1980).

[108] 15 U.S.C. § 1117 (1988).

[109] Champion Sparkplug Co. v. Sanders, 331 U.S. 125 (1947).

[110] Getty Petroleum Corp. v. Bartco Petroleum Corp., 858 F.2d 103, 8 U.S.P.Q.2d (BNA) 1336 (2d Cir. 1988), *cert. denied,* 109 S. Ct. 1642 (1989).

[111] 240 U.S. 251 (1916).

[112] Sheldon v. Metro-Goldwyn Pictures Corp., 309 U.S. 390 (1940).

[113] Truck Equip. Serv. Co. v. Fruehauf Corp., 536 F.2d 1210 (8th Cir. 1976).

[114] Holiday Inn v. Airport Holiday Hotel Corp., 493 F. Supp. 1025, 212 U.S.P.Q. (BNA) 208 (N.D. Tex.), *aff'd,* 683 F.2d 931, 216 U.S.P.Q. (BNA) 568 (5th Cir. 1980).

[115] Borg-Warner Corp. v. York-Shipley, Inc., 136 U.S.P.Q. (BNA) 255 (N.D. Ill. 1963).

$6 million on its original campaign.[116] Finally, a reasonable royalty may also contribute to an award of damages, that is, it bears a "national relationship to the rights appropriated."[117]

§ 4.53   —Award of Attorneys' Fees

The Lanham Act specifically permits the award of attorneys' fees in exceptional cases.[118] This cuts both ways. If the plaintiff's lawsuit fails to state a claim, is made in bad faith, or is harassing, the defendant may receive its attorneys' fees. For example, the defendant was awarded $1.1 million in attorneys' fees because the plaintiff brought a bad faith lawsuit against it for using Donkey Kong on its video game. The court was incensed because the plaintiff knew it did not own a trademark for King Kong.[119] Likewise, in another case, over $300,000 in attorneys' fees was awarded to the plaintiff when the defendant was found guilty of deliberate and willful trademark infringement.[120]

§ 4.54   Defenses

Traditional equitable defenses are also available to charges of trademark infringement. The defense of laches, unclean hands, fraud in obtaining trademark registrations, use of trademarks in violation of antitrust laws, and restriction of free speech have all been raised.

Laches lies when the plaintiff knows of the defendant's infringing use, delays in taking any action against that use, and knows that the defendant will be prejudiced as a result of the delay.[121] Making false representations in the applications or affidavits before the PTO may result in a finding of fraud and the cancellation of a federal registration.[122]

---

[116] U-Haul Int'l, Inc. v. Jartran, Inc., 793 F.2d 1034, 230 U.S.P.Q. (BNA) 343 (9th Cir. 1986).

[117] Bandag, Inc. v. A1 Boser's Tire Stores, Inc., 750 F.2d 903, 223 U.S.P.Q. 982 (Fed. Cir. 1984).

[118] 15 USC § 1117 (1988).

[119] Universal Studios, Inc. v. Nintendo Co., 797 F.2d 70, 230 U.S.P.Q. (BNA) 409 (2d Cir. 1986), *cert. denied,* 479 U.S. 987 (1986).

[120] Pillsbury Co. v. Southard, 5 U.S.P.Q.2d (BNA) 1928 (E.D. Okla. 1987).

[121] Citibank, N.A. v. Citytrust, 644 F. Supp. 1011, 231 U.S.P.Q. (BNA) 736 (E.D.N.Y. 1986).

[122] Torres v. Cantine Torresella S.r.l., 808 F.2d 46, 1 U.S.P.Q.2d (BNA) 1483 (Fed. Cir. 1986).

CHAPTER 5

COPYRIGHTS

§ 5.1 Introduction

Copyrights are often thought of as special territory for artists, composers, writers, and those connected with the entertainment industry. People in these activities, of course, have long been aware of the special value of copyright protection. What is not so well understood is that copyrights are at least as valuable to the commercial world, as well as to government operations and the fields of science and education.

The types of items eligible for copyright protection are advertisements, original labels, original designs incorporated on or in conjunction with useful items, writings, books, photographs, videos, and music, just to name a few. Customer lists, supply source lists, and compilations of readily available financial information (products of the "sweat of the brow," so the speak), are also subject to copyright protection. Coming just short of being absolutely free, copyright protection is the least expensive intellectual property protection you can get. The registration filing fee, for example, is only $10. In addition, a copyright has a long life. A corporation registering one of its copyrights would have the exclusive use of that copyright for a period of 75 years. Finally, there are a number of ancillary benefits that frequently flow from copyright registrations which, although not contemplated by the Copyright Act, provide long-term and quite valuable rewards to the copyright owner.

For instance, a copyright may serve an identification function, signifying to the public an association between a product or service and a given source, thereby acting as a common law trademark augmenting federal trademark protection. It may also become part of the trade dress of a product serving the same purpose as a trademark, even though trade dress as such is not registrable under the trademark statute. (See **Chapter 3** for further discussion of trade dress and trademarks.) A copyright also opens up vast expansions called *derivative works* that enjoy the same protection as the original copyright. Things like beverage mugs, tee-shirts, baseball caps, and "happy lunch" cardboard boxes may be derivative works. (See **§§ 5.3** and **5.10** for further discussions of compilations and derivative works.)

Three fields of intellectual property presently protected by statute are (1) patents (useful items or processes), (2) trademarks (identification of products or service and their sources), and (3) copyrights, the subject matter of this chapter. These protected types of property are not mutually exclusive, and, wherever possible, all three should be used for maximum intellectual property protection.

Protective programs and measures in general are discussed and illustrated in **Chapter 1**, "Trade Secrets." In addition, businesses and other enterprises that own copyrights should establish and maintain current catalogs of all protected works and should ensure that such works used in publications or advertisements always bear the copyright notice. Marketing and advertising personnel, in particular, should be kept current on the value of protecting copyright assets.

RESOURCES: The reference most frequently quoted in court decisions is Nimmer, Melville B. and David, *Nimmer on Copyright* (Matthew Bender: 11 Penn Plaza, New York, NY 10001) (1987). For a comprehensive collection of copyright decisions refer to *Copyright Law Decisions* (CCH). These decisions are also found in the *United States Patent Quarterly* (BNA).

Before proceeding to the substance of this chapter, a note about the copyright statute is in order. The first copyright statute was enacted by Congress in 1807 and was almost a copy of the British Statute of Anne. Throughout the course of the nineteenth century there were several minor revisions to the Copyright Act. A major overhaul of the copyright statute took place in 1909. That Copyright Act dominated the United States statutory copyright protection scene until December 31, 1977, when the 1978 Act went into effect. Consequently, most references, key words, and headnotes in treatises and reference books still refer to cases decided under the 1909 Act. In many, but not all, instances those cases may be relied on to answer the problems arising under the Copyright Act of 1976. Care must be taken in relying on older cases.

§ 5.2 Copyrightable Works

In its simplest terms, a *copyright* is a monopoly authorized by the United States Constitution and implemented by statute setting out specific categories of copyrightable works. The United States Constitution states: "The Congress shall have the power . . . to promote the Progress of Science and useful Arts, by securing for limited Times to Authors and Inventors the exclusive Right to their respective Writings and Discoveries."[1]

Things subject to copyright protection are called *works,* and *original work* means a work showing originality with at least a trace of creative input. Works are not copyrightable if they are mere ideas or ephemeral sounds or gestures. They must be in tangible form, which means in a form capable of either visually or audibly recreating the representation of the original work. The tangible form may be either a form that is now known to us, or one that may be developed in the future from which a work can be communicated either directly or with the aid of a machine or device.

---

[1] U.S. Const. art. I, § 8.

One of the very important distinctions we must make at the outset is that the idea behind a representation is simply not protected by copyright law. However, even a modicum of originality with respect to the representation of a threadbare idea is copyrightable.

For example, the idea of a fat, white-bearded older fellow in a red Santa Claus suit is not copyrightable, but the carrying out of the idea by a drawing or a puppet is.[2]

Similarly, a stick figure or the idea of stick figures is not copyrightable, but stick figures explaining exercises on aerobic machines that follow a sequence and pattern are copyrightable.[3] Directions on the labels of beauty products have also been held to be copyrightable.[4]

Compilations of names and addresses in alphabetical order or numerical order in a directory are copyrightable, even though every element in the compilation is easily ascertainable and no element has originated with the author.[5] The right to protection arises from the original efforts and labor of the author in seeking out and arranging or listing the contents in a new, original form not found in the public domain. On the other hand, words and phrases imprinted on envelopes describing contents or giving instructions are not copyrightable;[6] nor are blank forms, unless they convey information, rather than merely provide a place to record it.[7]

A photograph of a nondescript trashcan, or a beautiful model, is copyrightable as an original work.[8] But a "paddle-and-ball" video game is not copyrightable because it is "inseparable in any principled manner from the idea which it embodies."[9] Such a simple "hit and return" sequence is so prosaic as not to meet the originality standard of the Copyright Act.

---

[2] Doraw v. Sunset House Distrib. Corp., 197 F. Supp. 940, 131 U.S.P.Q. (BNA) 94 (S.D. Cal. 1961).

[3] Universal Athletic Sales Co. v. Salkind, 511 F.2d 904, 185 U.S.P.Q.2d (BNA) 76, *cert. denied,* 423 U.S. 863 (1975).

[4] Sebastian Int'l v. Consumer Contacts (PTY), Ltd., 664 F. Supp. 909, 3 U.S.P.Q.2d (BNA) 1401 (D.N.J. 1987).

[5] West Publishing Co. v. Mead Data Central, Inc., 799 F.2d 1219, 230 U.S.P.Q. (BNA) 801 (8th Cir. 1981), *cert. denied,* 479 U.S. 1070, 107 S. Ct. 962 (1987).

[6] Magic Mktg. v. Mailing Servs. of Pittsburgh, 634 F. Supp. 769, 230 U.S.P.Q. (BNA) 230 (W.D. Pa. 1986).

[7] Bibbero Sys., Inc. v. Colwell Sys., Inc., Copyright L. Dec. (CCH) ¶ 26,270 (N.D. Cal. 1988). *See also* Matthew Bender & Co. v. Kluwer Law Book Publishers, Inc., 672 F. Supp. 107, 5 U.S.P.Q.2d (BNA) 1363 (S.D.N.Y. 1987) (format and legal headings of charts in legal book conveyed no information and not protectable).

[8] Gross v. Seligman, 212 F. 930 (2d Cir. 1914); Estate of Vane v. The Fair, Inc., 676 F. Supp. 133, 4 U.S.P.Q.2d (BNA) 1333, *aff'd,* 849 F.2d 186, 7 U.S.P.Q.2d (BNA) 1479 (5th Cir. 1988), *cert. denied,* 57 U.S.L.W. 3452 (1989).

[9] Atari Games Corp. v. Oman, 693 F. Supp. 1204, 8 U.S.P.Q.2d (BNA) 426 (D.D.C. 1988), *rev'd,* 888 F.2d 878, 12 U.S.P.Q.2d (BNA) 1791 (D.C. Cir. 1989).

The photograph, however, involves elements of selection, composition, and a fleeting impression reduced to tangible form. Audiovisual displays of a copyrighted computer program may be copyrightable as pictorial or graphic works when their structure, sequence, and layout are dictated by artistic and aesthetic, rather than utilitarian or mechanical, considerations.[10]

An author's interpretive story of the life of a famous bank robber is susceptible to copyright, because the author's contributions to the relevant facts and ideas form a "protected expression."[11] Architectural plans have also been ruled eligible for copyright protection as drawings "of technical nature,"[12] although the Copyright Office has begun an inquiry regarding the degree of protection appropriate for architectural works. In addition, telecasts of baseball games have been ruled to involve sufficient "creative labor" for copyrightability.[13] Magazine covers are similarly protected as "original work[s] of authorship" with distinctive arrangements and layouts.[14]

Conversely, an ornamental bike rack, although it originated from a piece of wire sculpture artwork, has been denied copyright protection because it was "influenced in significant measure by utilitarian concern," thus making any aesthetic elements "conceptually inseparable from the utilitarian elements."[15] A professional soccer team's logo, which consisted of four angled lines forming an arrow with the word "Arrows" in cursive script under the word, was denied copyright protection on the basis that the design lacked a requisite minimum level of creativity.[16] The copyright statute itself sets out the following list of copyrightable works:[17]

1. Literary works
2. Musical works, including any accompanying words
3. Dramatic works, including any accompanying music
4. Pantomimes and choreographic works

---

[10] Broderbund Software, Inc. v. Unison World, Inc., 648 F. Supp. 1127, 231 U.S.P.Q. (BNA) 700 (N.D. Cal. 1986).

[11] Nash v. CBS, Inc., 691 F. Supp. 140, 143, 9 U.S.P.Q. (BNA) 684 (N.D. Ill. 1986).

[12] Demetriades v. Kautman, 680 F. Supp. 658, 665 U.S.P.Q.2d (BNA) 1737 (S.D.N.Y. 1988).

[13] Baltimore Orioles, Inc. v. Major League Baseball Players Assoc., 805 F.2d 663, 231 U.S.P.Q. (BNA) 673 (7th Cir. 1986), *cert. denied*, 480 U.S. 941 (1987).

[14] Reader's Digest Assoc. v. Conservative Digest, Inc., 821 F.2d 800, 3 U.S.P.Q.2d (BNA) 1276 (D.C. Cir. 1987).

[15] Brandir Int'l, Inc. v. Cascade Pac. Lumber Co., 834 F.2d 1142, 1147 5 U.S.P.Q.2d (BNA) 1089 (2d Cir. 1987).

[16] John Muller & Co. v. New York Arrows Soccer Team, Inc., 802 F.2d 989, 231 U.S.P.Q. (BNA) 319 (8th Cir. 1986).

[17] 17 U.S.C. § 102 (1988).

5. Pictorial, graphic, and sculptural works, including architectural plans
6. Motion pictures and other audiovisual works
7. Sound recordings.

§ 5.3 —Derivative Works

Derivative works derived from primary copyrightable works are also subject to copyright protection. (**Section 5.10** includes an expanded discussion on compilations and derivative works.) In general, a *compilation* is defined in the statute as "a work formed by the collection and assembling of pre-existing materials or of data that are selected, coordinated, or arranged in such a way that the resulting work as a whole constitutes an original work of authorship. The term 'compilation' includes collective works."[18] A compilation may include any work described in the Copyright Act or any matter not protected by copyright because it is in the public domain or any combination of copyrightable works or public domain items.

A *derivative work* is defined as "a work based upon one or more pre-existing works, such as a translation, musical arrangement, dramatization, fictionalization, motion picture version, sound recording, art reproduction, abridgement, condensation, or any other form in which a work may be recast, transformed, or adapted. A work consisting of editorial revisions, annotations, elaborations, or other modifications, which as a whole represent an original work of authorship, is a 'derivative work.'"[19] Derivative works are based on other previously copyrighted works.

§ 5.4 How to Obtain a Copyright

Some, although not much, copyright protection is available to a person who merely fixes an original representation in some tangible form capable of being reproduced so that others may see or hear it, without publishing or registering it. *Publication* is defined in the statute as "the distribution of copies or phonorecords of a work to the public."[20] The owner of such an unpublished, unregistered work cannot bring an action to enjoin another who copies his work. He can, however, sue an unauthorized copier for actual damages, if he can prove that he intended to claim a copyright and did not abandon it.[21] The owner of a published but unregistered work would have no greater choice of remedies.

---

[18] *Id.*

[19] 17 U.S.C. § 101 (1988).

[20] *Id.*

[21] 17 U.S.C. §§ 411, 412 (1988).

Stronger protection is available to a work that is unpublished but registered. All of the remedies provided by the statute (including injunctions, impoundment, and monetary damages)[22] are available to the owner of this sort of work. These same remedies are available to the owner of a published work that is also registered. The rights of the copyright owner are not only to use the copyrighted work for his own benefit, but also, and perhaps more importantly, to exclude others from copying and using the work without his permission.

As stated at the beginning of this section, one can acquire the simplest form of copyright simply by fixing in tangible form an original creation of the representation of an idea. This simple copyright requires no formalities, statutory or otherwise, but the creator must be careful not to indicate either by express words or actions, or by implication, that he does not intend to claim a copyright in the work or has abandoned any such claim.

§ 5.5   —Copyright Notice

The most widely utilized technique to avoid giving the impression of abandonment is to use a copyright notice. Although there is no statutory prescription for the form of an unpublished notice, a popular form of notice that has been used for decades is the phrase "All rights reserved." This notice is frequently followed by the name of the author, and may also be followed by another familiar phrase, "Not to be reproduced without the express permission of the author."

The Copyright Act requires that one of the three alternatives, "c," "copr," or "copyright," followed by the name of the author and year of publication, be placed on published copyrighted works produced in the United States prior to March 1, 1989. All three alternatives provide equal notice. It is also advisable to put notice of copyright on works produced within the United States after March 1, 1989 (the effective date of the Berne Convention Implementation Act of 1988, which amended the Copyright Act). The presence of such notice on copies to which an infringer had access deprives him of the defense of innocent infringement.[23]

§ 5.6   —Registration

A copyright can be strengthened by registration with the Register of Copyrights, Library of Congress, Washington, DC 20559. The present registration fee is a very modest $10 per work. The author need deposit two

---

[22] *Id.*

[23] 17 U.S.C. § 401(d) (1988).

complete copies of the best edition of a published work, or one copy of an unpublished work. A *best edition* is "an edition published in the United States at any time before the date of deposit, as the Library of Congress determines to be most suitable for its purposes."[24]

Registration forms for published works must be fully completed and executed and must accompany the $10 fee and the copy or copies submitted for registration. Forms are available at no charge from the Copyright Office. The present forms available are:

1. Form TX—Nondramatic Literary Work
2. Form PA—Performing Act
3. Form VA—Visual Act
4. Form SR—Sound Recording
5. Form RE—Renewal Registration
6. Form CA—Supplementary Registration
7. Form GR/CP—Group Registration for contributions to periodicals
8. Form IS—Issuance of an import statement.

The three most frequently used forms are the TX, VA, and PA. Completed samples of each of these, along with a transmittal letter and a request for special handling appear as **Forms 5–1** through **5–5**.

Form 5–1
LETTER TRANSMITTING MATERIAL FOR
COPYRIGHT REGISTRATION

Register of Copyrights
Library of Congress
Washington, D.C. 20559

Re: Copyright application for THREE KINGS

Dear Register:

I enclose copyright application Form TX for the original work "THREE KINGS," along with two of the best editions of the work and a check in the amount of $10.

This packet is being sent by certified mail with a return receipt requested.

In the event any questions arise during the examination for registration process, please call me at (000) 000-0000.

Sincerely,

---

[24] *Id.* at §§ 401 (1988).

FORM TX
UNITED STATES COPYRIGHT OFFICE

REGISTRATION NUMBER

TX	TXU

EFFECTIVE DATE OF REGISTRATION

Month	Day	Year

DO NOT WRITE ABOVE THIS LINE. IF YOU NEED MORE SPACE, USE A SEPARATE CONTINUATION SHEET.

1

TITLE OF THIS WORK ▼

FROGWARE - Version 1.1

PREVIOUS OR ALTERNATIVE TITLES ▼

PUBLICATION AS A CONTRIBUTION If this work was published as a contribution to a periodical, serial, or collection, give information about the collective work in which the contribution appeared. **Title of Collective Work ▼**

If published in a periodical or serial give: **Volume ▼**　　**Number ▼**　　**Issue Date ▼**　　**On Pages ▼**

2

a

NAME OF AUTHOR ▼

Pond, Inc.

DATES OF BIRTH AND DEATH
Year Born ▼　　Year Died ▼

Was this contribution to the work a "work made for hire"?
☒ Yes
☐ No

AUTHOR'S NATIONALITY OR DOMICILE
Name of Country
OR { Citizen of ▶
Domiciled in ▶ USA

WAS THIS AUTHOR'S CONTRIBUTION TO THE WORK
Anonymous? ☐ Yes ☒ No
Pseudonymous? ☐ Yes ☒ No
If the answer to either of these questions is "Yes," see detailed instructions.

NATURE OF AUTHORSHIP Briefly describe nature of the material created by this author in which copyright is claimed. ▼
Entire Test of Computer Program

NOTE

Under the law, the "author" of a "work made for hire" is generally the employer, not the employee (see instructions). For any part of this work that was "made for hire" check "Yes" in the space provided, give the employer (or other person for whom the work was prepared) as "Author" of that part, and leave the space for dates of birth and death blank.

b

NAME OF AUTHOR ▼

DATES OF BIRTH AND DEATH
Year Born ▼　　Year Died ▼

Was this contribution to the work a "work made for hire"?
☐ Yes
☐ No

AUTHOR'S NATIONALITY OR DOMICILE
Name of country
OR { Citizen of ▶
Domiciled in ▶

WAS THIS AUTHOR'S CONTRIBUTION TO THE WORK
Anonymous? ☐ Yes ☐ No
Pseudonymous? ☐ Yes ☐ No
If the answer to either of these questions is "Yes," see detailed instructions.

NATURE OF AUTHORSHIP Briefly describe nature of the material created by this author in which copyright is claimed. ▼

c

NAME OF AUTHOR ▼

DATES OF BIRTH AND DEATH
Year Born ▼　　Year Died ▼

Was this contribution to the work a "work made for hire"?
☐ Yes
☐ No

AUTHOR'S NATIONALITY OR DOMICILE
Name of Country
OR { Citizen of ▶
Domiciled in ▶

WAS THIS AUTHOR'S CONTRIBUTION TO THE WORK
Anonymous? ☐ Yes ☐ No
Pseudonymous? ☐ Yes ☐ No
If the answer to either of these questions is "Yes," see detailed instructions.

NATURE OF AUTHORSHIP Briefly describe nature of the material created by this author in which copyright is claimed. ▼

3

YEAR IN WHICH CREATION OF THIS WORK WAS COMPLETED This information must be given in all cases.
◀ Year

DATE AND NATION OF FIRST PUBLICATION OF THIS PARTICULAR WORK
Complete this information Month ▶ Dec.　Day ▶ 25　Year ▶ 1987
ONLY if this work has been published. U.S.A.　◀ Nation

4

See instructions before completing this space.

COPYRIGHT CLAIMANT(S) Name and address must be given even if the claimant is the same as the author given in space 2.▼

Pond, Inc.
(Address)

TRANSFER If the claimant(s) named here in space 4 are different from the author(s) named in space 2, give a brief statement of how the claimant(s) obtained ownership of the copyright.▼

APPLICATION RECEIVED

ONE DEPOSIT RECEIVED

TWO DEPOSITS RECEIVED

REMITTANCE NUMBER AND DATE

DO NOT WRITE HERE OFFICE USE ONLY

MORE ON BACK ▶
• Complete all applicable spaces (numbers 5-11) on the reverse side of this page.
• See detailed instructions.　• Sign the form at line 10.

DO NOT WRITE HERE
Page 1 of_____pages

Form 5–2. Registration application for nondramatic literary work (form TX).

EXAMINED BY

CHECKED BY

☐ CORRESPONDENCE
   Yes

☐ DEPOSIT ACCOUNT
   FUNDS USED

FORM TX

FOR
COPYRIGHT
OFFICE
USE
ONLY

DO NOT WRITE ABOVE THIS LINE. IF YOU NEED MORE SPACE, USE A SEPARATE CONTINUATION SHEET.

PREVIOUS REGISTRATION Has registration for this work, or for an earlier version of this work, already been made in the Copyright Office?
☐ Yes ☒ No If your answer is "Yes," why is another registration being sought? (Check appropriate box) ▼

☐ This is the first published edition of a work previously registered in unpublished form.

☐ This is the first application submitted by this author as copyright claimant.

☐ This is a changed version of the work, as shown by space 6 on this application.

If your answer is "Yes," give: **Previous Registration Number** ▼   **Year of Registration** ▼

5

DERIVATIVE WORK OR COMPILATION Complete both space 6a & 6b for a derivative work; complete only 6b for a compilation.
a. Preexisting Material Identify any preexisting work or works that this work is based on or incorporates. ▼

b. Material Added to This Work Give a brief, general statement of the material that has been added to this work and in which copyright is claimed. ▼

6

See instructions
before completing
this space

MANUFACTURERS AND LOCATIONS If this is a published work consisting preponderantly of nondramatic literary material in English, the law may require that the copies be manufactured in the United States or Canada for full protection. If so, the names of the manufacturers who performed certain processes, and the places where these processes were performed **must** be given. See instructions for details.
Names of Manufacturers ▼   **Places of Manufacture** ▼

7

REPRODUCTION FOR USE OF BLIND OR PHYSICALLY HANDICAPPED INDIVIDUALS   A signature on this form at space 10, and a check in one of the boxes here in space 8, constitutes a non-exclusive grant of permission to the Library of Congress to reproduce and distribute solely for the blind and physically handicapped and under the conditions and limitations prescribed by the regulations of the Copyright Office: (1) copies of the work identified in space 1 of this application in Braille (or similar tactile symbols); or (2) phonorecords embodying a fixation of a reading of that work; or (3) both.

     a ☐ Copies and Phonorecords   **b** ☐ Copies Only   **c** ☐ Phonorecords Only   See instructions

8

DEPOSIT ACCOUNT If the registration fee is to be charged to a Deposit Account established in the Copyright Office, give name and number of Account.
Name ▼   **Account Number** ▼

CORRESPONDENCE Give name and address to which correspondence about this application should be sent. Name/Address/Apt/City/State/Zip ▼

Dorr, Carson, Sloan & Peterson
3010 E. 6th Ave.
Denver, CO 80206

Area Code & Telephone Number ▶   (303) 333-3010

9

Be sure to
give your
daytime phone
◀ number

CERTIFICATION* I, the undersigned, hereby certify that I am the
Check one ▶

☐ author
☐ other copyright claimant
☐ owner of exclusive right(s)
☒ authorized agent of   Pond, Inc.
               Name of author or other copyright claimant, or owner of exclusive right(s) ▲

of the work identified in this application and that the statements made by me in this application are correct to the best of my knowledge.

Typed or printed name and date ▼ If this is a published work, this date must be the same as or later than the date of publication given in space 3.

Kermit   date ▶   Jan. 15, 1988

☞   Handwritten signature (X) ▼

10

MAIL CERTIFI-CATE TO

Name ▼

Dorr, Carson, Sloan & Peterson

Number/Street/Apartment Number ▼

3010 E. 6th Ave.

City/State/ZIP ▼

Denver, CO 80206

Certificate will be mailed in window envelope

Have you:
• Completed all necessary spaces?
• Signed your application in space 10?
• Enclosed check or money order for $10 payable to *Register of Copyrights*?
• Enclosed your deposit material with the application and fee?

MAIL TO: Register of Copyrights, Library of Congress, Washington, D.C. 20559.

11

* 17 U.S.C. § 506(e): Any person who knowingly makes a false representation of a material fact in the application for copyright registration provided for by section 409, or in any written statement filed in connection with the application, shall be fined not more than $2,500.

☆U.S. GOVERNMENT PRINTING OFFICE: 1987—181–531/40,024   April 1987—200,000

Form 5–2. *(Continued)*

FORM PA

UNITED STATES COPYRIGHT OFFICE

REGISTRATION NUMBER

PA   PAU

EFFECTIVE DATE OF REGISTRATION

....

(Month)   (Day)   (Year)

DO NOT WRITE ABOVE THIS LINE. IF YOU NEED MORE SPACE, USE CONTINUATION SHEET (FORM PA/CON)

(1)
Title

TITLE OF THIS WORK:

Lazycise

PREVIOUS OR ALTERNATIVE TITLES:

None

NATURE OF THIS WORK: (See instructions)

---

(2)
Author(s)

IMPORTANT: Under the law, the "author" of a "work made for hire" is generally the employer, not the employee (see instructions). If any part of this work was "made for hire" check "Yes" in the space provided, give the employer (or other person for whom the work was prepared) as "Author" of that part, and leave the space for dates blank.

1

NAME OF AUTHOR: Minimum Effort, Inc.

Was this author's contribution to the work a "work made for hire"?   Yes. X   No. :

AUTHOR'S NATIONALITY OR DOMICILE:

Citizen of .... } or { Domiciled in .... U.S.A. ....
(Name of Country)   (Name of Country)

AUTHOR OF: (Briefly describe nature of this author's contribution)
Creation & Performance of the exercise videotape

DATES OF BIRTH AND DEATH:

Born .... Died ....
          (Year)   (Year)

WAS THIS AUTHOR'S CONTRIBUTION TO THE WORK:

Anonymous?   Yes ......   No .. X
Pseudonymous?   Yes ......   No .. X

If the answer to either of these questions is "Yes," see detailed instructions attached.

2

NAME OF AUTHOR:

Was this author's contribution to the work a "work made for hire"?   Yes ......   No ......

AUTHOR'S NATIONALITY OR DOMICILE:

Citizen of .... } or { Domiciled in ....
(Name of Country)   (Name of Country)

AUTHOR OF: (Briefly describe nature of this author's contribution)

DATES OF BIRTH AND DEATH:

Born .... Died ....
          (Year)   (Year)

WAS THIS AUTHOR'S CONTRIBUTION TO THE WORK:

Anonymous?   Yes ......   No ......
Pseudonymous?   Yes ......   No ......

If the answer to either of these questions is "Yes," see detailed instructions attached.

3

NAME OF AUTHOR:

Was this author's contribution to the work a "work made for hire"?   Yes ......   No ......

AUTHOR'S NATIONALITY OR DOMICILE:

Citizen of .... } or { Domiciled in ....
(Name of Country)   (Name of Country)

AUTHOR OF: (Briefly describe nature of this author's contribution)

DATES OF BIRTH AND DEATH:

Born .... Died ....
          (Year)   (Year)

WAS THIS AUTHOR'S CONTRIBUTION TO THE WORK:

Anonymous?   Yes ......   No ......
Pseudonymous?   Yes ......   No ......

If the answer to either of these questions is "Yes," see detailed instructions attached.

---

(3)
Creation and Publication

YEAR IN WHICH CREATION OF THIS WORK WAS COMPLETED:

Year ....
(This information must be given in all cases.)

DATE AND NATION OF FIRST PUBLICATION:

Date ....
             (Month)   (Day)   (Year)

Nation ....
                        (Name of Country)

(Complete this block ONLY if this work has been published.)

---

(4)
Claimant(s)

NAME(S) AND ADDRESS(ES) OF COPYRIGHT CLAIMANT(S):
Minimum Effort, Inc.
110 Sleepy Hollow Road
Seldom Seen, PA 15022

TRANSFER: (If the copyright claimant(s) named here in space 4 are different from the author(s) named in space 2, give a brief statement of how the claimant(s) obtained ownership of the copyright.)

• Complete all applicable spaces (numbers 5-9) on the reverse side of this page
• Follow detailed instructions attached   • Sign the form at line 8

DO NOT WRITE HERE

Page 1 of .... pages

Form 5–3. Registration application for performing act (form PA).

EXAMINED BY:	APPLICATION RECEIVED:	
CHECKED BY:		FOR COPYRIGHT OFFICE USE ONLY
CORRESPONDENCE: ☐ Yes	DEPOSIT RECEIVED:	
DEPOSIT ACCOUNT FUNDS USED: ☐	REMITTANCE NUMBER AND DATE:	

DO NOT WRITE ABOVE THIS LINE. IF YOU NEED ADDITIONAL SPACE, USE CONTINUATION SHEET (FORM PA/CON)

PREVIOUS REGISTRATION:

⑤ Previous Registration

- Has registration for this work, or for an earlier version of this work, already been made in the Copyright Office? Yes .... No ... X ......

- If your answer is "Yes," why is another registration being sought? (Check appropriate box)
  - ☐ This is the first published edition of a work previously registered in unpublished form.
  - ☐ This is the first application submitted by this author as copyright claimant.
  - ☐ This is a changed version of the work, as shown by line 6 of the application.

- If your answer is "Yes," give: Previous Registration Number .... Year of Registration ....

COMPILATION OR DERIVATIVE WORK: (See instructions)

⑥ Compilation or Derivative Work

PREEXISTING MATERIAL: (Identify any preexisting work or works that the work is based on or incorporates.)
....
....
....

MATERIAL ADDED TO THIS WORK: (Give a brief, general statement of the material that has been added to this work and in which copyright is claimed.)
....
....
....

DEPOSIT ACCOUNT: (If the registration fee is to be charged to a Deposit Account established in the Copyright Office, give name and number of Account.)

Name: ....

Account Number: ....

CORRESPONDENCE: (Give name and address to which correspondence about this application should be sent.)

Name: .... Dorr, Carson, Sloan & Peterson ....

Address: .... 3010 East Sixth Avenue ....
(Apt.)

.... Denver .... Colorado 80206 ....
(City)   (State)   (ZIP)

⑦ Fee and Correspondence

CERTIFICATION: * I, the undersigned, hereby certify that I am the: (Check one)
☐ author ☐ other copyright claimant ☐ owner of exclusive right(s) ☒ authorized agent of: .... Minimum Effort, Inc. ....
(Name of author or other copyright claimant, or owner of exclusive right(s))
of the work identified in this application and that the statements made by me in this application are correct to the best of my knowledge.

Handwritten signature: (X) ....

Typed or printed name ..... Robert C. Dorr .... Date .. 9/19/89 ..

⑧ Certification (Application must be signed)

MAIL CERTIFICATE TO	⑨ Address For Return of Certificate

Dorr, Carson, Sloan and Peterson
(Name)

3010 East Sixth Avenue
(Number, Street and Apartment Number)

Denver, Colorado 80206
(City)   (State)   (ZIP code)

(Certificate will be mailed in window envelope)

* 17 U.S.C. §506(e) FALSE REPRESENTATION – Any person who knowingly makes a false representation of a material fact in the application for copyright registration provided for by section 409, or in any written statement filed in connection with the application, shall be fined not more than $2,500.

☆U.S. GOVERNMENT PRINTING OFFICE: 1978-261-022/17

April 1978-500,000

Form 5–3. *(Continued)*

FORM VA

UNITED STATES COPYRIGHT OFFICE

REGISTRATION NUMBER

VA   VAU

EFFECTIVE DATE OF REGISTRATION

(Month)   (Day)   (Year)

DO NOT WRITE ABOVE THIS LINE. IF YOU NEED MORE SPACE, USE CONTINUATION SHEET (FORM VA/CON)

① Title

TITLE OF THIS WORK:

Reclining Hamburger

Previous or Alternative Titles

NATURE OF THIS WORK: (See instructions)

PUBLICATION AS A CONTRIBUTION: (If this work was published as a contribution to a periodical, serial, or collection, give information about the collective work in which the contribution appeared.)

Title of Collective Work .... Vol ...... No ...... Date .... Pages ......

② Author(s)

IMPORTANT: Under the law, the "author" of a "work made for hire" is generally the employer, not the employee (see instructions). If any part of this work was "made for hire" check "Yes" in the space provided, give the employer (or other person for whom the work was prepared) as "Author" of that part, and leave the space for dates blank.

NAME OF AUTHOR:
Arthur Artist

Was this author's contribution to the work a "work made for hire"?   Yes .... No X

DATES OF BIRTH AND DEATH:
Born 3/7/21   Died ....
(Year)   (Year)

AUTHOR'S NATIONALITY OR DOMICILE:
Citizen of   U.S.A.   } or { Domiciled in ......
(Name of Country)   (Name of Country)

WAS THIS AUTHOR'S CONTRIBUTION TO THE WORK:
Anonymous?   Yes .... No X
Pseudonymous?   Yes .... No X
If the answer to either of these questions is "Yes," see detailed instructions attached.

AUTHOR OF: (Briefly describe nature of this author's contribution)
The Entire Oil Painting

1

NAME OF AUTHOR:

Was this author's contribution to the work a "work made for hire"?   Yes .... No ....

DATES OF BIRTH AND DEATH:
Born ....   Died ....
(Year)   (Year)

AUTHOR'S NATIONALITY OR DOMICILE:
Citizen of ...... } or { Domiciled in ......
(Name of Country)   (Name of Country)

WAS THIS AUTHOR'S CONTRIBUTION TO THE WORK:
Anonymous?   Yes .... No ....
Pseudonymous?   Yes .... No ....
If the answer to either of these questions is "Yes," see detailed instructions attached.

AUTHOR OF: (Briefly describe nature of this author's contribution)

2

NAME OF AUTHOR:

Was this author's contribution to the work a "work made for hire"?   Yes .... No ....

DATES OF BIRTH AND DEATH:
Born ....   Died ....
(Year)   (Year)

AUTHOR'S NATIONALITY OR DOMICILE:
Citizen of ...... } or { Domiciled in ......
(Name of Country)   (Name of Country)

WAS THIS AUTHOR'S CONTRIBUTION TO THE WORK:
Anonymous?   Yes .... No ....
Pseudonymous?   Yes .... No ....
If the answer to either of these questions is "Yes," see detailed instructions attached.

AUTHOR OF: (Briefly describe nature of this author's contribution)

3

③ Creation and Publication

YEAR IN WHICH CREATION OF THIS WORK WAS COMPLETED:
Year 1989
(This information must be given in all cases.)

DATE AND NATION OF FIRST PUBLICATION:
Date ...... (Month) ...... (Day) ...... (Year) ......
Nation ...... (Name of Country) ......
(Complete this block ONLY if this work has been published.)

④ Claimant(s)

NAME(S) AND ADDRESS(ES) OF COPYRIGHT CLAIMANT(S):

Arthur Artist
Garrett Apartments #18
Aurora, Colorado 80303

TRANSFER: (If the copyright claimant(s) named here in space 4 are different from the author(s) named in space 2, give a brief statement of how the claimant(s) obtained ownership of the copyright.)

• Complete all applicable spaces (numbers 5-9) on the reverse side of this page
• Follow detailed instructions attached   • Sign the form at line 8

DO NOT WRITE HERE
Page 1 of .... pages

Form 5–4. Registration application for visual act (form VA).

EXAMINED BY	APPLICATION RECEIVED	
CHECKED BY		
CORRESPONDENCE ☐ Yes	DEPOSIT RECEIVED	**FOR COPYRIGHT OFFICE USE ONLY**
DEPOSIT ACCOUNT FUNDS USED ☐	REMITTANCE NUMBER AND DATE	

DO NOT WRITE ABOVE THIS LINE. IF YOU NEED ADDITIONAL SPACE, USE CONTINUATION SHEET (FORM VA/CON)

PREVIOUS REGISTRATION:

- Has registration for this work, or for an earlier version of this work, already been made in the Copyright Office? Yes....... No ....

- If your answer is "Yes," why is another registration being sought? (Check appropriate box)
    ☐ This is the first published edition of a work previously registered in unpublished form.
    ☐ This is the first application submitted by this author as copyright claimant.
    ☐ This is a changed version of the work, as shown by line 6 of the application.

- If your answer is "Yes," give: Previous Registration Number........................Year of Registration........................

(5) Previous Registration

COMPILATION OR DERIVATIVE WORK: (See instructions)

PREEXISTING MATERIAL: (Identify any preexisting work or works that this work is based on or incorporates.)

MATERIAL ADDED TO THIS WORK: (Give a brief, general statement of the material that has been added to this work and in which copyright is claimed.)

(6) Compilation or Derivative Work

DEPOSIT ACCOUNT: (If the registration fee is to be charged to a Deposit Account established in the Copyright Office, give name and number of Account.)

Name:

Account Number:

CORRESPONDENCE: (Give name and address to which correspondence about this application should be sent.)

Name: Robert C. Dorr
Dorr, Sloan and Peterson
Address: 3010 East Sixth Avenue
(Apt.)
Denver, Colorado   80206
(City)   (State)   (ZIP)

(7) Fee and Correspondence

CERTIFICATION: ✱ I, the undersigned, hereby certify that I am the: (Check one)
☐ author ☐ other copyright claimant ☐ owner of exclusive right(s) ☑ authorized agent of   Arthur Artist
(Name of author or other copyright claimant, or owner of exclusive right(s))
of the work identified in this application and that the statements made by me in this application are correct to the best of my knowledge.

Handwritten signature: (X)..
Typed or printed name:.... Robert C. Dorr   Date: 9/19/89

(8) Certification (Application must be signed)

Robert C. Dorr
(Name)
3010 East Sixth Avenue
(Number, Street and Apartment Number)
Denver, Colorado 80206
(City)   (State)   (ZIP code)

**MAIL
CERTIFICATE
TO**

(Certificate will
be mailed in
window envelope)

(9) Address For Return of Certificate

✱ 17 U.S.C. § 506(e): FALSE REPRESENTATION—Any person who knowingly makes a false representation of a material fact in the application for copyright registration, provided for by section 409, or in any written statement filed in connection with the application, shall be fined not more than $2,500.
✩ U.S. GOVERNMENT PRINTING OFFICE: 1978—261-022/21

Sept. 1978—150,000

Form 5–4. *(Continued)*

Copyright Office • The Library of Congress • Washington, D.C. 20559

request for special handling

1

NOTE: The special handling of a claim severely disrupts the entire registration process. It is, therefore, granted only in the most urgent of cases. A request for special handling is subject to the approval of the Chief of the Acquisitions and Processing Division, who takes into account the workload situation of the office at the time the request is made. A minimum period of five working days is required to process a claim under our special handling procedures.

Why is there an urgent need for special handling?   Applicant believes that infringement

of its copyrights is occurring.

2

If special handling is needed because of litigation, please answer the following questions:

a. Is the litigation actual or prospective?   Prospective at this time.

b. Are you (or your client) the plaintiff or defendant in the action? Please specify.   Plaintiff.

c. What are the names of the parties and what is the name of the court where the action is pending or expected?

U.S. Federal District Court of Colorado   718 17th Street, Suite 147
                                                   Denver, Colorado 80202

d. What is the latest date on which the certificate(s) or other requested item(s) could be furnished to you and still be of use in this matter?

Monday, May 18, 1987

I certify that the statements made above are correct to the best of my knowledge.

(Signature)

(Address)

                                                              May 11, 1987
(Phone)   (Date)

FOR COPYRIGHT
OFFICE USE ONLY   Information Specialist handling matter

remarks

Form 5–5. Request for special handling.

§ 5.7 —Filling Out Forms

To observe some of the requirements of the forms, let's examine the form TX. *Section 1* asks for the title of the work. Every work submitted for registration *must* have a title. Spaces are provided for any previous title to the same work or alternative titles to the same work and, in the event the work was a contribution to a larger collection, the individual author may secure registered copyright protection by identifying the work submitted for registration as a contribution and identifying the work in which it was contained.

Section 2a of form TX requests the name of the author. The dates of birth and death need not be entered unless the author wishes to include them. However, you must check either the "yes" or "no" box as to whether the work was a "work made for hire," a concept we examine in further detail in § **5.17**, and fill in the author's domicile or citizenship. Section 2a then provides for identification of the work as either anonymous or pseudonymous; these boxes ("yes" or "no") must be checked.

Section 2a then requires a very brief description of the nature of the work created by the author. If there are co-authors, sections b and c and additional sections in "Form TX Continued" provide for the same information with respect to each author.

Section 3 requires entry of the year when the work was first created, and if, and only if, the work was published, the date and country of first publication.

Section 4 asks for the copyright owner's name and address. In the event the original authors have transferred their work, there is in Section 4 a space indicating the status of the claimants submitting the registration form.

Section 5 requires disclosure of previous registration. In most cases the block "no" would be checked, and no other information would be required.

Section 6 identifies the registration if it is a derivative work or a compilation. A derivative work, as discussed in § **5.3**, is another form of a previously copyrighted work, and subsections a & b both must be completed if the work being registered is derivative. Only 6b need be completed for a compilation. In 6a it is imperative to identify and disclaim rights to any federal government material. Failure to do so can void the entire copyright.

Section 7 of form TX is peculiar to this form. It is the so-called "manufacturing clause." If the material is in the English language, the printer's name and place of business are requested.

Section 8 provides for voluntary licensing of the work for use of blind and physically handicapped individuals.

Section 9 asks for the number of a deposit account in the event there is money on deposit with the Copyright Office for registering copyrights. If not, skip to the correspondence section of Section 9, which may or may not require different information from the name and address provided in either Section 4 or Section 11.

Section 10 is particularly important. It requires identification of the person certifying the form, including a printed name, a date, and a handwritten signature.

Section 11 simply requests the name and address to which the certificate should be mailed.

Thorough and accurate completion of the copyright registration form should not be taken lightly. The omission of any required bit of information, or an overbroad claim of the nature of the authorship, or the selection of the wrong form, will land the original application (after many months' delay) back in the lap of the author. The author will be instructed to resubmit a proper registration within a specified time or the registration will be deemed abandoned and the $10 registration fee forfeited.

This is of particular interest because the registration is effective on the date received by the Copyright Office. It is from that day forward that the benefits of registration accrue to the submitter. The receipt of an incomplete or improperly executed form does not constitute *receipt,* and the date of protection begins when the Copyright Office receives an acceptable registration form.

§ 5.8   Rights of Copyright Owners

Copyright owners have the exclusive rights to:

1. Reproduce copies of the copyrighted work.
2. Prepare derivative works.
3. Distribute copies or phonorecords by sale or any other transfer of ownership, or by rental, lease, or lending.
4. *If* the work is literary, musical, dramatic, choreographic, pantomime, motion picture, or another audiovisual work, to *perform* the work publicly.
5. *If* the work is literary, musical, dramatic, choreographic, pantomime, *or* pictorial, graphic, sculptural, individual images of a motion picture, or an audiovisual work, to *display* the copyrighted work publicly.

All of the above exclusive rights are limited by the doctrine of fair use, most of which is based on decided cases (common law). Other aspects of the doctrine of fair use are specifically enumerated in the copyright statute. See §§ **5.14** and **5.15** for further discussion of fair use.

The exclusive rights just examined endure for a relatively long time.[25] For example:

1. The copyright for a work of an individual author lasts for his or her lifetime plus 50 years.

---

[25] 17 U.S.C. §§ 302 (1988).

2. For joint works, the measuring lifetime is that of the last living author plus 50 years (coauthor your next book with your six-year-old
   child!).
3. For a work made for hire, the copyright lasts for 75 years from the
   first publication or 100 years from the creation.
4. For an unpublished work, the copyright lasts for 100 years from the
   time of creation.
5. For works created prior to the present Copyright Act (January 1,
   1978), copyrights in their first 27-year period must be renewed and
   the renewal period runs for 47 years. Copyrights that are in their renewal period are extended to last for 75 years from the date the
   copyright was originally obtained.

Section 203 of 17 U.S.C. gives rights to the author or authors of a work
to terminate otherwise exclusive or nonexclusive total grants or transfers
of rights in copyright, other than for works made for hire. In the event the
author is dead, the right belongs to the surviving spouse and children, if
any, of the deceased author. A termination may be effected during a five-
year window period, beginning at the end of 35 years from the date of the
original grant to the end of the 40th year after the date of the grant. It is
important to note that this right of termination is absolute and may be
exercised notwithstanding any agreement to the contrary by the original
author or authors, including any agreement to make a will or to make any
future grant. A similar provision for termination of copyrights in either
their first or second term under the earlier copyright statute (the 1900
Act) is granted to authors or their heirs under 17 U.S.C. § 304.

The Copyright Act also contains an unusual provision prohibiting involuntary transfer of exclusive rights under a copyright when those rights
have not previously been transferred voluntarily by the individual author.
It also prevents any governmental body from seizing, expropriating, or
otherwise exercising the rights of ownership.[26]

§ 5.9 Licensing Copyrights

The relinquishing of the copyright owner's exclusive rights, or part of
them, to another is customarily evidenced by a *license,* which is simply
either an oral or written grant of permission to use the otherwise exclusive
work. Perhaps the most common of these licenses is the nonexclusive right
to use a copyrighted work either for one single use or for inclusion in one
single work.

---

[26] 17 U.S.C. § 201(e) (1988).

For example, if an author wishes to include in an original book the copyrighted photograph of another, the author might request permission to use the copyrighted photograph in that book only, and the granting of that permission would constitute a nonexclusive license that could be granted by the owner of the copyright of the photograph, either gratis or for a fee. If the license is granted for a fee, the fee is called a *royalty*. One must be wary of the limitations of permitted use under a nonexclusive license, because the permission to use a photograph in a first edition may not necessarily extend to subsequent editions of the same book. Its use in subsequent editions might constitute an infringement. For example, rights to exhibit a film on television do not include the right to distribute video cassettes of the film.[27]

The owner of a nonexclusive license to use copyrighted material does not have the right to bring suit against others who infringe the copyright. Therefore recording a nonexclusive license would serve no serious purpose.

On the other hand, the copyright owner may grant to another an exclusive license either for use within a given area or for use for a certain period of time. The owner of an exclusive license has standing in its own name to sue for infringement of the copyright of the licensed work.[28] Although the Berne Convention Implementation Act of 1988 amending 17 U.S.C. § 205 makes recordation of a license or other instrument of transfer optional for causes of action arising after the amendment's effective date, recordation still provides constructive notice of ownership. The Berne Convention Implementation Act also makes it unnecessary to register a copyright, but unless and until the copyright itself is registered, an exclusive license or other instrument of transfer may not be recorded with the Copyright Office.[29]

§ 5.10 Derivative Works and Compilations

Derivative works and compilations are broad areas that expand the concept of originality. The term *derivative work* is explained in § 5.3. To restate it simply, it is the expression of the original creation either in a different media, format, or mode of expression. A *compilation*, on the other hand, is an original gathering and presentation of other works, possibly including or entirely consisting of works in the public domain.

---

[27] Cohen v. Paramount Pictures Corp., 845 F.2d 851, 6 U.S.P.Q.2d (BNA) 1773 (10th Cir. 1988).

[28] 17 U.S.C. § 501(b).

[29] 17 U.S.C. § 205(c)(2) (1989).

For example, a series of trite phrases in the public domain coupled with original artwork may constitute an original *compilation* protected by the Copyright Act.[30] Highway mileage guides[31] and plat maps[32] are also copyrightable as factual compilations. However, a derivative work of a public domain drawing must be sufficiently different to the eye of the ordinary observer for the creator to obtain a new copyright on it.[33] A recent case provides an example of a derivative work. The transferring of a copyrighted print from its sheet form to a decorative ceramic tile was held to constitute a derivative work and was, therefore, an infringement of the copyright on the print.[34] An interesting sidelight on derivative works is that if a derivative work is duly licensed by the owner of the underlying copyright, the terminations provisions of the Copyright Act do not apply to the derivative work. The licensee may continue to use the derivative work within the limits of the original license, even though the original author terminates a prior transfer of the underlying copyright to another.[35] A copyright owner also has rights to prevent the distortion of the copyrighted work.

If a compilation contains matter protected by another's copyright, permission to use such matter must first be obtained. Use of a permission form, such as the one shown as **Form 5–6**, may be efficient if a number of permissions are sought.

Form 5–6
COPYRIGHT PERMISSION FORM

Dear _____ :

I am in the process of writing a _____ on the subject of _____ for publication, and I request your permission to include the following items in my materials:

1. (The item), (place and year of publication)
2. (The item), (place and year of publication), etc.

---

[30] Roth Greeting Cards v. United Card Co., 429 F.2d 1106, 166 U.S.P.Q. (BNA) 291 (9th Cir. 1970).

[31] Rand McNally & Co. v. Fleet Management Sys., Inc., 634 F. Supp. 604, 230 U.S.P.Q. (BNA) 59 (N.D. Ill. 1986).

[32] Rockford Map Publishers, Inc. v. Directory Serv. Co. of Colo., Inc., 768 F.2d 145, 226 U.S.P.Q. (BNA) 1025 (7th Cir. 1985), *cert. denied,* 474 U.S. 1061 (1986).

[33] Sherry Mfg. Co. v. Towel King, Inc., 753 F.2d 1565, 225 U.S.P.Q. (BNA) 1005 (11th Cir. 1985).

[34] Mirage Edition, Inc. v. Albuquerque A.R.T. Co., 856 F.2d 1341, 8 U.S.P.Q.2d (BNA) 1171 (9th Cir. 1988).

[35] Miller Music, Inc. v. Snyder, 469 U.S. 153, 105 S. Ct. 638, 224 U.S.P.Q. (BNA) 313 (1985).

I request nonexclusive rights for this first publication and any revisions for publication in (the United States or worldwide). (If worldwide rights are sought, the right to translate should also be requested.)

I will give you full attribution as the author for any item I use. If someone else controls the right to give permission, please inform me.

Please sign and return the duplicate copy of this form in the stamped self-addressed envelope provided.

Sincerely,

Annie Author

Permission to use granted this _____ day of _____, 19____

_____

Copyright Owner

RESOURCES: For permission to use copyrighted music, contact:

American Society of Composers, Authors and Publishers, One Lincoln Plaza, New York, NY, 10023, telephone (217) 595-3050.

Broadcast Music, Inc., 320 West 57th Street, New York, NY 10019, telephone (212) 586-2000.

---

§ 5.11   Distortion of Work

A major stumbling block to the ratification by the United States of the Berne Convention was the convention's requirement for the recognition of the moral rights (*droit morale*) of an author or artist with respect to distortion of the work, attribution, and use of the work in a manner not in keeping with the artist's or author's current position or philosophy. While each of these elements is generally recognized by European members of the Berne Convention, the Berne Convention is not self-executing, and United States copyright law with respect to moral rights is changed only, if at all, by the Berne Convention Implementation Act of 1988. That Act provides that the provisions of the Berne Convention do not expand or reduce any right of an author to claim authorship of the work or to object to any distortion, mutilation, or other modification of or other derogatory action in relation to the work that would prejudice the author's honor or reputation.[36] See **§ 5.28** for the text of the Berne Convention Implementation Act of 1988.

---

[36] Public Law 100–568 (H.R. 4262) (Oct. 1988), 17 U.S.C. 104(c).

The recent phenomenon of "colorization" of older black and white motion pictures has not posed an infringement problem to date, no doubt because the process and exploitation has been done by permission of the copyright owners. If colorization in some future context is found to mutilate or distort the work (using psychedelic coloring, for example) or to seriously prejudice the author's honor or reputation, the author may have a remedy.

Neither the common law nor any state statutes with respect to moral rights have been restricted nor expanded by virtue of the United States' becoming a member of the Berne Convention. State law, by and large, gives copyright owners the right to prevent a licensee or assignee from distorting the copyrighted work, either by revisions or severe editing or the like, so as to destroy the original fabric or message or impact of the original work.[37]

§ 5.12   Infringement Actions

Remedies for infringement are described in the Copyright Act. Anyone who infringes the exclusive rights of the copyright owner may be sued in an infringement action. The remedies available under the Copyright Act include:

1. Temporary injunctions.
2. Final injunctions.
3. Impoundment and destruction of the infringing material.
4. Damages and profits: The copyright owner may be entitled to either: (a) actual damages and any additional profits the infringer made; or (b) statutory damages which normally run between $250 and $10,000. If the infringement is willful the court can increase statutory damages to $50,000.

   These statutory damages apply to registered works prior to the effective date of the Berne Convention Implementation Act of 1988. For works registered after the adoption of the Berne Convention Implementation Act, the statutory awards are raised from a minimum of $250 to $500 and from $10,000 to $20,000. Willful infringements permit the court to award a maximum of up to $100,000 and, for innocent infringements, the court may award a minimum of $200 rather than $100. Only infringements that arise after the effective

---

[37] Society of Survivors of Riga Ghetto v. Huttenbach, 1989 Copyright L. Dec. (CCH) ¶ 26,253 (1988); Salinger v. Random House, 811 F.2d 90, 1 U.S.P.Q.2d (BNA) 1673 (2d Cir.), *cert. denied,* 484 U.S. 890 (1987).

date of the Berne Amendments are affected by these statutory increases in statutory damages.

Copyright infringement actions may sometimes be barred by the *first sale* doctrine set forth in 17 U.S.C. § 109(a). This provision limits the copyright owner's distribution rights established in § 106 by permitting "the owner of a particular copy . . . to sell or otherwise dispose of the possession of that copy." In other words, the first sale doctrine prevents the copyright owner from controlling the future transfer of a copy once its material ownership has been transferred into the stream of commerce. For example, in a 1988 case involving a manufacturer of hair care products with copyrighted labels, the manufacturer failed in its infringement action against a foreign distribution company that bought a shipment of hair care products offshore, then reshipped some of the goods back into the United States. The court ruled that the first sale by the copyright owner had extinguished any right to later control over the importation of the sold copies.[38]

The owner's right to an injunction may be limited by the doctrine of fair use. See § 5.15. Attorney's fees may be granted to the prevailing party at the discretion of the court.[39]

§ 5.13   Noncopyrightable Works

While the Copyright Act provides copyright protection for original representations fixed in some tangible form, it does not provide protection for all representations, even though they may be fixed in a tangible form. The statute provides: "In no case does copyright protection for an original work of authorship extend to any idea, procedure, process, system, method of operation, concept, principle, or discovery, regardless of the form in which it is described, explained, illustrated, or embodied in such work."[40]

The plain meaning of this section is that while the representation of ideas, procedures, systems, and the like may be protected by copyright law, the ideas involved in any such procedure or system are not. They may be protected only by another legal concept such as patent law or the law of trade secrets.

---

[38] Sebastian Int'l, Inc. v. Consumer Contacts, 847 F.2d 1093, 7 U.S.P.Q.2d 1077 (3d. Cir. 1988).

[39] *See* Singh v. Famous Overseas, Inc., 680 F. Supp. 533, 6 U.S.P.Q.2d (BNA) 1969 (E.D.N.Y. 1988); Silverman v. CBS, Inc., 675 F. Supp. 870, 6 U.S.P.Q.2d (BNA) 1975 (S.D.N.Y. 1988).

[40] 17 U.S.C. § 102(b) (1988).

The same section also limits copyright protection to *original work* and excludes such things as short phrases, slogans, and simple drawings or figures in the public domain that have, by judicial decision, been deemed to contain insufficient *originality* to meet the statutory standard of an original work.[41] So-called "fact works" and industrial design are carefully scrutinized before they are found eligible for copyright protection. Forms are another special case. A useful approach in assessing copyright eligibility for a form is to ask whether it is simply a *check list record,* such as checking off steps performed in a physical examination, or whether the form also provides information or requires the user to read, understand, and make decisions, such as a standardized test form.[42]

What about copyright protection for articles that also have utility? Pictorial, graphic, and sculptural works provided protection by 17 U.S.C. § 113 may also be incorporated into useful articles such as vases, gift boxes, lamp bases, and other articles that fulfill purposes other than aesthetics. Section 113 freezes the copyright law with respect to such incorporation of a copyrightable work into a useful item to the law in effect on December 31, 1977, including the common law, the federal law, and statutes of any state. A general observation is that such copyrightable work does not lose its protection under federal copyright law simply because it is incorporated into a useful article, as long as the copyrightable characteristics of the work can be separated from or simply adorn the utilitarian function of the useful articles.[43]

If the alleged copyrightable work cannot be separated from the utility of the useful article, then, although no copyright protection may be available, the useful article might still be protected under a design patent.

§ 5.14   Fair Use

As explained in §§ **5.14** and **5.15**, a copyright owner's exclusive rights, while extensive, are limited by 17 U.S.C. § 107 and the doctrine of *fair use.* A pragmatic approach to fair use would measure it by the question: "What should a reasonable copyright owner expect of use by others that

---

[41] Magic Mktg. v. Mailing Servs. of Pittsburgh, 634 F. Supp. 769, 230 U.S.P.Q. (BNA) 230 (W.D. Pa. 1986).

[42] Baked v. Selden, 101 U.S. 99 (1880); Continental Casualty Co. v. Beardsley, 253 F.2d 702, 117 U.S.P.Q. (BNA) 1 (2d Cir.), *cert. denied,* 358 U.S. 816 (1958); Educational Testing Serv. v. Katzman, 793 F.2d 533, 230 U.S.P.Q. (BNA) 156 (3d Cir. 1986).

[43] Keiselstein-Cord v. Accessories By Pearl, Inc., 632 F.2d 989, 208 U.S.P.Q. (BNA) 1 (2d Cir. 1980). This case concerns the copyrightability of unique and original work adorning belt buckles.

would not substantially harm the copyright value?" Section 107 defines fair use and declares that fair use of a copyrighted work is not a copyright infringement. The examples given in § 107 include criticism, comment, news reporting, teaching, scholarship, and research.

In addition, § 107 lists four factors to be considered by courts in determining fair use situations. The factors are: (1) the purpose and character of the use (commercial or not-for-profit); (2) the nature of the copyrighted work; (3) the amount and substantiality of the portion used in relation to the work as a whole; and (4) the effect of use on the potential market or value of the copyrighted work.[44] As a very general rule of thumb, in examining whether the use of a copyrighted work without permission of the owner falls under the fair use exception, ask yourself whether a reasonable copyright owner would or should give permission for such a use. The answer to that question would depend on the four criteria listed above from § 107 of the Copyright Act.

The Copyright Act contains a few specific statutory provisions regarding fair use.

Section 108—reproduction of copyrighted works by libraries and archives.

Section 109—transfer rights of particular phonorecords or copies.

Section 110—exemption for face-to-face teaching activities and nonprofit institutions in a classroom or similar place; performance of nondramatic literary or musical works for teaching or instructional activity; performance of literary or musical works at a place of worship; and notfor-profit charitable performances.

Section 111—certain secondary transmissions.

Section 112—certain ephemeral recordings for purposes of archival preservation.

Section 115—provision for a compulsory license for making and distributing phonorecords.

Section 116—the so-called jukebox exception.

Section 117—archival copying of a computer program.

These specific provisions address very specialized activities and have little importance outside of those named activities.

---

[44] *See* Springsteen v. Plaza Roller Dome, Inc., 602 F. Supp. 1113, 225 U.S.P.Q. (BNA) 1008 (M.D.N.C. 1986) (small "putt putt" course with six small speakers using "off-the-air" songs fair use). Pacific S. Co. v. Duncan, 749 F.2d 733 (11th Cir. 1984), *cert. denied,* 471 U.S. 1004 (1985).

§ 5.15　—Case Law

Since there is no precise statutory definition of fair use, each case is decided on the particular use balanced with the fair expectations of the copyright owner. Many examples of the courts' approaches to fair use are contained in case law.

In *Keep Thompson Governor Committee v. Citizens for Gallen Committee,*[45] the court examined the four factors set out in § **5.14** in a case alleging infringement by a rival political party of a political advertisement. The court decided that the purpose and character of the use by the defendant was noncommercial, that the nature of the copyrighted work was political, that the defendant's alleged infringement amounted to 15 seconds out of a 3-minute ad, and that the plaintiff had not lost customers because of the defendant's actions. The court decided that the defendant's use of the 15-second portion of the plaintiff's ad was fair use and that no infringement occurred.

In *Key Maps, Inc. v. Pruitt,*[46] the defendant county fire marshall obtained an already copyrighted map from the plaintiff owner and adapted it for the use of fire districts. After the owner delayed in making copies, the defendant had it reproduced elsewhere and distributed it to the various fire districts. The court held that the defendant's use of the map was fair use under the four § 107 factors.

Rosemont Enterprises v. Random House, Inc.,[47] involved a biography of Howard Hughes that was held not to infringe the plaintiff's copyright in articles published 12 years previously. The articles' author could not monopolize the narration of historical events.

In *Times, Inc. v. Bernard Geis Associates,*[48] reproduction in a book of charcoal drawings of film frames of the assassination of President Kennedy was held fair use because it was in the public interest to have available as much information as possible about the event.

The court found in *Benny v. Loews, Inc.,*[49] that no permission was obtained by Jack Benny before performing a second burlesque TV reproduction of *Gaslight.* This second performance was held not to be fair use.

In *Toksvig v. Bruce Publishing Co.,*[50] a biography of Hans Christian Andersen was held to infringe on an earlier copyrighted biography and was not considered fair use. Here, the court was influenced by the fact that the infringer wrote the second biography in one-third the time that

---

[45] 457 F. Supp. 957, 199 U.S.P.Q. (BNA) 788 (D.N.H. 1978).

[46] 470 F. Supp. 33, 203 U.S.P.Q. (BNA) 282 (S.D. Tex. 1978).

[47] 366 F.2d 303, 150 U.S.P.Q. (BNA) 715 (2d Cir. 1966), *cert. denied,* 385 U.S. 1009 (1967).

[48] 293 F. Supp. 130, 159 U.S.P.Q. (BNA) 663 (S.D.N.Y. 1968).

[49] 239 F.2d 532, 112 U.S.P.Q. (BNA) 11 (9th Cir. 1956), *aff'd,* 356 U.S. 43 (1958).

[50] 181 F.2d 664, 85 U.S.P.Q. (BNA) 339 (7th Cir. 1950).

the original biographer took and that the infringer did not read Danish, the language in which the primary source material was written.

In *American Institute of Architects v. Fenichal,*[51] the Institute had compiled a booklet of forms intended to be used in construction agreements. The defendant's use of the forms was held fair use.

In *Thompson v. Gernsback,*[52] a defendant was not allowed to plead the defense of fair use to the charge that he infringed a psychiatrist's copyrighted article dealing with scientific material on homosexuality.

Williams & Wilkins Co. v. United States[53] involved the unauthorized photocopying of medical journal articles for research. Fair use was found (pre-1978 Act).

A home economics teacher used copyrighted pages verbatim for instruction in cooking classes, without credit to or permission from the copyright owner in *Marcus v. Rowley.*[54] This was held to be infringement, going beyond fair use.

Synopsizing another's reports is not fair use. In *Wainright Securities v. Wall Street Transcript,*[55] the court declined to "strain" to apply fair use to a copier making a profit on extensive verbatim use of copyrighted materials.

In *Franklin Mint Corp. v. Natural Wildlife Art Exchange, Inc.,*[56] an artist's making a second drawing of a cardinal, after selling the copyright on the first, was held not to be copying because the second drawing contained a "pattern of differences," and was not "just an echo."

Hustler Magazine was involved in two recent fair use cases. In *Haberman v. Hustler Magazine, Inc.,*[57] Hustler prevailed on a fair use defense where the magazine's use of a photographer's photos was found not intended to increase the sales of the magazine and therefore did not injure the market for the photos. Indeed, the market for the photographer's photos actually increased. However, in *Hustler v. Moral Majority, Inc.,*[58] the Moral Majority's use of *Hustler's* parodies of Jerry Falwell were found to constitute fair use when used in fundraising letters.

Extensive quotations from J. D. Salinger's private letters were held not to be fair use and therefore their utilization by Random House was enjoined in *Salinger v. Random House.*[59] But in an action to enjoin the publication

---

[51] 41 F. Supp. 146, 51 U.S.P.Q. (BNA) 29 (S.D.N.Y. 1941).

[52] 94 F. Supp. 453 (S.D.N.Y. 1950).

[53] 172 U.S.P.Q. (BNA) 670 (Ct. Cl. 1972).

[54] 695 F.2d 1171, 217 U.S.P.Q. (BNA) 691 (9th Cir. 1983).

[55] 558 F.2d 91, 194 U.S.P.Q. (BNA) 401 (2d Cir. 1978).

[56] 575 F.2d 62, 197 U.S.P.Q. (BNA) 721 (3d Cir.), *cert. denied,* 439 U.S. 880 (1978).

[57] 626 F. Supp. 201, 229 U.S.P.Q. (BNA) 15 (D. Mass. 1986).

[58] 606 F. Supp. 1526, 226 U.S.P.Q. (BNA) 721 (C.D. Cal. 1985).

[59] 811 F.2d 90, 1 U.S.P.Q.2d (BNA) 1673 (2d Cir.), *cert. denied,* 484 U.S. 890 (1987).

of a critical biography of L. Ron Hubbard, founder of the Church of Scientology, a New York district court, although recognizing that the biography's inclusion of some of Hubbard's unpublished, copyrighted material did not constitute fair use, ruled that the "interests of free speech overwhelmingly exceeded the plaintiff's" interest in an injunction.[60]

§ 5.16   Misuse of Copyrights

Misuse of a copyright by the owner is the use of federal copyright law or the ownership of a registered copyright for purposes other than reasonable compensation for the creation of the copyrighted work. There is no apparent private right under the Copyright Act, even for persons injured by misuse of the copyright laws, to force cancellation of copyright or to obtain other remedies against a misuser of the Copyright Act. However, the Copyright Office has recently promulgated regulations which permit it to cancel copyrights obtained improperly. Such cancellation is a matter totally within the discretion of the Register of Copyrights.

In the few reported cases in this area, the courts have in the exercise of their equity jurisdiction, refused to grant relief in areas of relatively clear misuse of the copyright statute. For example, the legitimate purchase of previous copyrights, motivated solely for the purpose of preventing the publication of a major work about a public figure on the eve of publication, has been viewed as inequitable conduct, and any remedy under the Copyright Act was denied.[61]

In summary, the courts have tangentially approached the issue of the misuse of the copyright laws by the owner but, as of this writing, the remedy appears to be denial of rights that might otherwise conceivably be enforced, rather than any punitive action including cancellation of copyright against the malfeasor.

Misuse of the copyright laws by a competitor is covered by the extensive remedies for infringement of registered works discussed in § 5.19. These give relief to the aggrieved owner in most situations. However, consider the situation of a competitor improperly registering public domain material contained in software similar to already copyrighted software, then threatening infringement suits unless users obtain a license. The commercial harm is evident, but relief under the Copyright Act may be unsatisfactory. Relief in such a case may be available under the Trademark Act on an unfair competition basis as discussed in **Chapter 3**.

---

[60] New Era Publications v. Henry Holt & Sons, 695 F. Supp. 1493 U.S.P.Q.2d (BNA) 1713 (S.D.N.Y. 1988), *aff'd,* 873 F.2d 576, 10 U.S.P.Q.2d (BNA) 1561 (1989).

[61] Rosemont Enters., Inc. v. Random House, Inc., 366 F.2d 303, 150 U.S.P.Q. (BNA) 715 (2d Cir. 1966), *cert. denied,* 385 U.S. 1009 (1967).

§ 5.17   Works Made for Hire

The concept of *works made for hire* focuses on who owns a work. Generally the employer owns the creations of its employees.

Prior to *Community for Creative Nonviolence v. Reid*,[62] the federal courts of appeal were split on how to determine whether a work was made for hire.[63] The view of the Fifth Circuit Court of Appeals,[64] sustained by the Supreme Court in *Reid*, was that the creator of the work must be an employee and not an independent contractor. If the creator of the work is an independent contractor, then the work must fit into one of the nine statutory categories of "specially ordered or commissioned works,"[65] and there must be an agreement signed by the parties that the commissioned work is intended as a work made for hire.

The other approaches, now overruled, concentrated on whether the person or entity who paid for the work either controlled in some substantial measure the end product of the work or controlled the activities of the actual author of the work. It seems clear after the *Reid* case that the only safe course of conduct is to have the party paying for the work and the party authorizing the work agree in writing that the work is made for hire, and to add a safety net clause that, if the work is found not to be a work made for hire, the author by the same document assigns, sells, bargains, and conveys all the author's rights in copyright to the person paying for the work. A sample form accomplishing such an arrangement is shown as **Form 5–7**.

The unresolved issue in both the Fifth Circuit case and the Supreme Court case is whether the participation by the party paying for the works amounts to joint authorship between the party paying for the work and the author. That depends upon a finding of an intention that the two contributions be merged into inseparable or interdependent parts of a whole as described in 17 U.S.C. § 103.

Form 5–7
WORK FOR HIRE AGREEMENT

THIS AGREEMENT is entered into and effective this _____ day of _____, 19____, by and between ABC Contractor, Inc., a Colorado corporation having its principal place of business at _____ (hereinafter referred to as "ABC"), and XYZ Contractee, Inc. (hereinafter

---

[62] 109 S. Ct. 2166, 10 U.S.P.Q.2d (BNA) 1985 (1989).

[63] *See* 17 U.S.C. §§ 101, 201(b) (1988).

[64] Easter Seal Soc'y for Crippled Children v. Playboy Enters., 815 F.2d 323, 2 U.S.P.Q.2d (BNA) 1585 (5th Cir. 1987).

[65] 17 U.S.C. § 101 (1988).

referred to as "XYZ"), a Colorado corporation having its principal place of business at _____.

WITNESSETH

WHEREAS, ABC has undertaken the design and development of a computer software program to _____ ("program"); and

WHEREAS, ABC desires to own a computer software program and supportive documentation to _____ (hereafter "program"); and

WHEREAS, XYZ is willing to work on the program under a "work made for hire" agreement as that term is defined by the United States Copyright Laws but with the full control of ABC;

NOW THEREFORE, in consideration of the sum of ten dollars ($10); the mutual promises and covenants contained herein; and for other good and valuable consideration; the parties hereto agree as follows:

1. XYZ and ABC acknowledge that the program is being created under the direction and control of ABC, and agree that the program shall be deemed a work made for hire by an independent contractor under the United States Copyright Laws (17 U.S.C. § 101) and, by virtue of this agreement, is the sole property of ABC free and clear from all claims of any nature relating to XYZ's contributions and other efforts, including the right to copyright the work in the name of ABC as author and proprietor thereof and any termination rights thereto. XYZ understands and agrees that ABC owns all right, title, and interest in the program and has the right to register all copyrights therein in its own name, as author, in the United States of America and in all foreign countries.

2. ABC shall pay XYZ the amounts set forth in Attachment A for its services in the creation of the program.

3. XYZ agrees that ABC shall have the unlimited right to supervise and control XYZ and to direct XYZ during the creation of the program. ABC shall have the right to use the whole program, any part or parts thereof, or none of the program, as it sees fit. ABC may alter the program, add to it, or combine it with any other program or programs, at its sole discretion. Notwithstanding the foregoing, all original material submitted by ABC to XYZ as part of the program or as part of the process of creating the program, including but not limited to programs, listings, printouts, documentation, notes, flow charts, and programming aids, shall be the property of ABC whether or not ABC uses such material. XYZ, after the performance of its services under this agreement, shall return all such original materials and copies thereof and XYZ shall have no right to make any other use of this material.

4(a). The parties to this agreement intend that ABC shall have full ownership of the program with no rights of ownership in XYZ. XYZ agrees that in the event this agreement is determined by a court of competent jurisdiction not to be a work for hire under the federal copyright laws, this agreement shall operate as an irrevocable assignment by XYZ to ABC of the copyright in the program including all rights thereunder in perpetuity. Under this irrevocable assignment, XYZ hereby assigns to ABC the sole and exclusive right, title, and interest in and to the program, without further consideration, and agrees to assist ABC in registering and from time to time enforcing all copyrights and other rights and protections relating to the program in any and all countries. It is XYZ's specific intent to assign all right, title, and interest whatsoever in any and all copyright right in the aforesaid program, in any media, and for any purpose, to ABC including all rights of renewal and extensions. To that end, XYZ agrees to execute and deliver all necessary documents requested by ABC in connection therewith and appoints ABC as its agent and attorney-in-fact to act for and in its behalf and stead to execute, register, and file any such applications, and to do all other lawfully permitted acts to further the registration, prosecution, issuance, renewals, and extensions of copyrights or other protections with the same legal force and effect as if executed by XYZ.

(b).   The parties stipulate that in the event of any dispute arising out of or concerning this agreement, no acts of ABC undertaken for the purpose of securing, maintaining, or preserving the copyright in the program, including but not limited to recordation of this agreement with the United States Copyright Office, shall be considered by any finder of fact or determiner of law in determining the character of the program as a work made for hire, unless expressly authorized in writing by ABC. Any such authorized use shall be limited to such use or uses as are expressly and unambiguously stated in the authorizing writing, and such writing shall be narrowly and strictly construed. The parties further stipulate that ABC shall not be estopped to assert that the program is a work made for hire by virtue of any act taken by ABC to secure, maintain, or preserve the copyright of the work. XYZ agrees that all types of information relating to the program, including but not limited to this contract and its attachments, and all original material submitted by ABC to XYZ as specified in Paragraph 3 above, are to be considered the trade secrets of ABC.

5.   In the event ABC shall bring an infringement suit against any third parties or shall be sued by any third parties as a result of XYZ's authorship of the program, XYZ agrees to cooperate reasonably with ABC in defending against or prosecuting any such suit. This right shall be cumulative to any other rights of ABC hereunder. XYZ shall keep all trade secrets of ABC confidential and shall sign nondisclosure agreements when requested by ABC to do so.

6.   XYZ agrees that it shall not, at any time hereafter, dispute, contest, or aid or assist others in disputing or contesting, either directly or indirectly, ABC's exclusive right, title, and interest in the program, copyrights, or other proprietary rights therein claimed by ABC.

7.   XYZ warrants that the material in the program written by XYZ is original and does not infringe the rights of any other work.

8.   The terms and provisions of this agreement shall be binding upon the parties and their heirs, legal representatives, successors, and assigns.

9.   This agreement shall be governed by the laws of the state of Colorado.

10. This agreement constitutes the entire understanding between the parties hereto. This agreement, including this paragraph, may be amended or modified only by an instrument in writing signed by both of the parties hereto or their authorized representatives.

This agreement is executed by the parties hereto.

Date: _____   XYZ CONTRACTEE, INC.

By: _____

Title: _____

Date: _____   ABC CONTRACTOR, INC.

By: _____

Title: _____

§ 5.18   Enforcement of Rights

The remedies for copyright infringement provided by the Copyright Act have been discussed briefly in § 5.12. This section includes a more detailed discussion of remedies from the standpoint of protecting the rights of the copyright owner. The impact of the recent amendment of the 1976 Copyright Act by the Berne Convention Implementation Act (see § 5.28) is highlighted for the benefit of those readers already familiar with the principal provisions of the 1976 Act prior to the Berne Convention Amendment. One must realize, however, that the Berne Convention Implementation Act has been integrated into and is now part of 17 U.S.C. It is simply the most recent amendment to 17 U.S.C.

Even though the Berne Convention has rendered notice of copyright claim no longer as important as it was prior to March 1989, under the Implementation Act notice still has both a practical and a legal impact on protecting a copyright owner's rights against an infringer. It notifies honest and conscientious parties desiring to use the work that there is a property right involved and that the rights of the owner should be respected. It also takes away from unscrupulous users the defense of innocent infringement.[66] In addition, the United States is also a subscriber to the Universal Copyright Convention and, from an international standpoint, the notice requirements of nations that are members of that convention have not necessarily been changed or altered by the Berne Convention. Therefore, the protection of a copyright owner's rights in Universal Copyright Convention nations may still depend upon adequate copyright notice.

---

[66] 17 U.S.C. §§ 401–405 (1990).

Although the Berne Convention makes registration of a copyright for a work originating in other countries voluntary in or after March, 1989, there are still strong incentives to register copyrights for works originating in the United States. Statutory damages and attorneys' fees will be awarded only if the copyright owner has registered the copyright within three months of the work's publication.

§ 5.19   —Remedies

The remedies for infringement are provided in 17 U.S.C. §§ 502 through 505. The first remedy provided in § 502 is injunction, both temporary and final, which usually restrains future infringement of the copyright. The injunction is a remedy that is fashioned by the court in the broad discretion of the court and may not only be prohibitory in nature but may also require the infringer to perform affirmative acts.[67] The copyright owner may obtain a preliminary injunction by showing: (1) irreparable injury; (2) ownership; (3) likelihood of success on the merits; and, of course, (4) infringement.[68]

The prospect of impounding and disposition of offending articles provided in 17 U.S.C. § 509 is also provided in cases of criminal infringement. The "offending article" may include devices by which the infringing works may be reproduced, such as plates, molds, and matrices. Impounding sequesters the articles during litigation, and the final order of the court may also provide for the destruction of the offending articles.[69]

In addition to an injunction, the copyright owner may claim either actual damages or, at the owner's election, statutory damages. Only actual damages may be claimed for infringements of unpublished works occurring before registration, or for published works infringed before registration, unless registration is made within three months after the first publication of the work.[70]

The infringer's profits, if any, may be recovered if they are not already accounted for in the owner's actual damages. In that event, the owner need show only the infringer's gross revenue, and the infringer has the burden of proving actual deductible expenses.[71]

If the work is registered, however, the owner may elect to receive statutory damages and avoid the problem of proving actual damages. The

---

[67] *Id.* at §§ 502–505 (1988).

[68] *See* American Code Co. v. Bersinger, 282 F. 829 (2d Cir. 1922); Houghton Mifflin Co. v. Stackpole Son, Inc., 104 F.2d 306, 42 U.S.P.Q. (BNA) 96 (2d Cir. 1939), *cert. denied,* 308 U.S. 597 (1939).

[69] 17 U.S.C. §§ 503(a) and (b) (1988).

[70] *Id.* § 504(b) (1988).

[71] *Id.*

amount of these damages for infringement to any one work is a minimum of $500 and no more than $20,000 as the court considers just. If the court finds willful infringement, the award may be raised to $100,000 as part of the infringement action. If the work is registered, the court may also award, at its discretion, attorneys' fees to the prevailing party and may assess costs against any party.[72] Although penalties for criminal offenses are not remedies under the control of the copyright owner, § 506 of the Act also provides penalties for criminal infringement, false copyright notice, fraudulent removal of copyright notice, and false representation of a material fact in the application for registration.[73]

The importance of contract law in copyright licensing has been alluded to but should be emphasized once more. Breaches of a licensing agreement are not only infringements under copyright law but may also result in additional causes of action under the common law of contracts.

If an infringement is suspected or apparent from a nonlicensee infringer, it is imperative that the copyright owner police the exclusivity of its work by cease and desist letters, accompanied or followed by an offer to license the use. If that fails, one must weigh the costs and benefits of infringement litigation. An example of a cease and desist letter follows as **Form 5–8**.

Form 5–8
CEASE AND DESIST LETTER

Dear _____:

I am the owner of the U.S. Copyright in a photograph entitled "Dusky Dawn," Registration Number _____. I am informed that you have been selling as your own work copies of my work in the form of wall plaques. I demand that you immediately cease any reproduction and sale of my work, and that you turn over to me any copies in your possession along with the original negative, and that you provide me with a complete account of the persons to whom you have sold or to whom you may have transferred any of the offending works, along with all profits you have made from the infringements.

Your actions may have also induced others to infringe by distributing the offending works and showing them publicly. They also violate 15 U.S.C. § 1125(a) because they constitute a false designation of origin and a false description of goods in commerce.

Please communicate with me immediately as to steps you are taking to comply with these demands or I will be forced to institute more formal action.

Sincerely,

_____   _____
Date   Signature of Copyright Owner

---

[72] 17 U.S.C. § 504(c) (1988).

[73] *Id.* § 506 (1988).

§ 5.20   Federal Preemption

Section 301 of 17 U.S.C. preempts all state law that might provide rights equivalent to any of the exclusive rights specified in § 106 and within the subject matter specified in §§ 102 and 103 of the Copyright Act. Section 301 specifically pertains only to works "fixed in a tangible medium of expression." Oral works such as improvised speeches, live jazz performances, and live demonstrations are frequently never fixed in a tangible medium of expression and thus are not covered by the § 301 preemption. In these cases, state law may still be relied on to resolve disputes.

Even though architectural drawings are subject to copyright law, a contract made under state law requiring the party using the plans to buy supplies only from the architect is not preempted (voided) by the Copyright Act.[74] Common law fraud and the unfair competition practices of passing off or palming off are determined by state law.[75] Similarly, misappropriation of a celebrity's voice for an audio commercial may violate a state statute forbidding stealing one's identity, and would also appear to support an action under the unfair competition doctrine of right of publicity.[76]

Section 301(d) expressly excludes from preemption "any other federal statute." Among the most prominent federal intellectual property statutes not preempted by the Copyright Act is § 43(a) of the Lanham Act discussed in **Chapter 3**.[77]

The common law and various state statutes may still apply to owners of intellectual property in the areas of (1) confidential disclosures;[78] (2) rights of privacy;[79] (3) defamation; (4) unfair business practices; and (5) contracts.[80] An initial rule of thumb analyzing whether rights have been preempted by the Copyright Act is to discern whether the situation in question contains an element that is distinguishable and separate from the exclusive rights granted by the copyright statute.

---

[74] Acorn Structures, Inc. v. Swantz, 846 F.2d 923 (4th Cir. 1988).

[75] Warrington Assocs., Inc. v. Real-Time Eng'g Sys., Inc., 522 F. Supp. 367, 216 U.S.P.Q. (BNA) 1024 (N.D. Ill. 1981) (law of trade secrets and misappropriation not per se preempted by copyright law). *See also* Videotronics, Inc. v. Bend Elecs., 564 F. Supp. 1471 (D. Nev. 1983).

[76] Ippolito v. Ono—Lennon, 526 N.Y.S.2d 877, 139 Misc. 2d 230 (1988).

[77] 15 U.S.C. § 1125 (1988).

[78] Smith v. Weinstein, 738 F.2d 419 (2d Cir. 1984) (an express or implied contract to either keep secret or pay for ideas contained in a written unregistered script held not preempted).

[79] Baltimore Orioles, Inc. v. Major League Baseball Players Assoc., 805 F.2d 663 (7th Cir. 1986) (copyrighted telecasts of baseball games preempt the individual player's right of publicity in their gametime performances).

[80] Mayer v. Josiah Wedgewood & Son, Ltd., 609 F. Supp. 1523 (S.D.N.Y. 1985) (required "extra element" necessary to preserve unfair competition from preemption under the copyright law must be one which changes the nature of the action).

§ 5.21 Protection of Computer Software

By an amendment to the copyright statute, computer programs have been given statutory standing as copyrightable works.[81] Computer program registrations are accomplished on form TX, an example of which appears as **Form 5–2**. Both source code programs (English words or signs) and object code (machine language) are registrable.[82] The Copyright Office now regularly issues registrations for computer programs. Although source code, source code and object code, and object code applications have been registered, the Copyright Office will issue a so-called "rule of doubt" registration for applications that include object code, because of the inability of the Copyright Office to examine these works.

Video displays, even though each operator may generate a different set of images, are audiovisual works and are protected by registration of the computer chip. Similarly, registration of the audiovisual portion of the work protects the chips.[83]

RESOURCE: Pearsen, "An Annotated Guide to Establishing and Registering U.S. Computer Software Copyright," *Colorado Lawyer,* Vol. 3, p. 22 (Feb. 1986).

A sample form for assignment of software copyright follows as **Form 5–9.**

Form 5–9
ASSIGNMENT OF SOFTWARE COPYRIGHT

WHEREAS, _____, whose residence address is _____ (hereinafter called the "Assignor") warrants that it has authored software entitled "_____" with United States copyright notice duly affixed thereto; and

WHEREAS, the Assignor is the sole owner of the copyright identified as Registration No. _____ in the United States Copyright Office for the aforesaid software and desires to transfer the same to _____, located and doing business at _____, (hereinafter called the "Assignee");

---

[81] 17 U.S.C. § 101 (1988).

[82] Williams Elecs., Inc. v. Artic Int'l, Inc., 685 F.2d 870, 215 U.S.P.Q. (BNA) 405 (3d Cir. 1982).

[83] *See* Apple Computer, Inc. v. Formula Int'l, Inc., 725 F.2d 521, 221 U.S.P.Q. (BNA) 762 (9th Cir. 1984); Apple Computer, Inc. v. Franklin Computer Corp., 714 F.2d 1240, 219 U.S.P.Q. (BNA) 113 (3d Cir. 1983); Midway Mfg. Co. v. Artic Int'l, Inc., 547 F. Supp. 999, 216 U.S.P.Q. (BNA) 413 (N.D. Ill. 1982), *aff'd,* 704 F.2d 1009, 218 U.S.P.Q. (BNA) 791 (7th Cir. 1983), *cert. denied,* 464 U.S. 823, 220 U.S.P.Q. (BNA) 480 (1983).

NOW, THEREFORE, for good and valuable consideration paid by the Assignee, receipt of which is hereby acknowledged by the Assignor, Assignor hereby sells, assigns, transfers, and sets over unto Assignee all the right, title, and interest whatsoever in and to the copyright in the software entitled "_____;" any and all renewals and extensions of such copyright that may be secured under the laws now or hereafter pertaining thereto in the United States; and any and all causes of action heretofore accrued in the Assignor's favor for infringement of said copyright.

This Assignment vests unto the Assignee, its successors and assigns, to have and to hold, for the duration and the existence of the copyrights and all renewals and extensions thereof, any and all copyrights in each of the above versions and in the software.

This Assignment is executed at _____ this _____ day of _____, 19____.

Date: _____   By: _____

STATE OF   :
                      : ss.
COUNTY OF   :

Before me, a Notary Public in and for the said County and State, personally appeared _____ known to me to be the person whose name is subscribed to the foregoing instrument, and acknowledges to me that he/she executed the same for the purposes and considerations therein expressed.

Given under my hand and seal of office this _____ day of _____, 19____.

My commission expires:

_____

Notary Public

_____

Address

§ 5.22   —Notice Requirements

Notice is now optional under the Berne Convention. All pre-March 1, 1989, software must have notice on all copies of the work when published. Under the Berne Convention, notice is voluntary and, if used, may eliminate the innocent infringer defense. Notice still consists of encircled "c" or the word "copyright" or the abbreviation "copr." (The use of simply the letter "c" is not proper, even though a "c" enclosed in a hexagon has been held sufficient.[84]) Include in the notice the year of first publication of the work, and the name of the copyright owner.

The notice must be affixed to the copies in such a way as to provide reasonable notice of the claimed copyright. In *Innovative Concepts in Entertainment v. Entertainment Enterprises Co.,*[85] the court denied a temporary restraining order but granted a preliminary injunction based upon plaintiff's copyrights. The case involved plaintiff's Chexx Miniature Hockey Game, and defendant's similar game called Face-Off. The court found copying to have taken place and said: "As copying may be found from evidence that a defendant had access to the copyrighted work and that the defendant's work is substantially similar to plaintiffs, plaintiff here has demonstrated copying."[86]

The plaintiff's first attorney had failed to advise him to register copyrights. The plaintiff then marketed the game and a second attorney subsequently advised registration. Because the game had already been marketed without a copyright notice, the plaintiff applied stickers to all subsequent games and mailed stickers to distributors in an effort to place notice on the games already distributed. The court found that this was a sufficient curative act under 17 U.S.C. § 405(a), despite the admonition under 17 U.S.C. § 410(c) that publications without notice are in the public domain unless excused. Random appearance of the copyright notice in the video *Joker Poker* was held insufficient.[87] Initial registration in these cases would have helped avoid substantial frustration, anxiety, and expense.

The *unit publication* rule was discussed by the court in *Koontz v. Jaffarian,*[88] in which the author wrote a manual containing data necessary for estimating bids for electrical construction contracts. A computer program was subsequently developed for automating the method. The manual contained a copyright notice but the computer software did not. Although the manual was sold separately, the computer software was sold only in conjunction with the manual. Koontz had registered both the manual and the software together as a *unit publication.* The court found that the notice on the manual was effective to protect the copyright in the associated software. It should be noted that the computer program was in fact a *derivative work* flowing from the underlying manual.

---

[84] Videotronics, Inc. v. Bend Elecs., 586 F. Supp. 478 (D. Nev. 1984).

[85] 576 F. Supp. 457, 221 U.S.P.Q. (BNA) 376 (E.D.N.Y. 1983).

[86] *Id.* at 460, 221 U.S.P.Q. (BNA) at 377.

[87] Videotronics, Inc. v. Bend Elecs., 586 F. Supp. 478, 222 U.S.P.Q. (BNA) 936 (D. Nev. 1984).

[88] 617 F. Supp. 1108, 226 U.S.P.Q. (BNA) 418 (E.D. Va. 1985), *aff'd,* 787 F.2d 906, 229 U.S.P.Q. (BNA) 381 (4th Cir. 1986).

§ 5.23   —Deposit Requirements

Deposit requirements for programs containing trade secrets are found in currently published regulations of the Copyright Office. As published, they provide for four deposit alternatives (March 31, 1989):

1. Deposit of first and last 25 pages of source code with some, but not all, portions of the code blocked out.
2. At least the first and last 10 pages of source code with no blocked-out pages.
3. First and last 25 pages of object code plus any 10 pages of source code with no blocked-out pages.
4. For programs of 25 pages or less, no more than 50% of the program blocked out or withheld, provided the remaining portion shows sufficient copyrightable authorship.[89]

The Copyright Office reports that over 90 percent of computer programs filed simply submit the required 50 pages of source code without portions blocked out. The remaining 10 percent fall within one of the three automatic grants of special relief described in alternatives 1, 2, and 3.

Final regulations[90] now provide that:

1. The source code must be specified.
2. There is no longer any requirement to state the total number of lines of code in a program.
3. Blocking of deposits is permitted only with respect to trade secret material, and unblocked portions must contain "an appreciable amount of the original computer code."
4. When registration is made based on deposited object code, it is made under the "rule of doubt" with no determination of copyrightable authorship.
5. Source code marked in a manner that virtually blocks out all computer code expression will not be an acceptable form of deposit.
6. Continued availability of special relief from filing the entire work in readily readable form for computer programs is affirmed.

Screen displays are also *works* and on June 10, 1988, the Copyright Office published notice that it would require a single registration of all copyrightable expression embodied in a computer program owned by the same claimant, including related computer graphic screen displays.

---

[89] 37 C.F.R. 202.20 vii A.
[90] 37 C.F.R. 202.20 vii B.

Presently an applicant has the option to include or omit on the registration application any specific reference to a claim in computer screen matter. If computer screen material is specifically claimed, the deposit must include appropriate reproductions of the screen displays such as visual reproductions in the form of printouts, photographs, or drawings. These materials are preferred. They should be no smaller than 3″ × 3″ and no larger than 9″ × 12″. A 1/2″ VHS videotape is acceptable when authorship is primarily visual, for example, a videogame, but not when literary authorship predominates. The reproduction should not merely show the functioning of the computer program. A computer program manual will not constitute an acceptable deposit to identify the computer screen authorship.

§ 5.24 —Protection of Databases

Information databases are constantly changing. As of this writing a single registration of a database may be made if:

1. Updates are made by the same copyright claimant.
2. Updates bear the same general title.
3. All updates are similar in their general content.
4. All updates are similar in general organization.
5. Each update was first published within three months of the previous form in a single calendar year.
6. Deposit requirements are all met.

The applicant must also provide information distinguishing separate files, file names, subjects, content, approximate number of records, and frequency of updating.[91]

§ 5.25 —Infringement

Infringement of computer programs is still a developing area of copyright law.[92]

For example, a device which enabled the purchaser to make copies of Atari home video games has been held to be a "contributory" infringement of the game.[93] Unless there is a copying of the work, however, there

---

[91] 37 C.F.R. 202.20 vii D6(v).

[92] M. Kramer Mfg., Inc. v. Andrews, 783 F.2d 421, 228 U.S.P.Q. (BNA) 705 (4th Cir. 1986). *See also* Lasercomb Am. v. Holiday Steel Rule Die Co., 829 F.2d 36 (4th Cir. 1987).

[93] Atari, Inc. v. JS&A, Inc., 597 F. Supp. 5 (N.D. Ill. 1983).

is no copyright infringement, even though the software owner's trade secrets have been appropriated.[94] A software version of a written manual is a derivative work and therefore copying it is an infringement.[95] Reverse engineering, which is discussed in **Chapter 1,** is known as *disassembly* in the computer software copyright area. Obtaining a machine-readable version of a program by disassembly of the copyrighted computer chip is an infringement.[96]

We have already seen that the term *infringement* contemplates two elements: access to the copyrighted work and copying of the copyrighted work. Proof of copying is frequently submitted simply on the basis that the original work and the alleged infringing work are strikingly similar. In the field of computer software, the proof of copying must be established by a less simplistic approach, and the recent cases look to structure, sequence, and layout, also sometimes called *look and feel* of a program.[97]

Copyright owners, understandably eager to protect their software from unauthorized copying, implant many sorts of anticopying "bugs" in software that can be neutralized for properly licensed users by trade secret computer instructions provided by the copyright owner. However, an independent and original disassembly procedure to unlock a copyright owner's anticopying protection devices, since it does not involve copying the program itself, is not a copyright infringement.[98]

One final observation is that a state government's unauthorized copying of a copyrighted computer program gives the copyright owner no remedy, because the state is immune from suit under the 11th Amendment of the United States Constitution.[99]

RESOURCES: Beutel, "Copyright Infringement and Derivative Software," *Computer Lawyer,* Vol. 4, p. 12 (Mar. 1987). Siegal, "Copyright Infringement of the 'Look and Feel' of an Operating System," *Computer Lawyer,* Vol. 4, p. 1 (Jan. 1987).

---

[94] Q-CO Indus., Inc. v. Hoffman, 625 F. Supp. 608, 228 U.S.P.Q. (BNA) 554 (S.D.N.Y. 1985).

[95] Williams v. Arndt, 626 F. Supp. 571, 227 U.S.P.Q. (BNA) 615 (D. Mass. 1985).

[96] E.F. Johnson Co. v. Uniden Corp., 623 F. Supp. 1485, 228 U.S.P.Q. (BNA) 891 (D. Minn. 1985).

[97] Broderbund Software, Inc. v. Unison World, Inc., 648 F. Supp. 1127, 213 U.S.P.Q. (BNA) 700 (N.D. Cal. 1986); Whelan Assocs., Inc. v. Jaslow Dental Laboratory, 797 F.2d 1222, 230 U.S.P.Q. (BNA) 481 (3d Cir. 1986).

[98] Vault Corp. v. Quaid Software, Ltd., 847 F.2d 255, 7 U.S.P.Q.2d (BNA) 1281 (5th Cir. 1988). 17 U.S.C. § 901 (1988).

[99] B.V. Eng'g v. University of Cal., 858 F.2d 1394, 8 U.S.P.Q.2d (BNA) 1421 (9th Cir. 1988), *cert. denied,* 109 S. Ct. 1557 (1989).

§ 5.26   Protection of Computer Chips

In 1984 Chapter 9, entitled "Protection of Semi-Conductor Chip Products,"[100] was added to Title 17 of the United States Code. The reason Congress added this chapter was to counteract a line of federal decisions that held that chips (mask works) were solely useful articles and as such were not subject to copyright protection. The new Chapter 9 permits registration of such chips with the Copyright Office, but:

1. The protection is for ten years from the date of first use, provided registration takes place within two years of the first exploitation. This term is considerably shorter than the term provided for other copyrightable works, and failure to complete registration may negate all protection.
2. Reverse engineering is permitted.
3. Registration forms similar to the regular copyright forms are provided by the Copyright Office, but the fee is $20 instead of the $10 fee required for regular copyrighted works.
4. "Substantial copying" would subject the infringer to actual or statutory damages, the amount of which is within the sound discretion of the federal court. In addition, the offending products may be impounded.

The Chip Protection Act does not carry with it any criminal penalties.

§ 5.27   Excerpts from 1976 Copyright Act

17 U.S.C. § 101.   Definitions

As used in this title, the following terms and their variant forms mean the following:

An "anonymous work" is a work on the copies or phonorecords of which no natural person is identified as author.

"Audiovisual works" are works that consist of a series of related images which are intrinsically intended to be shown by the use of machines or devices such as projectors, viewers, or electronic equipment, together with accompanying sounds, if any, regardless of the nature of the material objects, such as films or tapes, in which the works are embodied.

---

[100] 17 U.S.C. § 901 (1988).

The "Berne Convention" is the Convention for the Protection of Literary and Artistic Works, signed at Berne, Switzerland, on September 9, 1886, and all acts, protocols, and revisions thereto.

A work is a "Berne Convention work" if—

(1)   in the case of an unpublished work, one or more of the authors is a national of a nation adhering to the Berne Convention, or in the case of a published work, one or more of the authors is a national of a nation adhering to the Berne Convention on the date of first publication:

(2)   the work was first published in a nation adhering to the Berne Convention, or was simultaneously first published in a nation adhering to the Berne Convention and in a foreign nation that does not adhere to the Berne Convention;

(3)   in the case of an audiovisual work—

(A)   if one or more of the authors is a legal entity, that author has its headquarters in a nation adhering to the Berne Convention; or

(B)   if one or more of the authors is an individual, that author is domiciled, or has his or her habitual residence in, a nation adhering to the Berne Convention; or

(4)   in the case of a pictorial, graphic, or sculptural work that is incorporated in a building or other structure, the building or structure is located in a nation adhering to the Berne Convention.

For purposes of paragraph (1), an author who is domiciled in or has his or her habitual residence in, a nation adhering to the Berne Convention is considered to be a national of that nation. For purposes of paragraph (2), a work is considered to have been simultaneously published in two or more nations if its dates of publication are within 30 days of one another.

The "best edition" of a work is the edition, published in the United States at any time before the date of deposit, that the Library of Congress determines to be most suitable for its purposes.

A person's "children" are that person's immediate offspring, whether legitimate or not, and any children legally adopted by that person.

A "collective work" is a work, such as a periodical issue, anthology, or encyclopedia, in which a number of contributions, constituting separate and independent works in themselves, are assembled into a collective whole.

A "compilation" is a work formed by the collection and assembling of preexisting materials or of data that are selected, coordinated, or arranged in such a way that the resulting work as a whole constitutes an original work of authorship. The term "compilation" includes collective works.

"Copies" are material objects, other than phonorecords, in which a work is fixed by any method now known or later developed, and from which the work can be perceived, reproduced, or otherwise communicated, either directly or with the aid of a machine or device. The term "copies" includes the material object, other than a phonorecord, in which the work is first fixed.

"Copyright owner", with respect to any one of the exclusive rights comprised in a copyright, refers to the owner of that particular rights.

The "country of origin" of a Berne Convention work, for purposes of section 411, is the United States if—

(1)   in the case of a published work, the work is first published—

(A) in the United States;

(B) simultaneously in the United States and another nation or nations adhering to the Berne Convention, whose law grants a term of copyright protection that is the same as or longer than the term provided in the United States;

(C) simultaneously in the United States and a foreign nation that does not adhere to the Berne Convention; or

(D) in a foreign nation that does not adhere to the Berne Convention, and all of the authors of the work are nationals, domiciliaries, or habitual residents of, or in the case of an audiovisual work, legal entities with headquarters in the United States;

(2)   in the case of an unpublished work, all the authors of the work are nationals, domiciliaries, or habitual residents of the United States, or, in the case of an unpublished audiovisual work all the authors are legal entities with headquarters in the United States; or

(3)   in the case of a pictorial, graphic, or sculptural work incorporated in a building or structure, the building or structure is located in the United States.

For the purposes of section 411, the "country of origin" of any other Berne Convention work is not the United States.

A work is "created" when it is fixed in a copy or phonorecord for the first time; where a work is prepared over a period of time, the portion of it that has been fixed at any particular time constitutes the work as of that time, and where the work has been prepared in different versions, each version constitutes a separate work.

A "derivative work" is a work based upon one or more preexisting works, such as a translation, musical arrangement, dramatization, fictionalization, motion picture version, sound recording, art reproduction, abridgement, condensation, or any other form in which a work may be recast, transformed, or adapted. A work consisting of editorial revisions, annotations, elaborations, or other modifications which, as a whole, represent an original work of authorship, is a "derivative work."

A "device", "machine", or "process" is one now known or later developed.

To "display" a work means to show a copy of it, either directly or by means of a film, slide, television image, or any other device or process or, in the case of a motion picture or other audiovisual work, to show individual images nonsequentially.

A work is "fixed" in a tangible medium of expression when its embodiment in a copy or phonorecord, by or under the authority of the author, is sufficiently permanent or stable to permit it to be perceived, reproduced, or otherwise communicated for a period of more than transitory duration. A work consisting of sound, images, or both, that are being transmitted, is "fixed" for purposes of this title if a fixation of the work is being made simultaneously with its transmission.

The terms "including" and "such as" are illustrative and not limitative.

A "joint work" is a work prepared by two or more authors with the intention that their contributions be merged into inseparable or interdependent parts of a unitary whole.

"Literary works" are works, other than audiovisual works, expressed in words, numbers, or other verbal or numerical symbols or indicia, regardless of the nature of the material objects, such as books, periodicals, manuscripts, phonorecords, film, tapes, disks, or cards, in which they are embodied.

"Motion pictures" are audiovisual works consisting of a series of related images which, when shown in succession, impart an impression of motion, together with accompanying sounds, if any.

To "perform" a work means to recite, render, play, dance, or act it, either directly or by means of any device or process or, in the case of a motion picture or other audiovisual work, to show its images in any sequence or to make the sounds accompanying it audible.

"Phonorecords" are material objects in which sounds, other than those accompanying a motion picture or other audiovisual work, are fixed by any method now known or later developed, and from which the sounds can be perceived, reproduced, or otherwise communicated, either directly or with the aid of a machine or device. The term "phonorecords" includes the material object in which the sounds are first fixed.

"Pictorial, graphic, and sculptural works" include two-dimensional and three-dimensional works of fine, graphic, and applied art, photographs, prints and art reproductions, maps, globes, charts, diagrams, models, and technical drawings, including architectural plans. Such works shall include works of artistic craftsmanship insofar as their form but not their mechanical or utilitarian aspects are concerned; the design of a useful article, as defined in this section, shall be considered a pictorial, graphic, or sculptural work only if, and only to the extent that, such design incorporates pictorial, graphic, or sculptural features that can be identified separately from, and are capable of existing independently of, the utilitarian aspects of the article.

A "pseudonymous work" is a work on the copies or phonorecords of which the author is identified under a fictitious name.

"Publication" is the distribution of copies or phonorecords of a work to the public by sale or other transfer of ownership, or by rental, lease, or lending. The offering to distribute copies or phonorecords to a group of persons for purposes of further distribution, public performance, or public display, constitutes publication. A public performance or display of a work does not of itself constitute publication.

To perform or display a work "publicly" means—

(1)   to perform or display it at a place open to the public or at any place where a substantial number of persons outside of a normal circle of a family and its social acquaintances is gathered; or

(2)   to transmit or otherwise communicate a performance or display of the work to a place specified by clause (1) or to be public, by means of any

device or process, whether the members of the public capable of receiving the performance or display receive it in the same place or in separate places and at the same time or at different times.

"Sound recordings" are works that result from the fixation of a series of musical, spoken, or other sounds, but not including the sounds accompanying a motion picture or other audiovisual work, regardless of the nature of the material objects, such as disks, tapes, or other phonorecords, in which they are embodied.

"State" includes the District of Columbia and the Commonwealth of Puerto Rico, and any territories to which this title is made applicable by an act of Congress.

A "transfer of copyright ownership" is an assignment, mortgage, exclusive license, or any other conveyance, alienation, or hypothecation of a copyright or of any of the exclusive rights comprised in a copyright, whether or not it is limited in time or place of effect, but not including a nonexclusive license.

A "transmission program" is a body of material that, as an aggregate, has been produced for the sole purpose of transmission to the public in sequence and as a unit.

To "transmit" a performance or display is to communicate it by any device or process whereby images or sounds are received beyond the place from which they are sent.

The "United States", when used in a geographical sense, comprises the several States, the District of Columbia and the Commonwealth of Puerto Rico, and the organized territories under the jurisdiction of the United States Government.

A "useful article" is an article having an intrinsic utilitarian function that is not merely to portray the appearance of the article or to convey information. An article that is normally a part of a useful article is considered a "useful article".

The author's "widow" or "widower" is the author's surviving spouse under the law of the author's domicile at the time of his or her death, whether or not the spouse has later remarried.

A "work of the United States Government" is a work prepared by an officer or employee of the United States Government as part of that person's official duties.

A "work made for hire" is—

    (1)   a work prepared by an employee within the scope of his or employment or

    (2)   a work specially ordered or commissioned for use as a contribution to a collective work, as a part, of a motion picture or other audiovisual work, as a translation, as a supplementary work, as a compilation, as an instructional text, as a test, as answer material for a test, or as an atlas, if the parties expressly agree in a written instrument signed by them that the work shall be considered a work made for hire. For the purpose of the foregoing sentence, a "supplementary work" is a work prepared for publication as a secondary adjunct to a work by another author for the purpose of introducing, concluding, illustrating, explaining, revising, commenting upon, or assisting in the use of the other work, such as forewords, afterwords, pictorial illustrations,

maps, charts, tables, editorial notes, musical arrangements, answer material for tests, bibliographies, appendixes, and indexes, and an "instructional text" is a literary, pictorial, or graphic work prepared for publication and with the purpose of use in systematic instructional activities.

A "computer program" is a set of statements or instructions to be used directly or indirectly in a computer in order to bring about a certain result.

§ 102.   Subject matter of copyright: In general

(a)   Copyright protection subsists, in accordance with this title, in original works of authorship fixed in any tangible medium of expression, now known or later developed, from which they can be perceived, reproduced, or otherwise communicated, either directly or with the aid of a machine or device. Works of authorship include the following categories:

(1)   literary works;
(2)   musical works, including any accompanying words;
(3)   dramatic works, including any accompanying music;
(4)   pantomimes and choreographic works;
(5)   pictorial, graphic, and sculptural works;
(6)   motion pictures and other audiovisual works; and
(7)   sound recordings.

(b)   In no case does copyright protection for an original work of authorship extend to any idea, procedure, process, system, method or operation, concept, principle, or discovery, regardless of the form in which it is described, explained, illustrated, or embodied in such work.

§ 103.   Subject matter of copyright: Compilations and derivative works

(a)   The subject matter of copyright as specified by section 102 includes compilations and derivative works, but protection for a work employing pre-existing material in which copyright subsists does not extend to any part of the work in which such material has been used unlawfully.

(b)   The copyright in a compilation or derivative work extends only to the material contributed by the author of such work, as distinguished from the pre-existing material employed in the work, and does not imply any exclusive right in the preexisting material. The copyright in such work is independent of, and does not affect or enlarge the scope, duration, ownership, or subsistence of, any copyright protection in the preexisting material.

§ 104.   Subject matter of copyright: National origin

(a)   Unpublished Works.—The works specified by sections 102 and 103, while unpublished, are subject to protection under this title without regard to the nationality or domicile of the author.

(b)   Published Works.—The works specified by sections 102 and 103, when published, are subject to protection under this title if—

(1)   on the date of first publication, one or more of the authors is a national or domiciliary of the United States, or is a national, domiciliary, or sovereign authority of a foreign nation that is a party to a copyright treaty to which the United States is also a party, or is a stateless person, wherever that person may be domiciled; or

(2)   the work is first published in the United States or in a foreign nation that, on the date of first publication, is a party to the Universal Copyright Convention; or

(3)   the work is first published by the United Nations or any of its specialized agencies, or by the Organization of American States; or

(4)   the work is a Berne Convention work; or

(5)   the work comes within the scope of a Presidential proclamation. Whenever the President finds that a particular foreign nation extends, to works by authors who are nationals or domiciliaries of the United States or to works that are first published in the United States, copyright protection on substantially the same basis as that on which the foreign nation extends protection to works of its own nationals and domiciliaries and works first published in that nation, the President may by proclamation extend protection under this title to works of which one or more of the authors is, on the date of first publication, a national, domiciliary, or sovereign authority of that nation, or which was first published in that nation. The President may revise, suspend, or revoke any such proclamation or impose any conditions or limitations on protection under a proclamation.

(c)   Effect of Berne Convention.—No right or interest in a work eligible for protection under this title may be claimed by virtue of, or in reliance upon, the provisions of the Berne Convention, or the adherence of the United States thereto. Any rights in a work eligible for protection under this title that derive from this title, other Federal or State statutes, or the common law, shall not be expanded or reduced by virtue of, or in reliance upon, the provisions of the Berne Convention, or the adherence of the United States thereto.

§ 106.   Exclusive rights in copyrighted works

Subject to sections 107 through 118, the owner of copyright under this title has the exclusive rights to do and to authorize any of the following:

(1)   to reproduce the copyrighted work in copies or phonorecords;

(2)   to prepare derivative works based upon the copyrighted work;

(3)   to distribute copies or phonorecords of the copyrighted work to the public by sale or other transfer of ownership, or by rental, lease, or lending;

(4)   in the case of literary, musical, dramatic, and choreographic works, pantomimes, and motion pictures and other audiovisual works, to perform the copyrighted work publicly; and

(5)   in the case of literary, musical, dramatic, and choreographic works, pantomimes, and pictorial, graphic, or sculptural works, including the individual images of a motion picture or other audiovisual work, to display the copyrighted work publicly.

§ 107.   Limitations on exclusive rights: Fair use

Notwithstanding the provisions of section 106, the fair use of a copyrighted work, including such use by reproduction in copies or phonorecords or by any other means specified by that section, for purposes such as criticism, comment, news reporting, teaching (including multiple copies for classroom use), scholarship, or research, is not an infringement of copyright. In determining whether the use made of a work in any particular case is a fair use the factors to be considered shall include—

(1)   the purpose and character of the use, including whether such use is of a commercial nature or is for nonprofit educational purposes;

(2)   the nature of the copyrighted work;

(3)   the amount and substantiality of the portion used in relation to the copyrighted work as a whole; and

(4)   the effect of the use upon the potential market for or value of the copyrighted work.

§ 117.   Limitations on exclusive rights: Computer programs

Notwithstanding the provisions of section 106, it is not an infringement for the owner of a copy of a computer program to make or authorize the making of another copy or adaptation of that computer program provided:

(1)   that such a new copy or adaptation is created as an essential step in the utilization of the computer program in conjunction with a machine and that it is used in no other manner, or

(2)   that such new copy or adaptation is for archival purposes only and that all archival copies are destroyed in the event that continued possession of the computer program should cease to be rightful.

Any exact copies prepared in accordance with the provisions of this section may be leased, sold, or otherwise transferred, along with the copy from which such copies were prepared, only as part of the lease, sale, or other transfer of all rights in the program. Adaptations so prepared may be transferred only with the authorization of the copyright owner.

§ 201.   Ownership of copyright

(a)   Initial Ownership.—Copyright in a work protected under this title vests initially in the author or authors of the work. The authors of a joint work are coowners of copyright in the work.

(b)   Works Made for Hire.—In the case of a work made for hire, the employer or other person for whom the work was prepared is considered the author for purposes of this title, and, unless the parties have expressly agreed otherwise in a written instrument signed by them, owns all of the rights comprised in the copyright.

(c)   Contributions to Collective Works.—Copyright in each separate contribution to a collective work is distinct from copyright in the collective work as a whole, and vests initially in the author of the contribution. In the absence of an express transfer of the copyright or of any rights under it, the owner of copyright in the collective work is presumed to have acquired only the privilege of reproducing and distributing the contribution as part of the particular collective work, any revision of that collective work, and any later collective work in the same series.

(d)   Transfer of Ownership.—

(1)   The ownership of a copyright may be transferred in whole or in part by any means of conveyance or by operation of law, and may be bequeathed by will or pass as personal property by the applicable laws of intestate succession.

(2)   Any of the exclusive rights comprised in a copyright including any subdivision of any of the rights specified by section 106, may be transferred as provided by clause (1) and owned separately. The owner of any particular exclusive right is entitled, to the extent of that right, to all of the protection and remedies accorded to the copyright owner by this title.

(e)   Involuntary Transfer.—When an individual author's ownership of a copyright, or of any of the exclusive rights under a copyright, has not previously been transferred voluntarily by that individual author, no action by any governmental body other official or organization purporting to seize, expropriate, transfer, or exercise right of ownership with respect to the copyright, or any of the exclusive rights under a copyright, shall be given effect under this title except as provided under Title 11.

§ 202.   Ownership of copyright as distinct from ownership of material object

Ownership of a copyright, or of any of the exclusive rights under a copyright, is distinct from ownership of any material object in which the work is embodied. Transfer of ownership of any material object, including the copy or phonorecord in which the work is first fixed, does not of itself convey any rights in the copyrighted work embodied in the object; nor, in the absence of an agreement, does transfer of ownership of a copyright or of any exclusive rights under a copyright convey property rights in any material object.

§ 301.   Preemption with respect to other laws

(a)   On and after January 1, 1978, all legal or equitable rights that are equivalent to any of the exclusive rights within the general scope of copyright as specified by section 106 in works of authorship that are fixed in a tangible medium of expression and come within the subject matter of copyright as specified by sections 102 and 103, whether created before or after that date and whether published or unpublished, are governed exclusively by this title. Thereafter, no person is entitled to any such right or equivalent right in any such work under the common law or statutes of any State.

(b)   Nothing in this title annuls or limits any rights or remedies under the common law or statutes or any State with respect to—

(1)   subject matter that does not come within the subject matter of copyright as specified by sections 102 and 103, including works of authorship not fixed in any tangible medium of expression; or

(2)   any cause of action arising from undertakings commenced before January 1, 1978; or

(3)   activities violating legal or equitable rights that are not equivalent to any of the exclusive rights within the general scope of copyright as specified by section 106.

(c)   With respect to sound recordings fixed before February 15, 1972, any rights or remedies under the common law or statutes of any State shall not be annulled or limited by this title until February 15, 2047. The preemptive provisions of subsection (a) shall apply to any such rights and remedies pertaining to any cause of action arising from undertakings commenced on and after February 15, 2047. Notwithstanding the provisions of sections 303, no sound recording fixed before February 15, 1972, shall be subject to copyright under this title before, on, or after February 15, 2047.

(d)   Nothing in this title annuls or limits any right or remedies under any other Federal statute.

(e)   The scope of Federal preemption under this section is not affected by the adherence of the United States to the Berne Convention or the satisfaction of obligations of the United States thereunder.

§ 401.   Notice of copyright: Visually perceptible copies

(a)   General Provisions.—Whenever a work protected under this title is published in the United States or elsewhere by authority of the copyright owner, a notice of copyright as provided by this section may be placed on publicly distributed copies from which the work can be visually perceived, either directly or with the aid of a machine or device.

(b)   Form of Notice.—If a notice appears on the copies, it shall consist of the following three elements:

(1)   the symbol © (the letter C in a circle), or the word "Copyright", or the abbreviation "Copr."; and

(2)   the year of first publication of the work; in the case of compilations or derivative works incorporating previously published material, the year date of first publication of the compilation or derivative work is sufficient. The year date may be omitted where a pictorial, graphic, or sculptural work, with accompanying text matter, if any, is reproduced in or on greeting cards, postcards, stationery, jewelry, dolls, toys, or any useful articles; and

(3)   the name of the owner of copyright in the work, or an abbreviation by which the name can be recognized, or a generally known alternative designation of the owner.

(c)   Position of Notice.—The notice shall be affixed to the copies in such manner and location as to give reasonable notice of the claim of copyright.

The Register of Copyrights shall prescribe by regulation, as examples, specific methods of affixation and positions of the notice on various types of works that will satisfy this requirement, but these specifications shall not be considered exhaustive.

(d)   Evidentiary Weight of Notice.—If a notice of copyright in the form and position specified by this section appears on the published copy or copies to which a defendant in a copyright infringement suit had access, then no weight shall be given to such a defendant's interposition of a defense based on innocent infringement in mitigation of actual or statutory damages, except as provided in the last sentence of section 504(c)(2).

§ 402.   Notice of Copyright: Phonorecords of sound recordings

(a)   General Provisions.—Whenever a sound recording protected under this title is published in the United States or elsewhere by authority of the copyright owner, a notice of copyright as provided by this section may be placed on publicly distributed phonorecords of the sound recording.

(b)   Form of Notice.—If a notice appears on the phonorecords, it shall consist of the following three elements:

(1)   the symbol ℗ (the letter P in a circle); and

(2)   the year of first publication of the sound recording; and

(3)   the name of the owner of copyright in the sound recording, or an abbreviation by which the name can be recognized, or a generally known alternative designation of the owner, if the producer of the sound recording is named on the phonorecord labels or containers, and if no other name appears in conjunction with the notice, the producer's name shall be considered a part of the notice.

(c)   Position of Notice.—The notice shall be placed on the surface of the phonorecord, or on the phonorecord label or container, in such manner and location as to give reasonable notice of the claim of copyright.

(d)   Evidentiary Weight of Notice.—If a notice of copyright in the form and position specified by this section appears on the published phonorecord or phonorecords to which a defendant in a copyright infringement suit had access, then no weight shall be given to such a defendant's interposition of a defense based on innocent infringement in mitigation of actual or statutory damages, except as provided in the last sentence of section 504(c)(2).

§ 411.   Registration and infringement actions

(a)   Except for actions for infringement of copyright in Berne Convention works whose country of origin is not the United States, and subject to the provisions of subsection (b), no action for infringement of the copyright in any work shall be instituted until registration of the copyright claim has been made in accordance with this title. In any case, however, where the deposit, application, and fee required for registration have been delivered to the Copyright Office in proper form and registration has been refused, the applicant is entitled to institute an action for infringement if notice thereof, with a copy of the complaint, is served on the Register of Copyrights. The Register may, at his or her option, become a party to the action with respect to the issue of registrability of the copyright claim by entering an appearance within sixty days after such service, but the Register's failure to become a party shall not deprive the court of jurisdiction to determine that issue.

(b)   In the case of a work consisting of sounds, images, or both, the first fixation of which is made simultaneously with its transmission, the copyright owner may, either before or after such fixation takes place, institute an action for infringement under section 501, fully subject to the remedies provided by sections 502 through 506 and sections 509 and 510, if, in accordance with requirements that the Register of Copyrights shall prescribe by regulation, the copyright owner—

(1)   serves notice upon the infringer, not less than ten or more than thirty days before such fixation, identifying the work and the specific time and source of its first transmission, and declaring an intention to secure copyright in the work; and

(2)   makes registration for the work, if required by subsection (a), within three months after its first transmission.

§ 412.   Registration as prerequisite to certain remedies for infringement

In any action under this title, other than an action instituted under section 411(b), no award of statutory damages or of attorney's fees, as provided by sections 504 and 505, shall be made for—

(1)   any infringement of copyright in an unpublished work commenced before the effective date of its registration; or

(2)   any infringement of copyright commenced after first publication of the work and before the effective date of its registration, unless such registration is made within three months after the first publication of the work.

§ 501.   Infringement of copyright

(a)   Anyone who violates any of the exclusive rights of the copyright owner as provided by sections 106 through 118, or who imports copies or phonorecords into the United States in violation of section 602, is an infringer of the copyright.

(b)   The legal or beneficial owner of an exclusive right under a copyright is entitled, subject to the requirements of section 411, to institute an action for any infringement of that particular right committed while he or she is the owner of it. The court may require such owner to serve written notice of the action with a copy of the complaint upon any person shown, by the records of the Copyright Office or otherwise, to have or claim an interest in the copyright, and shall require that such notice be served upon any person whose interest is likely to be affected by a decision in the case. The court may require the joinder, and shall permit the intervention, of any person having or claiming an interest in the copyright.

   (c)   For any secondary transmission by a cable system that embodies a performance or a display of a work which is actionable as an act of infringement under subsection (c) of section 111, a television broadcast station holding a copyright or other license to transmit or perform the same version of that work shall, for purposes of subsection (b) of this section, be treated as a legal or beneficial owner if such secondary transmission occurs within the local service area of that television station.

   (d)   For any secondary transmission by a cable system that is actionable as an act of infringement pursuant to section 111(c)(3), the following shall also have standing to sue: (i) the primary transmitter whose transmission has been altered by the cable system; and (ii) any broadcast station within whose local service area the secondary transmission occurs.

   (e)   With respect to any secondary transmission that is made by a satellite carrier of a primary transmission embodying the performance or display of a work and is actionable as an act of infringement under section 119(a)(5), a network station holding a copyright or other license to transmit or perform the same version of that work shall, for purposes of subsection (b) of this section, be treated as a legal or beneficial owner if such secondary transmission occurs within the local service area of that station.

§ 502.   Remedies for infringement: Injunctions

   (a)   Any court having jurisdiction of a civil action arising under this title may, subject to the provisions of section 1498 of title 28, grant temporary and final injunctions on such terms as it may deem reasonable to prevent or restrain infringement of a copyright.

   (b)   Any such injunction may be served anywhere in the United States on the person enjoined; it shall be operative throughout the United States and shall be enforceable, by proceedings in contempt or otherwise, by any United States court having jurisdiction of that person. The clerk of the court granting the injunction shall, when requested by any other court in which enforcement of the injunction is sought, transmit promptly to the other court a certified copy of all the papers in the case on file in such clerk's office.

§ 503.   Remedies for infringement: Impounding and disposition of infringing articles

   (a)   At any time while an action under this title is pending, the court may order the impounding, on such terms as it may deem reasonable, of all copies or phonorecords claimed to have been made or used in violation of the copyright's owner's exclusive rights, and of all plates, molds, matrices, masters, tapes, film negatives, or other articles by means of which such copies or phonorecords may be reproduced.

(b)   As part of a final judgment or decree, the court may order the destruction or other reasonable disposition of all copies or phonorecords found to have been made or used in violation of the copyright owner's exclusive rights, and of all plates, molds, matrices, masters, tapes, film negatives, or other articles by means of which such copies or phonorecords may be reproduced.

§ 504.   Remedies for infringement: Damages and profits

(a)   In General.—Except as otherwise provided by this title, an infringer of copyright is liable for either—

(1)   the copyright owner's actual damages and any additional profits of the infringer, as provided by subsection (b); or

(2)   statutory damages, as provided by subsection (c).

(b)   Actual Damages and Profits.—The copyright owner is entitled to recover the actual damages suffered by him or her as a result of the infringement, and any profits of the infringer that are attributable to the infringement and are not taken into account in computing the actual damages. In establishing the infringer's profits, the copyright owner is required to present proof only of the infringer's gross revenue, and the infringer is required to prove his or her deductible expenses and the elements of profit attributable to factors other than the copyrighted work.

(c)   Statutory Damages.—

(1)   Except as provided by clause (2) of this subsection, the copyright owner may elect, at any time before final judgment is rendered, to recover, instead of actual damages and profits, an award of statutory damages for all infringements involved in the action, with respect to any one work, for which any one infringer is liable individually, or for which any two or more infringers are liable jointly and severally, in a sum of not less than $500 or more than $20,000 as the court considers just. For the purposes of this subsection, all the parts of a compilation or derivative work constitute one work.

(2)   In a case where the copyright owner sustains the burden of proving, and the court finds, that infringement was committed willfully, the court in its discretion may increase the award of statutory damages to a sum of not more than $100,000. In a case where the infringer sustains the burden of proving, and the court finds, that such infringer was not aware and had no reason to believe that his or her acts constituted an infringement of copyright, the court in its discretion may reduce the award of statutory damages to a sum of not less than $200. The court shall remit statutory damages in any case where an infringer believed and had reasonable grounds for believing that his or her use of the copyrighted work was a fair use under section 107, if the infringer was: (i) an employee or agent of a nonprofit educational institution, library, or archives acting within the scope of his or her employment who, or such institution, library, or archives itself, which infringed by reproducing the work in copies or phonorecords;

or (ii) a public broadcasting entity which or a person who, as a regular part of the nonprofit activities of a public broadcasting entity (as defined in subsection (g) of section 118) infringed by performing a published nondramatic literary work or by reproducing a transmission program embodying a performance of such a work.

§ 505.   Remedies for infringement: Costs and attorney's fees

In any civil action under this title, the court in its discretion may allow the recovery of full costs by or against any party other than the United States or an officer thereof. Except as otherwise provided by this title, the court may also award a reasonable attorney's fee to the prevailing party as part of the costs.

§ 5.28   Berne Convention Implementation Act

THE BERNE CONVENTION IMPLEMENTATION ACT
OF 1988
(Pub. L. 100-568, 102 Stat. 2853)

Sec. 1.   Short Title and References to Title 17, United States Code

(a)   Short title.—This Act may be cited as the "Berne Convention Implementation Act of 1988".

(b)   References to Title 17, United States Code.—Whenever in this Act an amendment or repeal is expressed in terms of an amendment to or a repeal of a section or other provision, the reference shall be considered to be made to a section or other provision of title 17, United States Code.

Sec. 2.   Declarations

The Congress makes the following declarations:

(1)   The Convention for the Protection of Literary and Artistic Works, signed at Berne, Switzerland, on September 9, 1886, and all acts, protocols, and revisions thereto (hereafter in this Act referred to as the "Berne Convention") are not self-executing under the Constitution and laws of the United States.

(2)   The obligations of the United States under the Berne Convention may be performed only pursuant to appropriate domestic law.

(3)   The amendments made by this Act, together with the law as it exists on the date of the enactment of this Act, satisfy the obligations of the United States in adhering to the Berne Convention and no further rights or interests shall be recognized or created for that purpose.

Sec. 3.   Construction of the Berne Convention

(a)   Relationship with Domestic Law.—The provisions of the Berne Convention—

(1)   shall be given effect under title 17, as amended by this Act, and any other relevant provision of Federal or State law, including the common law; and

(C)   by inserting after the definition of "Copyright owner", the following:

"The 'country of origin' of a Berne Convention work, for purposes of section 411, is the United States if—

"(1)   in the case of a published work, the work is first published—

"(A)   in the United States;

"(B)   simultaneously in the United States and another nation or nations adhering to the Berne Convention, whose law grants a term of copyright protection that is the same as or longer than the term provided in the United States;

"(C)   simultaneously in the United States and a foreign nation that does not adhere to the Berne Convention; or

"(D)   in a foreign nation that does not adhere to the Berne Convention, and all of the authors of the work are nationals, domiciliaries, or habitual residents of, or in the case of an audiovisual work legal entities with headquarters in, the United States;

"(2)   in the case of an unpublished work, all the authors of the work are nationals, domiciliaries, or habitual residents of the United States, or, in the case of an unpublished audiovisual work, all the authors are legal entities with headquarters in the United States; or

"(3)   in the case of a pictorial, graphic, or sculptural work incorporated in a building or structure, the building or sculpture is located in the United States.

"For the purposes of section 411, the 'country of origin' of any other Berne Convention work is not in the United States.";

(2)   in section 104(b)—

(A)   by redesignating paragraph (4) as paragraph (5); and

(B)   by inserting after paragraph (3) the following new paragraph;

"(4)   the work is a Berne Convention work; or";

(3)   in section 104 by adding at the end thereof the following:

"(c)   Effect of Berne Convention.—No right or interest in a work eligible for protection under this title may be claimed by virtue of, or in reliance upon, the provisions of the Berne Convention, or the adherence of the United States thereto. Any rights in a work eligible for protection under this title that derive from this title, other Federal or State statutes, or the common law, shall not be expanded or reduced by virtue of, or in reliance upon, the provisions of the Berne Convention, or the adherence of the United States thereto."; and

(4)   by inserting after section 116 the following new section:

"§ 116A.   Negotiated licenses for public performances by means of coin-operated phonorecord players

"(a)   Applicability of Section.—This section applies to any non-dramatic musical work embodied in a phonorecord.

"(b)   Limitation on Exclusive Right if Licenses Not Negotiated.—

"(1)   Applicability.—In the case of a work to which this section applies, the exclusive right under clause (4) of section 106 to perform the work publicly by means of a coin-operated phono-record player is limited by section 116 to the extent provided in this section.

"(2)   Determination by Copyright Royalty Tribunal.—The Copyright Royalty Tribunal, at the end of the 1-year period beginning on the effective date of the Berne Convention Implementation Act of 1988, and periodically thereafter to the extent necessary to carry out subsection (f), shall determine whether or not negotiated licenses authorized by subsection (c) are in effect so as to provide permission to use a quantity of musical works not substantially smaller than the quantity of such works performed on coin-operated phonorecord players during the 1-year period ending on the effective date of that Act. If the Copyright Royalty Tribunal determines that such negotiated licenses are not so in effect, the Tribunal shall, upon making the determination, publish the determination in the Federal Register. Upon such publication, section 116 shall apply with respect to musical works that are not the subject of such negotiated licenses.

"(c)   Negotiated Licenses.—

"(1) Authority for Negotiations.—Any owners of copyright in works to which this section applies and any operators of coin-operated phonorecord players may negotiate and agree upon the terms and rates of royalty payments for the performance of such works, and the proportionate division of fees paid among copyright owners, and may designate common agents to negotiate, agree to, pay, or receive such royalty payments.

"(2) Arbitration.—Parties to such a negotiation, within such time as may be specified by the Copyright Royalty Tribunal by regulation, may determine the result of the negotiation by arbitration. Such arbitration shall be governed by the provisions of title 9, to the extent such title is not inconsistent with this section. The parties shall give notice to the Copyright Royalty Tribunal of any determination reached by arbitration and any such determination shall, as between the parties to the arbitration, be dispositive of the issues to which it relates.

"(d) License Agreements Superior to Copy Royalty Tribunal Determinations.—License agreements between one or more copyright owners and one or more operators of coin-operated phonorecord players, which are negotiated in accordance with subsection (c), shall be given effect in lieu of any otherwise applicable determination by the Copyright Royalty Tribunal.

"(e) Negotiation Schedule.—Not later than 60 days after the effective date of the Berne Convention Implementation Act of 1988, if the Chairman of the Copyright Royalty Tribunal has not received notice, from copyright owners and operators of coin-operated phonorecord players referred to in subsection (c)(1), of the date and location of the first meeting between such copyright owners and such operators to commence negotiations authorized by subsection (c), the Chairman shall announce the date and location of such meeting. Such meeting may not be held more than 90 days after the effective date of such Act.

"(f) Copyright Royalty Tribunal to Suspend Various Activities.— The Copyright Royalty Tribunal shall not conduct any ratemaking activity with respect to coin-operated phonorecord players unless, at any time more than one year after the effective date of the Berne Convention Implementation Act of 1988, the negotiated licenses adopted by the parties under this section do not provide permission to use a quantity of musical works not substantially smaller than the quantity of such works performed on coin-operated phonorecord players during the one-year period ending on the effective date of such Act.

"(g) Transition Provisions; Retention of Copyright Royalty Tribunal Jurisdiction.—Until such time as licensing provisions are determined by the parties under this section, the terms of the compulsory license under section 116, with respect to the public performance of nondramatic musical works by means of coin-operated phonorecord players, which is in effect on the day before the effective date of the Berne Convention Implementation Act of 1988, shall remain in force. If a negotiated license authorized by this section comes into force so as to supersede previous determinations of the Copyright Royalty Tribunal, as provided in subsection (d), but thereafter is terminated or expires and is not replaced by another licensing agreement, then section 116 shall be effective with respect to musical works that were the subject of such terminated or expired licenses.".

(b) Technical Amendments.—

(1) Section 116 is amended—

(A) by amending the section heading to read as follows:

"§ 116. Scope of exclusive rights in nondramatic musical works: compulsory licenses for public performances by means of coin-operated phonorecord players";

(B)   in subsection (a) in the matter preceding paragraph (1), by inserting after "in a phonorecord," the following: "the performance of which is subject to this section as provided in section 116A,"; and

(C)   in subsection (e), by inserting "and section 116A" after "As used in this section".

(2)   The table of sections at the beginning of chapter 1 is amended by striking out the item relating to section 116, and inserting in lieu thereof the following:

"116.   Scope of exclusive rights in nondramatic musical works: Compulsory licenses for public performances by means of coin-operated phonorecord players.

"116A.   Negotiated licenses for public performances by means of coin-operated phonorecord players.".

Sec. 5.   Recordation

Section 205 is amended—

(1)   by striking out subsection (d); and

(2)   by redesignating subsections (e) and (f) as subsections (d) and (e), respectively.

Sec. 6.   Preemption with Respect to Other Laws Not Affected

Section 301 is amended by adding at the end thereof the following:

"(e) The scope of Federal preemption under this section is not affected by the adherence of the United States to the Berne Convention or the satisfaction of obligations of the United States thereunder.".

Sec. 7.   Notice of Copyright

(a)   Visually Perceptible Copies.—Section 401 is amended—

(1)   in subsection (a), by amending the subsection heading to read as follows:

"(a)   General Provisions.—";

(2)   in subsection (a), by striking out "shall be placed on all" and inserting in lieu thereof "may be placed on";

(3)   in subsection (b), by striking out "The notice appearing on the copies" and inserting in lieu thereof "If a notice appears on the copies, it"; and

(4)   by adding at the end the following:

"(d)   Evidentiary Weight of Notice.—If a notice of copyright in the form and position specified by this section appears on the published copy or copies to which a defendant in a copyright infringement suit had access, then no weight shall be given to such a defendant's interposition of a defense based on innocent infringement in mitigation of actual or statutory damages, except as provided in the last sentence of section 504(c)(2).".

(b)   Phonorecords of Sound Recordings.—Section 402 is amended—

(1)   in subsection (a), by amending the subsection heading to read as follows:

"(a)   General Provisions.—";

(2)   in subsection (a), by striking out "shall be placed on all" and inserting in lieu thereof "may be placed on";

(3)   in subsection (b), by striking out "The notice appearing on the phonorecords" and inserting in lieu thereof "If a notice appears on the phonorecords, it"; and

(4)   by adding at the end thereof the following new subsection:

"(d)   Evidentiary Weight of Notice.—If a notice of copyright in the form and position specified by this section appears on the published phonorecord or phonorecords to which a defendant in a copyright infringement suit had access, then no weight shall be given to such a defendant's interposition of a defense based on innocent infringement in mitigation of actual or statutory damages, except as provided in the last sentence of section 504(c)(2).".

(c)   Publications Incorporating United States Government Works.—Section 403 is amended to read as follows:

"Sections 401(d) and 402(d) shall not apply to a work published in copies or phonorecords consisting predominantly of one or more works of the United States Government unless the notice of copyright appearing on the published copies or phonorecords to which a defendant in the copyright infringement suit had access includes a statement identifying, either affirmatively or negatively, those portions of the copies or phonorecords embodying any work or works protected under this title.".

(d)   Notice of Copyright: Contributions to Collective Works.—Section 404 is amended—

(1)   in subsection (a), by striking out "to satisfy the requirements of sections 401 through 403", and inserting in lieu thereof "to invoke the provisions of section 401(d) or 402(d), as applicable"; and

(2)   in subsection (b), by striking out "Where" and inserting in lieu thereof "With respect to copies and phonorecords publicly distributed by authority of the copyright owner before the effective date of the Berne Convention Implementation Act of 1988, where".

(e)   Omission of Notice.—Section 405 is amended—

(1)   in subsection (a), by striking out "The omission of the copyright notice prescribed by" and inserting in lieu thereof "With respect to copies and phonorecords publicly distributed by authority of the copyright owner before the effective date of the Berne Convention Implementation Act of 1988, the omission of the copyright notice described in";

(2)   in subsection (b), by striking out "omitted," in the first sentence and inserting in lieu thereof, "omitted and which was publicly distributed by authority of the copyright owner before the effective date of the Berne Convention Implementation Act of 1988,"; and

(3)   by amending the section heading to read as follows:

"§ 405.   Notice of copyright: Omission of notice on certain copies and phonorecords"

(f)   Error in Name or Date.—Section 406 is amended—

(1)   in subsection (a) by striking out "Where" and inserting in lieu thereof "With respect to copies and phonorecords publicly distributed by authority of the copyright owner before the effective date of the Berne Convention Implementation Act of 1988, where";

(2)   in subsection (b) by inserting "before the effective date of the Berne Convention Implementation Act of 1988" after "distribution";

(3)   in subsection (c)—

(A)   by inserting "before the effective date of the Berne Convention Implementation Act of 1988" after "publicly distributed"; and

(B)   by inserting after "405" the following: "as in effect on the day before the effective date of the Berne Convention Implementation Act of 1988"; and

(4)   by amending the section heading to read as follows:

"Sec. 406.   Notice of copyright: Error in name or date on certain copies and phonorecords".

(g)   Clerical Amendment.—The table of sections at the beginning of chapter 4 is amended by striking out the items relating to sections 405 and 406 and inserting in lieu thereof the following:

"405.   Notice of copyright: Omission of notice on certain copies and phonorecords.

"406.   Notice of copyright: Error in name or date on certain copies and phonorecords".

Sec. 8.   Deposit of Copies or Phonorecords for Library of Congress

Section 407(a) is amended by striking out "with notice of copyright".

Sec. 9.   Copyright Registration

(a)   Registration in General.—Section 408 is amended—

(1)   in subsection (a), by striking out "Subject to the provisions of section 405(a), such" in the second sentence and inserting in lieu thereof "Such";

(2)   in subsection (c)(2)—

(A)   by striking out "all of the following conditions—" and inserting in lieu thereof "the following conditions";

(B)   by striking out subparagraph (A); and

(C)   by redesignating subparagraphs (B) and (C) as subparagraphs (A) and (B), respectively.

(b)   Infringement Actions.—

(1)   Registration as a Prerequisite.—Section 411 is amended—

(A)   by amending the section heading to read as follows:

"§ 411.   Registration and infringement actions";

(B)   in subsection (a) by striking out "Subject" and inserting in lieu thereof "Except for actions for infringement of copyright in Berne Conventions works whose country of origin is not the United States, and subject"; and

(C)   in subsection (b)(2) by inserting ", if required by subsection (a)," after "work".

(2)   Table of Sections.—The table of sections at the beginning of chapter 4 is amended by striking out the item relating to section 411 and inserting in lieu thereof the following:

"411.   Registration and infringement actions.".

Sec. 10.   Copyright Infringement and Remedies

(a)   Infringement.—Section 501(b) is amended by striking out "sections 205(d) and 411," and inserting in lieu thereof "section 411.".

(b)   Damages and Profits.—Section 504(c) is amended—

(1)   in paragraph (1)—

(A)   by striking out "$250", and inserting in lieu thereof "$500"; and

(B)   by striking out "$10,000", and inserting in lieu thereof "$20,000"; and

(2)   in paragraph (2)—

(A)   by striking out "$50,000.", and inserting in lieu thereof "$100,000."; and

(B)   by striking out "$100.", and inserting in lieu thereof "$200.".

Sec. 11.   Copyright Royalty Tribunal

Chapter 8 is amended—

(1)   in section 801, by adding at the end of subsection (b) the following:

"In determining whether a return to a copyright owner under section 116 is fair, appropriate weight shall be given to—

"(i)   the rates previously determined by the Tribunal to provide a fair return to the copyright owner, and

"(ii)   the rates contained in any license negotiated pursuant to section 116A of this title."; and

(2)   by amending section 804(a)(2)(C) to read as follows:

"(C)(i)   In proceedings under section 801(b)(1) concerning the adjustment of royalty rates as provided in section 11[6], such petition may be filed in 1990 and in each subsequent tenth calendar year, and at any time within 1 year after negotiated licenses authorized by section 116A are terminated or expire and are not replaced by subsequent agreements.

"(ii)   If negotiated licenses authorized by section 116A come into force so as to supersede previous determinations of the Tribunal, as provided in section 116A(d), but thereafter are terminated or expire and are not replaced by subsequent agreements, the Tribunal shall, upon petition of any party to such terminated or expired negotiated license agreement, promptly establish an interim royalty rate or rates for the public performance by means of a coin-operated phonorecord player of nondramatic musical works embodied in phonorecords which had been subject to the terminated or expired negotiated license agreement. Such interim royalty rate or rates shall be the same as the last such rate or rates and shall remain in force until the conclusion of proceedings to adjust the royalty rates applicable to such works, or until superseded by a new negotiated license agreement, as provided in section 116A(d).".

Sec. 12.   Works in the Public Domain

Title 17, United States Code, as amended by this Act, does not provide copyright protection for any work that is in the public domain in the United States.

Sec. 13.   Effective Date; Effect on Pending Cases

(a)   Effective Date.—This Act and the amendments made by this Act take effect on the date on which the Berne Convention (as defined in section 101 of title 17, United States Code) enters into force with respect to the United States.

(b)   Effect on Pending Cases.—Any cause of action arising under title 17, United States Code, before the effective date of this Act shall be governed by the provisions of such title as in effect when the cause of action arose.

CHAPTER 6

OFFICER AND DIRECTOR PERSONAL LIABILITY

§ 6.1   A Popular Misconception

Most corporate executives believe that the company they work for will shield them from personal liability for improper acts they might commit. In the intellectual property arena however, officers and directors are increasingly being found personally liable for willful acts of patent, copyright, and trademark infringement. In addition, this liability may, depending upon the state, also apply in the case of trade secret misappropriation.

This chapter explores officer and director personal liability in the area of intellectual property. It simply is not worth risking a home, family savings, or the college education of children by willfully infringing another's intellectual property rights. It is important to follow the simple guidelines set forth at the end of this chapter to minimize such legal risks. Do not let corporate arrogance become personal catastrophe. See the guidelines set forth in **§ 6.12.**

RESOURCE: Coolley, "Personal Liability of Corporate Officers and Directors for Infringement of Intellectual Property," *Journal of Patent & Trademark Office Society,* Vol. 68, No. 5, pp. 228–241 (May 1986).

---

§ 6.2   Willful Infringement

The issue of willful infringement is important because a court's finding of willful infringement acts as a trigger for consideration of officer and director personal liability. The courts have always made a fundamental distinction between intentional and unintentional violation of the laws. Compare the example of one driver who aims a car at another person, hitting that person with the intent to cause substantial bodily harm, with another driver who accidentally strikes someone, such as a child at play, who jumps out in front of the car. The former situation evokes hatred, the latter, sorrow. So it is with patent, trademark, and copyright infringement. Those who intentionally or flagrantly infringe another's intellectual property are likely to bear the wrath of the court.

In the patent infringement arena, the Federal Circuit follows a *totality of the circumstances* test in determining willful patent infringement, that is, whether a reasonable person would prudently conduct himself with any confidence that the courts might hold the patent invalid (or not infringed).[1] Once a person becomes aware of a patent, he or she has an affirmative duty of care. Among the factors to be considered in the issue of willful infringement are whether the officer or director:

1. Sought a license which could either be an admission of willful infringement or a show of good faith (that is, as an alternative to expensive litigation).[2] The act of "seeking a license" has always carried with it a belief that the patent is valid and infringed—otherwise, why would a party be willing to pay a royalty? However, if a party believes the patent invalid or not infringed and the party does not want to encumber its business with a lengthy and perhaps expensive lawsuit, then "seeking a license" may be an act of good faith.

2. Sought advice from outside counsel, which mitigates against willfulness if outside counsel's advice is followed[3]

3. Flagrantly disregarded the patent rights[4]

---

[1] Studiengesellschaft Kohle v. Dart Indus., 666 F. Supp. 677, 4 U.S.P.Q.2d (BNA) 1817 (D. Del. 1987), *aff'd,* 862 F.2d 1564, 9 U.S.P.Q.2d (BNA) 1273 (Fed. Cir. 1988).

[2] King Instrument Corp. v. Otari Corp., 767 F.2d 853, 867, 226 U.S.P.Q. (BNA) 402 (Fed. Cir. 1985), *cert. denied,* 475 U.S. 1016 (1986).

[3] *Id.*

[4] *Id.*

4. Fully appreciated the commercial significance of the patented product but copied it anyway[5]

5. Made an effort to "design around" the patent.[6]

A company has an affirmative duty of care to obtain competent outside legal advice so that it can fully understand its rights in a possible patent infringement scenario.

The Lanham Act permits the court to increase the amount of recovery up to three times at its discretion "as the court shall find to be just, according to the circumstances of the case."[7]

The Copyright Act also permits a court, at its discretion, to increase the award of statutory damages from a maximum of $20,000 to $100,000 in cases of willful infringement.[8] Although the Copyright Act does not define willfulness, case law requires that the defendant knew, had reason to know, or recklessly disregarded the fact that his or her conduct constituted copyright infringement.

Because of the state-by-state interpretation of trade secret law, the exemplary or punitive damage law of each state, or as provided by each state's version of the Uniform Trade Secret Act, must be carefully considered.

§ 6.3   Personal Liability for Patent Infringement

An analysis of personal liability for officers, directors, and shareholders in patent infringement cases appears in §§ 6.4 through 6.8. This area is discussed in depth because it represents a universal area of concern over increasingly large damage awards in patent infringement cases. Sections 6.9 and 6.10 present illustrative copyright and trademark infringement cases in which individual officers, directors, or shareholders have been found liable. The chapter concludes with practical procedures one can follow to minimize personal liability risks (§ 6.11).

§ 6.4   —Standards for Liability

Early in the history of United States patent law, corporate officers and directors were individually enjoined from patent infringement when they

---

[5] Spindlefabrik v. Schubert, 829 F.2d 1075, 4 U.S.P.Q.2d (BNA) 1044 (Fed. Cir. 1987), *cert. denied,* 484 U.S. 1063 (1988).

[6] *Id.*

[7] Lanham Act § 35, 15 U.S.C. § 1117(a) (Supp. IV 1986). *See* Getty Petroleum Corp. v. Bartco Petroleum Corp., 858 F.2d 103, 8 U.S.P.Q.2d (BNA) 1336 (2d Cir. 1988) (thorough discussion of the role of § 35 of the Lanham Act).

[8] 17 U.S.C. § 504(c)(2) (1988).

directed the manufacturing and selling of allegedly infringing articles.[9] Although the application of injunctive relief against such officers and directors appeared to be universal, the early cases split on extending the remedy to damages.

In *United Nickel Co. v. Worthington,*[10] Justice Lowell stated:

> Infringement is not a trespass. The form of action is case; and this is because the act done is not of itself a direct interference with the tangible property of the plaintiff, but an indirect interference with his paramount right. . . . It would be a great hardship if the directors of a railway or manufacturing corporation were bound, at their personal peril, to find out that every machine which the company uses is free of all claim of monopoly. . . . I am of opinion that the only persons who can be held for damages are those who should have taken a license, and that they are those who own or have some interest in the business of making, using, or selling the thing which is an infringement; and that an action at law cannot be maintained against the directors, shareholders, or workmen of a corporation which infringes a patented improvement.

It was held by other courts, however, that all who join in an infringement are liable for damages as defendants even though they are merely officers, shareholders, or directors of the corporation.[11] William Robinson, in his famous 1890 treatise, *The Law of Patents for Useful Inventions,* agreed with the latter viewpoint and stated:

> [This] is in harmony with other doctrines of the law, sufficiently protects the patentee, and justly punishes those whose willful acts place them on the same footing with individual infringers. Under this opinion, all agents who perform acts of infringement, and all stockholders, directors, and other officers who in the prosecution of the business or the corporation authorize them, participate in the infringement and are personally responsible to the patentee.[12]

The Seventh Circuit subsequently announced the rule that became a guiding precedent in this area. In *Dangler v. Imperial Machine Co.,*[13] the court held that the general rule was that corporate officers and directors were not liable without some special showing, such as a deliberate use of the corporation as an instrument to infringe. The Seventh Circuit stated:

---

[9] Goodyear v. Phelps, 10 F. Cas. 711, 3 Blatch. 91 (C.C.N.D.N.Y. 1853); Consolidated Safety Valve Co. v. Ashton Valve Co., 26 F. 319 (C.C.D. Mass. 1886).

[10] 13 F. 392, 393 (C.C.D. Mass. 1882).

[11] National Car Brake Shoe Co. v. Terre Haute Car Mfg. Co., 19 F. 514 (C.C.D. Ind. 1884); Smith v. Standard Laundry Mach. Co., 19 F. 826 (C.C.D.N.Y. 1883).

[12] W. Robinson, *The Law of Patents for Useful Inventions,* § 913, at 82 (1984).

[13] 11 F.2d 945, 947 (7th Cir. 1926).

We . . . hold that, in the absence of some special showing, the managing officers of a corporation are not liable for the infringements of such corporation, though committed under their general direction. The uncertainty surrounding the questions of validity and infringement make[s] any other rule unduly harsh and oppressive.

It is when the officer acts willfully and knowingly—that is, when he personally participates in the manufacture or sale of the infringing article (acts other than as an officer), or when he uses the corporation as an instrument to carry out his own willful and deliberate infringements, or when he knowingly uses an irresponsible corporation with the purpose of avoiding personal liabilities—that officers are held jointly with the company. The foregoing are by no means cited as the only instances when the officers may be held liable, but they are sufficient for the present case.[14]

In *Dangler,* the defendants were the president and secretary of the corporation, who together held 40 percent of its stock. They relied on the advice of a "reputable patent attorney" who stated the "machine could be lawfully made." The corporation was subsequently declared bankrupt, even though the defendant took out a number of personal loans to keep it going. The district court held the defendants liable for damages and profits, but the Seventh Circuit reversed.

A number of decisions were made following this case in which the actual language of the courts is important:

1. "The facts tend to indicate a preconceived deliberate conduct on the part of the officers to use the corporation merely to carry on the infringing and unfair practices and that these practices constituted conduct so palpable and so alien to the purpose of a bona fide corporation that from this alone it might be concluded that the conduct was willful, deliberate and personal on the part of the officials."[15]

2. Defendant deliberately designed the infringing device and "was at all times in control of the administrative and managerial policy of the corporation."[16]

3. "[Defendant] was the moving, active conscious force behind International's infringement. Under 35 U.S.C. Section 271(b) he is therefore subject to personal liability without regard to whether International is his alter ego."[17]

---

[14] *Id.* at 947.

[15] General Motors Corp. v. Provus, 100 F.2d 562, 564 (7th Cir. 1938).

[16] Weller Mfg. Co. v. Wen Prods. Inc., 231 F.2d 795, 801, 109 U.S.P.Q. (BNA) 73, 77 (7th Cir. 1956).

[17] International Mfg. Co. v. Landon, Inc., 336 F.2d 723, 729, 142 U.S.P.Q. (BNA) 421, 426 (9th Cir. 1964), *cert. denied,* 379 U.S. 988, *reh'g denied,* 380 U.S. 938 (1965).

4. "[Defendant] was one of the original incorporators of the corporate defendant. He had been its president, director, and majority stockholder since its inception. He personally participated in the design of the accused devices and of the sales bulletin therefor."[18]

5. "Defendant's argument that he acted only as president of Mar-Bel and then only with the advice of counsel has a hollow ring. He was the incorporator, president, majority stockholder, and moving force which resulted in the manufacture of the accused device. He participated in the development and promotion of the sale of his machine."[19]

6. Defendant was the "moving force" behind both the infringing company and the specific infringing activity.[20]

7. Liability under 35 U.S.C. § 271(b) may include "liability of corporate officials who actively aid and abet their corporation's infringements."[21]

8. "The evidence firmly establishes that [the individuals] were directly responsible for the design and production of the infringing chairs."[22]

Without question, each court was incensed by the officer's or director's conduct.

On the other hand, courts have also held officers and directors in certain situations to be not liable:

1. "[A] corporate officer is generally not personally liable for an infringement when he acts solely within his duties as an officer and director." Though defendant was chief administrative officer, one of four founders of the corporation, and a large shareholder, he "in no way directed or instigated the infringing method of manufacture."[23]

2. "Corporate officers are not liable for patent infringement where they have not been active other than as officers."[24]

---

[18] Rex Chainbelt, Inc. v. General Kinematics Corp., 363 F.2d 336, 348, 150 U.S.P.Q. (BNA) 319 (7th Cir. 1966).

[19] White v. Mar-Bel, Inc., 509 F.2d 287, 292, 185 U.S.P.Q. (BNA) 129, 134 (5th Cir.), *reh'g denied,* 511 F.2d 1402 (5th Cir. 1975).

[20] Rohm & Haas v. Crystal Chem. Co., 722 F.2d 1556, 220 U.S.P.Q. (BNA) 289 (Fed. Cir. 1983).

[21] Power Lift, Inc. v. Lange Tool, 774 F.2d 478, 481, 227 U.S.P.Q. (BNA) 435, 437 (Fed. Cir. 1985).

[22] Orthokinetics, Inc. v. Safety Travel Chairs, Inc., 806 F.2d 1565, 1577, 1 U.S.P.Q.2d (BNA) 1081, 1091 (Fed. Cir. 1986).

[23] U.S. Phillips Corp. v. National Micronetics, Inc., 410 F. Supp. 449, 468, 188 U.S.P.Q. (BNA) 662, 678 (S.D.N.Y. 1976), *aff'd,* 550 F.2d 716, 193 U.S.P.Q. (BNA) 65, *cert. denied,* 434 U.S. 859 (1977).

[24] Bewal, Inc. v. Minnesota Mining & Mfg. Co., 292 F.2d 159, 166, 129 U.S.P.Q. (BNA) 440, 446 (10th Cir. 1961).

3. There is "little justification for making [officers, agents and servants] defendants except in rare instances where it is shown that they have infringed the patent as individuals or have personally directed the infringement."[25]

In *Power Lift, Inc. v. Lange Tools, Inc.,*[26] Judge Rich affirmed the lower court's final judgment upholding the jury's determination of willful infringement, corporate officer liability, and the award of attorneys' fees as being not clearly erroneous. The jury awarded lost profits damages in the amount of $229,655, together with prejudgment interest and attorneys' fees. In this case, the individual, Mr. Lange, was president, founder, majority owner, and director of Lange Tools. He was not sued for direct infringement under 35 U.S.C. § 271(a) but only on the theory that Lange induced the corporation to infringe the patents under § 271(b). Lange argued on appeal that, technically speaking, the statute prohibited inducement of "another" to infringe the patent. His argument was simply that "[a] corporation and its president do not, in law, constitute separate entities." Judge Rich relied on legislative history indicating that the purpose of § 271 was to be broadly interpreted.

In *White v. Mar-Bel, Inc.,*[27] the individual corporate officer was the incorporator, president, majority stockholder, and moving force that resulted in the manufacture of the accused device. The jury and the Fifth Circuit found him liable under § 271(b) for inducing infringement, although the district court judge did not in his judgment notwithstanding the verdict. The Fifth Circuit affirmed the jury's award of $94,500 in compensatory damages.

§ 6.5   —Statutory Basis for Liability

A number of decisions have based liability on direct infringement (35 U.S.C. § 271(a)) when knowledge of the patent is not a necessary element. In *Orthokinetics, Inc. v. Safety Travel Chairs, Inc.,*[28] Chief Judge Markey stated:

> [3] Corporate officers are presumably aware of what they are doing, and in that sense they can be said to have acted "willfully." However, that does not mean that their acts must rise to the level recognized by the law as constituting willful infringement as a prerequisite for the imposition of personal liability for the corporation's direct infringement.

---

[25] Hutter v. De Q. Bottle Stopper Co., 128 F. 283 (2d Cir. 1904).

[26] 774 F.2d 478, 227 U.S.P.Q. (BNA) 435 (Fed. Cir. 1985).

[27] 509 F.2d 287, 185 U.S.P.Q. (BNA) 129 (5th Cir.), *reh'g denied,* 511 F.2d 1402 (5th Cir. 1975).

[28] 806 F.2d 1565, 1 U.S.P.Q.2d (BNA) 1081 (Fed. Cir. 1986).

To determine whether corporate officers are personally liable for the direct infringement of the corporation under § 271(a) requires invocation of those general principles relating to piercing the corporate veil.

Infringement is a tort, . . . and officers of a corporation are personally liable for tortious conduct of the corporation if they personally took part in the commission of the tort or specially directed other officers, agents, or employees of the corporation to commit the tortious act. . . . The cases are legion in which courts have recognized and imposed personal liability on corporate officers for participating in, inducing, and approving acts of patent infringement.

The evidence established the makeup and control of STC and Entron, Pivacek testified that he was at all material times the President and sole stockholder of Entron and that he elected its Board of Directors. He also testified that he is the President of STC and that he, Cole, and Chipman held all of STC's directorships and owned all of the stock in STC. The evidence firmly establishes that Pivacek, Cole and Chipman were directly responsible for the design and production of the infringing chairs and that they were the only ones who stood to benefit from sales of those chairs. That evidence was fully sufficient to support the jury's imposition of personal liability on Pivacek, Cole, and Chipman for the direct infringement of STC and Entron and for STC's contributory infringement. The district court's setting aside of the jury's findings on personal liability must therefore be reversed.[29]

Other decisions base liability upon inducement or contributory infringement under 35 U.S.C. §§ 271(b) and (c), in which knowledge of the patent is important.[30]

§ 6.6   —Other Theories for Liability

Corporate officers are individually liable for torts they commit.[31] This tortious liability is distinct from any liability resulting from the alter ego doctrine or from the doctrine of piercing the corporate veil. The effect of piercing a corporate veil is simply to hold the owner liable. Piercing the corporate veil is resorted to when the court finds that the corporation is not a bona fide independent entity.[32]

---

[29] *Id.* at 1577, 1 U.S.P.Q.2d (BNA) at 1091.

[30] *Id.* at 1577, 1 U.S.P.Q.2d (BNA) at 1091. *See also* Power Lift, Inc. v. Lange Tool, 774 F.2d 478, 227 U.S.P.Q. (BNA) 435 (Fed. Cir. 1985).

[31] Solo Cup Co. v. Paper Mach. Corp., 359 F.2d 754, 149 U.S.P.Q. (BNA) 239 (7th Cir. 1966).

[32] Donsco, Inc. v. Casper Corp., 587 F.2d 602, 199 U.S.P.Q. (BNA) 705 (3d Cir. 1978).

§ 6.7   —Injunctive Relief

There is no doubt that an injunctive decree against a guilty infringing corporation is individually binding upon its officers and agents, even if they were not parties to the lawsuit personally. Injunctions, under the Federal Rules of Civil Procedure, broadly cover not only the parties but their "officers, agents, servants, employees, and attorneys."[33]

§ 6.8   —Salaried Employees

Salaried employees have not been held liable for patent infringement. In *Wilden Pump & Engineering Co. v. Pressed & Welded Products Co.,*[34] the court stated, "No cases have been cited where a non-management, salaried employee, without more, was found to be an individually liable infringer. . . . "

§ 6.9   Personal Liability for Copyright Infringement

In determining personal liability for copyright infringement, the courts inquire whether a person had (1) the right and ability to supervise the infringing activity; and (2) an obvious and direct financial interest in exploitation of copyrighted materials, or (3) personally participated in the infringing activity.[35]

In the copyright area, vicarious liability may even be imposed on a controlling person who had no actual knowledge of the infringement but had the ability to supervise and control the infringing activity. For example, when a husband and wife owned a radio station that played music not covered by an ASCAP (American Society of Composers, Authors, and Publishers) license, ASCAP prevailed in finding the wife to be jointly and severally liable for damages because she participated both in management decisions and in the selection of the music. She was also the bookkeeper of the station and an equal owner. Hence, even though she was not aware of the actual infringement, she was held to be jointly and severally liable.[36]

---

[33] 33 Rule 65(d), Federal Rules of Civil Procedure.

[34] 655 F.2d 984, 990, 213 U.S.P.Q. (BNA) 282 (9th Cir. 1981).

[35] Major League Baseball Promotion Corp. v. Colour-Tex Inc., 14 U.S.P.Q.2d (BNA) 1177, 1183 (D.N.J. 1990).

[36] Collins Court Music, Inc. v. Pulley, 704 F. Supp. 963, 9 U.S.P.Q.2d (BNA) 1804 (W.D. Mo. 1988). *See also* RCA/Ariola Int'l, Inc. v. Thomas & Grayston Co., 845 F.2d 773, 6 U.S.P.Q.2d (BNA) 1692 (8th Cir. 1988).

§ 6.10   Personal Liability for
Trademark Infringement

In a leading trademark case, this ruling on personal liability was made:

> A corporate officer is individually liable for the torts he personally com-
> mits and cannot shield himself behind a corporation when he is an actual
> participant in the tort. . . . This principle applies when the conduct con-
> stitutes unfair competition. . . . The fact that an officer is acting for a
> corporation also may make the corporation vicariously or secondarily li-
> able under the doctrine of respondeat superior; it does not however relieve
> the individual of his responsibility.[37]

It is useful here to mention *Bambu Sales, Inc. v. Sultana Crackers,
Inc.,*[38] in which the plaintiff brought a lawsuit against the defendants for
unauthorized use of the Bambu trademark for cigarette paper. The court
evaluated the facts of the case and stated:

> Turning to the facts of this case, it is uncontested that defendant
> Bernard Gulack, the manager of defendant Gulack Trading (who attests
> that he "runs the company and makes the decisions"), purchased the coun-
> terfeit BAMBU paper from a "Spanish jobber . . . named Eddie" and
> resold it to "various jobbers", including defendant Sultana. It is similarly
> uncontested that defendant William Brooks, the president and a director
> and shareholder of Nu Service, specifically instructed his buyer concern-
> ing the purchase and subsequent resale of the infringing merchandise,
> approved these transactions and personally examined the goods. Likewise
> it is undisputed that defendant Brian Gold, the sales manager of Sultana,
> arranged for the purchase and resale of the counterfeit paper, personally
> received the merchandise, and was in fact the only individual at Sultana
> who was involved in the transactions.
>
> Because these established facts demonstrate that Gulack, Brooks and
> Brian Gold are the "moving, active conscious forces behind [their respec-
> tive corporations'] infringement," plaintiff is entitled to summary judg-
> ment against them on the issue of liability on each claim.[39]

§ 6.11   Guidelines for Minimizing Personal Liability

Because courts are finding a greater liability for participating officers, directors, or shareholders in infringement cases, steps should be taken by

---

[37] Donsco, Inc. v. Casper Corp., 587 F.2d 602, 606, 199 U.S.P.Q. (BNA) 705, 707–08 (3d
Cir. 1978).

[38] 7 U.S.P.Q.2d (BNA) 1177 (E.D.N.Y. 1988).

[39] *Id.* at 1189.

such individuals to minimize the risk of being named as co-defendants for intellectual property infringement. The following steps may be taken to minimize this risk, whether patents, trademarks, or copyrights are involved:

1. Avoid personal participation in infringement or misappropriation of another's intellectual property rights.

2. Seek outside counsel and obtain an opinion in writing.

3. Seek board of director or shareholder ratification.

4. Be careful to document that all acts are solely within the duties of an officer or director of the corporation and do not constitute directing or instigating infringing acts.

5. Avoid being labeled the "moving, active conscious force behind infringement."

6. Do not deliberately copy another's product or trademark without a duly diligent investigation.

7. Take seriously any charge of infringement made by another party and carefully document a good faith course of investigation as a followup to the threat.

8. Do not make any public statements boasting that you are not concerned about a competitor's particular patents, trademarks, or copyrights.

9. Be careful in seeking a license for another's intellectual property. If the license is not granted, be sure to take a prudent course in carefully avoiding infringement of the other party's intellectual property rights.

10. Be sure all corporate records reflect a policy of prudence, respect for others' intellectual property rights, and adherence to a course of action advised by outside counsel.

CHAPTER 7

ADVERTISING

§ 7.1   Introduction

This chapter is not meant to be a tutorial in the complex area involving the legal issues of advertising. Rather, it concentrates on a number of key intellectual property issues that affect advertising practices. Adhering to the guidelines set forth in this chapter will minimize the legal risks of business advertising. For an in-depth analysis of the law of advertising, the reader is referred to the following resources.

RESOURCES:

1. Rosden, George and Peter, *The Law of Advertising* (Matthew Bender: 1275 Broadway, Albany, NY 12201) (1990). A four-volume set, this treatise is the bible of advertising law.
2. Plevin, Kenneth, and Miriam Siroky, *Advertising Compliance Handbook* (Practising Law Institute: New York, NY) (1988). This handy 460-page book should be in every corporate counsel's library.

3.   Kent, Felix, and Douglas Wood, "Legal Problems in Advertising," *Business Law Monograph* (Matthew Bender: 1275 Broadway, Albany, NY 12201) (1989). This short practical guide contains forms and other source materials.

---

§ 7.2   Comparative Advertising Guidelines

Many advertisements contain comparisons between two similar products. Mercedes Benz cars are compared to Lincolns; Sun computers are compared to Hewlett Packard computers for processing power, storage, speed, and so forth. Without question, comparative advertising, as long as the comparison is truthful, constitutes fair competition and is legally proper under the First Amendment as free commercial speech.

Indeed, it is well known that marketing can also "puff" or exaggerate the quality or characteristics of a company's products; even such puffing is fair competition and perfectly legal.[1] For example, in a Toyota advertisement, the ad puffed: "No other compact 4×4 can out-muscle the Toyota V6." Does anyone really know what "out-muscle" means? Pure puffery! Professor Prosser in his treatise of torts states:"The 'puffing rule' amounts to a seller's privilege to lie his head off, so long as he says nothing specific, on the theory that no reasonable man would believe him, or that no reasonable man would be influenced by such talk."[2] The rights to compare truthfully and to puff in the sales of one's own product are protected under the First Amendment of the Constitution as commercial free speech. However, the First Amendment does not protect false and misleading misrepresentations in advertising. The four cases reviewed in the following discussion help to illustrate the legal issues involved in comparative advertising.

Bristol-Myers launched an aggressive advertising campaign on national television depicting Christina Ferrare holding a bottle of Body on Tap shampoo.[3] In the commercial Ms. Ferrare stated: "In shampoo tests with over 900 women like me, Body on Tap got higher ratings than Prell for body. Higher than Flex for conditioning. Higher than Sassoon for strong, healthy looking hair." An independent market research company actually conducted the tests for Bristol-Myers. However, upon analysis of the 900 women tested, approximately one-third of the "women like Christina

---

[1] Testing Sys., Inc. v. Magnaflux Corp., 251 F. Supp. 286, 149 U.S.P.Q. (BNA) 129 (E.D. Pa. 1966).

[2] W. Prosser, *Prosser on Torts,* § 109 (4th ed. 1971).

[3] Vidal Sassoon, Inc. v. Bristol-Myers Co., 661 F.2d 272, 213 U.S.P.Q. (BNA) 24 (2d Cir. 1981).

Ferrare" were actually young women aged 13 to 18 and not adult women. The court stated:

> Whether or not the statements made in the advertisements are literally true, § 43(a) of the Lanham Act encompasses more than blatant falsehoods. It embraces "innuendo, indirect intimations, and ambiguous suggestions" evidenced by the consuming public's misapprehension of the hard facts underlying an advertisement. . . . The inaccuracies alleged concern the number and age of the women in the tests, how the comparisons were made, and how the results were tabulated. . . . [W]e are persuaded that § 43(a) does prohibit the misrepresentations alleged here.[4]

In a significant case involving comparative advertising, Jartran had advertised in newspapers and magazines by comparing a U-Haul trailer side-by-side with a Jartran trailer.[5] The heading of the ad was "COMPARE BEFORE YOU MAKE A MOVE" and the ad stated:

> Only Jartran can rent you trailers designed for the times. BRAND NEW TRAILERS: Lightweight, perfectly balanced trailers that are easy to hook up. GAS SAVING DESIGN: all Jartran trailers are aerodynamically designed to save gas and provide exceptional road stability. Who can rent you a trailer that won't push you around? Jartran can.

Jartran claimed that its advertisement amounted only to puffery. The court disagreed and preliminarily enjoined Jartran. The court found the statement "only Jartran can rent you trailers designed for the times" to be actually false, as well as the phrases "greater stability and safety," and "exceptional road stability." In a later proceeding, the court awarded $40 million plus reasonable attorneys' fees.[6]

In these two cases, direct comparisons to a competitor's product were made. Not surprisingly, the competitor was the plaintiff in each comparative advertising lawsuit. In the following two cases, although not specifically named, the competitor was impliedly referred to in the offending advertisement.

Procter & Gamble issued a series of commercials for its Citrus Hill orange juice emphasizing a "heart of the orange" theme. Coca-Cola brought a lawsuit claiming that the "heart of the orange" theme implied that Citrus Hill orange juice was made from the heart or cubed center of the orange, making it sweeter and better tasting than other juices. In actuality,

---

[4] *Id.* at 277, 213 U.S.P.Q. (BNA) at 27.

[5] U-Haul Int'l Inc. v. Jartran, Inc., 522 F. Supp. 1238, 212 U.S.P.Q. (BNA) 49 (D. Ariz. 1981), *aff'd,* 681 F.2d 1159, 216 U.S.P.Q. (BNA) 1077 (9th Cir. 1982).

[6] U-Haul Int'l Inc. v. Jartran, Inc., 601 F. Supp. 1140, 225 U.S.P.Q. (BNA) 306 (D. Ariz. 1984), *aff'd in part and rev'd in part,* 793 F.2d 1034, 230 U.S.P.Q. (BNA) 343 (9th Cir. 1986).

Coca-Cola claimed, Procter & Gamble, like all of its competitors, made Citrus Hill juice from the entire interior portion of the orange. The court agreed with Coca-Cola that the advertisement was misleading.[7]

Warner Lambert advertised its E.P.T. Plus home pregnancy kit as the fastest test and capable of producing determinations of pregnancy in 10 minutes. Tambrands sued Warner Lambert and prevailed because Warner Lambert's own study indicated that 48 percent of pregnant women did not receive accurate results in 10 minutes.[8]

Following are comparative advertising guidelines which, if followed, will substantially minimize comparative advertising legal risks:

1. Use only true statements in the advertisement.
2. Accurately identify any competitive products appearing in the advertisement.
3. Do not cast expressly or impliedly disparagements on the competitor.
4. Use objective statements of the type that can be substantiated by the consumer. For example, if two cars are being compared regarding horsepower, the consumer can easily check the specifications of each individual car.
5. Avoid making subjective statements in the advertisement. Be sure to use an independent testing company to substantiate comparisons based upon actual tests among competing products. It is important to have the testing company maintain accurate records of the test.
6. Be sure to comply with the advertising codes of a particular association, industry, or media. For example, the major networks usually have policies for accepting comparative advertisements.
7. Avoid using superiority statements and puffery such as "This computer operates at warp speed!"

RESOURCE: Federal Trade Commission, 6th Street and Pennsylvania Ave., NW, Washington, DC 20580, telephone 202-326-2222. The FTC has a Public Reference Branch that will provide businesses with a number of comparative advertising guides.

---

§ 7.3 Use of Another's Trademark in Advertising

It is entirely proper to use another's trademark in advertising the products and services of a business. This is especially important in the areas

---

[7] Coca-Cola Co. v. Procter & Gamble Co., 822 F.2d 28, 3 U.S.P.Q.2d (BNA) 1364 (6th Cir. 1987).

[8] Tambrands, Inc. v. Warner Lambert Co., 673 F. Supp. 1190 (S.D.N.Y. 1987).

of manufactured parts, repair and reconditioning, and using photographs of competitors' products. These three topics are discussed in §§ **7.4** through **7.6**.

§ 7.4 —Manufactured Parts

A manufacturer has the right to inform the public that its manufactured components will fit with, operate in, or support another's trademarked product. For example, if a business is manufacturing a computer peripheral accessory that operates with IBM hardware and Lotus software, it is entirely proper to use the IBM and Lotus trademarks in the text of the ad. In the following example, proper reference to another's trademark is being made:

> The POORHORSE accelerator card is fully compatible with the IBM* personal computer and is fully operational with all LOTUS* software including 1-2-3.*
>
> * IBM is a registered trademark of International Business Machines Corporation. LOTUS and 1-2-3 are registered trademarks of Lotus Development Corporation.

But using the IBM or Lotus trademarks in the banner or headline of the advertisement or prominently elsewhere, however, one might falsely create the impression that the product is somehow sponsored by or affiliated with IBM or Lotus. Hence, the use of another's trademark should be relegated to the textual portion of the advertisement and should not appear elsewhere in the advertisement in bold or enlarged lettering. This is a general guideline, not an absolute legal rule.

It is generally improper to make use of another's trademark when the product is "buried" or "forms a part of" a new manufactured product. For example, the defendant in the *Bulova Watch* case[9] had purchased original Bulova watch movements and inserted them into new watch cases. He applied the trademark Bulova on the watch dial. Bulova Watch Co. sued and successfully enjoined the defendant from using the Bulova mark.

§ 7.5 —Repair or Recondition

The right to use another's trademark in repairing or reconditioning products is clear. This was decided early in the 1947 United States Supreme

---

[9] Bulova Watch Co. v. Allerton Co., 328 F.2d 20, 140 U.S.P.Q. (BNA) 440 (7th Cir. 1964).

Court case of *Champion Sparkplug Co. v. Sanders.*[10] In such use, however, the product must be stamped with the word "repaired" or "used." Furthermore, a legend must appear on all cartons, containers, advertising, and business communications making it clear that the products are used and reconditioned.

Frequent problems arise in Yellow Page advertising. These problems are usually caused when an advertising company improperly prepares the advertisement. For example, in a case that held that a defendant had improperly used the Bandag logo in advertising its tire recapping services,[11] the court recognized that the defendant nevertheless had the legal right to use the Bandag mark in a truthful statement of its services. That is, the defendant could truthfully advertise to others that it had the ability to sell tires that had been recapped by other authentic Bandag franchises. In this case, an advertising agency apparently prepared the Yellow Page ad for the defendant. The court stated:

> An independent dealer may properly advertise that he sells merchandise associated by the public with a well-known trade or service mark so long as this does not mislead customers into thinking that he is an authorized agent of, or directly connected with, the owner of that mark. In order to communicate accurate information about a product, a right is implied to use any mark fairly associated with that product.[12]

In another situation, the defendant placed his Yellow Page ad for Volkswagen repair service near the listings of authorized Volkswagen dealers. In finding the defendant liable, the court observed: "Some of the defendant's Yellow Page listings prominently display plaintiff's mark and occupy more space than, and immediately precede, the listing of licensed dealerships."[13] Without question, a business has the right to use another's trademark in a truthful reference. Furthermore, if the products involve repaired or used products, positive statements that the products have been used or repaired must be made.

§ 7.6 —Use of Another's Photographs

Comparative advertisements may incorporate a photograph of the competitor's product. This commonly occurs in both automobile and computer comparative advertisements. Again, if the guidelines set forth in § 7.2 are

---

[10] 331 U.S. 125 (1947).

[11] Bandag, Inc. v. Al Bolser's Tire Stores, Inc., 750 F.2d 903, 223 U.S.P.Q. (BNA) 982 (Fed. Cir. 1984).

[12] *Id.* at 910, 223 U.S.P.Q. (BNA) at 986.

[13] Volkswagen Aktiengesellschaft v. Brewer, 170 U.S.P.Q. (BNA) 560 (D. Ariz. 1971).

followed so that a true comparison can be made with full statement of the ownership of the trademark of the product displayed in the photograph, then the legal risks of comparative advertising are minimal. In some situations, however, the photograph of the competitor's product is altered and is displayed as the actual product of another. For example, when defendants used photographs of the plaintiff's lamp to solicit orders, the plaintiff sued under the Lanham Act.[14] The court found that the defendants' advertisements utilizing a photograph of the plaintiff's lamp were misleading and stated:

> Defendants falsely represented to prospective customers that plaintiff's lamp was of defendants' own manufacture, undertaking to supply such lamps for sale. This it was not yet prepared to do. It is further unfair for defendant to take advantage of plaintiff's product development and good will to usurp a share of the market.[15]

The defendant was enjoined from using all photographs and ordered to cancel all of the orders it had taken based upon the advertisement.

In another case, the defendant utilized a photograph of the plaintiff's twin-bottom grain semitrailers in its sales literature to advertise its entry into the business. The court found defendant's conduct to be so intentional and accompanied by such bad faith that it increased the lower court's award of profits by 500 percent![16]

§ 7.7   First Amendment Free Commercial Speech

First Amendment free commercial speech rights are well recognized and perhaps constitute one of the broadest and most liberal legal rights granted under our Constitution. It is not surprising that defendants in advertising lawsuits rely on the First Amendment to limit the copyright and trademark rights of plaintiffs. It has been stated that the First Amendment is not a license to trample on legally recognized rights in intellectual property.[17] Rightly or wrongly, the First Amendment has been extended to protect free commercial speech.[18] In the area of comparative advertising,

---

[14] Sublime Prods., Inc. v. Gerber Prods., Inc., 579 F. Supp. 248, 223 U.S.P.Q. (BNA) 383 (S.D.N.Y. 1984).

[15] *Id.* at 250.

[16] Truck Equip. Serv. Co. v. Fruehauf Corp., 536 F.2d 1210, 191 U.S.P.Q. (BNA) 79 (8th Cir.), *cert. denied,* 429 U.S. 861 (1976).

[17] Dallas Cowboys Cheerleaders, Inc. v. Scoreboard Posters, Inc., 600 F.2d 1184, 1188, 203 U.S.P.Q. (BNA) 321, 323 (5th Cir. 1979).

[18] Triangle Publications, Inc. v. Knight-Ridder Newspapers, Inc., 445 F. Supp. 875, 884, 198 U.S.P.Q. (BNA) 28, 36 (S.D. Fla. 1978), *aff'd,* 626 F.2d 1171, 207 U.S.P.Q. (BNA) 977 (5th Cir. 1980).

in which a competitor's trademark, product photograph, or other reference appears, comparative advertising has been considered "an important source of information for the education of consumers" and is to be protected.[19] However, misleading advertising, as discussed in §§ 7.2 through 7.6, is not protected.[20]

A struggle exists between copyright protection and First Amendment free commercial speech. Both are based upon rights guaranteed by the Constitution. A current legal trend grants free commercial speech primacy over constitutionally protected copyright rights.[21] With respect to the First Amendment versus the copyright rights dilemma, one court has stated that: when the First Amendment and the Copyright Act "operate at cross-purposes, the primacy of the First Amendment mandates that the Copyright Act be deprived of effectuation . . . the recent extension of First Amendment protection to commercial speech induces a conflict between the Copyright Act and the First Amendment."[22]

When a newspaper used "name-calling" television commercials to advertise its new television supplement by using an image of the competing *TV Guide,* the court ruled against *TV Guide.* It stated, "Such comparative advertising, when undertaken in the serious manner that defendant did herein, represents an important source of information for the education of consumers in a free enterprise system."[23]

Without question, significant litigation occurs in the comparative advertising arena. Large corporations carefully use to the fullest legal extent possible their First Amendment rights to compare their products in a favorable light against their competitors' products. Likewise, those companies suffering the brunt of such comparison will vigorously litigate to prevent it from occurring. Most businesses, however, cannot afford the luxury of this type of expensive and extensive litigation. Therefore, this chapter provides practical legal guidelines for smaller businesses to follow in order to minimize their advertising litigation risks.

§ 7.8   Use of Disclaimers

Positive disclaimers are effectively used in many advertisements, especially those on television. For example, in its popular magazine *Consumer*

---

[19] *Id.* at 883, 198 U.S.P.Q. (BNA) at 36.

[20] Vidal Sassoon, Inc. v. Bristol-Myers Co., 661 F.2d 272, 276 n.8, 213 U.S.P.Q. (BNA) 24, 27 n.8 (2d Cir. 1981).

[21] Triangle Publications, Inc. v. Knight-Ridder Newspapers, Inc., 445 F. Supp. 875, 884, 198 U.S.P.Q. (BNA) 28, 36 (S.D. Fla. 1978), *aff'd,* 626 F.2d 1171, 207 U.S.P.Q. (BNA) 977 (5th Cir. 1980).

[22] *Id.* at 882, 198 U.S.P.Q. (BNA) at 36.

[23] *Id.* at 883, 198 U.S.P.Q. (BNA) at 36.

Reports, Consumers Union gave Regina vacuum cleaners a high rating. The defendant used this rating in its television commercial as follows: "[Regina] is the only lightweight that *Consumer Reports* says 'was an adequate substitute for a full-size vacuum.'"[24] Superimposed on the screen was the following disclaimer: "*Consumer Reports* is not affiliated with Regina and does not endorse products." The court ruled in favor of Regina and stated:

> The district court erred in enjoining Regina from making any reference to the favorable CONSUMER REPORTS rating. If the record truly evinced a likelihood of confusion (which it does not), the proper course would have been to require a clear disclaimer. The First Amendment demands use of a disclaimer when there is a reasonable possibility that it will suffice to alleviate consumer confusion.[25]

§ 7.9   Rights of Publicity or Privacy

The unauthorized use of a person's name or likeness is a violation of his or her right of publicity or privacy. Indeed, the unauthorized use of the image of an object such as a building or a car may also be actionable. A written agreement or release must be entered into with such persons or owners of such objects. An example of such a written release is shown as **Form 7–1**.

Form 7–1
RELEASE OF RIGHT TO USE NAME AND LIKENESS

For good and valuable consideration, the receipt of which is acknowledged, I hereby grant to Poorhorse Corp. (address) and to its agents, assigns, licensees, and legal representatives the irrevocable, perpetual, and worldwide right to use my name and my physical likeness in an advertisement. This right shall extend to any and all uses of my name and physical likeness in other promotion or for any other lawful trade purposes. I waive any right to inspect or approve the finished advertisement or such other uses that may be created in connection therewith. Poorhorse Corp. shall have the full right at its discretion to edit, modify, add to, and/or delete material or juxtapose any part of the advertisement with any other advertisement. I hereby release Poorhorse Corp. from any and all claims, demands, or causes of action including but not limited to defamation and my rights of publicity or privacy in

---

[24] Consumers Union v. General Signal Corp., 724 F.2d 1044, 1047, 221 U.S.P.Q. (BNA) 400, 402 (2d Cir. 1983), *reh'g denied,* 730 F.2d 47 (2d Cir.), *cert. denied,* 469 U.S. 823 (1984).

[25] *Id.* at 1053, 221 U.S.P.Q. (BNA) 400 at 406.

the use by Poorhorse Corp. of my name and physical likeness. I have read this release and I understand its contents and intend to be legally bound hereby.

Name: _____
(Print Full Name)   (Age)

Witness: _____   Signed: _____

Address: _____   Address: _____

_____   _____

Telephone: _____   Telephone: _____

                                              Date: _____ 19_____

If the person is a minor, the information contained in **Form 7–2** should be added to the Release:

Form 7–2
PARENT'S CONSENT FOR MINOR TO RELEASE RIGHT TO USE NAME AND LIKENESS

I am the parent and guardian of the minor named above and have the legal authority to execute the above release. I approve all the foregoing and intend myself and my minor to be fully bound thereby.

Name: _____
(Print Full Name)   (Age)

Witness: _____   Signed: _____

Address: _____   Address: _____

_____   _____

Telephone: _____   Telephone: _____

                                              Date: _____ 19_____

The following set of guidelines should be reviewed by personnel responsible for obtaining signed releases:

1. A release (see **Forms 7–1** and **7–2**) must be used for all advertisements whenever a person's name is used, the person is recognizable, or the person is well known.
2. A release is not needed if a person is part of a crowd scene or is shown in the fleeting background. There are no specific guidelines on what constitutes a crowd.
3. Each release should be witnessed.
4. Obtain the full name, full address, and the phone number of the subject person. If possible, attach the person's business card to the release.

5. The person's address and phone number should be verified by calling or looking them up in the phone book.

6. Ten dollars ($10) must be paid to the person and a copy of the returned check should be kept in the file with the signed release.

7. It is important to verify the age of the person signing the release. What constitutes minor status varies from state to state. A rule of thumb is that anyone under the age of 18 should be considered a minor and parent or guardian signatures should be obtained.

Form 7–3 should be used when using film or photographs showing another's building or product.

Form 7–3
PROPERTY OR PRODUCT RELEASE

For consideration of _____ dollars and for other good and valuable consideration paid by Poorhorse Corp. (address), the undersigned hereby grants irrevocable, perpetual, and worldwide permission to Poorhorse Corp., its agents, assigns, licensees, and legal representatives, to film, photograph, display, and distribute for use in a commercial or advertisement the property or product described below. This right shall extend to any and all uses in advertising and promotion or for any other lawful trade purpose. I waive any right to inspect or approve the finished commercial or advertisement.

The undersigned warrants that it is the owner or authorized agent of the owner of the property or product and has the full power and authority to grant this permission.

Description of Property or Product: _____

_____

Address (if property): _____

_____

IF COMPANY: IF INDIVIDUAL:

_____   _____
(Name of Company)   (Name)

Address: _____   _____

_____   _____

By: _____   Telephone: _____

Title: _____   Date: _____

Telephone: _____

Date: _____

CHAPTER 8

PROTECTING SOFTWARE

§ 8.1   Introduction

In the 1980s, the impact of computer software on the world economy became significant. The impact was first seen in the United States, but it quickly spread to Europe and the Orient. High school and college students coming up with new software video games became instant millionaires. The young creators of dBASE and Lotus founded multibillion dollar companies on their software efforts.

Software is a new type of property over which the courts have struggled to afford protection. In the early cases regarding software protection, the difficulty facing the courts was to gain an understanding of the technology. Court decisions went out of their way to define carefully such words as *software, bit, byte, source code,* and *object code.* The law governing computer use has matured since those early days and this chapter presents current, practical approaches toward legal protection of software through copyrights, patents, and trade secrets. This chapter is designed to supplement the preceding chapters and to hone in on the cutting edge of legal issues.

RESOURCES:

1. Nimmer, Raymond T., *The Law of Computer Technology* (Warren, Gorham & Lamont: 210 South St., Boston, MA 02111 (Supp. 1990). The bible of computer law, this book is an essential reference written in clear and concise language.

2. Hoffman, Paul S., *The Software Legal Book* (Shafer Books, Inc.: 139 Grand Street, P.O. Box 40, Croton-on-Hudson, NY 10520). An excellent looseleaf book in two volumes, this work is specifically designed for the nonattorney and contains numerous forms.

3. *The Computer Lawyer* (Prentice Hall Law & Business: 910 Sylvan Ave., Englewood Cliffs, NJ 07632, (telephone 1-800-223-0231). A must have monthly periodical, the magazine is a bargain at $275 per year.

4. *Guide to Computer Law* (Commerce Clearing House: 4025 W. Peterson Ave., Chicago, IL 60646). This two-volume legal treatise, which is continuously updated, is detailed, thorough, and essential for the computer law practitioner.

---

§ 8.2   Copyrighting Software

The door first opened to copyright protection of software with the passage of the 1976 Copyright Act.[1] Although not specifically enumerated in the new Copyright Act, the fact that computer programs were proper copyrightable subject matter was stated in the legislative history of the Act. In 1980 Congress specifically amended the 1976 Act by adding a broad definition of a computer program.[2]

Attempting to follow the mandate of the 1980 amendments, the Copyright Office, then composed mostly of liberal arts graduates, struggled with such strange terms as *source code* and *object code*. *Source code* essentially constitutes the language in which a programmer writes a program. It appears to be filled with unintelligible words and symbols. *Object code* is the version of the program existing in binary ones and zeroes that actually

---

[1] 17 U.S.C. § 90 (1978).

[2] Computer Software Act of 1980, Pub. L. No. 96-517, 94 Stat. 3015 (1980), amending 17 U.S.C. §§ 101–810.

operates the machine. Source code and object code listings were mystifying to the Copyright Office. Even today when object code is registered, the Copyright Office will issue a so-called "rule of doubt" registration simply because it cannot examine such works to determine originality. A rule of doubt registration means that the examiner believes that the software is an original work of authorship but she cannot verify it through her own examination process as she can in the case of a painting or a novel.[3] Now the Copyright Office is more comfortable with these strange documents than it was in the early days.

The Ninth Circuit resolved the legal difficulty as to the form of the software in a 1983 California case involving the Apple Computer company.[4] The court emphatically stated that computer programs, whether existing in a paper listing, in a floppy disk, in a hard disk, or in a ROM, were protected under the 1980 amendments:

> Either all computer programs so embodied are within the terms "idea, procedure, system, method of operation" and are excluded, or all of them are outside those terms and thus protectible. There is nothing in any of the statutory terms which suggest[s] a different result for different types of computer programs based upon the function they serve within the machine.[5]

The physical form of the software does not now pose a legal problem with the courts.

A different screen presentation on the video monitor, even though produced by the same underlying software, does not preclude a finding of copyright infringement.

In 1983, a court found infringement of the famous Pacman object code ROMs even though the defendant's audiovisual characters were found not to infringe the Pacman characters.[6] In a case that has caused some concern in the software world with respect to the development of add-on software, the defendant had sold printed circuit boards (that is, hardware) for use in video game machines that would speed up the play of the famous Galaxian video game.[7] The Seventh Circuit held the hardware speedup to be a derivative work and, therefore, unless authorized by the

---

[3] Library of Congress, Compendium II on Copyright Office Practices § 324.04 (1984).

[4] Apple Computer, Inc. v. Formula Int'l, Inc., 562 F. Supp. 775, 218 U.S.P.Q. (BNA) 47 (C.D. Cal. 1983), aff'd, 725 F.2d 521, 221 U.S.P.Q. (BNA) 762 (9th Cir. 1984).

[5] Id. at 780, 218 U.S.P.Q. at 51.

[6] Midway Mfg. Co. v. Strohon, 564 F. Supp. 741, 219 U.S.P.Q. (BNA) 42 (N.D. Ill. 1983).

[7] Midway Mfg. Co. v. Artic Int'l, Inc., 547 F. Supp. 999, 216 U.S.P.Q. (BNA) 413 (N.D. Ill. 1982), aff'd, 704 F.2d 1009, 218 U.S.P.Q. (BNA) 791 (Fed. Cir. 1983), cert. denied, 464 U.S. 823 (1983). See Stern, Framing Prints, Giving the Mona Lisa a Moustache, Speeding Up Video Games, and Marketing Add-On Software: A Comment on the Mirage Case, 37 Pat. Trademark & Copyright J. (BNA) 305 (Feb. 2, 1989).

copyright owner, a copyright infringement. Clearly, video game businesses purchased such printed circuit boards in an effort to keep Galaxian interesting and challenging to players, and to increase their profits. Without such speedup, video businesses were losing revenue because good players could keep Galaxian in the playing mode for a long time. The Fourth Circuit has held that a federal copyright registration of the software contained in an integrated circuit chip also protects the audiovideo screen display presentation.[8]

The above cases are interesting to study because each represents a new, if not gigantic, step in the technological understanding of the courts regarding the actual legal ramifications of the 1980 copyright amendment.

§ 8.3 —Proper Copyright Subject Matter

Copyright law is not designed to protect functionality or the basic underlying idea. The Ninth Circuit found no copyright infringement involving the two video games Tricky Trapper and Mouser.[9] The court stated: "Although there are numerous similar features . . . each . . . constitutes a basic idea of the videogames and, to the extent each feature is expressive . . . the expression is 'as a practical matter indispensable, or at least standard, in the treatment of a given [idea].'"[10]

Figure 8–1 sets forth the *levels of abstraction test,* used to identify what is proper copyright subject matter. This test was first expressed by Judge Learned Hand, one of copyright's most articulate and thoughtful analysts:

> Upon any work, and especially upon a play, a great number of patterns of increasing generality will fit equally well, as more and more of the incident is left out. The last may perhaps be no more than the most general statement of what the play is all about, and at times might consist only of its title; but there is a point in this series of abstractions where they are no longer protected, since otherwise the playwright could prevent the use of his "ideas" to which, apart from their expression, his property is never extended.[11]

In **Figure 8–1**, the apex of the triangle represents an idea and the bottom layer of the triangle is the expression of the idea. For example, the idea could be a movie about a war staged in outer space between good and evil, and the expression could be the actual screenplay for the movie

---

[8] M. Kramer Mfg. Co. v. Andrews, 783 F.2d 421, 228 U.S.P.Q. (BNA) 705 (4th Cir. 1986).

[9] Frybarger v. IBM, 812 F.2d 525, 2 U.S.P.Q.2d (BNA) 1135 (9th Cir. 1987).

[10] *Id.* at 529, 2 U.S.P.Q. 2d at 1138.

[11] Nichols v. Universal Pictures Corp., 45 F.2d 119, 121 (2d Cir. 1930), *cert. denied,* 282 U.S. 902 (1931).

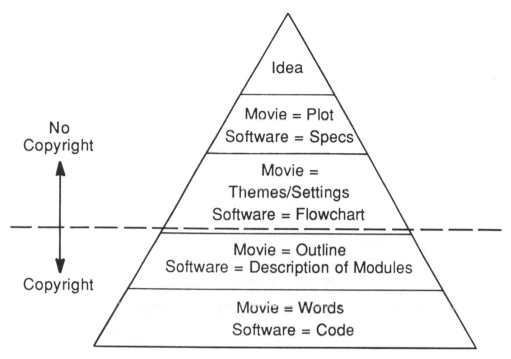

Figure 8–1. Levels of abstraction test.

such as *Star Wars.* Somewhere between the idea and the actual expression, a demarcation line is drawn (shown by the dotted line); the levels of abstraction above that line are not protectable under copyright law, but the levels of abstraction below that line are. As shown in the figure, the levels for a movie may be represented as actual words, an outline, the detailed settings and themes, or the overall plot.

In the area of software, these levels of abstraction could be code, detailed description of modules, flow chart of functional modules, or the design specifications (for example, the requirements for word processing). The location of the demarcation line varies from case to case, and the levels of abstraction test is designed to be functional, based upon the facts of a particular case. For example, if the expression at the bottom of the triangle is mostly dictated by functional software requirements, then the demarcation line is lowered. If the software concept is unique and novel, the line of demarcation may be much closer to the top of the triangle.

In the context of software law, the Seventh Circuit adopted Judge Learned Hand's levels of abstraction test and found the plaintiff's software to be "dictated by the externalities of the cotton market," held the plaintiff's creative contribution not to be sufficient to give it a monopoly, and therefore found no infringement.[12] The court found the line of demarcation to be lower than the plaintiff claimed.

The Third Circuit is responsible for the famous "look and feel" software doctrine of infringement that uses copyright law to protect the sequence, structure, and organization (commonly called SSO) of the software.[13] That court held that the defendant's software infringed the plaintiff's subroutine and file structures.[14]

In reaching this conclusion, the Third Circuit ruled that "copyright principles derived from other areas are applicable in the field of computer programs" and that "paraphrasing" a copyrighted work (despite lack of identity of expression) has been actionable. The court then stated: "[T]he purpose or function of a utilitarian work would be the work's idea, and everything that is not necessary to that purpose or function would be part of the expression of the idea."[15]

This look and feel test is interesting in that it places the demarcation line of the levels of abstraction test very close to the apex of the triangle. This test also suggests that other competing software packages should be evaluated to determine whether the defendant's software infringes the plaintiff's software. In other words, have other competitors created software performing the same function, but with an entirely different look and feel? The look and feel test is the law in several circuits but has been criticized by other circuits that have adopted the levels of abstraction test. This split among the circuits creates an opportunity for a plaintiff to look for the circuit court most favorable to its case. Legally, this is called *forum shopping,* and it will continue to be possible until this split in circuits is resolved by the Supreme Court.

§ 8.4　—Protection of Software Written in Symbols

The Copyright Office has issued a certificate of copyright registration for a software program written in onscreen icons.[16] Essentially, the author had created a program called Client Portrait by using icons appearing on the screen. No words or grammar appeared in the created program, only icons. The underlying software was Double Helix. The copyright examiner, although issuing the registration, cautioned that any copyright in

---

[12] Plains Cotton Coop. Ass'n v. Goodpasture Computer Serv., 807 F.2d 1256, 2 U.S.P.Q. 2d (BNA) 1635 (5th Cir.), *reh'g denied,* 813 F.2d 407 (5th Cir.), *cert. denied,* 484 U.S. 821 (1987).

[13] Whelan Assoc., Inc. v. Jaslow Dental Laboratory, Inc., 797 F.2d 1222, 230 U.S.P.Q. (BNA) 481 (3d Cir. 1986), *cert. denied,* 479 U.S. 1031 (1987).

[14] *Id.* at 1240, 230 U.S.P.Q. at 494.

[15] *Id.* at 1236, 230 U.S.P.Q. at 490.

[16] Copyright Registration No. TX 2-466-876, CCH Guide to Computer Law (CCH) ¶ 60,011 (1990).

Client Portrait did not imply a copyright claim in the underlying Double Helix language. Several letters were written between the Copyright Office and the attorneys for the author of Client Portrait, questioning whether the author or a computer designed the material. This matter of protecting programs authored by a computer will be a substantial issue in the near future.

§ 8.5   —Copyright Registration

RESOURCE:

1. The Copyright Office has much free information (circulars and leaflets) that assists in filing software applications: Register of Copyrights, Library of Congress, Washington, DC, telephone 202-707-1812.

The procedure for registering software, along with an actual example, is fully discussed in **Chapter 5**.

It is important when registering software to understand that only a single registration is necessary to cover both the computer program and the accompanying visual screen displays, along with any audio.[17] This issue, with which the Copyright Office has struggled for years, has been resolved in favor of simplicity. A single registration suffices, and the deposit need only be the computer program, not videos of the screen displays. This is true only if the copyright application claims rights to the software in the application by using one of the following terms: (1) *Entire work,* or (2) *Entire computer program.* If one desires to deposit identifying material for the visual screen displays, then the following language is used: (1) *Entire computer program including audiovisual materials,* or (2) *Entire computer program including artwork on screen displays.*[18]

§ 8.6   —Copyright Notice

Although United States adoption of the Berne Convention has eliminated the requirement of copyright notice, it is simply good practice always to use the standard copyright notice because it eliminates the innocent infringer defense. There has been some litigation in the past as to what

---

[17] Copyright Office Notice of Registration Decision No. 87-4, 53 Fed. Reg. 21,817, CCH Guide to Computer Law (CCH) ¶ 20,496 (June 10, 1988).

[18] Copyright Office, Computer Programs & Related Screen Displays, CCH Guide to Computer Law (CCH) ¶ 60,059 (Oct. 19, 1989).

constitutes proper copyright notice in software. From a practical point of view, the copyright notice should be:

1. Placed in the software itself so that it is printed out in a listing of the source code
2. Visibly flashed on the screen for a period of time so that it can be read and understood
3. Placed on a label on the software storage medium such as a label on a floppy disk
4. Placed on the accompanying manual of operation
5. Printed on input formats whether printed or appearing on the screen
6. Placed on printed output formats.

The copyright notice must be affixed to the copies in such a way as to provide reasonable notice of the claimed copyright.

§ 8.7 —Copyright Infringement

RESOURCES:

1. Beutel, "Copyright Infringement and Derivative Software," *The Computer Lawyer* Vol. 4, No. 1, pp. 12–19 (Mar. 1987).
2. Siegal, "Copyright Infringement of the 'Look and Feel' of an Operating System," *The Computer Lawyer* Vol. 4, No. 1, pp. 1–17 (Jan. 1987).

In copyright infringement cases, there is a three-year statute of limitations in which to bring an infringement action. This is a relatively short period of time; therefore, it is important that the software copyright owner promptly evaluate any possible infringements of its copyrights. The following cases illustrate the state of flux that copyright infringement cases have undergone and are presently undergoing.

Atari sued and enjoined JS&A as a "contributory" infringer in the sale of JS&A's Prom Blaster software. The Prom Blaster enabled the purchaser to make copies of Atari home video games. JS&A argued that the device was being sold to persons who would make archival copies of the Atari home video game, a practice that is fully permitted by the copyright law. The court disagreed with this argument.[19]

In another case, the defendant did not have access to the plaintiff's source code. Rather, the defendant obtained a machine-readable version

---

[19] Atari, Inc. v. JS&A, Inc., No. 83 Civ. 8333 (N.D. Ill. Dec. 6, 1983).

from the computer chip of the plaintiff's copyrighted program by using a reverse engineering process known as *disassembly*. After the defendant came out with its software, the plaintiff filed suit and won.[20]

In an interesting Massachusetts case, the plaintiff owned a copyright in a commodities trading method that was written in a manual. The defendant purchased the manual and produced a software version of the trading method and system. The court found copyright infringement, concluding that the software was a derivative work of the written material.[21]

In a look and feel case, the plaintiff owned the copyright to the famous Print Shop software that was found to be infringed by the defendant's Printmaster software. The court stated:

> In the present case, it is clear that the structure, sequence, and layout of the audiovisual displays in "Print Shop" were dictated primarily by artistic and aesthetic considerations, not by utilitarian or mechanical ones. Repeatedly, the testimony of David Balsam showed that, in creating the screens of "Print Shop," he based textual and graphic decisions on the basis of aesthetic and artistic preferences. . . . The bottom line is that the designer of any program that performed the same functions as "Print Shop" had available a wide range of expression governed predominately by artistic and not utilitarian considerations. Thus, the Court cannot accept defendant's argument that the audiovisual displays of "Print Shop" fall outside the scope of "pictorial" or "graphic" works as set forth in § 101. . . . Put simply, "Printmaster" looks like a copy of "Print Shop" with a few embellishments scattered about in no particular order. The "total concept and feel" of these programs . . . is virtually identical. The application of the intrinsic test in the present case compels the finding that their expression is substantially similar.[22]

In a case illustrating the substantial value that software copyrights may have, the Commercial Arbitration Tribunal of the American Arbitration Association ruled that Fujitsu would be permitted to have access to certain types of IBM programs over the next 10 years, at the same time assuring IBM full compensation for their use.[23] Under the award, Fujitsu would receive the necessary IBM interface information that would allow its own independent engineering staff to create an IBM-compatible operating system software. IBM, on the other hand, obtained not only compensation but assurances that Fujitsu would not use other IBM information in the development of the compatible software.

---

[20] E.F. Johnson Co. v. Uniden Corp., 623 F. Supp. 1485, 228 U.S.P.Q. (BNA) 891 (D. Minn. 1985).

[21] Williams v. Arndt, 626 F. Supp. 571, 227 U.S.P.Q. (BNA) 615 (D. Mass. 1985).

[22] Broderbund Software, Inc. v. Unison World, Inc., 648 F. Supp. 1127, 1134, 231 U.S.P.Q. (BNA) 700, 704–06 (N.D. Cal. 1986).

[23] American Arbitration Ass'n Commercial Arbitration Tribunal, Case No. 13T-117-0636-85 (Nov. 29, 1988), CCH Guide to Copyright Law (CCH) ¶ 20,517.

§ 8.8 —Unauthorized Corporate Copying of Software

Without question, in many corporations and organizations there is an underlying belief that only one copy of software needs to be purchased. Once purchased, copies of the software are made and distributed throughout the organization. If your organization does this—stop! The Software Publishers Association (SPA), which includes as members Ashton-Tate, Lotus Development Corp., Microsoft, MicroPro International, and Word-Perfect Corp., is enforcing copyrights against the unauthorized copying of software in the business environment. For example, in a lawsuit against a New York book publisher, Facts on File, Inc., the SPA received a settlement in excess of $100,000. The President of Facts on File stated:

> Regrettably, unauthorized copies were loaded onto the hard disk of some of our office PCs. In the press of daily business, we did not give this matter the thought we should have in order to recognize that this might infringe on the plaintiff's copyrights. We regret our carelessness and have made amends. As publishers ourselves, we expect our copyrights to be respected and we should make a special effort to respect the copyrights of others. We have adopted a very firm policy warning our employees not to loan any software on their personal hard drives without demonstrating to management that they can do so without infringement on any copyright. We think that other firms should adopt similar guidelines.[24]

It is important to remind employees periodically not to engage in unauthorized copying of software. In most states, such copying is also a criminal offense.

The SPA has more than 500 member software companies and has already filed a number of similar lawsuits.[25] The SPA, which uses the proceeds from each lawsuit to fund future litigation, can be contacted at: Software Publishers Association, 1101 Connecticut Avenue, NW, Washington, DC 20036.

---

[24] CCH Guide to Computer Law (CCH) ¶ 60,028 (1990).

[25] The Copyright Office has studied copyright litigation in the field of motion pictures. Copyright L. Rep. (CCH) ¶ 20,420 (1990). The following briefly summarizes the results of copyright litigation in this area during 1984 and 1985. The results are based on a survey of 233 lawyers and senior corporate executives:

 1. Disputes initiated involving copyrights—3,900
 2. Disputes settled prior to the initiation of litigation—3,100
 3. Disputes resulting in a lawsuit being filed—747
 4. Disputes settled prior to judgment or during trial—651
 5. Disputes resulting in the award of a judgment—96.

With respect to the latter 96 lawsuits, the total cost of the lawsuits was estimated a $5 million, with total settlement awards to the plaintiffs in the range of $11.5 million. The lesson to be learned from this study is that only 2½ percent of copyright disputes resulted in actual trial.

§ 8.9 —Database Protection

RESOURCE: Pearson, "Computer Databases: Copyright and Other Protection," *The Computer Lawyer* Vol. 4, No. 6, pp. 28–36 (June, 1987).

Almost every business has a corporate database that contains substantial trade secret information. The database may range from a simple customer list to valuable chemical formulations. On a daily, if not hourly basis, most businesses access databases owned and managed by others, such as the DIALOG collection of databases. Computer databases have been held to be copyrightable under copyright law.[26] However, if there is a lack of sufficient creativity, it will not be held protectable. For example, if there is no exercise of creativity or judgment in the creation of the database and creating it was a simple clerical function, the database will not be protected under copyright law. One court has held that if the database was compiled through "industrious collection," then it will be eligible for copyright protection.[27] If a business desires to protect its database under copyright law, then it is imperative that it take proper steps to show care, discretion, and industrious collection in selecting, editing, and monitoring the data going into the database.

§ 8.10 Patenting Software

Historically, software was not patentable. The United States Supreme Court, in the 1981 case of *Diamond v. Diehr,*[28] changed things by holding that a process for curing synthetic rubber using a mathematical formula in a programmed digital computer was proper subject matter for a patent. This decision set the stage for a flurry of clarifying legal decisions holding software to be proper subject matter for a patent. For example, a method for seismic exploration using a summing algorithm was also held to be proper subject matter for a patent.[29] A CAT scan imaging technique utilizing a mathematical alogrithm was also held to be patentable.[30]

Now an explosion of software patents is taking place, with 40 percent of United States software patents being issued to Japanese companies.[31]

---

[26] Financial Information, Inc. v. Moody's Investors Serv., Inc., 751 F.2d 501, 224 U.S.P.Q. (BNA) 632 (2d Cir. 1984), *on remand,* 231 U.S.P.Q. (BNA) 803 (S.D.N.Y.), *aff'd,* 808 F.2d 204, 1 U.S.P.Q.2d (BNA) 1279 (2d Cir. 1986), *cert. denied,* 484 U.S. 820 (1987).

[27] National Business Lists, Inc. v. Dun & Bradstreet, Inc., 552 F. Supp. 89, 215 U.S.P.Q. (BNA) 595 (N.D. Ill. 1982).

[28] 450 U.S. 175 (1981).

[29] *In re* Taner, 681 F.2d 787, 214 U.S.P.Q. (BNA) 678 (C.C.P.A. 1982).

[30] *In re* Abele, 684 F.2d 902, 214 U.S.P.Q. (BNA) 682 (C.C.P.A. 1982).

[31] Kahin, *The Software Patent Crisis,* 93 Tech. Rev. 53-58 (Apr. 1990).

Software programmers traditionally have freely used programming concepts, features, and methods to create their individual software. The ramifications of issuing patents on such products are just now being realized, and what the future holds is unclear.

§ 8.11   —Proper Patent Subject Matter

The following software patent illustrates the characteristics of a software invention that was initially rejected by the Patent Office as not being proper subject matter but then reversed by an appellate court.[32] The invention involved patenting a method for controlling the internal operations of the computer. The invention performed as follows.

Suppose a user provides the following information:

(1)   values for a, b, c, and d;
(2) $A = X + Y$;
(3) $X = a + b$; and
(4) $Y = c + d$.

Obviously, a computer cannot execute these operations in the order presented because step (2) cannot be performed until the results of steps (3) and (4) are obtained. What the appellants' algorithm does is rearrange the order of the formulas as presented by the user so that the computer can execute the operations. Thus, using our example, the appellants' algorithmic process would rearrange the formulas as follows:

(1)   values for a, b, c, and d;
(2) $X = a + b$;
(3) $Y = c + d$; and
(4) $A = X + Y$.

These formulas, as arranged, can be executed by the computer in a logical, sequential fashion.[33]

The 17-year patent monopoly as stated in the patent claim also stated:

48.   A general purpose data processor of known type operating under the control of a stored program containing a set of instructions for enabling the data processor to execute formulas in an object program comprising a plurality of formulas, such that the same results will be produced when using the same given data, regardless of the sequence in which said formulas are presented in said object program, said data processor performing the following functions:

(a)   examining each of said formulas in a storage area of the data processor to determine which formulas can be designated as defined;

---

[32] *In re Pardo*, 684 F.2d 912, 214 U.S.P.Q. (BNA) 673 (C.C.P.A. 1982).

[33] *Id.* at 914, 214 U.S.P.Q. at 674.

(b)   executing, in the sequence in which each formula is designated as defined, said formulas designated as defined;

(c)   repeating steps (a) and (b) for at least undefined formulas as many times as required until all said formulas have been designated as defined and have been executed;

whereby to produce the same results upon execution of the formulas in the sequence recited in step (b) when using the same given data, regardless of the order in which said formulas were presented in the object program prior to said functions.[34]

A software engineer, upon understanding this invention and the above claim language, will also fully appreciate the breadth and nature of software patents that can be obtained. Without question, software patents are being vigorously sought by software houses, businesses, and programmers.

In another example, Merrill Lynch received a patent on its *Cash Management Account* (CMA) program that Paine Webber sought to invalidate based on the ground that it "merely describe[d] a series of manipulative steps" that could be "performed by and with the aid of paper, pencil, and telephone."[35] The court held the patent valid and stated that computer programs are recognized as being proper subject matter for patents. The court found the claimed invention to be neither an "alogrithm" nor a "method of doing business," stating:

[T]his Court has carefully examined the claims in this case and is unable to find any direct or indirect recitation of a procedure for solving a mathematical problem. Rather, the patent allegedly claims a methodology to effectuate a highly efficient business system and does not restate a mathematical formula.[36]

This case was settled but served as a signal to patent attorneys to commence writing patent applications on software for controlling business operations and methods.

§ 8.12   —Examples of Issued Software Patents

The abstract shown in **Figure 8–2** is obtained from the *Official Gazette* and sets forth a good example of an issued patent in the software area. It shows that a software patent with broad claims was issued. This patent is now owned by Refac International and Refac has sued Lotus, Ashton-Tate, Microsoft, and others for patent infringement. The patent was

---

[34] *Id.* at 913, 214 U.S.P.Q. at 674.

[35] Paine, Webber, Jackson & Curtis, Inc. v. Merrill Lynch, Pierce, Fenner & Smith, Inc., 564 F. Supp. 1358, 1365, 218 U.S.P.Q. (BNA) 212, 217 (D. Del. 1983).

[36] *Id.* at 1368, 218 U.S.P.Q. at 219.

4,398,249
PROCESS AND APPARATUS FOR CONVERTING A
SOURCE PROGRAM INTO AN OBJECT PROGRAM
Rene K. Pardo, and Remy Landau, both of 12 Romney Rd.,
Downsview, Ontario, both of Canada M3H 1H2
Filed Aug. 12, 1970, Ser. No. 63,185
Int. Cl.³ G06F *15/06*

U.S. Cl. 364—300   **36 Claims**

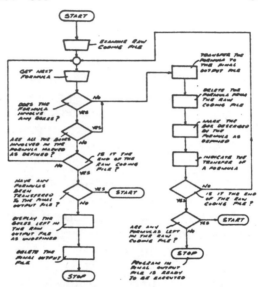

1. A process of operating a general purpose data processor
of known type to enable the data processor to execute formulas
in an object program comprising a plurality of formulas, such
that the same results will be produced when using the same
given data, regardless of the sequence in which said formulas
are presented in said object program, comprising the steps of:
  (a) examining each of said formulas in a storage area of the
    data processor to determine which formulas can be desig-
    nated as defined;
  (b) storing, in the sequence in which each formula is desig-
    nated as defined, said formulas which are designated as
    defined;
  (c) repeating steps (a) and (b) for at least undefined formulas
    as many times as required until all said formulas have been
    designated as defined and have been stored;
  whereby to produce the same results upon sequential execu-
    tion of the formulas stored by said process when using the
    same given data, regardless of the order in which said
    formulas were presented in the object program prior to
    said process.

Figure 8–2. Abstract of software patent in the *Official
Gazette of the United States Patent Office.*

United States Patent [19]

Vincent et al.

[11] Patent Number: 4,645,238

[45] Date of Patent: * Feb. 24, 1987

[54] ANNOTATED CALENDAR ASSEMBLY

[75] Inventors: James P. Vincent, Arlington; Mary
                   E. Weidmann, Irving; Donald E.
                   Curtis, Garland, all of Tex.

[73] Assignee: International Business Machines
                   Corporation, Armonk, N.Y.

[*] Notice: The portion of the term of this patent
                  subsequent to May 27, 2003 has been
                  disclaimed.

[21] Appl. No.: 487,375

[22] Filed: Apr. 21, 1983

[51] Int. Cl.⁴ G09G 3/04; G06F 7/00;
                                         G04B 19/24
[52] U.S. Cl. 283/67; 340/700;
                                    364/300; 368/28
[58] Field of Search 283/67, 360/20, 29,
                   368/30, 40; 281/15 B; 364/900, 300, 200;
                                         340/700, 706

[56]   References Cited
          U.S. PATENT DOCUMENTS

3,594,935	7/1971	Blattstein	281/15 B
3,999,050	12/1976	Pitroda .	
4,162,610	7/1979	Levine	368/28
4,247,927	1/1981	Oooka et al.	368/30
4,270,192	5/1981	Kudo	368/29
4,353,178	10/1982	Meezawa	368/30
4,428,681	1/1984	Icashio	368/29
4,591,840	5/1986	Curtis et al.	340/700 X

FOREIGN PATENT DOCUMENTS

0005661	5/1979	European Pat. Off. .	
84102530	11/1984	European Pat. Off. .	
2517400	2/1977	Fed. Rep. of Germany .	
2904664	8/1980	Fed. Rep. of Germany .	
2026736	2/1980	United Kingdom	368/30

OTHER PUBLICATIONS

Keith Clark Inc. Catalogue, Work-A-Day 1972 Calendars, face page and pp. 2 & 6.
IBM Bulletin, vol. 19, No. 7, Dec. 1976.
IBM Bulletin, vol. 26, Nov. 1, 1984.

Primary Examiner—Robert L. Spruill
Assistant Examiner—Paul M. Heyrana, Sr.
Attorney, Agent, or Firm—J. H. Barksdale

[57]   ABSTRACT

A method of assembling, for display, a monthly calendar annotated with exterior current day narrative notes and embedded abbreviated notes. Notes related to a specific day can be prepared on a time independent basis by calling, and keying to, a day screen for the specific day. In addition, keying is used to distinguish between normal and special notes which are to be later displayed in abbreviated and narrative forms, respectively. Upon the occurrence of the specific day and the calling of a calendar screen, the notes are displayed along with an updated calendar. Special notes appear as narrative footnotes and normal notes appear in abbreviated form with the day indications. In the absence of further day screen calling and keying, the footnotes change on a daily basis, while the abbreviated notes remain fixed.

12 Claims, 4 Drawing Figures

Figure 8-3. Entire software patent in the *Official Gazette of the United States Patent Office.*

LOOK AT THE WHOLE MONTH

SCHEDULE FOR: G. J. JOHNSON   DATE: 07/19/83

SUNDAY	MONDAY	TUESDAY	WEDNESDAY	THURSDAY	FRIDAY	SATURDAY
					1 MM...I.	2 ...L.W.
3	4	5 <MM	6 .1.	7 MMM	8	9 >
10	11	12 *	13	14 I	15	16 ...m.
17	18	19 <D- --	20 ..D>	21	22	23
24	25	26	27	28 --	29	30 VVVV>
31						

NOTE: REMEMBER THAT WILSON WANTED AUGUST'S FIGURES

PF1 LOOK AT THE DAY   PF2 SCHEDULES   PF3 ROOMS   PF4 NEXT DAY   PF5 PREVIOUS DAY
PF7 GROUPS   PF8 PRINT   PF9 HELP   PF10 NEXT MONTH   PF11 PREV. MONTH   PF12 RETURN

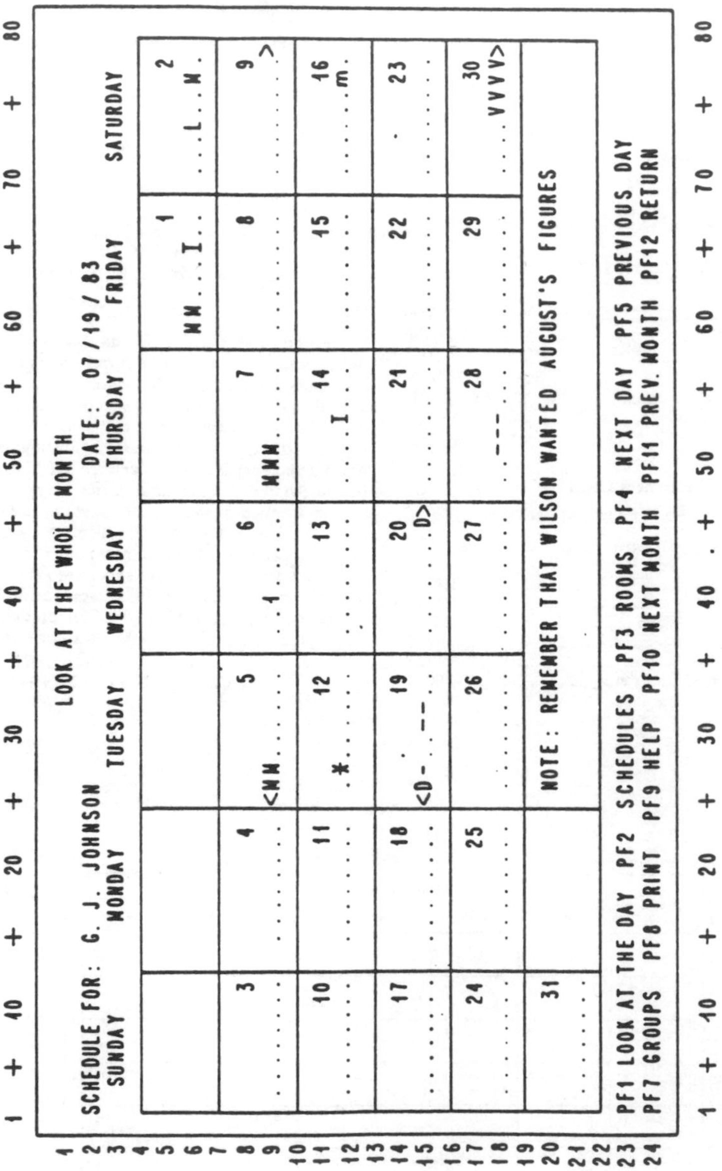

FIG. 1

Figure 8–3. *(Continued)*

U.S. Patent   Feb. 24, 1987   Sheet 2 of 4   4,645,238

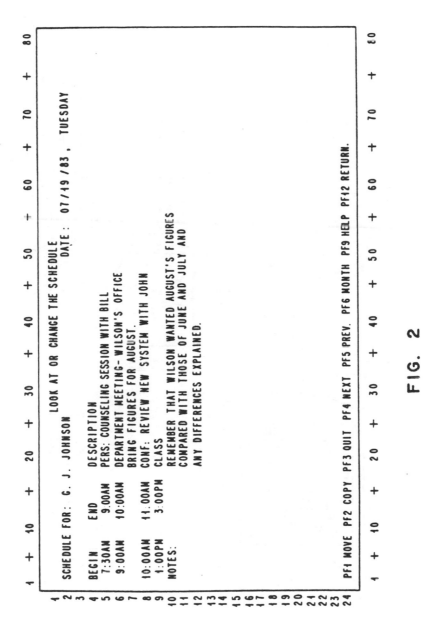

FIG. 2

Figure 8–3. *(Continued)*

U.S. Patent Feb. 24, 1987 Sheet 3 of 4 4,645,238

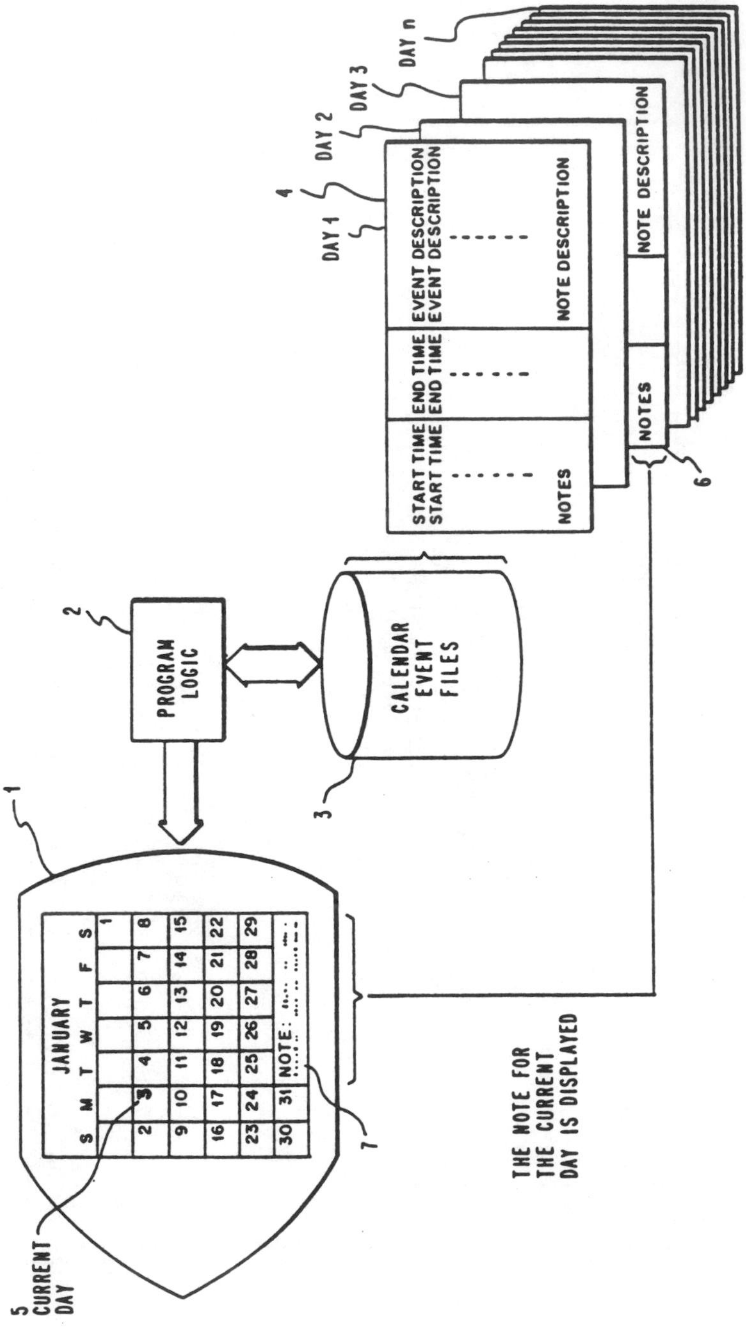

FIG. 3

Figure 8–3. *(Continued)*

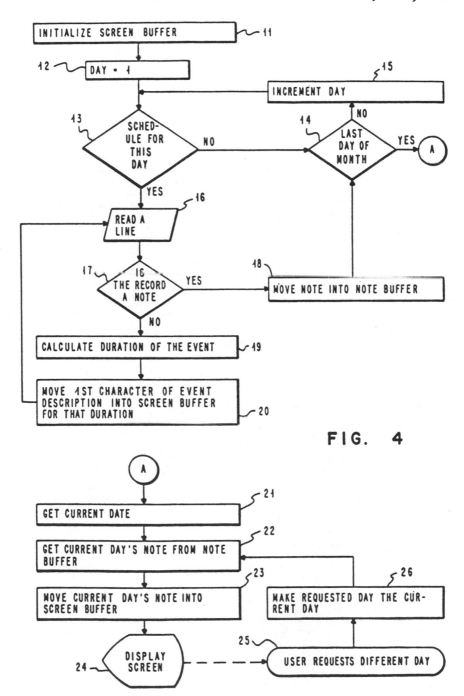

FIG. 4

Figure 8–3. *(Continued)*

4,645,238

ANNOTATED CALENDAR ASSEMBLY

TECHNICAL FIELD

This invention relates generally to calendaring, and more specifically to assembly of an annotated calendar containing abbreviated event notes and narrative event related notes.

BACKGROUND ART

Calendars and uses thereof are many and vary widely. By calendar is meant any medium carrying a plurality of past, present, or future day indications. The day indications can be spelled out with alphabetical characters and/or made up of numeric characters. One type of popular calendar in use today is a day oriented ring binder having a separate page or sheet of paper for each day. Each page has imprinted thereon a date and two pages are dedicated to each date. A monthly calendar related to the date is imprinted on one of the pages. The pages occur consecutively in the binder according to date. Blank space is provided a user for preparing or writing in event notes related to the page date. The event notes can be information related to a meeting, conference, appointment, etc. The notes can be narrative, abbreviated, etc. The user can be the owner of the calendar as well as a visual reviewer of the calendar.

Another type of popular calendar has a month or portion thereof depicted on each page in grid form. This type of calendar has day blocks containing day numbers. Blank space surrounds the numbers in the blocks and is used by a user for entering event notes. The extensiveness of the notes which can be entered is directly related to the size of the blocks, user writing, etc. For a heavily scheduled user such as someone having different meetings every hour or so each day, providing sufficient space for meaningful notes would require a calendar of unwieldly size. A more manageable alternative is reversion to the previously described day oriented ring binder. Underlying major problems still exists, though. One is the excessive time required to leaf back and forth through the pages in search of a desired date for entering a note. Another is clutter. As the number of notes grows, the time required to read and decipher the notes increases.

With the advent of application driven keyboard/display work stations, the door was opened for application programmers to create a so-called electronic calendars. The most pertinent known work of others includes the creation of a monthly calendar grid similar to that described above and having embedded note abbreviations for timed day events. This annotated calendar is created from both month and day screens. That is, based on a clock, day blocks on the monthly calendar grid screen are filled in with appropriate day numbers on one line in each of the blocks. Then, based on keying and creating filled in day screens, abbreviations are filled in on another line in the blocks. No narrative information is provided for on the calendar screen. As is the case in certain instances, there is a need to obtain meaningful detail related to an abbreviation. This requires recall of a day screen. An example is an important reminder non-correlatible to the abbreviation, such as a note to bring materials to a meeting in conference room F. The fact of a meeting is provided for with an abbreviation such as "M". However, the reminder is not provided for and recall is in order.

Another problem with the above-mentioned prior work of others is that excessive day screen keying is required to handle abbreviations. That is, abbreviations have to be keyed in on the day screen. This requires time and thought. Yet another problem with the prior work of others is that the positional relationship to time of the abbreviation is not readily discernible. That is, a user can not always accurately correlate a meeting time with the location of the abbreviation in the day block.

In addition to the above, with the advent of application driven keyboard/display work stations, document footnoting become more readily manageable. That is, correlating footnotes and pages such that the footnotes appear on the same page with a corresponding footnote references is now a system operation. Drawing any analogy between document footnoting and the instant invention requires that the body text for a page of a footnoted document be equivalent to a monthly calendar grid. The two are not equivalent, though. Calendar day oriented footnotes must change on a daily basis in relation to a relatively fixed monthly calendar. As such, the footnoting of documents, taken alone or in combination with work of others, is not considered to either anticipate the instant invention or render the instant invention obvious.

The invention of this application presents advances over known art or work of others in that the flexibility in the use and creation of day screens is improved, and day screen event related information in narrative form is available as a footnote upon combined screen creation. The advantages of these advances are that screen size does not have to be increased, more meaningful information can be presented to a user, and information is readily available in uncluttered form.

DISCLOSURE OF THE INVENTION

A unique method of assembling an annotated calendar is provided in order that time related information is presented to a user in an uncluttered and readily retrievable and understandable manner. The calendar is assembled from day and month screens. The month screens are built in grid form such that blocks are provided for each day of the month. Within the blocks are day indications made up of a number of numeric characters. Surrounding each day indication is blank space for carrying event information which is abbreviated from a corresponding day screen. Abbreviations are used for standard items such as meetings. Located adjacent the bottom of the grid is space for carrying event related information in narrative form from a day screen. The information which is to appear in narrative form has special significance, such as a reminder to bring materials to a meeting.

Day screens are built by keying in a date, a time, information about the keyed in time, and narrative event related notes. Based on date keying, an appropriate month grid is built. Based on time and related information keying, the first character of the related information is positionally located time-wise in the blank space in the appropriate block. Based on narrative event related note keying and a clock, the note is positioned adjacent the bottom of the grid as a footnote on the appropriate day's screen. As day screens are updated, the assembled calendar is updated. However, updating of the footnote will only be effective on the assembled calendar on the current date.

Figure 8–3. *(Continued)*

4,645,238

3

BRIEF DESCRIPTION OF THE DRAWING

FIG. 1 is a pictorial representation of an annotated calendar assembled according to this invention.

FIG. 2 is a pictorial representation of a filled in day screen or daily appointment schedule for a current day which is used in assembling the calendar of FIG. 1.

FIG. 3 illustrates a day and month screen relationship, and in generalized block diagram form, the structure for assembling the calendar of FIG. 1.

FIG. 4 shows a flow diagram of the software operations performed by the structure of FIG. 3 for assembling the calendar of FIG. 1.

BEST MODE FOR CARRYING OUT THE INVENTION

For a more detailed understanding of the invention, reference is first made to FIG. 1. In this figure, a calendar for the month of July 1983 is depicted in grid form, and is annotated with hourly event abbreviations and a narrative event related footnote. The depicted grid is a rectangular array of seven by six day blocks with Sundays occupying the first or left column of blocks. The bottom row has two blocks on the left hand side of the grid. With this arrangement, any given month having 31 days and beginning on the Saturday in the top right hand corner of the grid, will end no later than Monday.

When the whole month is displayed on a display device of at least 24 lines of 80 characters, each day block can be two character rows high and 10 characters wide. Within each day block, numeric characters appear on the top row to indicate the date. On the bottom row a single character abbreviation can be used to represent each event note. Referring to Friday, July 1, the "M" positionally located at both the 9:00 and 10:00 a.m. time slots can be an abbreviation for the events "Meeting in Bill's office" and "Meeting in conference room G", respectively. It is to be noted that periods follow the M's. Each of these periods represent an hour of the day, assumed here to begin at 9:00 a.m. and end at 5:00 p.m., and appear to aid a user in visually correlating the time of the abbreviation. Without the periods, determining that the "I" is at 2:00 p.m. is not that easy a chore. The abbreviations can be assigned by the user or selected by the system. For example, when two events overlap, a flagging character, "*" can be assigned. As alluded to above, a period is used for unscheduled times. When the whole month is displayed in this manner, the free and unscheduled times of each day can be readily determined.

The equivalent of the rightmost five block positions on the bottom row is unused with the above described grid arrangement. As will be explained in greater detail hereinafter, this heretofore unused space can be used for narrative event related notes concerning a current date. The current date in most instances is "today's date". It can also be a specified date. That is, the current date can be the date specified for viewing a calendar of a different date.

Again, the annotated calendar of FIG. 1 is built from day and month screens. The month screen is built including the grid outline of FIG. 1 with the date indications appropriately located in the blocks for the month of the screen. For May 1983, the day indication "1" would appear in the top left hand block (under the Sunday column and in the top row). In building the month screen, the days of the week appear along the top of the grid, the name of the screen "Look at the Whole

4

Month" appears at the top, a help chart appears at the bottom, etc.

Referring next to FIG. 2, there is illustrated a filled in day screen. When initially called, the screen contains all entries with the exception of those immediately under the headings "BEGIN", "END", and "DESCRIPTION". The date opposite "Date:" is initially today's date as determined by a clock.

By entering times under the BEGIN and END headings, positional locations for event note abbreviations and codes in a subsequently built annotated calendar are established. For a standard eight hour day beginning, for example, at 9:00 a.m. and ending at 5:00 p.m., the abbreviations are system selected as the first character of the event note under the DESCRIPTION heading. Since the current date (July 19, 1983) events begin on the half hour and before 9:00 a.m., a code or "<" character is positioned in the screen of FIG. 1 against the left border of the day block. This is to alert a user that an other than normal schedule has been established. In like manner, a ">" indicates that the day's events will extend beyond 5:00 p.m. The hyphens appearing following the "D" are coded indications that the events corresponding to the times are personal or private in nature and the viewer in this case only need know that events are scheduled during the corresponding times.

The term "NOTES:" under BEGIN is operator entered. The system will recognize any narrative event related note entered opposite thereto as being scheduled for inclusion as a footnote during later annotated calendar assembly. Depending on the extensiveness of the note and available space in the screen of FIG. 1, the note will be included in full, or partially as shown in FIG. 1.

From the above, normal event notes are abbreviated and embedded during an annotated calendar assembly operation, while narrative event related notes having special significance are set out in narrative form as footnotes exterior of the grid.

Refer next to FIG. 3. In this figure is shown in a generalized form the structure for creating or assembling an annotated calendar. In response to a request to assemble and display a monthly annotated calendar on display device 1, program logic 2 reads each of the daily files 4 from mass storage 3 for a given month and condenses the hourly events into an abbreviated format. When the file for the current day 5 is processed, the note section 6 from the daily file is formatted into the unused portion of the calendar display as a footnote 7. When the current day is changed on the monthly display, the program logic 2 does not need to reformat the abbreviated events, but simply finds the special narrative event related note for the new day, and moves it to the footnote area.

Reference is next made to FIG. 4 wherein there is illustrated in greater detail the operations performed by program logic 2 in assembling the annotated calendar of FIG. 1. To begin with, a screen buffer included in a standard general purpose computer system such as the system of FIG. 3 is initialized. This is indicated by block 11 with the monthly grid as if there are no events scheduled at any time during the month. Next, a counter included in the system is set to the first day of the month as indicated by block 12. Thereafter, a determination is made as to whether there are any events scheduled for the first day. This operation is indicated by logic sequence 13. If not, a determination is made by logic sequence 14 as to whether there are any more days in

Figure 8–3. *(Continued)*

5   4,645,238   6

the month. If there are more days in the month, the day is incremented as indicated by block 15, and processing continues at logic sequence 13.

If there are events scheduled on the day represented by the count of block 15, a line is read from the corresponding daily schedule as indicated by block 16. Next, a determination is made by logic sequence 17 as to whether the line read is a special event related note or an hourly or other timed event. If it is a special narrative note, the note is written into a special buffer included in the system. The special buffer will contain all notes to be displayed in narrative form for the month as indicated by block 18. Since only the first of the narrative event related notes are displayed, processing continues with logic sequence 14.

If the line read is an event note to be abbreviated, the duration of the event is calculated as indicated by logic sequence 19. The first character of the event note description is moved into the screen buffer and repeated to indicate the duration of the event as indicated by block 20. The duration may be from 9:00 to 11:00 a.m., for example.

When all of the days in the month have been processed, today's date is retrieved from a clock as indicated by block 21. The number of the day is used to find the current day's narrative event related note in the special note buffer included in the system. This is indicated by block 22. This narrative event related note is moved to the bottom right hand portion of the screen buffer as indicated by block 23. Thereafter, the assembled annotated monthly calendar screen is displayed as indicated by block 24. If the user requests to view a different day's notes by keying in the number of the day as indicated by block 25, the requested day is made the "current" day as indicated by block 26, and processing continues with block 22.

From the above, in the absence of further day screen editing, abbreviated notes for a whole month remain fixed while special narrative notes change on a daily basis.

In summary, a unique method of assembling an annotated calendar is provided in order that time related information is presented to a user in an uncluttered and readily retrievable and understandable manner. The calendar is assembled from day and month screens. The month screens are built in grid form such that blocks are provided for each day of the month. Within the blocks are day indications made up of a number of numeric characters. Surrounding each day indication is blank space for carrying event information which is abbreviated from a corresponding day screen. Abbreviations are used for standard items such as meetings. Located adjacent the bottom of the grid is space for carrying event related information in narrative form from a day screen. The information which is to appear in narrative form has special significance, such as a reminder to bring materials to a meeting.

Day screens are built by keying in a date, a time, information about the keyed in time, and narrative event related notes. Based on date keying, an appropriate month grid is built. Based on time and related information keying, the first character of the related information

mation is positionally located time-wise in the blank space in the appropriate block. Based on narrative event related note keying and a clock, the note is positioned adjacent the bottom of the grid as a footnote on the appropriate day's screen. As day screens are updated, the assembled calendar is updated. However, updating of the footnote will only be effective on the assembled calendar on the current date.

While the invention has been particularly shown and described with reference to a preferred embodiment, it will be understood by those skilled in the art that various changes in form and detail may be made without departing from the spirit and scope of the invention.

We claim:

1. A method of assembling and displaying an annotated calendar, said method comprising:
   (1) creating a combined screen from separate calendar and day screens;
   (2) including a footnote applicable to a current date in said combined screen to form said annotated calendar; and
   (3) displaying said annotated calendar.

2. A method according to claim 1 including locating said footnote exterior or said calendar.

3. A method according to claim 2 including creating said calendar in grid form forming blocks for a plurality of dates with each block having associated therewith a different date indication.

4. A method according to claim 3 including creating said calendar screen based on a clock.

5. A method according to claim 4 including creating said combined screen based on said clock.

6. A method according to claim 5 including creating said day screen independent of said clock.

7. A method according to claim 6 including creating said day screen based on an entry related to time and a note entry.

8. A method according to claim 7 including creating said combined screen with entries related to time from each day screen corresponding to said calendar screen indicated in appropriate ones of said blocks in abbreviated form.

9. A method according to claim 8 including creating said calendar screen with date indications within said blocks.

10. A method according to claim 8 including creating said combined screen with said note entry as a footnote.

11. In a computer system, a method of aiding a user of a computer created calendar in visually ascertaining a time of an abbreviated event, said method comprising:
   (a) displaying on a display device an abbreviation for a scheduled event for a day on said calendar, said abbreviation being positioned timewise for said day; and
   (b) displaying on a display device an unscheduled time representation for a time for which no event has been scheduled.

12. A method according to claim 11 including displaying a period as said representation for unscheduled time.

* * * * *

65

Figure 8–3. *(Continued)*

originally filed in 1970 and issued in 1983, 13 years later! Six years after issuance, the lawsuits were brought. A lot has happened in the 19-year period since the patent was filed, and this patent will serve as a portent for the future.

In **Figure 8–3**, a 1987 software patent issued to IBM is set forth in its entirety. It is important to review this patent carefully for a number of reasons:

1. The invention pertains to annotating a calendar. Read Claim 1 and witness the breadth of the claim!
2. The patent is short and was, therefore, inexpensive to obtain.
3. The patent was filed in 1983 and issued in 1987, a four-year delay. Software patents take longer to issue than patents of other inventions.

§ 8.13   —Practical Considerations in Obtaining Patents on Software

The following guidelines set forth five considerations that should be evaluated before deciding whether to proceed with a software patent application:

1. What is the commercial life of the software in the marketplace? If the commercial life is one, two, or three years, keep in mind that it takes about this length of time for a patent to issue. Why go to the time and expense of obtaining a patent if no patent protection is available during the commercial life of the software?
2. Does the proposed software patent cover an invention of significant commercial value? If the proposed software product has value for other software products or for other applications, serious consideration should be given to patenting the particular software feature. If, however, the software feature is of minor commercial value and can be implemented in many different ways, then a patent should not be pursued.
3. Does the software incorporate a mathematical algorithm? If the software feature is nothing more than a mathematical algorithm, even under existing case law that liberally weighs in favor of software patents, the software feature is probably not proper subject matter. In this case your investment in obtaining a patent may become substantial and your application mired down in a debate with the Patent Office and in the appellate courts.
4. Does the software represent a novel and nonobvious procedure? The principles of novelty and nonobviousness in patents in **Chapter 2**

should be reviewed. Most software programmers believe that their contribution is well within ordinary skill and that they are doing nothing unusual or out of the ordinary. Management should not fall into this trap and should carefully investigate the novelty and nonobviousness of the proposed software features for patent consideration.

5. Will the software be copied by competitors? Perhaps this is the bottom line. If the answer to this question is yes, then serious consideration should be given to obtaining patent protection. Simply stated, if it is likely to be copied, the software most likely has a substantial commercial lifetime, has commercial value, represents more than simply a mathematical algorithm, and is novel and nonobvious.

§ 8.14   Trademarks in the Software Arena

Without question, the trademark principles set forth in **Chapter 4** should be followed because they are equally applicable in the computer software context.

The Patent and Trademark Office has issued a special rule[37] permitting filing a photograph of a computer screen projecting the trademark as evidence of trademark use. This rule came about because purchasers of computer programs often could not see the mark before purchasing the programs. It was only upon installation of the software that the trademarks came up on the computer's screen.

Software is normally registered in International Class 9 (goods) and in International Class 42 (services). The filing fee is $175 per class, and five identical specimens must accompany the mark for trademark applications based on actual use.

If software is being advertised as "compatible with" a particular hardware system or software package, it is crucial that it actually be fully operable with the other trademarked hardware or software.

The following cases represent a sample of the types of trademarks involved in computer trademark litigation:

1. A likelihood of confusion was found to exist between Apple and Pineapple, which are both used for personal computers[38]

---

[37] Patent and Trademark Office, Trademark Manual of Examining Procedures § 808.04(d) (rev. ed. 1986).

[38] Apple Computer, Inc. v. Formula Int'l, Inc., 725 F.2d 521, 221 U.S.P.Q. (BNA) 762 (9th Cir. 1984).

2. Software News was held to be a generic title for a software newspaper[39]

3. Data Safe, used for offsite storage of business records, was held to be not confusingly similar to Databank, a title designating safes for storing computer media.[40]

§ 8.15   Trade Secrets and Software

Trade secret litigation is an important part of protecting software. For example, when a software owner licensed another to use a number of report writing, financial planning, and modeling programs and the licensee then proceeded to incorporate the software owner's programs into its own general ledger system that was marketed both within and without the United States, the court awarded compensatory damages of $1.4 million and exemplary damages of $968,000 for such willful and malicious trade secret misappropriation.[41]

Likewise, when two former employees of Bell Telephone Laboratories left to work for General Instrument Corp. on a similar project, Bell sued for trade secret misappropriation. Although the two employees did not take any physical property from Bell, they did carry information in their minds. The trade secrets involved 81,000 lines of source code for a highly sophisticated videotex system. At the time, General Instrument was also working on a videotex system. The court found that Bell's selection and arrangement of algorithms and routines "created the novel result of implementing these videotex functions." The court concluded that the two employees could not have memorized all 81,000 lines of the source code, but stated:

> We are convinced that Gabby and Mansky took with them more than mere experience. It is true that they took no documents and could not possibly recreate the source code from memory. Yet, the evidence establishes that both were more than casually associated with Bell's software. When they departed, they took with them not only general knowledge and experience, but the specifics of Bell's software. This information would of necessity be used in their new job just as would previously acquired general knowledge and experience.[42]

---

[39] Technical Publishing Co. v. Lebhar-Friedman, Inc., 729 F.2d 1136, 222 U.S.P.Q. (BNA) 839 (7th Cir. 1984).

[40] Wright Line, Inc. v. Data Safe Servs. Corp., 769 U.S.P.Q. (BNA) 229 (T.T.A.B. 1985).

[41] McCormack & Dodge Corp. v. ABC Management Sys., Inc., 222 U.S.P.Q. (BNA) 432 (Wash. 1983).

[42] Bell Tel. Laboratories v. General Instrument Corp., 26 Pat. Trademark & Copyright J. (BNA) 328 (Aug. 11, 1983).

§ 8.16   Shrink-Wrapped Licenses

Shrink-wrapped licenses, also known as "blister package contracts," are clearly the most popular method of protecting mass-marketed computer software.

RESOURCE: Levy, "Software Warranties: Multiple Issues and Drafting Considerations," *The Computer Lawyer,* Vol. 5, No. 1, pp. 14–19 (Jan. 1988).

One goal of a shrink-wrapped software license is to inhibit application of 17 U.S.C. § 109 (the first sale doctrine) (see **Chapter 5**) by characterizing the transfer of possession of the software as a lease, license, or loan instead of a sale. A second goal of a shrink-wrapped license is to inhibit the purchaser's rights under 17 U.S.C. § 117 of the Copyright Act (which allows a purchaser to make an adaptation or decompilation of the program) by requiring the purchaser to maintain the trade secret status of the software.

Most shrink-wrapped software licenses include the following provisions:

1. Requirement that statement of title shall remain in the name of the copyright owner
2. Prohibition against transfer of possession of the copy by sale, lease, or otherwise
3. Either a prohibition against decompilation or a clause protecting the trade secrets
4. Prohibition against multi-user or multimachine uses
5. Merger clause
6. Choice of law
7. Term and termination clause
8. Disclaimer of warranty or limitation of remedies clauses.

Significant debate has taken place as to the enforceability of shrink-wrapped licenses. In the 1916 United States Supreme Court case, *Straus v. Victor Talking Machine,*[43] license notices were attached to record players, which contained many patented parts. The notice granted the owner only the right to use the record player and prohibited the modification of the player, forbade the resale of the player, and stated that use of the player constituted acceptance of the license. The Supreme Court declared the license void and, in extremely strong language, stated: "[such agreements]

---

[43] 243 U.S. 490 (1917).

have been hateful to the law from Lord Cook's day to ours because [they are] obnoxious to the public's interest."[44] Despite such strong language, shrink-wrapped licenses of software are commonly used in the modern commercial marketplace.

It becomes imperative that the license should specify retention of title to the software in the licensor in order to prevent the licensee from gaining substantial rights under 17 U.S.C. §§ 109 and 117 wherein she may feel free to rent, sublicense, loan, sell, or decompile her own copy. Furthermore, the license agreement should grant the right under 17 U.S.C. § 117 of the Copyright Act (that is, the right to make an archival copy) specifically to the licensee while forbidding the licensee from making other copies for other purposes. A shrink-wrapped license that prohibited making even archival copies has been held to be invalid.[45]

Form 8–1 (reproduced with permission) is an example of a shrink-wrapped software license agreement.

Form 8–1
LICENSE AGREEMENT
IMPORTANT!

THE OPENING OF THESE DISKETTES SIGNIFIES YOUR ACCEPTANCE OF THIS AGREEMENT. DO NOT OPEN THIS PACKAGE IF YOU DO NOT ACCEPT THESE TERMS AND CONDITIONS. THIS PACKAGE MAY BE RETURNED, UN-OPENED, WITH YOUR RECEIPT FOR A FULL REFUND.

FROGWARE software constitutes a disk having copyrighted computer software accompanied by a copyrighted user manual in which all copyrights and ownership rights are owned only by Frogware, Inc. FROGWARE software contains certain confidential information also owned by Frogware, Inc.

FROGWARE, Inc. grants to you a nonexclusive license to use a copy of FROG-WARE software on a single microcomputer, and the term of this grant is effective until terminated. You may make one archival copy of the software for use with the same microcomputer provided you mark the copy "ARCHIVAL COPY" and include our copyright notice. Both the archival copy and original copy of the software must be destroyed when your use stops or when this Agreement terminates.

You may call and discuss with us by telephone any questions about the installation and use of FROGWARE software (303) 333-3010. We reserve the right to discontinue technical support at any time without notice to you.

---

[44] *Id.* at 500–01.

[45] Vault Corp. v. Quaid Software Ltd., 655 F. Supp. 750, 2 U.S.P.Q.2d (BNA) 1407, (E.D. La. 1987), *aff'd,* 847 F.2d 255, 7 U.S.P.Q.2d (BNA) 1281 (5th Cir. 1988).

You are not entitled to sublicense, rent, lease, sell, pledge, or otherwise transfer or distribute the original copy or archival copy of FROGWARE software. Modification, disassembly, reverse engineering, or creating derivative works based on the software or any portion thereof is expressly prohibited. Copying of the manual is also prohibited. Breach of these provisions automatically terminates this Agreement.

FROGWARE software is warranted for ninety (90) days from the date of purchase to be free from defects in materials and workmanship under normal use. To obtain replacement of any material under this warranty, you must return the inaccurate disk or copy of the manual to us within the warranty period, or notify us in writing within the warranty period that you have found an inaccuracy in FROGWARE software and then return the materials to us. This limited warranty only covers the original user, and FROGWARE, Inc. makes no other express warranties.

ANY AND ALL IMPLIED WARRANTIES RELATING HERETO ARE LIMITED IN DURATION TO THIS NINETY-DAY WARRANTY PERIOD. REPLACEMENT OF THE DISK OR THE MANUAL IS YOUR EXCLUSIVE REMEDY AND SOLE MEASURE OF RECOVERABLE DAMAGES.

SOME STATES DO NOT ALLOW LIMITATIONS ON HOW LONG AN IMPLIED WARRANTY LASTS, SO THE ABOVE LIMITATIONS MAY NOT APPLY TO YOU. THIS WARRANTY GIVES YOU SPECIFIC LEGAL RIGHTS, AND YOU MAY ALSO HAVE OTHER RIGHTS WHICH VARY FROM STATE TO STATE.

THE DISK AND THE MANUAL IS LICENSED "AS IS" WITHOUT WARRANTY OR ANY KIND, EITHER EXPRESS OR IMPLIED, INCLUDING BUT NOT LIMITED TO THE IMPLIED WARRANTIES OF MERCHANTABILITY AND FITNESS FOR A PARTICULAR PURPOSE. WITHOUT LIMITATION, ALL WARRANTIES AGAINST INFRINGEMENT OR THE LIKE RESPECTING THE PROGRAM ARE HEREBY DISCLAIMED BY FROGWARE, INC. FROGWARE, INC. DOES NOT WARRANT THAT ANY FUNCTIONS CONTAINED IN THIS PACKAGE WILL MEET YOUR MANUAL REQUIREMENTS OR THAT YOUR USE OF THE PACKAGE WILL BE UNINTERRUPTED OR ERROR FREE.

WE SHALL HAVE NO LIABILITY TO YOU OR ANY THIRD PARTY REGARDING FROGWARE SOFTWARE IN WARRANTY, CONTRACT, TORT, OR OTHERWISE. IN NO EVENT WILL FROGWARE, INC. BE LIABLE FOR ANY DIRECT, INCIDENTAL, SPECIAL, INDIRECT, GENERAL, OR CONSEQUENTIAL DAMAGE OR LOSS OF ANY NATURE (SUCH AS DAMAGE TO PROPERTY, DAMAGES RESULTING FROM DELAY, CLAIMS, OR THIRD PARTIES, LOSS OF PROFITS, OR INJURY TO PERSON) WHICH MAY ARISE IN CONNECTION WITH THE USE OF OR INABILITY TO USE THE PROGRAM OR MANUAL. THIS CLAUSE SHALL SURVIVE FAILURE OF ANY EXCLUSIVE REMEDY.

SOME STATES DO NOT ALLOW THE EXCLUSION OR LIMITATION OF INCI-
DENTAL OR CONSEQUENTIAL DAMAGES, SO THE ABOVE LIMITATION OR
EXCLUSION MAY NOT APPLY TO YOU.

The construction and performance of this Agreement shall be governed by the
laws, jurisdiction, and venue of the State of Montana. The prevailing party in
any action or proceeding brought in connection with an alleged breach of this
Agreement shall be awarded reasonable attorneys fees to be paid by the other
party. This Agreement contains the entire understanding between the parties
and supersedes any proposal or prior agreement regarding the subject matter
hereof.

Should you have any questions, please write: FROGWARE, INC., P.O. Box
007, Pondville, Montana 07770.

§ 8.17   State Virus Laws

California, Illinois, Minnesota, and Texas[46] have enacted criminal laws to
counter the attack by illegal "viruses" or "worms." A business should not
rely only on state criminal prosecution, but should take significant technological steps to inoculate its software against viral attacks.

RESOURCE: Stoll, *The Cuckoo's Egg* (Doubleday: 666 Fifth Avenue,
New York, NY 10103) (1990). This is a true story of the Hannover, West
Germany, undercover hacker spy ring and of the infection of 6,000 com-
puters on the Internet telephone lines within several hours.

---

[46] Cal. Penal Code § 502(b)(10) (West 1990); Ill. Ann. Stat. ch. 38, para. 160-3(a)(4)
(Smith-Hurd 1979); Minn. Stat. Ann. § 609.87(12) (West 1990); Tex. Penal Code Ann.
§ 33.01(10) (Vernon 1990) *reported in* CCH Guide to Computer Law (CCH) ¶ 60,067
(1989).

BIBLIOGRAPHY

Altman, Louis, *Callman Unfair Competition, Trademarks & Monopolies: 1945–1989* (Callaghan & Co.: 155 Pfingsten Rd., Deerfield, IL 60015) (Callman, R., ed., 4th ed. 1989).

Aspelund, Donald J., *Employee Noncompetition Law* (Clark Boardman Co.: 375 Hudson St., New York, NY 10014) (1989).

Bahrick, "Security Interests in Intellectual Property," *AIPLA Quarterly Journal,* Vol. 15:30, pp. 30–49 (1987).

Beutel, "Copyright Infringement and Derivative Software," *The Computer Lawyer,* Vol. 4, No. 1, pp. 12–19 (Mar. 1987).

Computer Lawyer, The (Prentice Hall Law & Business: 910 Sylvan Ave., Englewood Cliffs, NJ 07632, telephone 1-800-223-0231).

Cooley, "Personal Liability of Corporate Officers and Directors for Infringement of Intellectual Property," *Journal of Patent and Trademark Office Society,* Vol. 68, No. 3, pp. 228–41 (May 1986).

Corporate Counsel's Guide to Protecting Trade Secrets (Business Laws, Inc.: 8828 Mayfield Rd., Chesterfield, OH 44026) (1990).

Creel, Thomas L., ed., *Guide to Patent Arbitration* (BNA: 1231 25th St., NW, Washington, DC 20037) (1987).

Efficiency of Consideration for Employee's Covenant Not to Compete, Entered into after Inception of Employment, 51 A.L.R.3d 825 (1987).

Guide to Computer Law (Commerce Clearing House: 4025 W. Peterson Ave., Chicago, IL 60646) (1981).

Hawes, James E., *Trademark Registration Practice* (Clark Boardman Co.: 375 Hudson St., New York, NY 10014) (1987).

Hoffman, Paul S., *The Software Legal Book* (Shafer Books, Inc.: 139 Grand St., PO Box 40, Croton-on-Hudson, NY 10520) (1990).

Kane, Siegrun D., *Trademark Law—A Practitioner's Guide* (Practising Law Institute: 810 Seventh Ave., New York, NY 10019) (1987).

Kent, Felix, & Douglas Wood, "Legal Problems in Advertising," *Business Law Monograph BLM 5* (Matthew Bender: 11 Penn Plaza, New York, NY 10001) (1989).

Kramer, Barry, & Allen D. Brufsky, *Trademark Law Practice Forms* (Clark Boardman Co.: 375 Hudson St., New York, NY 10014) (1988).

Laurie, "Protection of Trade Secrets in Object Form Software: The Case for Reverse Engineering," *The Computer Lawyer,* Vol. 1, No. 6, pp. 1–11 (July 1984).

Levy, "Software Warranties: Multiple Issues and Drafting Considerations," *The Computer Lawyer,* Vol. 5, No. 1, pp. 14–19 (Jan. 1988).

Mayers, Harry R., & Brian G. Brunsvold, *Drafting Patent License Agreements* (BNA: 1231 25th St., NW, Washington, DC 20037) (1984).

McCarthy, J. Thomas, *Trademarks and Unfair Competition* (Bancroft Whitney Co.: Lawyers Cooperative Publishing Co., Aqueduct Bldg., Rochester, NY 14694 (2d ed. 1989).

McCarthy, Kevin R., & John W. Kornemeier, *Protecting the Confidentiality of Business Information Submitted to the Federal Government* (Matthew Bender: 11 Penn Plaza, New York, NY 10001) (1988).

Milgrim, Roger M., *Trade Secrets* (Matthew Bender: 11 Penn Plaza, New York, NY 10001) (1990).

Nimmer, Melville B., *Nimmer on Copyright* (Matthew Bender: 11 Penn Plaza, New York, NY 10001) (1978).

Nimmer, Raymond J., *The Law of Computer Technology* (Warren, Gorham & Lamont: 210 South St., Boston, MA 02111) (Supp. 1990).

Nordhaus, Raymond C., *Patent License Agreements* (Jurst Publishing Co.: 7122 N. Clark St., Chicago, IL 60626) (1990).

Note, *Consideration for Employee Non-Competition Covenants in Employments-at-Will,* 54 Fordham L. Rev. 1123 (1986).

Official Gazette: Trademarks (Superintendent of Documents, Government Printing Office, Washington, DC 20402) (weekly).

Pearson, "Computer Databases: Copyright and Other Protection," *The Computer Lawyer,* Vol. 4, No. 6, pp. 28–36 (June 1987).

Pinckney, *Products Comparison Manual for Trademark Users* (BNA: 1231 25th St., NW, Washington, DC 20037) (1988).

Plevin, Kenneth, & Miriam Siroky, *Advertising Compliance Handbook* (Practising Law Institute: 810 Seventh Ave., New York, NY 10019) (1988).

Register of Copyrights, Library of Congress, Washington, DC, telephone 202-707-1812 (free circulars and leaflets).

Rosden, George & Peter, *The Law of Advertising* (Matthew Bender: 11 Penn Plaza, New York, NY 10001) (1990).

Rosenberg, Peter D., *Patent Law Fundamentals* (Clark Boardman Co.: 375 Hudson St., New York, NY 10014) (1990).

Rubin, James S., *HOW: Working with the NEW Process Patent Law* (National Association of Manufacturers: 1331 Pennsylvania Ave., NW, Suite 1500, North Lobby, Washington, DC 20004-1703) (1989).

Siegal, "Copyright Infringement of the 'Look and Feel' of an Operating System," *The Computer Lawyer,* Vol. 4, No. 1, pp. 1–17 (Jan. 1987).

State Trademark and Unfair Competition Law, United States Trademark Association (Clark Boardman Co.: 375 Hudson St., New York, NY 12201) (1989).

Stoll, *The Cuckoo's Egg* (Doubleday: 666 Fifth Ave., New York, NY 10103) (1990).

Superintendent of Documents, United States Government Printing Office, Washington, DC 20402, offers these publications:

Directory of Registered Patent Attorneys and Agents Arranged by States and Country.

Index of Patents.

Manual of Classification.

Manual of Patent Examining Procedure.

Story of the United States Patent Office.

Title 37 Code of Federal Regulations.

"The Trademark Revision Act of 1988," *The Trademark Reporter,* Vol. 79, No. 3 (U.S. Trademark Ass'n: 6 E. 45th St., New York, NY 10017) (May–June 1989).

Valiulis, Anthony C., *Covenants Not to Compete* (John Wiley & Sons: 605 Third Ave., New York, NY 10158) (1988).

TABLE OF AUTHORITIES

Case	*Book §*
Department of Justice v. Calspon Corp., 578 F.2d 295, 198 U.S.P.Q. (BNA) 147 (C.C.P.A. 1978)	§ 4.23
Diamond v. Chakrabarty, 447 U.S. 303, 206 U.S.P.Q. (BNA) 193 (1980)	§ 2.7
Diamond v. Diehr, 450 U.S. 175, 209 U.S.P.Q. (BNA) 1 (1981)	§§ 2.7, 8.11
Diehl & Sons, Inc. v. International Harvester Co., 445 F. Supp. 282 (1978)	§ 3.6
Digital Dev. Corp. v. International Memory Sys., 185 U.S.P.Q. (BNA) 136 (S.D. Cal. 1973)	§§ 1.4, 1.8
Distillerie Filli Ramazzoti S.P.A. v. Banfi Prod. Corp., 52 Misc. 2d 593, 276 N.Y.S.2d 413, 151 U.S.P.Q. (BNA) 551 (1966), *aff'd,* 27 A.D.2d 905, 280 N.Y.S.2d 892 (1967)	§§ 3.7, 3.24
Diversified Mktg., Inc. v. Estee Lauder, Inc., 705 F. Supp. 128, 9 U.S.P.Q.2d (BNA) 1882 (S.D.N.Y. 1988)	§ 7.11
Donsco, Inc. v. Casper Corp., 587 F.2d 602, 199 U.S.P.Q. (BNA) 705 (3d Cir. 1978)	§§ 6.6, 6.10
Doraw v. Sunset House Distrib. Corp., 197 F. Supp. 940, 131 U.S.P.Q. (BNA) 94 (S.D.Cal. 1961)	§ 5.2
Easter Seal Soc'y for Crippled Children v. Playboy Enters., 815 F.2d 323, 2 U.S.P.Q. (BNA) 1585 (5th Cir. 1987)	§ 5.17
Echo Travel, Inc. v. Travel Assocs., 870 F.2d 126, 10 U.S.P.Q.2d (BNA) 1368 (7th Cir. 1989)	§ 3.22
Eco-Separator Co. v. Shell Canada Ltd., 872 F.2d 427, 12 U.S.P.Q.2d (BNA) 1635 (9th Cir. 1989)	§ 1.8
Educational Dev. Corp. v. Economy Co., 562 F.2d 26, 195 U.S.P.Q. (BNA) 482 (10th Cir. 1977)	§§ 4.25, 4.44
Educational Testing Serv. v. Katzman, 793 F.2d 533, 230 U.S.P.Q. (BNA) 156, (3d Cir. 1986)	§ 5.13
E.F. Johnson Co. v. Uniden Corp., 623 F. Supp. 1485, 228 U.S.P.Q. (BNA) 891 (D. Minn. 1985)	§§ 5.25, 8.7
Egbert v. Lippmann, 104 U.S. 333 (1881)	§ 2.13
Electronics Corp. of Am. v. Honeywell, Inc., 428 F.2d 191 (1st Cir. 1970)	§ 3.16
Fabrica, Inc. v. Eldorado Corp., 697 F.2d 890 (9th Cir. 1983)	§ 3.7
Factors Etc., Inc. v. Pro Arts, Inc., 579 F.2d 215, 205 U.S.P.Q. (BNA) 751 (2d Cir. 1978), *cert. denied,* 440 U.S. 908 (1979), *on remand,* 496 F. Supp. 1090, 208 U.S.P.Q. (BNA) 529 (S.D.N.Y. 1980), *rev'd,* 625 F.2d 278, 211 U.S.P.Q. (BNA) 1 (2d Cir. 1981), *cert. denied,* 456 U.S. 927 (1982), *on remand,* 541 F. Supp. 231 (S.D.N.Y. 1982), *vacated,* 562 F. Supp. 304 (S.D.N.Y. 1983), *reh'g denied,* 701 F.2d 11 (2d Cir. 1983)	§ 3.17
Federal Trade Comm'n v. Raladum Co., 283 U.S. 643 (1931)	§ 3.20

Case	*Book §*
Shurie v. Richmond, 699 F.2d 1156, 216 U.S.P.Q. (BNA) 1042 (Fed. Cir. 1983)	§ 2.19
Siegel v. Chicken Delight, Inc., 448 F.2d 43, 171 U.S.P.Q. (BNA) 269 (9th Cir. 1971), *cert. denied,* 405 U.S. 955 (1972)	§ 4.40
SI Handling Sys., Inc. v. Heisley, 581 F. Supp. 1553, 222 U.S.P.Q. (BNA) 52 (E.D. Pa. 1984)	§§ 1.3, 1.11
Silverman v. CBS, Inc., 675 F. Supp. 870, 6 U.S.P.Q.2d (BNA) 1975 (S.D.N.Y. 1988)	§ 5.12
Simmons Fastener Corp. v. Illinois Tool Works, Inc., 739 F.2d 1573, 222 U.S.P.Q. (BNA) 744 (Fed. Cir. 1984)	§ 2.9
Singh v. Famous Overseas, Inc., 680 F. Supp. 533, 6 U.S.P.Q.2d (BNA) 1969 (E.D.N.Y. 1988)	§ 5.12
Smith v. Bic Corp., 869 F.2d 194, 10 U.S.P.Q.2d (BNA) 1052 (3d Cir. 1989)	§ 1.23
Smith v. Standard Laundry Mach. Co., 19 F. 826 (C.C.D.N.Y. 1883)	§ 6.4
Smith v. Weinstein, 738 F.2d 419 (2d Cir. 1984)	§ 5.20
Smith Int'l v. Hughes Tool Co., 229 U.S.P.Q. (BNA) 81 (C.D. Cal. 1986), *appeal dismissed as moot,* 839 F.2d 663, 5 U.S.P.Q.2d (BNA) 1686 (Fed. Cir. 1988)	§ 2.4
Society of Survivors of Riga Getto v. Huttenbach, 1989 Copyright L. Dec. (CCH) 26,253 (1988)	§ 5.10
Solo Cup Co. v. Paper Mach. Corp., 359 F.2d 754, 149 U.S.P.Q. (BNA) 239 (7th Cir. 1966)	§ 6.6
Spindlefabrik v. Schubert, 829 F.2d 1075, 4 U.S.P.Q.2d (BNA) 1044 (Fed. Cir. 1987), *cert. denied,* 484 U.S. 1063 (1988)	§ 6.2
Springsteen v. Plaza Roller Dome, Inc., 602 F. Supp. 1113, 225 U.S.P.Q. (BNA) 1008 (M.D.N.C. 1986)	§ 5.14
Standard Brands, Inc. v. Smidler, 151 F.2d 34 (2d Cir. 1945)	§ 4.14
Stanley Aviation Corp. v. United States, 196 U.S.P.Q. (BNA) 612 (D. Colo. 1977)	§§ 1.6, 1.12
Stix Products, Inc. v. United Merchants & Mfgrs., Inc., 295 F. Supp. 479, 160 U.S.P.Q. (BNA) 777 (S.D.N.Y. 1968)	§§ 4.15, 4.16
Straus v. Victor Talking Machine, 243 U.S. 490 (1917)	§ 8.16
Studiengesellschaft Kohle v. Dart Indus., 666 F. Supp. 677, 4 U.S.P.Q. 2d (BNA) 1817 (D. Del. 1987), *aff'd,* 862 F.2d 1564, 9 U.S.P.Q.2d (BNA) 1273 (Fed. Cir. 1988)	§ 6.2
Sublime Prods., Inc. v. Gerber Prods., Inc., 579 F. Supp. 248, 223 U.S.P.Q. (BNA) 383 (S.D.N.Y. 1984)	§ 7.6
Suozzi, *ex parte,* 125 U.S.P.Q. (BNA) 445, 453 (Pat. & Trademark App. Bd. 1959)	§ 2.15
Surgical Supply Servs., Inc. v. Adler, 321 F.2d 536, 138 U.S.P.Q. (BNA) 263 (E.D. Pa. 1962)	§ 3.3

TABLE OF FORMS

INDEX

327